Information Visualization in Data Mining and Knowledge Discovery

The Morgan Kaufmann Series in Data Management Systems

Series Editor: Jim Gray, Microsoft Research

Information Visualization in Data Mining and Knowledge Discovery

Edited by

USAMA FAYYAD

digiMine, Inc.

GEORGES G. GRINSTEIN

University of Massachusetts, Lowell

ANDREAS WIERSE

VirCinity IT-Consulting GmbH

MORGAN KAUFMANN PUBLISHERS

AN IMPRINT OF ACADEMIC PRESS

A Harcourt Science and Technology Company

SAN FRANCISCO   SAN DIEGO   NEW YORK   BOSTON
LONDON   SYDNEY   TOKYO

Executive Editor Diane D. Cerra
Publishing Services Manager Scott Norton
Senior Production Editor Cheri Palmer
Assistant Developmental Editor Marilyn Alan
Editorial Assistant Mona Buehler
Cover Design Ross Carron Design
Cover Image Neal Mishler/Tony Stone Images
Text Design/Composition Rebecca Evans & Associates
Technical Illustration Technologies 'N Typography
Copyeditor Daril Bentley
Proofreader Jennifer McClain
Indexer Bill Meyers
Printer Courier Corporation

Morgan Kaufmann Publishers
340 Pine Street, Sixth Floor, San Francisco, CA 94104-3205, USA
http://www.mkp.com

ACADEMIC PRESS
A Harcourt Science and Technology Company
525 B Street, Suite 1900, San Diego, CA 92101-4495, USA
http://www.academicpress.com

Academic Press
Harcourt Place, 32 Jamestown Road, London, NW1 7BY, United Kingdom
http://www.academicpress.com

Library of Congress Control Number: 2001090601

ISBN 1-55860-689-0

This book is printed on acid-free paper.

Foreword

From the Series Editor

Jim Gray

Microsoft Research

Data visualization has lagged its sister disciplines of data capture, data storage, data analysis, and knowledge discovery. The KDD tools now exist, but there is still a huge gap between our ability to extract answers and our ability to present the information in meaningful ways.

Today, most data mining systems are chauffeur driven, requiring experts in the arcane languages and techniques that comprise the system's plumbing. When results emerge, they often need a second class of expert graphic artists to render them in easily comprehensible forms.

There is consensus that the next breakthroughs will come from integrated solutions that allow end users to explore their data using graphical metaphors—the goal is to unify data mining algorithms and visual human interfaces. This will bring users into direct contact with their data and will make data mining and knowledge discovery available to everyone, not just those rich enough to be able to afford data mining and graphics chauffeurs.

This book summarizes the current state of this rapidly evolving field. It includes both tutorial information that gives the background needed to understand the issues, and it also gives first-hand descriptions of the academic and industrial research in this area. The book gives quick and very informative tutorials on the psychology and technology of visual data representation. It also gives a quick summary of data mining and modeling tools. Once these preliminaries are out of the way, the chapters describe the current product and research scene and give benchmarks and goals for evaluating these efforts. Later chapters tell some success stories of applying KDD visualization to real problems.

Having all this information in a consistent and organized collection makes this book an ideal basis for anyone wanting a current synopsis of visual knowledge and data discovery.

Foreword

STEPHEN G. EICK

Chief Technical Officer, Visual Insights

As a participant in the first database visualization workshop, it gives me great pleasure to see the progress that has occurred over the last eight years. This early workshop, held in 1993 as an adjunct to IEEE's visualization conference in San Jose, was a small, tight-knit meeting where a few of us exchanged ideas on how we had applied visualization to understand databases. Thinking back on that original meeting, much is the same, but the really exciting aspects are the differences. The themes of this early workshop involved trying to apply visualization to understand complexity in databases, using visual interfaces as an interface into the data, and factoring out common visual techniques.

Progress has occurred along three significant dimensions. First, our original ideas have matured, and the field of *information visualization* has been created. Information visualization captures the themes from this early workshop by extending scientific visualization—which focused on 3D scientific data—toward understanding nonspatial, higher-dimension data. Second, the research focus has grown beyond visualization to include data mining and analytics as integrated components of the knowledge discovery process. Third, the applications have grown in number, depth, significance, and sophistication.

Part of the reason for the increased interest in visualization and knowledge discovery involves fundamental technology trends. With the decreasing cost of silicon, it is now possible to instrument processes and collect fine-grained data. The growth in networking and increased storage capacity has made it possible to assemble large data sets in warehouses. Web-based interfaces now provide ubiquitous access to the data. The research problem is how to make sense of all this data. This fundamental trend is repeating itself in domain after domain as it becomes possible to collect finer-grained data, and users struggle to make sense of it all.

This book's focus on the intersection between visualization, data mining, and knowledge discovery is particularly important. Visualization involves constructing graphical interfaces that enable humans to understand complex data sets. Visualization is the link between the two most powerful information-processing systems: humans and the modern computer. Humans, unfortunately, have many limitations. In particular, we are quite limited in our ability to handle scale and are easily overwhelmed by the volumes of data that are now routinely connected. Data mining, an automated process, is a natural reduction technique that complements human capabilities. Combining these two approaches for knowledge discovery is clearly a great idea.

There seems to be a standard approach toward knowledge discovery that is being repeated in problem domain after domain. Technology trends make it feasible to collect a new class of data. Domain-specific transforms are created that involve cleaning, schema, and integration. Data mining analytics are layered on top as a reduction and sense-making operation. In scientific domains the results become discoveries, and in business domains the results are linked into operational systems that drive actions. As the chapters in this book illustrate, visualization contributes to each step of the process where humans are involved.

My highest compliments go to Fayyad, Grinstein, and Wierse for assembling this collection of papers and rounding it out with an excellent introduction. The chapters in this book knit together contributions from the leading scientists and engineers. Bundled together, the contributions are much more useful than the sum of the individual components. The contributions include reusable ideas that are assembled for easy distribution to a much wider audience.

Contents

Acknowledgments

We would like to give special thanks to UMass Lowell past and current graduate students who provided extensive support preparing for and holding the
workshops that led to this book. They spent many hours from concept to
implementation dealing with logistics and editorial activities. In particular,
special thanks go to Dr. Claudio Meneses and Dr. Pat Hoffman for helping
make the workshops successful while in the midst of their dissertation research and yet still finished. We also especially thank Alex Gee for the innu-
merable hours spent editing and reorganizing the chapters and their figures,
all while participating as a founder in a startup! His suggestions and attention to detail have made the book a superb reference.

We thank Morgan Kaufmann for making this book possible. We appreciate the support provided by Diane Cerra and Marilyn Alan in reviving the
aspirations we had in holding the workshops and encouraging us to look
beyond the problems and their associated delays. Their steadfastness and
ability have made the book a reality.

And of course thanks go to our wives for their patience and support that
continue to provide an environment where intense productivity is attainable.

About the Web Site

Some of the book's color figures appear in the color insert following page 194.
You can view nearly all of the book's figures in color at Morgan Kaufmann's
Information Visualization in Data Mining and Knowledge Discovery Web site
at *http://www.mkp.com/infovis_in_datamining/*.

Introduction

Usama Fayyad

digiMine, Inc.

Georges G. Grinstein

University of Masssachusetts, Lowell

Brief History of Related Fields

With the closing of the millennium, our experience in dealing with ever-growing databases has not halted but rather steadfastly continues [Abb00]. The explosive generation of massive data sets and our need to extract the data's inherent information has continued to spawn research in several significant areas, each of which aims to increase our understanding of the data, what useful information is latent within it, and how to detect portions of it that are of strong interest. The primary relevant fields to this endeavor are statistics, data visualization, databases, and the combined fields of data mining, pattern recognition, machine learning, and artificial intelligence.

With its early historical connection to data analysis, statistics applies various mathematical and numerical methods to determine the fit of mathematical models to the data. The majority of the work in statistics has focused on methods for verifying a priori hypotheses about the data. Most such methods rely on determining the degree of fit of a statistical model or model family to a set of observations (data points)—usually small in number. The decision of what model to use, how to fit the model, and how to assess the degree of fit is performed by the human expert: the statistician [Sta01].

Deeply rooted in exploratory data analysis or EDA (statistical data presentation techniques), data visualization provides graphical displays for data manipulation and comprehension [Tuk77, Vel81, Cle85, Cle95]. The methods in this field have focused primarily on the visual presentation of the data or information contained within it. The reliance on deciding what gets presented and how it is displayed has largely been left to the human expert: the data visualization expert. Furthermore, the bulk of the challenges tackled in this field have been about the visualization of the data directly, with a good portion of the effort focused on making it easier to visualize more dimensions effectively given the limited 2D and 3D display technology available. Visualization research has successfully brought together researchers from computer science, user interfaces, psychology and perception, and statistics [Car00, Baj99, Fol94, Sen90].

Stemming from a purely computational approach, two distinct camps working on two fundamental aspects of data mining have emerged out of the field of computer science. The first is focused on data storage and retrieval technology as related to database theory and practice. The second is centered on the notion of the algorithmic principles that enable the detection or extraction of patterns and statistical models from data. This latter branch evolved early under the field of pattern recognition, and later under artificial intelligence (AI), machine learning (ML), and most recently the field of data mining and knowledge discovery in databases (KDD) proper [Fay96a, Fay96b, Fay96c]. With the primary goal of applying computational algorithms to identify structural organization in the data, it is safe to say that the emphasis was on algorithms and relatively little attention was paid to the visualization aspects of the problem. Unlike data visualization and statistics, the approaches emerging from these algorithmic fields have focused on "automation" rather than on the human driving the process. The driver for this has primarily been twofold. The first is the (sometimes misguided, but often true) belief that for large databases with large numbers of variables (dimensions), human intuition can be more of a hindrance than a helpful factor in approaching preliminary analysis tasks. The second driver has been the fascination with automation as a means of understanding how people detect and find patterns in data [Adr96, Ber97, Big96, Bur98, Cha98].

Algorithms developed on the database side of the field tended to incorporate few, if any, statistical techniques while focusing on scalability to large databases, with special focus on practical and systems-oriented considerations. On the other hand, pattern recognition, AI, ML, and KDD techniques focused on more intensive search algorithms, as well as advanced statistical techniques, with a lesser emphasis on scalability. The last three or four years of the twentieth century saw the successful merging of database-inspired techniques with KDD algorithms to produce the next generation of work, which combined sophisticated modeling, statistical considerations, scalability, and integration with database systems. This was the emergence of the data mining and KDD field as represented in a large set of academic and industry conferences, represented most notably by the KDD conference series and the ACM SIGKDD (Special Interest Group on Knowledge Discovery and Data Mining) [Fay96b].

Each of these data exploration fields provides valuable tools in an effort to extract knowledge from ever-growing and increasingly pervasive databases. The focus of this book is on an aspect of KDD that has to date received relatively little attention in the literature: the combination of data visualization with data mining techniques [Gri96].

Data Mining and Visualization

The analysis of collected data is not a new activity. On the contrary, statisticians have been defining the mathematical descriptions of data for many years. The various concepts of data *moments*—means, modes, variances, and standard deviations—are well understood and regularly used with other known statistical approaches. It is from this statistical foundation of data analysis that results are often validated, and made comprehensible and appropriate. The early set of techniques and "technologies" used to analyze and model early data sets revolved around visualization of the data using graphs, charts, and tables. Digital computers and data storage dramatically changed the picture. The data volumes ruled out traditional "manual" approaches to analysis. Humans are, by nature and history, dwellers of low-dimensional worlds. Our senses and instincts can help us deal with three to five dimensions, perhaps as many as ten if we count all the natural senses and their derivatives. How are we to deal with 100 dimensions? 1000 dimensions? Even tens of thousands, as we see today in e-commerce, the Web, and in scientific observation?

With the reality of massive data sets came the realization of the difficulty and complexity of constructing computational tools extending our human analysis capabilities to higher dimensions. Today's data mining algorithms, which determine statistical models that fit the data, or reliable patterns that appear within it, are fairly complex and draw on mathematical techniques from probability theory, information theory, estimation, uncertainty, graph theory, and database techniques [Che96a, Che96b, Big96, Bur98, Cha98, Eld96, Gly97, Hec97, Hol95, Imi96, Koh96, Man96, Man97].

Computers contributed to the data analysis problem they are now helping to solve. Data grew unmanageable for the human-generated table and for tabulation manipulation and analysis. We cannot imagine performing computations of, say, one million records with several hundred variables by hand, or even with a set of modern tools. Consequently, automation became necessary.

Data mining is one of the central areas of activity associated with understanding, navigating, and exploiting this new world of large and complex databases. Let's begin with a definition of data mining:

Data mining ■ Mechanized process of identifying or discovering useful structure in data.

We use the term *structure* to refer to patterns, models, or relations over the data. A *pattern* is classically described as a parsimonious description of a subset of data points. A *model* is a (statistical) description of the entire data set. A *relation* is simply a property specifying some dependency between fields (attributes) over a subset of the data; for example, a disproportionately large set of people who own a computer happen to also buy online. While fairly straightforward, this definition of data mining turns out to have some fundamental implications—it implies tackling and solving some of the most challenging questions we face today: What does it mean for a pattern to be true? What does it mean for a summary to be interesting or useful? Which of the multitude of models and patterns that can possibly describe any given finite data set do we choose to believe? What is our basis for "preferring" one pattern over another? When is a reliable correlation indicative of a causal relationship?

However, as we developed the ability to extract increasingly more complex or subtle structure from data, two new serious problems emerged. The first is that automation of the structure discovery process distances the data exploration process from the user. The effective human explorer now needs to understand both the structure of the data and the subtleties of the exploration process that leads to these structures. The second problem is related to the first: the challenge of effectively visualizing the resulting models (or structures) can be quite complex, as it typically involves many variables instead of viewing 2D or 3D plots of data.

Visualization, well done, harnesses the perceptual capabilities of humans to provide visual insight into data [Gre98, Gri89, Gri90, Hea96, Hea98, Lev99, Rob90, Smi90]. Early statistical methods provided reasonable visual support for data explorers. Similarly, modern graphical techniques help provide visual comprehension of the various computational approaches. Moreover, visualization is also being used to display properties of data that have complex relations—possibly patterns not obtainable by current computation methods [Baj99, Buj91, Fel97, Fri74, Lee96, Mic98, Swa96, War94].

Although visualization can be applied directly to data, visualization also represents an interface to the software developed in these other areas and as such plays another significant role. This special role is what provides the mechanism to more tightly couple the user to the various applications and to harness the creative and exploratory capabilities of the human within the data analysis loop.

Effective Data Reduction

Whereas the previous section provides a basic definition of data mining, we present here our functional view of data mining as it pertains to visualization. Finding patterns or models in data is fundamentally about data reduction. Be it a model, pattern, or relation, data mining can be viewed as the determination of a summary of the data or some form of it under consideration. This view is very much aligned with the primary goals of data visualization: finding a view or projection of the data that reduces complexity while capturing important information. The goal is to reduce complexity while losing the least amount of information. Let's consider a couple of basic data mining tasks.

For example, in a *prediction task*, the goal of data mining is to select the dimensions (variables or attributes) relevant to accurately predicting one variable based on others. It is hence possible for an algorithm to home in on a few dimensions out of the possibly hundreds or thousands necessary to determine a predicted variable. As such, a data mining algorithm can be viewed as a pre-processor for a visualization engine, discarding the bulk of the irrelevant dimensions and avoiding the combinatorial number of subsets of dimensions that could be considered, to focus the analyst's attention on the few relevant variables. It is still a challenge to visualize the selected dimensions in such a way that humans find it easier to understand the relevant dependencies, but now the challenge has been simplified and focused: it has at least been significantly reduced.

Another example of a major data mining task is clustering (also known as segmentation) of data: finding groups in the data, such as the data points within each group (segment) being similar to one another by some metric. Clustering can be viewed as a form of separating a data set into the constituent distributions that when "mixed" form the generative density distribution of the overall data set. For example, a database of customer profiles containing age, income, gender, and a history of products purchased from a store can be segmented into clusters of customers having similar purchasing tendencies, gender, and age. Although any attempt to visualize the data set as a whole may result in complicated views of the data, if you were able to iden-tify the homogeneous subpopulations in the data, each of the subpopula-tions would be much easier to visualize. In this case, a data mining tech-nique, clustering, can help us separate the data into subsets, each of which is easier to visualize, understand, and summarize. This is another valuable pre-processing step toward effective data reduction. Whereas prediction can be helpful in selecting variables (or columns) of the data, clustering is help-ful in selecting subsets (or rows) of the data.

Examples can be obtained also for the other tasks of data mining, includ-ing dependency modeling, data summarization (finding relations between fields over data subsets), and sequence and deviation detection (capturing patterns in sequences and series). The basic view here is that data mining can be viewed as yet another form of determining the right projections on subsets of the data to help visualize it.

Of course, not all models are necessarily easier to visualize than the origi-nal data. For example, a neural network model might combine attributes in complicated nonlinear combinations that are difficult to disentangle. How-ever, this is primarily due to our lack of good techniques for inferring the degrees of dependencies from nonlinear models, It is often possible to use such models to home in on interesting simplifying views. The visualization of models and patterns is still an open and challenging research area.

In summary, the role of visualization remains extremely important in helping people understand phenomena of interest in data. Data visualiza-tion has been around for a while, but data mining now adds new challenges of visualizing models extracted from data. Without the proper visualization techniques, data mining models, though a reduced form of the original data, may not give us the desired insight to help humans understand the phenom-ena of interest. Hence, data mining helps us tackle larger problems, but does not entirely solve the problem of getting the insights needed for true under-standing. These can only be obtained by ensuring that humans can actually visualize and understand models.

About This Book

Exploring the integration of the various related data analysis disciplines was the goal of two workshops held in the early 1990s. The first of these was held in conjunction with the IEEE Visualization 1993 Conference in San Jose, fol-lowed two years later by a second workshop in Atlanta at the IEEE Visualiza-tion 1995 Conference—both published as Springer-Verlag Lecture Notes in

Computer Science [Lee94, Wie95]. The goal was to think of visualization as a user interface component that supports queries not just in the classical windows sense but also as part of the data exploration process. Important conclusions from these two workshops were the emerging importance of data mining as a field unto itself, the similarity of related problems, and the advantage of cross-field research discussions.

As a result, researchers from the data exploration areas of statistics, data mining, and data visualization have been working on developing and integrating tools and methods. The idea was to bridge the differences in approaches and encourage research to help produce new methodologies that combine the best of both. For example, data mining is primarily centered on computational number crunching techniques, with minimal user involvement as the machine attempts to extract various features of the data. Data visualization, at the other extreme, emphasizes user interactions and manipulations of graphical data representations for visual feature recognition and understanding. Each approach has its advantages and its major weaknesses. Whereas algorithms working in isolation can miss out on the "wisdom" that is readily available from human knowledge of the problem and the data, strictly manually guided approaches can easily cause users to lose their way in high-dimensional spaces. Between data mining and data visualization, the statistical camp employs user-applied numerical methods with standard graphical displays for visual interpretation.

It is our belief that the joint efforts of these three disciplines can provide breakthroughs in the most difficult analysis problems, along with helping overcome hurdles within individual fields. With this in mind, workshops were held at two highly recognized and pertinent conferences. The first workshop, geared toward data miners and statisticians, was held at the Third International Conference on Knowledge Discovery and Data Mining (KDD'97) in Newport Beach, California, in August of 1997. The second workshop was held at the IEEE Visualization 1997 Conference (VIS'97) in Phoenix, Arizona, in October of 1997, which focused on research in data visualization. The two workshops were organized to make sure that sufficient involvement and interaction took place between two key communities that had not historically attended each other's meetings.

The goal of both workshops was to provide an open forum for the discussion of the many issues involved in the integration of data mining and data visualization. Through the participation of expert researchers attending either or both workshops, several important problems were identified and solutions suggested. These problems, as well as other topics by specialists, comprise the major topics of discussion in this book.

This volume is designed as a reference work containing the collection of thoughts and ideas of noted researchers from the fields of data mining and data visualization. The book consists of three parts.

Part I provides an introduction to and survey of visualization, and focuses on visualization components. Two exemplary applications of visualization are provided. General visualization references can also be found in [Vis01].

"Introduction to Data Visualization" by Georges G. Grinstein and Matthew O. Ward provides a broad overview of the field of data visualization. Terminology, visual perception, data classification, display techniques, and tools for interaction are reviewed. Methodologies for designing effective visualizations and existing visualization systems are discussed, and modern technologies for data visualization are examined.

Data mining algorithms often flatten the large data sets involved. In "A Survey of Visualizations for High-Dimensional Data Mining," Patrick E. Hoffman and Georges G. Grinstein provide a survey of the common and novel flat file or table visualizations focusing on those that can handle more than three dimensions. This chapter is complementary to Chapter 11, "Benchmark Development for the Evaluation of Visualization for Data Mining," which provides preliminary evaluations of some of these visualizations.

Ronald M. Pickett and Georges G. Grinstein discuss the need for "Evaluation of Visualization Systems." We need to determine quantitatively the relative merits of competing displays or systems, and to be able to tell, when we adjust parameters, whether we have made a display or system better or worse.

In "The Data Visualization Environment," Mike Foster and Alexander G. Gee present the issues for the development of visualization and interaction techniques within exploration environments. Discussions include the requirements for supporting users and the possible addition of computer-assisted techniques. The development of a taxonomy for visualization techniques and interaction methods is recommended, and a generalized collaborative exploration environment that supports multiple users and various computers is introduced, providing a look at future data mining and visualization systems.

"Visualizing Massive Multivariate Time-Series Data" by Dennis DeCoste summarizes experiences and a philosophy in developing tools for mining and visualizing massive multivariate time-series data. The primary task is discovering nominal relationships among sensors from large-scale historic data sets of NASA spacecraft, such as the Space Shuttle, typically consisting of thousands of sensors, each sampled over millions of time points. The chapter focuses on discovering context-sensitive high- and low-envelope functions that are particularly useful for detecting future abnormalities and faults during health monitoring operations. However, the visualization issues addressed in the chapter are applicable to general large-scale time-series data mining tasks and are relatively underexplored to date in the data mining community.

According to John Light in "Portable Document Indexes," visualization should be a means of involving the user in a search for results, rather than creating visualizations to present results to the user. Too much visualization attempts to create, either directly or indirectly, a single picture that shows *the answer.* Instead, the visuals should be part of a process that allows the user to find the answer in his own mind.

Is the use of high-quality graphics an essential ingredient of data visualization? In "Character-Based Data Visualization for Data Mining," Michel Pilote and Madeleine Fillion identify some core mechanisms that will benefit any data visualization system, independently of the degree of graphical sophistication.

Part II provides an introduction to KDD and a brief background of data mining, incorporating visualization as well as case studies. Also found in this part are several seminal chapters on model visualization.

In "Visualization in the Knowledge Discovery Process," Ken Collier, Muralidhar Medidi, and Donald Sautter hold that data visualization must permeate the knowledge discovery process from data cleansing and warehousing through data mining and exploration. This advance is likely to improve the understanding users have about their data, thereby increasing the likelihood that new and useful insights about the data will be gained.

Data mining is a technology closely coupled to databases. Andreas Wierse asks the question, "What Can Visualization Do for Data Mining?" Visualization comes in when the results of such mining are analyzed; the iteration of visualization and mining makes it easier for users to find the interesting patterns.

Many modern visualizations invented in the past few years have not yet been integrated with the blossoming data mining tools of neural networks, rule-based classifiers, and other exciting machine-learning algorithms. Patrick E. Hoffman and Georges G. Grinstein identify visualizations for data mining in "Multidimensional Information Visualizations for Data Mining." In addition, they discuss the need for visualization to help understand the "black box" functions learned with neural nets and complex rule-based classifiers.

New sets of powerful data visualization tools have appeared in the marketplace and in the research community. However, it is difficult to judge the effectiveness of these tools for supporting large-scale information exploration and knowledge discovery. In "Benchmark Development for the Evaluation of Visualization for Data Mining," Georges G. Grinstein, Patrick E.

Hoffman, Ronald M. Pickett, and Sharon J. Laskowski describe a set of issues critical to benchmarking and evaluation in this domain.

According to Henry S. Gertzman in "Data Visualization for Decision Support Activities," with such large amounts of data, visualization—as a part of the exploration process—becomes imperative. Yet, it is not obvious how to effectively visualize the results of mining large amounts of data in N dimensions, where N can be as large as 1200!

"A Visualization-Driven Approach for Strategic Knowledge Discovery" by David Law Yuh Foong describes an interactive visualization approach for knowledge discovery and highlights the pivotal roles of visualization in the KDD process, particularly in the data pre-processing and data mining phases.

In "A Visual Metaphor for Knowledge Discovery: An Integrated Approach to Visualizing the Task, Data, and Results," Peter Docherty and Allan Beck investigate two main areas in an attempt to formulate an integrated approach to visualizing the knowledge discovery task, the data required within that task, and the results of the task: how to describe a complete knowledge discovery task in an intuitive visual manner and how to visualize the actual data being mined (the transformation process and the data mining algorithms, respectively).

"Visualizing Data Mining Models" by Kurt Thearling, Barry Becker, Dennis DeCoste, William D. Mawby, Michel Pilote, and Dan Sommerfield discusses a number of methods used to visualize data mining models. The driving forces behind visualizing data mining models can be broken down into two key areas: understanding and trust.

In "Model Visualization," Wesley Johnston describes a wish list of what data visualization needs to provide to support the knowledge discovery process, emphasizing "model visualization." Currently the focus is on "data visualization." The best solution is to have both model and data visualization and to integrate them well to aid in the improvement of spatial and temporal data mining.

Data exploration has traditionally been considered in terms of user interface issues for interactive browsing. As the quantity of data to be examined increases, however, it becomes even more important to blend the boundaries between the visual presentation of a data mining process and of user-driven data exploration. This is the problem addressed in "Issues in Time-Series and Categorical Data Exploration" by Nancy Grady, Raymond Flanery, Jr., June Donato, and Jack Schryver.

The simple Bayesian classifier (SBC), sometimes called naive Bayes, is built based on a conditional independence model of each attribute, given the class. The SBC can serve as an excellent tool for initial exploratory data analysis when coupled with a visualizer that makes its structure comprehensible. "Visualizing the Simple Bayesian Classifier" by Barry Becker, Ron Kohavi, and Dan Sommerfield describes such a visual representation of the SBC model that has been successfully implemented.

The DB-Discover system is a research software tool for knowledge discovery from databases. "Visualizating Data Mining Results with Domain Generalization Graphs" by Robert J. Hilderman, Liangchun Li, and Howard J. Hamilton presents the design of the data visualization capabilities of DB-Discover, how the data visualization techniques help manage the many possible summaries, and how potentially interesting summaries are selected from them.

There are a multitude of issues remaining to be addressed to achieve our vision for exploration of LSDBs. However, Martin R. Stytz and Sheila B. Banks, in "An Adaptive Interface Approach for Real-Time Data Exploration," describe six issues of critical importance.

Part III deals with the knowledge discovery process. Here the roles for data mining algorithms and data visualization techniques are combined to provide exploration environments. The first chapter begins with an overview of the KDD process and is followed by those that describe how data mining and visualization can work together. The possibilities for data mining algorithms supporting smart visualizations and visualizations manipulating data mining models before, during, and after data analysis are then presented. This part concludes with chapters discussing the handling of text documents, massive data sets, and two case studies.

In "Discovering New Relationships: A Brief Overview of Data Mining and Knowledge Discovery," Philip J. Rhodes outlines the KDD process and the goals, methods, and algorithms of data mining. "A Taxonomy for Integrating Data Mining and Data Visualization" by Thomas H. Hinke and Timothy S. Newman presents a visualization taxonomy that can be used to characterize the integration of data visualization and data mining. "Integrating Data Mining and Visualization Processes" by Nancy Grady, Loretta Auvill, Allan Beck, Peter R. Bono, Mary Dimmock, and Claudio J. Meneses discusses research issues and requirements for the overall process of data exploration to be under the control of end users.

When the advantages of visual mining are desired but the number of variables is prohibitively large, algorithms can be useful in selecting the best subset of dimensions to be used by the visualization. In "Multidimensional Education: Visual and Algorithmic Data Mining Domains and Symbiosis," Ted W. Mihalisin describes the circumstances under which visualization may be useful when algorithmic approaches are appropriate.

In "Robust Beta Mining," R. Douglas Martin and Tim Simin describe the use of S-PLUS to build a robust beta miner tool that will allow the user to quickly isolate firms for which the conventional beta calculation is suspect, and automatically provide visualizations of the time-series and scatter-plot data for such firms. William D. Mawby discusses the use of visualizations to manipulate underlying models in "Use of the Manifold Concept in Model Visualization."

What is clearly called for is multidimensional education that will allow companies to discern which tools are powerful and which are not. "Data Warfare and Multidimensional Education" by Ted W. Mihalisin is an attempt to start the educational process.

The application of data mining and visualization tools to textual material is a topic of increasing interest as the number of text document collections continues to increase. In "Document Mining and Visualization," Alexander G. Gee and John Light discuss the unification of text retrieval and data mining techniques to broaden tools, including visualization, for data mining of text archives.

"Research Issues in the Analysis and Visualization of Massive Data Sets" by Claudio J. Meneses and Georges G. Grinstein identifies and discusses some research issues related to the analysis and visualization of massive data sets, in the context of the KDD process.

Marc Ringuette argues that knowledge derived from data mining is not enough to achieve a real return on an investment; the organization must have some tools to operationalize that knowledge for problem solving. In "Toward Smarter Databases: A Case-Building Toolkit," the author outlines Inference Corporation's plan to fuse data mining and visualization, inductive learning and clustering routines, and the Case-Based Reasoning paradigm.

"The NASD Regulation Advanced Detection System: Integrating Data Mining and Visualization for Break Detection in the NASDAQ Stock Market" by Ted E. Senator, Henry G. Goldberg, Ping Shyr, Scott Bennett, Steve Donoho, and Craig Lovell discusses a system under development by NASD Regulation, Inc., and SRA International, Inc., for use by NASD Regulation, Inc., as part of its responsibility for surveillance of the NASDAQ stock market.

It is our hope that this collection will inspire future research on work that combines methodologies and technologies from the various related fields. Although the works in this book represent some of the earliest steps and thoughts toward understanding the problems that lie at the interface between data mining and visualization, collecting them in a reference will help in documenting the early state of this emerging area, as well as serve as a starting point for researchers interested in advancing the state of the art.

References

[Abb00]   A. E. Abbadi, M. L. Brodie, S. Chakravarthy, U. Dayal, N. Kamel, G. Schlageter, K. Whang (editors). "VLDB 2000," *Proceedings of the 26th International Conference on Very Large Data Bases,* Cairo, Egypt, September 10–14, 2000. San Francisco. Morgan Kaufmann, 2000. ISBN 1-55860-715-3. See also the previous VLDB conferences.

[Adr96]   P. Adriaans and D. Zantinge. *Data Mining.* Reading, MA. Addison-Wesley, Harlow, 1996.

[Baj99]   C. Bajaj (editor) and B. Krishnamurthy. *Data Visualization Techniques (Trends in Software, 6).* New York. John Wiley & Sons, 1999.

[Ber97]   M. J. Berry and G. Linoff. *Data Mining Techniques.* New York. John Wiley & Sons, 1997.

[Big96]   J. P. Bigus. *Data Mining with Neural Networks.* New York. McGraw-Hill, 1996.

[Buj91]   A. Buja, J. A. McDonald, J. Michalak, and W. Stuetzle. "Interactive Data Visualization Using Focusing and Linking," *Proceedings Visualization '91.* Los Alamitos, CA. IEEE Computer Society Press, pp.156–163, 1991.

[Buj96]   A. Buja, D. Cook, and D. F. Swayne. "Interactive High-Dimensional Data Visualization." *Journal of Computational and Graphical Statistics 5,* pp. 78–99, 1996.

[Bur98]   C.J.C. Burges. "A Tutorial on Support Vector Machines for Pattern Recognition." *Data Mining and Knowledge Discovery,* 2(2):955–974, 1998.

[Car00]   S. K. Card, J. D. MacKinlay, and B. Shneiderman (editors). *Readings in Information Visualization: Using Vision to Think.* San Francisco. Morgan Kaufmann, 2000.

[Cha98]   S. Chaudhuri. "Data Mining and Database Systems: Where Is the Intersection?" *Bulletin of the Technical Committee on Data Engineering,* 21:4–8, March 1998.

[Che96a] P. Cheeseman and J. Stutz. "Bayesian Classification (AutoClass): Theory and Results." U. M. Fayyad, G. Piatetsky-Shapiro, P. Smyth, and R. Uthurusamy (editors), *Advances in Knowledge Discovery and Data Mining,* pp. 153–180. Cambridge, MA. AAAI/MIT Press, 1996.

[Che96b] M. Chen, J. Han, and P. Yu. "Data Mining: An Overview from Database Perspective." *IEEE Transactions on Knowledge and Data Engineering,* 8(6):866–883, December 1996.

[Cle85]   W. S. Cleveland. *The Elements of Graphing Data.* Summit, NJ. Hobart Press, 1985.

[Cle95]   W. S. Cleveland. *Visualizing Data.* Summit, NJ. Hobart Press, 1995.

[Eld96]   J. Elder IV and D. Pregibon. "A Statistical Perspective on Knowledge Discovery in Databases." U. M. Fayyad, G. Piatetsky-Shapiro, P. Smyth, and R. Uthurusamy (editors), *Advances in Knowledge Discovery and Data Mining*, pp. 83–115. Cambridge, MA. AAAI/MIT Press, 1996.

[Est97]   M. Ester, H. Kriegel, and J. Sander. "Spatial Data Mining: A Database Approach," *Proceedings of the 5th International Symposium on Spatial Databases* (SSD), pp. 47–66, 1997.

[Fay96a] U. M. Fayyad. "Data Mining and Knowledge Discovery: Making Sense Out of Data." *IEEE Expert*, pp. 20–25, October 1996.

[Fay96b] U. Fayyad. G. Piatetsky-Shapiro, P. Smyth, and R. Uthurusamy (editors). *Advances in Knowledge Discovery and Data Mining.* Cambridge, MA. MIT Press, 1996.

[Fay96c] U. Fayyad and R. Uthurusamy. "Data Mining and Knowledge Discovery in Databases." *Communications of the ACM: Data Mining and Knowledge Discovery in Databases* (special issue), 39(11), November 1996.

[Fel97]   R. Feldman, W. Klosgen, and A. Zilberstein. "Visualization Techniques to Explore Data Mining Results for Document Collections." KDD'97, pp. 16–23. Menlo Park, CA. AAAI Press, 1997.

[Fle99]   A. Flexer. "On the Use of Self-Organizing Maps for Clustering and Visualization." J. M. Zytkow and J. Rauch (editors), *Principles of Data Mining and Knowledge Discovery*, Third European Conference, PKDD'99, Prague, Czech Republic. Proceedings, Lecture Notes in Artificial Intelligence 1704, pp. 80–88. Berlin. Springer, 1999.

[Fol94]   J. Foley and B. Ribarsky. "Next-Generation Data Visualization Tools." L. Rosenblum, R. A. Earnshaw, J. Encarnacao, H. Hagen, A. Kaufman, S. Klimenko, G. Nielson, F. Post, and D. Thalmann (editors), *Scientific Visualization: Advances and Challenges*, Chapter 7, pp. 103–127. London. Academic Press, 1994.

[Fri74]   J. Friedman and J. Tukey. "A Projection Pursuit Algorithm for Exploratory Data Analysis." *IEEE Transactions on Computers*, pp. 881–890, October 1974.

[Gly97]   C. Glymour, D. Madigan, D. Pregibon, and P. Smyth. "Statistical Themes and Lessons for Data Mining." *Data Mining and Knowledge Discovery* 1(1):11–28, 1997.

[Gre98]   M. Green. *Toward a Perceptual Science of Multidimensional Data Visualization: Bertin and Beyond. http://www.ergogero.com/dataviz/dviz0.html*, 1998.

[Gri89]   G. Grinstein, R. Pickett, and M. Williams. "EXVIS: An Exploratory Data Visualization Environment," *Proceedings Graphics Interface '89*, pp. 254–261, 1989.

[Gri90]   G. Grinstein and S. Smith. "Perceptualization of Scientific Data." E. Farrell (editor). *Proceedings of the 1990 SPIE/SPSE Conference #1259, Extracting Meaning from Complex Data*, pp. 190–199. Bellingham, WA. The Society for Imaging and Technology, 1990.

[Gri96]   G. Grinstein. "Visualization and Data Mining," *Proceedings of the 1996 International Conference on Knowledge Discovery in Databases (KDD'96)*, pp. 384–385, 1996.

[Hea96]   C. G. Healey. "Choosing Effective Colours for Data Visualization," *Proceedings Visualization '96*, pp. 263–270, San Francisco, 1996.

[Hea98]   C. G. Healey. "On the Use of Perceptual Cues and Data Mining for Effective Visualization of Scientific Datasets," *Proceedings Graphics Interface '98*, pp. 177–184, Vancouver, 1998.

[Hec97]   D. Heckerman. "Bayesian Networks For Data Mining." *Data Mining and Knowledge Discovery*, 1(1), 1997.

[Hol95]   M. Holsheimer, M. Kersten, H. Mannila, and H. Toivonen. "A Perspective on Databases and Data Mining." First International Conference on Knowledge Discovery and Data Mining, August 1995.

[Imi96]   T. Imielinski. "From File Mining to Database Mining." R. Ng (editor), *Proceedings of the 1996 ACM SIGMOD Workshop on Research Issues on Data Mining and Knowledge Discovery*, pp. 35–39, Montreal, June 1996.

[Kei94a]   D. Keim, H. Kriegel, and T. Seidl. "Supporting Data Mining of Large Databases by Visual Feedback Queries," *Proceedings of the 10th International Conference on Data Engineering*, Houston, February 1994.

[Kei94b]   D. Keim, R. D. Bergeron, and R. Pickett. "Test Data Sets for Evaluating Data Visualization Techniques." *Database Issues for Data Visualization*, IEEE Visualization '93 Workshop. Berlin. Springer-Verlag, 1994.

[Kei96]   D. A. Keim and H. P. Kriegel. "Visualization Techniques for Mining Large Databases: A Comparison." IEEE Transactions on Knowledge and Data Engineering TKDE'96, Special Issue on Data Mining, 8(6):923–938, 1996.

[Koh96]   R. Kohavi, D. Sommerfield, and J. Dougherty. "Data Mining Using MLC++ : A Machine Learning Library in C++." *Tools with Artificial Intelligence*, pp. 234–245. Los Alamitos, CA. IEEE Computer Society Press, 1996. See also *http://www.sgi. com/Technology/mlc*.

[Kop96]   K. Koperski, J. Adhikary, and J. Han. "Spatial Data Mining: Progress and Challenges," *SIGMOD Workshop on Research Issues on Data Mining and Knowledge Discovery (DMKD)*, 1996.

[Lee94]   J. P. Lee and G. G. Grinstein (editors). *Database Issues for Data Visualization.* Berlin. Springer-Verlag, 1994. CSLN No. 871, ISBN 3-540-58519-2.

[Lee96]   H-Y. Lee and H-L. Ong. "Visualization Support for Data Mining." *IEEE Expert*, pp. 69–75, October 1996.

[Lev99]   H. Levkowitz. *Color Theory and Modeling for Computer Graphics, Visualization, and Multimedia Applications.* Boston. Kluwer Academic Publishers, 1999.

[Man96]   H. Mannila. "Data Mining: Machine Learning, Statistics, and Databases," *Proceedings of the 8th International Conference on Scientific and Statistical Database Management*, pp. 1–6, 1996.

[Man97]   H. Mannila. "Methods and Problems in Data Mining," *Proceedings of the International Conference on Database Theory*, F. Afrati and P. Kolaitis (editors). Berlin. Springer-Verlag, January 1997.

[Mic98]   G. S. Michaels, D. B. Carr, M. Askenazi, S. Fuhrman, X. Wen, and R. Somogyi. "Cluster Analysis and Data Visualization of Large-Scale Gene Expression Data," *Pacific Symposium on Biocomputing* 3:42–53, 1998.

[Pau99]   M. C. Paulk. "Toward Quantitative Process Management with Exploratory Data Analysis," *Proceedings of the Ninth International Conference on Software Quality*, pp. 35–42, Cambridge, MA, October 1999.

[Pro97]   F. Provost and T. Fawcett. "Analysis and Visualization of Classifier Performance: Comparison Under Imprecise Class and Cost Distributions," *Proceedings of the Third International Conference on Knowledge Discovery and Data Mining*, pp. 43–48, 1997.

[Ray96]   M. L. Raymer, W. F. Punch, E. D. Goodman, and L. A. Kuhn. "Genetic Programming for Improved Data Mining: Application to the Biochemistry of Protein Interactions," *First International Conference on Genetic Programming (GP96)*, pp. 375–380. Cambridge, MA. MIT Press, 1996.

[Rob90]   P. K. Robertson. "A Methodology for Scientific Data Visualization: Choosing Representations Based on a Natural Scene Paradigm." A. Kaufman (editor), *Proceedings of Visualization '90*, pp. 114–123. Los Alamitos, CA. IEEE Computer Society Press, 1990.

[Sal97]   L. Salzberg. "On Comparing Classifiers: Pitfalls to Avoid and a Recommended Approach." *Data Mining and Knowledge Discovery*, 1:317–328, 1997.

[Sen90]   H. Senay and E. Ignatius. *Rules and Principles of Scientific Data Visualization*. SIGGRAPH '90 Course Notes #27, State of the Art in Data Visualization, 1990.

[Sen91]   H. Senay and E. Ignatius. "Compositional Analysis and Synthesis of Scientific Data Visualization Techniques," *Proceedings of Computer Graphics International*, pp. 262–282, 1991.

[Smi90]   S. Smith, R. D. Bergeron, and G. G. Grinstein. "Stereophonic and Surface Sound Generation for Exploratory Data Analysis," *Proceedings CHI '90 Conference on Human Factors in Computing Systems*, pp. 125–132, 1990.

[Sta01]   *Journal of Computational and Graphical Statistics, Exploratory Data Analysis Journal, Journal of Applied Stochastic Models and Data Analysis, Proceedings of the American Statistical Society, Journal of Computational Statistics,* and the *Journal of Computational Statistics and Data Analysis.*

[StA98]   R. St. Amant and P. R. Cohen. "Intelligent Support for Exploratory Data Analysis." *Journal of Computational and Graphical Statistics*, 7(4):545–558, 1998.

[Swa96]   D. F. Swayne, D. Cook, and A. Buja. *XGobi: Interactive Dynamic Data Visualization in the X Window System.* Technical report, Bellcore, Iowa State University, and AT&T Labs, 1996.

[Tuk77]   J. W. Tukey. *Exploratory Data Analysis.* Reading, MA. Addison-Wesley, 1977.

[Vel81]   P. F. Velleman and D. C. Hoaglin. *Applications, Basics, and Computing of Exploratory Data Analysis.* Boston. Duxbury Press, 1981.

[Ves99]   J. Vesanto. "SOM-Based Data Visualization Methods." *Intelligent Data Analysis*, vol. 3, April 1999.

[Vis01]   *IEEE Visualization and Computer Graphics Journal*, the Proceedings of the IEEE Visualization Conferences, and the Proceedings of the IEEE Information Visualization Conference.

[War94]   M. O. Ward. "XmdvTool: Integrating Multiple Methods for Visualizing Multivariate Data," *Visualization '94*, pp. 326–336, Washington, DC, 1994.

[Wie95]   A. Wierse, J. P. Lee, and G. Grinstein (editors). *2nd Workshop on Database Issues for Data Visualization.* Atlanta, Georgia, Database Issues for Data Visualization: IEEE Visualization '95 Workshop. London. Springer-Verlag, LNCS No. 1471, 1995.

Part I

DATA VISUALIZATION

Chapter 1

Introduction to Data Visualization

GEORGES G. GRINSTEIN

University of Massachusetts, Lowell

MATTHEW O. WARD

Worcester Polytechnic Institute

1.1 Goals of This Chapter

In this brief and intensive chapter we provide a broad overview of the field of data visualization. We discuss terminology, visual perception, data classification, display techniques, and tools for interaction. We present methodologies for designing effective visualizations and discuss existing visualization systems. We also examine modern technologies for data visualization.

1.1.1 Purpose of Data Visualization

Human beings look for structure, features, patterns, trends, anomalies, and relationships in data. Visualization supports this by presenting the data in various forms with differing interactions. A visualization can provide a qualitative overview of large and complex data sets, can summarize data, and can assist in identifying regions of interest and appropriate parameters for more focused quantitative analysis. In an ideal system, visualization harnesses the perceptual capabilities of the human visual system.

1.2 Classification of Visualization Techniques

The sections that follow discuss visualization techniques, components, and interactions. Subsequent sections address basic visualization terminology, as well as the structure and representation of data, including examples.

1.2.1 Visualization Techniques

Visualization techniques can be classified in a number of ways: based on the task at hand, based on the structure of the underlying data set, or based on the dimension of the display.

Visualizations can be used to explore data, to confirm a hypothesis, or to manipulate a viewer such as in a marketing brochure. In exploratory visualizations, the user does not necessarily know what he is looking for. This creates a dynamic scenario in which interaction is critical. The user is searching for structure or trends and is attempting to arrive at some hypothesis. In a confirmatory visualization, the user has a hypothesis that needs to be tested. This scenario is more stable and predictable. System parameters are often predetermined. Analytic tools are especially necessary to be able to confirm or refute the hypothesis. In production visualizations, the user has a validated hypothesis and so knows exactly what is to be presented and focuses on refining the visualization to optimize that presentation (think of a marketing campaign). This is the most stable and predictable of visualizations. Often, the author may not even be present. Visualizations can also be classified as to whether the underlying data is spatial or nonspatial or whether the displayed data is to be 2D (such as contour lines) or 3D (such as cloud vapor).

1.2.2 Visualization Components

Data can be either stable or dynamic. A PET scan, for example, is static, whereas cloud vapor over time is dynamic. A visualization can be stationary, animated, or interactive: respectively, for example, a set of MRI images, a simulation of a finite element analysis over time, or a real-time representation of wind flow across an automobile. The processing of the data in the visualization system can be batch or interactive: batch for the analysis of a set of images; interactive for pre-surgery analysis.

1.2.3 Visualization Interactions

The user can interact with the data in a variety of ways. These include browsing, to get "the big picture"; sampling, to reduce data size; directed, for "ad hoc" querying; and associative, to access related data.

The user can also interact with the visualization system. For example, the user can create, edit, or manipulate the visualization networks; the user can specify data files to be retrieved, data fields to be displayed, specify visualization pipeline parameters, create or manipulate the output (for further queries), or display further available information about the data.

1.2.4 Basic Visualization Terminology

Visualization ■ The graphical (as opposed to textual or verbal) communication of information (e.g, data, documents, structure)

Interaction ■ A fundamental component of visualization that permits user-specified modifications to visualization parameters

Data model ■ A representation of data that may include structure, attributes, relationships, behavior, and semantics, as well as a repository for data values themselves

Graphical attributes ■ User-controllable aspects of the image generation process, including position, size, color, shape, orientation, speed, texture, and transparency of graphical entities

Mapping ■ An association of data values and attributes to graphical entities and attributes

Rendering ■ Creating and displaying an image

Field ■ A grid of data points that may be uniform or nonuniform

Scalar ■ A single numeric data value

Vector ■ A 1D list of values associated with a single datum

Tensor ■ A 2D array of values associated with a single datum

Isosurface ■ Contours or boundaries in a field with a common value, usually dependent on interpolating between values in the field

Glyph ■ A shape or image generated by mapping data components to graphical attributes (also called an icon)

1.2.5 Structure and Representation of Data

Data is specific to a particular domain or application. A datum has one or more components (scalar, vector, tensor), possibly with geometric and structural attributes such as location and connectivity. Each component may be nominal or ordinal and discrete or continuous. Each component may be ordered, may have a distance relationship, or may have an absolute zero (mathematicians call this *scale*). The location attribute is relevant only for data from a physical domain, and may be on a regular or irregular grid. The connectivity of data specifies the neighborhood relationship among data points, and is most often used for resampling or interpolation.

1.2.6 Examples

MRI (magnetic resonance imagery) ■ Density, with three spatial attributes, 3D grid connectivity

CFD (computational fluid dynamics) ■ Magnitude, with three spatial and three orientation attributes, 3D grid connectivity (uniform or nonuniform)

Financial ■ No geometric structure, n possibly independent components, nominal and ordinal

CAD (computer-aided design) ■ Three spatial attributes with edge and polygon connections, surface properties

Remote sensing ■ Multiple channels, with two or three spatial attributes, grid connectivity

Census ■ Multiple fields of all types, spatial attributes (e.g, address), connectivity implied by similarities in fields

1.3 Perception in Visualization

The study of human visual perception can be extremely beneficial to the process of designing effective visualizations. In particular, perceptual studies can help us answer questions such as:

■ What graphical primitives do humans detect quickly (preattentive)?

■ What graphical attributes can be accurately measured?

- How many distinct values for a particular attribute can be used without confusion?

- How do we combine primitives to recognize complex phenomena?

- How should color be used?

In this section, we review some of the experiments that have been performed to evaluate human performance in perceptual tasks and attempt to summarize their implications to visualization.

1.3.1 Human Perception and Information Theory

Many important experiments have been performed in the field of perceptual psychology. An impressive compilation of tests were reported in a seminal work by George Miller in 1956 [Mil56]. In this paper, the author conjectured that a human's ability to measure visual, auditory, tactile, and other stimuli is quite limited. The format of his analysis is as follows.

Assume that a human being is a communication channel, taking input and generating output, with the overlap being the amount of transmitted information. For each primitive (visual, auditory, tactile, and so on), measure the number of distinct levels the average participant can identify with a high degree of accuracy. The amount of information will follow an asymptotic behavior. Label this level the channel capacity for information transfer by the human and measure it in bits. To limit bias in the experiments, results from specialists in image interpretation were ignored, and the amount of training given to the participants was limited. Only noise-free data was used. The next two sections summarize some of the experiments with single and multiple stimuli.

1.3.2 Absolute Judgment of 1D Stimuli

Sound Pitches (Pollack) ■ Using equal logarithmic steps from 100 to 8000 cps, performance leveled off at 2.5 bits (we can choose six pitches a listener will never confuse). Varying the range did not change the results appreciably. Persons recognizing five high pitches or five low pitches did not recognize ten when combined.

Sound Loudness (Gardner) ■ Varying the spacing between 15 and 110 dbs, it levels off at 2.3 bits (five volumes).

Salinity (Beebe-Center) ■ Varying concentration from .3 to 34.7 gm NcCl per 100 cc water, responses leveled off at 1.9 bits (four levels).

Position on a Line (Hake/Gardner) ■ Using a pointer at an arbitrary position between two markers, participants labeled either from a list of possibilities or number between 0 and 100. Results were approximately 3.25 bits, although improvements were noted after long exposure (10 to 15 levels).

Sizes of Squares (Eriksen/Hake) ■ Results were 2.2 bits. Color (Eriksen): results were 3.1 bits for hue, 2.3 bits for brightness. Touch (Gelard): by placing vibrators on the chest area, participants were able to accurately measure four intensities, five durations, and seven locations.

Line Geometry (Pollack) ■ Results for line length were 2.6 to 3 bits (depends on duration), direction was 2.8 to 3.3 bits, curvature was 2.2 bits for constant arc length and 1.6 bits for constant chord length.

Thus there appears to be some built-in limit on our capability to perceive 1D signals. The mean from the experiments was 2.6 bits, with a standard deviation of .6 bits.

1.3.3 Absolute Judgment of Multidimensional Stimuli

Dot in a Square (Klemmer/Frick) ■ Should be twice that of position on a line (6.5 bits), but measured at 4.6 bits.

Salinity and Sweetness (Beebe-Center) ■ Combined sucrose and salt solutions. Should be twice salinity (3.8 bits), but measured at 2.3 bits.

Loudness and Pitch (Pollack) ■ Should be combination of pitch and loudness (4.8 bits), but measured at 3.1 bits.

Hue and Saturation (Halsey/Chapanis) ■ Should be 5.3 bits, but measured at 3.6 bits.

Size, Brightness, and Hue (Eriksen) ■ Should be 7.6 bits, but measured at 4.1 bits.

Multiple Sound Parameters (Pollack/Ficks) ■ Six variables: frequency, intensity, rate of interruption, on-time fraction, duration, and location. Each could have five values for a total of 15.6K combinations. Results were 7.2 bits, or 150 different categories.

In summary, having a little information about a lot of parameters seems to be the way we do things. This agrees with linguistic theory, which identifies 8 to 10 dimensions, where each distinction is binary or ternary.

1.3.4 Measurement Versus Detection

Many visualization tasks involve detection of differences rather than measurement of absolute values. It turns out that our ability to detect small changes (relative judgment) is much stronger than performing measurement (absolute judgment). Cleveland reported a study performed to rank various graphical attributes in terms of human ability to perceive and classify change [Cle85]. The particular attributes tested were angle, area, color hue, color saturation, density (amount of black), length (distance), position along a common scale, position along identical, nonaligned scales, slope, and volume. The experiments showed errors in perception ordered as follows (increasing error):

1. Position along a common scale

2. Position along identical, nonaligned scales

3. Length

4. Angle/slope (depends greatly on orientation and type)

5. Area

6. Volume

7. Color hue, saturation, density (only informal testing)

The major distinction between position and length is that position is a relative judgment (a proportion of a whole), whereas length is an absolute measurement. Another interesting finding is Weber's Law, which states that the likelihood of detection is proportional to the relative change, not the absolute change, of a graphical attribute. This means that regardless of the absolute size of a graphical entity, our ability to detect changes is based on relative (some proportion) changes, such as a 5% increase or decrease.

The dimensionality of the graphical attribute also plays an important role. Stevens's Law states that the perceived scale in absolute measurements is the actual scale raised to a power. For linear features, the power is between .9 and 1.1, for area features it is between .6 and .9, and for volume features it is between .5 and .8. Thus, mapping single values to attributes such as area and volume is more likely to result in errors in judgment than mapping to simpler attributes, such as length.

1.3.5 Expanding Capabilities

This section is from [Mil56]. Given our seemingly limited ability to accurately measure graphical attributes, you might wonder how we are capable of recognizing hundreds of individual faces, tastes, voices, and other stimuli. We can certainly increase the dimensionality, which leads to larger bit rates. However, there is likely to be a "span of perceptual dimensionality," hypothesized to be approximately 10, beyond which adding dimensions does not increase recognition rate. One approach is to reconfigure the problem as a sequence of different absolute judgments, which leads to the analysis of immediate memory. Studies show that the span of immediate memory is approximately seven items. Each item may be a single, simple stimuli, or some combination or complex chunk. Several experiments dealing with binary digits, decimal digits, letters, syllables, words, and mixtures have shown the number of chunks we are capable of remembering accurately is relatively constant. An interesting observation is that we can remember six or so multisyllabic words, but also six or so monosyllabic words. Thus, we chunk things at the largest logical unit (probably).

Recoding is the process of reorganizing information into fewer chunks with more bits of information per chunk (e.g., the process of learning Morse code). Experiments in recalling long strings of binary digits show nearly linear improvement with chunk size. We remember events by creating a verbal recoding of the event, and then elaborate from this coded version (this accounts for variations in witness testimony). As everyone recodes differently, this can also account for differences in people's abilities to notice changes in appearance, such as the reactions (or lack thereof) you get after getting a haircut or switching to wearing contact lenses.

1.3.6 Summary of Perceptual Experiments

It is clear that our span of absolute judgment and immediate memory limits our ability to perceive information accurately. We can expand on this ability by reformatting perceptual tasks into multiple dimensions or sequences of chunks, but this does not account for the large number of sensory stimuli we are capable of recognizing. Clearly, context plays a role in this process.

The implications of this in the field of visualization cannot be ignored. In applications in which absolute judgment is required, the best we can do with a single graphical attribute (without training) is between four and seven values. To get a larger range of recognizable levels, we must re-pose the problem in multiple dimensions, make a series of simple decisions, or perform some type of chunking. Alternatively, we can attempt to redefine the problem such that relative, rather than absolute, judgment could be used to focus attention, with a second, more quantitatively accurate, stage following the initial focus of attention.

1.4 Classification of Display Techniques

There are many ways to look at data. How can we get a handle on this plethora of techniques? One way is to try to group them in some orderly fashion. There are several approaches to doing this.

1.4.1 Visualization Techniques

Visualization techniques can be classified as to whether their focus is geometric or symbolic, whether the stimulus is 2D or 3D, or whether the display is static or dynamic. Geometric techniques include representing data as a scatter plot, lines, surfaces, or volumes. In such cases, the data typically has several fields that can be mapped to axes for these graphs to be displayed. Here, the data is most often the result of some physical model, simulation, or computation.

Symbolic representations focus on representing especially nonnumeric data using pixels, icons, arrays, or graphs (networks, relations, and so on). The focus here is more on displaying the relationships between the data elements. Hence, topological considerations may be more important. In both the geometric and symbolic cases, the visual representation on the screen may be 2D, 3D, stereoscopic, or even immersed, as in looking through a stereoscopic headset.

Finally, one classification that is key, and relates to the importance of interaction, is whether the display technique presents static or dynamic data. These impose a number of implications for the system and its relationship to the user.

Not all techniques fall precisely into one of the foregoing classifications. The lines of separation are not precise, and many displays are hybrids of various techniques.

1.4.2 Techniques for Graphical Data Presentation

We can order the visualization techniques based on the amount of structure the technique requires. At the lowest level, the techniques are representative of a typical graphical API. This low geometric level is the one most often used by developers of visualization systems and some specialized applications. These low-level primitives are broadly available in almost every visualization application. Middle-level systems embed more structure in the technique and can be found in more specialized visualization environments such as CAD or simulation systems. Many middle-level techniques are the ones we most typically see as mainstream visualizations. Finally, the higher-level visualization techniques require much more structure, involve more parameters to be set up, and are most often found in very specialized systems such as medical visualizations and network intrusion systems. Low-level primitives with the most often used attributes include:

- Point with position, color, and size
- Line with location, length, width, color, and style
- Polygon with location, shape, size, orientation, color, texture, translucency
- Image with pattern, range of values, colormap, size, and scale

    Medium-level primitives include:

- Image such as 2D or 3D scalar fields
- Point plots with position coordinates
- Wire frames with connection components (edges)
- Isosurface with contours or surfaces extracted from a field
- Rubber sheet with 3D surface computed from 2D scalars
- Streamline flow, such as the path of a particle through a static vector field
- Streakline flow, such as the path of a particle through a dynamic vector field
- Ribbons and tubes, extensions to the previous two flow visualizations
- Icons and glyphs, such as arrows, spheres, boxes, stars, stick figures, and faces

- Parallel coordinates taking a multivariate point and mapping it to a polyline across N vertical axes
- Dimensional stacking taking multivariate points and mapping them to space recursively partitioned

High-level primitives include:

- Multiple objects of like type (streamlines, slices, glyphs) differentiated by style, position, or color
- Mapping data onto objects (e.g., a surface)
- Translucent surfaces with glyphs, slices
- Multiple simultaneous views
- Surface geometry with streamlines

1.5 Examples of Data Visualization Techniques

The following examples were generated with either IBM Visualization Data Explorer or XmdvTool, a public-domain multivariate visualization package.

1. *Line Graph:* A line graph is formed by connecting points whose positions are determined by a variable (y dimension) for which you have values over a sequence of another variable (x dimension), such as temperature at distinct time periods (Figure 1.1(a)).

2. *Scatter Plots:* A 2D scatter plot is generated by plotting points or markers whose positions are driven by two variables. Unlike line graphs, multiple points can map to the same x or y coordinate. A scatter-plot matrix is a tool for displaying multivariate data, in which each plot of the matrix shows the data points based on two data dimensions/variables (Figure 1.1(b)).

3. *2D Isosurfaces:* An isosurface is a boundary on which every point has the same value. It is typically generated from a discrete grid of values, with interpolation used to identify where the boundary is crossed. In 2D, this manifests itself as contour lines, such as lines of constant elevation or density (see Figure 1.2(a)).

4. *3D Isosurfaces:* 3D isosurfaces are created in a manner similar to that which creates 2D isosurfaces, but instead of forming contour lines, the result is a 3D surface consisting of connected (usually) triangular

Figure 1.1

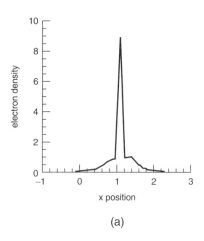

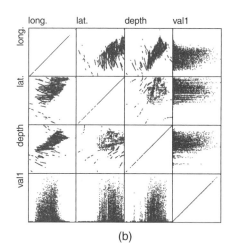

(a)   (b)

(a) Line graph and (b) scatter plot.

Figure 1.2

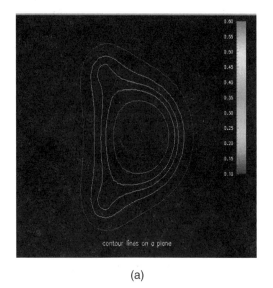

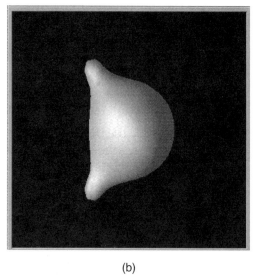

(a)   (b)

(a) 2D and (b) 3D isosurfaces. (See also color plate for Figure 1.2(a).)

Figure 1.3

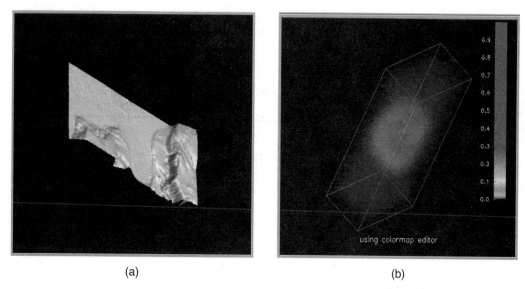

(a)   (b)

(a) Rubber sheet visualization and (b) volume visualization. (See also color plate for Figure 1.3(b).)

patches. Examples include the isolation of bone structure in tomographic data and isotherms in computational fluid dynamics models (see Figure 1.2(b)).

5. *Rubber Sheet:* A rubber sheet is a 3D surface formed by mapping the values in a 2D field to elevation and connecting the points with a triangular mesh (see Figure 1.3(a)).

6. *Volume Visualization:* In volume visualization, a 3D scalar data grid is rendered by casting rays through the projection plane and into the scalar field. The resulting pixel value is determined either as some combination of all data values encountered by the ray, or, for isosurfaces, as a particular isovalue exceeded along the ray. Shading is performed by computing local gradients in the data field. Color and opacity can be used to isolate or highlight value ranges of interest (see Figure 1.3(b)).

7. *Scalar Glyphs:* Glyphs map data values to graphical attributes such as size, color, and shape. Scalar (1D) glyphs each convey a single value. The size of a cube or sphere is an attribute commonly associated with 3D scalar data, such as mapping water density in a cloud (Figure 1.4(a)).

Figure 1.4

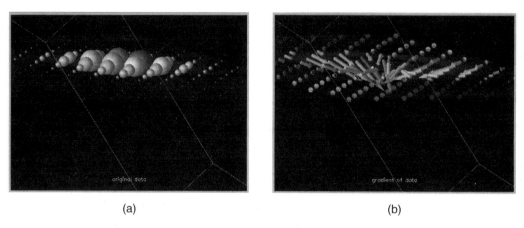

(a)   (b)

(a) Scalar glyph and (b) vector glyph. (See also color plate.)

8. *Vector Glyphs:* Vector glyphs are often used to convey flow information, such as magnitude and direction of wind fields. Arrows are the most prevalent form of vector glyphs, but others exist as well (Figure 1.4(b)).

9. *Star Glyphs:* For data with large numbers of dimensions/variables, shape coding is a common visualization tactic. In a star glyph, each dimension controls the length of a ray emanating from a center point. Each data point will have a given center point and a number of equally angled rays based on the number of dimensions. The endpoints of the rays for a given glyph are often connected to reduce misinterpretation when glyphs overlap (Figure 1.5(a)).

10. *Parallel Coordinates:* Another method of displaying multivariate data employs parallel coordinates. For n-dimensional data there are n equally spaced vertical (or horizontal) axes, and each data point is represented as a polyline that crosses each axis at a position proportional to its value for that dimension (the ends of the axis correspond to minimum and maximum values for each dimension) (Figure 1.5(b)).

11. *Dimensional Stacking:* Dimensional stacking is a recursive embedding technique for displaying high-dimensional data. Each dimension is discretized into a small number of bins, and the display area is broken into a grid of sub-images. The number of sub-images is based on the number of bins associated with the two "outer" dimensions (user specified). The sub-images are decomposed further based on the number of bins for two more dimensions. This continues until all dimensions have been assigned (Figure 1.6(a)).

Figure 1.5

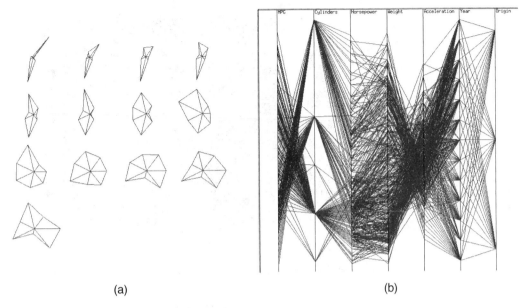

(a)   (b)

(a) Star glyphs and (b) parallel coordinates.

Figure 1.6

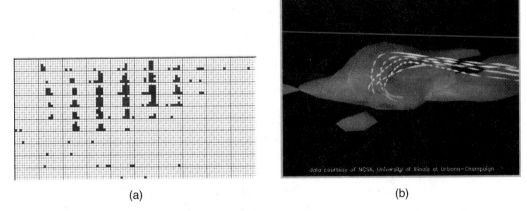

(a)   (b)

(a) Dimensional stacking and (b) ribbons. (See also color plate for Figure 1.6(b).)

Figure 1.7

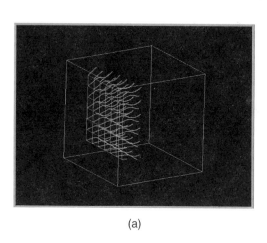 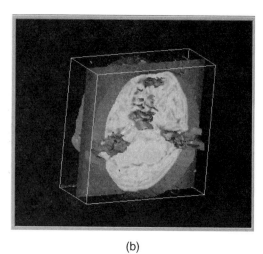

(a)   (b)

(a) Streaklines and (b) combined isosurface and slicing. (See also color plate for Figure 1.7(b).)

12. *Ribbons with Twists Based on Vorticity:* Streamlines are a method of computing the path of a particle through a velocity field via a process called particle advection. By connecting the points along the particle path, flow behavior can be observed. By changing the line to a ribbon, other information can be displayed as well, such as mapping data to color, texture, thickness, and orientation (Figure 1.6(b)).

13. *Streaklines Using Three Time Frames:* Streaklines are like streamlines, with the difference being that data exists for several time frames. Thus, instead of advecting particles through a static (steady-state) flow field, the path can be perturbed by changes within the flow (Figure 1.7(a)).

14. *Combining Slicing and Isosurface:* It is possible to integrate several distinct visualizations into a composite, using the strengths of one visualization to counterbalance the weaknesses of another. A common method of exploring volume data is to generate an isosurface for a value of interest, but then pass a cutting plane through the volume to show all values for a slice as an image on the plane (Figure 1.7(b)).

15. *Other Visualization Techniques:* This list is far from exhaustive. New techniques are being developed each year as the complexity and size of data sets increase. Methods and systems from the literature in-

clude BEAD, Benediktine Space, Cityscapes, Cone Trees and Cam Trees, Fish-eye Views, HyperSpace, Iconographics, Information Cube, Information Visualizer, Landscapes, Narcissus, NetSee, Perspective Walls, Radviz, Rooms, Sage and Visage, SeeSoft, Sphere Visualization, SPIRE, VIBE and VR-VIBE, and VizNet.

1.6 Interactive Data Exploration

Exploratory visualization is an interactive data mining process that can be structured in the following pipeline:

Databases ■ One or more data repositories, potentially distributed, containing the raw data and metadata relevant to the exploration task.

Database subsets ■ Via some query mechanism, a specific subset of the data is retrieved. Queries can be based on ranges of particular data attributes or on metadata associated with the desired subset.

Representation mappings ■ Data attributes require transformations to map to the graphical attributes to be used.

Visualization settings ■ Colormaps, lighting configuration, and geometric constraints must be specified for the view to be rendered.

Data displays ■ The visualization is presented to the user.

There are many critical design decisions that need to be made along this pipeline, such as how to select the best visualization for the particular domain and task, what forms of interaction need to be supported, and how best to integrate analytical tools into the visualization. These are briefly elaborated upon in the following.

1.6.1 Selecting a Visualization

There are several important factors that must be considered when selecting an appropriate visualization. Some of these include:

■ Current display technology supports between one and three million pixels, whereas typical data sets contain anywhere from hundreds of bytes to gigabytes or terabytes of information. How can you use this space effectively? Can other attributes, such as time and sound, be used to supplement limitations imposed by screen resolution?

- Similarly, the density/sparseness of the data, in conjunction with the visualization mapping chosen, may require interpolation/subsampling of the data prior to display. This may result in both artifacts and miscommunication in the presentation. For example, data may appear smoother than it really is, features may be lost via subsampling, and users may be led to believe that data has been gathered at a much higher resolution than it really was.

- Data can be presented at its original dimensionality or via projections/subsetting at lower dimensionalities. Display technology is predominantly 2D. There are trade-offs to consider between the benefits and limitations (e.g., occlusion) when selecting the dimensionality of the resulting visualization.

- The task being performed (e.g., detection/measurement of patterns/anomalies) and the purpose of the visualization (exploration, confirmation, presentation) can determine which visualizations are likely to be more effective than others. A successful visualization is one that emphasizes the information of interest and presents it at a resolution sufficient to perform the task.

1.6.2 Interactions to Support Exploration

There are several classes of interaction operations that can and should be integrated into the visualization process. These include:

Data selection operations ■ To retrieve subset of interest at a particular resolution

Data manipulation operations ■ To smooth, filter, interpolate, or otherwise manipulate the raw data

Representation operations ■ To set/modify the specific attribute mappings being used, such as changing the colormap

Image orientation/viewing operations ■ To pan, zoom, rotate, or otherwise modify the window/viewport mappings

Visualization interactions ■ To navigate or perform selection via directly manipulating the elements being displayed

A powerful class of interaction operations is referred to as *probes*. These allow the user to isolate a section of the data being visualized and present it in a secondary visualization that is often of reduced dimensionality. For example, a 1D probe, as found in Exvis, maps an individual data point selected with the mouse to multidimensional sound parameters. Examples of 2D probes are slices within a volume or a region of interest in an image. An *n*-D probe, such as the data-driven brush found in XmdvTool, creates a subspace of the same dimensionality as the data being analyzed and allows the user to control the location and extents of the subspace.

1.6.3 Integrating Analysis into the Visualization

Visualization is not a substitute for quantitative analysis. Rather, it is a quali-tative means for focusing analytic approaches and helping users select the most appropriate parameters for quantitative techniques. Packages such as S-PLUS and Mathematica integrate statistical tools with visualizations to allow users to interactively formulate a model to describe the data being analyzed. Packages such as SGI's MineSet and IBM's Intelligent Miner com-bine data mining operations such as association rule generators, clustering, and decision tree classifiers with visualizations that can be used for both assessing the results (hypothesis confirmation) and adjusting the parame-ters of the mining operations. Analytic tools can also be used to guide the visualization process. For example, XGobi uses projection pursuit algorithms to locate views within multivariate data sets that have potentially high infor-mation content. Keys to successful integration are a shared data model and intuitive navigation and selection tools to facilitate the creation, iterative refinement, and validation of hypotheses regarding structures within data sets.

1.7 Designing Effective Visualizations

Although creating a visualization for a particular data set is relatively straight-forward, creating an effective visualization—that is, one that communicates information accurately and in a way that helps the viewer perform his or her task—can be quite difficult. It is unlikely that there will ever be a procedure you can follow to guarantee that the resulting visualization will be good; however, there are a number of "rules of thumb" (many derived from Tufte) that you can follow to avoid common problems and increase the likelihood that the visualization will be useful. Some of these include the following:

- Include a key (legend) to the symbols and/or color mappings, as well as labels for all axes. These are essential for proper interpretation.

- Use "intuitive" mappings where possible (e.g., spatial to spatial, temperature to color), though remember that sometimes nonintuitive mappings can reveal interesting features.

- Use color with care. Be aware of context-sensitive color expectations, as well as perceptual limitations. Provide ready access to alternate color-maps and user customization, and consider redundantly mapping to data controlling the color to a different graphical attribute.

- Provide easy methods for view selection and modification, such as direct manipulation panning, zooming, and rotation.

- Avoid overcrowding images. Provide users with opportunities to enable or disable features or components of the visualization.

- Avoid distorting data (known as "viz lies"). Differences and similarities in the graphical depiction of the data should be comparable to the relationships within the data being shown.

- Scale your data with care, and convey the scaling in a key. Scaling can reveal essential features of the data, but can also be easily misinterpreted.

- Do not compare apples and oranges. For example, drawing a correlation between sunspots and the stock market is rather a stretch. People assume that data appearing in the same visualization have some semantic relationship to one another.

- Be concise. Avoid excessive gimmickry (e.g., 3D graphics for 1D data). The temptation is often to use all of the features a visualization tool provides. A key rule is to keep things simple.

- Avoid dependence on absolute judgments. Relative judgment is more reliable. As described in the section on perception, our ability to make absolute measurements on graphical attributes is limited.

- Differentiate original data from derived (e.g., interpolated, smoothed) data. There is often a temptation to discard data that detracts from the main features you are hoping to convey in the visualization. Although this can be useful and effective, it is important to inform the user that what she is viewing has been modified from the original.

- Don't forget aesthetics (visualizations should be appealing to the eye). Although we can't all be artists, we can all strive for balance, simplicity, and pleasing color combinations while avoiding garish gimmickry, excessive texture variation, and distracting flashes, beeps, and any other component of the visualization that adds little to the communication of information.

1.8 Visualization Systems

There are a number of public-domain, shareware, and commercial visualization systems that incorporate many of the techniques we have described. In this section we describe a number of such systems. Some visualization systems provide an environment that supports the development of a wide variety of applications. They provide a number of techniques and in some cases a visual programming environment. These include AVS, IBM Visualization Data Explorer, SGI Explorer, Khoros, and SciAn. Some packages focus on a specific visualization; others on a set of related visualizations. These include Xmdv, Xgobi, Xsauci, and NetMap. Finally, some packages incorporate analytic and simulation techniques with visualizations. These include S-PLUS, SPSS, MatLab, Mathematica, and MAPLE.

AVS ■ A powerful environment for the visualization of geometry and field data. It provides a large library of modules for data import, filtering, transformation, and display. Users can employ existing applications or create custom applications via visual programming. Modules are connected in a network using a point-drag-click mechanism. Modules include both analysis and display techniques, and users can develop their own modules. A large (and growing) library of free user-written modules is available through North Carolina State University. Each module provides a customizable control panel for easy interactions, and users can animate various parameters of the data flow pipeline.

NetMap ■ A visualization tool for exploring relational databases. Data nodes are ordered by one parameter in a linear or circular fashion on the screen. Relations formed by other parameters are displayed using the edges between nodes or by the color of the nodes. NetMap has the ability to handle millions of records using powerful view editing and zooming facilities. It has been successfully applied to many diverse fields (e.g., crime and stock market databases).

MatLab and Mathematica ■ Numeric computation and visualization software systems. They both provide analytic and visualization techniques. The numerous data analysis and transformations include Fourier analysis, matrix functions and operations, polynomial interpolation, special functions, and matrices (including sparse matrices). The numerous graphics techniques include 2D, 3D (surface contours, line trajectories, volume slice plots), lighting, and color models. It is also one of the few systems providing sound processing. A number of signal processing techniques are available in MatLab, including filter design and analysis, special operations, waveform generators, linear system transformations, and other transforms (Hilbert, DCT, Fourier, Z). Mathematica also provides differential equation libraries as well as other very specialized analysis and visualization packages.

Xsauci ■ A public-domain program for visual comparison of genetic sequences and similar domains (text, shapes) based on correlation images. Each row of the image corresponds to a distinct alignment of two sequences. Each pixel is colored based on a similarity metric applied to overlapping sequence elements. Sequence relationships appear as readily perceived patterns of lines. Dynamic filtering is used for removing short, spurious sequences of matches. A number of special tools are available, including database operations, feature-preserving compression, user-specified gap filling, and graphical presentation of density and distribution of sequence elements.

Xgobi ■ A public-domain program for visualizing multivariate data using 2D and 3D scatter plots. It supports brushing for highlighting, masking, and textual data identification. It also includes automated projection pursuit techniques for exploring high-dimensional spaces.

S-PLUS ■ A commercial package providing rich statistical computations with reasonable graphics output. It provides support for fitting models, prediction, dynamic loading of large data sets (30 Gb, for example), correlation measures, regression models, randomness tests, time-series, and nearest neighbor routines. It supports simulation methods and works with both spatial data and databases. S+SpatialData deals best with data sets with geostatistical data; that is, data observed at fixed locations, point patterns, data consisting of a finite number of locations in an observed spatial location, lattice data, and regularly or irregularly spaced spatial regions. Here too a number of specialized tools are provided. These include variogram visualization and estimation, kriging, spatial smoothing, Ripley's K functions, hexagonal bin plots, and point maps.

Finally, S+Datablade represents the marriage of the Illustra object-relational database and S-PLUS. It provides SQL access to databases with visualization of databases and statistical functions on the data.

1.8.1 WWW Visualization Interfaces

Most of the previously described visualization systems have their own special interfaces, ranging from a network programming interface (AVS) to Xsauci, a custom interface. There is a trend toward using a browser as the key interface for new applications. This makes sense, as we deal more and more with distributed information with the browser as the interface to search and retrieval engines. As such, having the browser as the interface to your data exploration environment also makes sense. We find thus that a browser interface to a visualization environment

- Extends Internet access
- Provides a visual interface to distributed multimedia information
- Provides transparent network access
- Is distributed (worldwide)
- Provides extensive use of graphics, video, and sound
- Provides a window interface, even to 3D data

1.9 Summary

We have provided a rapid overview of the field of data visualization. We looked at a simple taxonomy and gave a number of examples of different systems. For further information, explore the following Web sites:

www.nas.nasa.gov/RNR/Visualization/annotatedURLs.html

www-ocean.tamu.edu/7Ebaum/graphics-graph-systems.html

Slides associated with this chapter can be found at *www.cs.wpi.edu/~matt /v97tut/* and *www.cs.uml.edu/~grinstei/tut/v96tut2.html.*

There are many companies making commercial visualization technologies. These include (at the time of writing): Abacus Concepts, Advanced

Visual Systems, Alta Analytics, Autodesk, BBN, BMDP Statistical Software, Borland, BUSS, David Sarnoff Research Center, Harlequin, IBM, Information Builders, Insight Consulting, Lucent Technology, MapInfo, The Mathworks, ParaSoft, SAS Institute, Silicon Graphics, Spyglass, StaSci, Visible Decisions, Visual Numerics, and Xerox.

References

Books

[Ber73]   J. Bertin. *The Semiology of Graphics*. Madison, WI. University of Wisconsin Press (translation), 1973.

[Bro95]   J. Brown, R. Earnshaw, M. Jern, and J. Vince. *Visualization*. New York. John Wiley and Sons, 1995.

[Cle85]   W. Cleveland. *The Elements of Graphing Data*. Monterey, CA. Wadsworth, 1985.

[Cle93]   W. Cleveland. *Visualizing Data*. Summit, NJ. Hobart Press, 1993.

[Fri89]   R. Friedhoff and W. Benzon. *Visualization: The Second Computer Revolution*. New York. Harry N. Abrams, 1989.

[Hen97]   W. Hendee and P. Wells (editors). *The Perception of Visual Information*. New York. Springer-Verlag, 1997.

[Kel93]   P. Keller and M. Keller. *Visual Cues: Practical Data Visualization*. Los Alamitos, CA. IEEE Computer Society Press, 1993.

[Mil56]   G. Miller. "The Magical Number Seven, Plus or Minus Two: Some Limits on Our Capacity for Processing Information," *Psychological Review* 63:2, pp. 81–96, 1956.

[Nei90]   G. Neilson, B. Shriver, and L. Rosenblum (editors). *Visualization in Scientific Computing*. Los Alamitos, CA. IEEE Computer Society Press, 1990.

[Tha90]   D. Thalman (editor). *Scientific Visualization and Graphics Simulation*. New York. John Wiley and Sons, 1990.

[Tuf83]   E. Tufte. *The Visual Display of Quantitative Information*. Cheshire, CT. Graphics Press, 1983.

[Tuf90]   E. Tufte. *Envisioning Information*. Cheshire, CT. Graphics Press, 1990.

[Tuf97]   E. Tufte. *Visual Explanations*. Cheshire, CT. Graphics Press, 1997.

Recommended Reading

Journals

IEEE Transactions on Visualization and Computer Graphics

IEEE Computer Graphics and Applications

Computers in Physics

Computers and Graphics

Computer Graphics Forum

Computer Graphics (ACM SIGGRAPH)

ACM Transactions on Computer Graphics

Journal of Computational and Graphical Statistics

Conferences

Proceedings of IEEE Visualization Conferences

Proceedings of SPIE Conferences on Visual Data Exploration and Analysis

Proceedings of IEEE Volume Visualization Symposia

Proceedings of IEEE Information Visualization Symposia

Proceedings of ACM SIGGRAPH Conferences

Proceedings of Eurographics Conferences

Chapter 2

A Survey of Visualizations for High-Dimensional Data Mining

Patrick E. Hoffman
Georges G. Grinstein

University of Massachusetts, Lowell

Introduction

Data mining algorithms often flatten the large data sets involved. This chapter provides a survey of the common and novel flat file or table visualizations focusing on those that can handle more than three dimensions. This chapter is complementary to the chapter "Benchmark Development for the Evaluation of Visualization for Data Mining," which provides preliminary evaluations of some of these visualizations and is also found in this volume.

2.1 Data Sets Used

We selected two of the most common benchmarking data sets for use in most of our visualization examples. These are the automobile and the Iris Flower data sets. Nearly all data mining packages include at least one of these data sets. These data sets are available from the UC Irvine Machine Learning Repository [Uci97].

Iris Plant Flowers ■ From Fischer 1936, physical measurements from three types of flowers

Car (Automobile) ■ Data concerning cars manufactured in America, Japan, and Europe from 1970 to 1982

2.2 Table Visualizations

A 2D table of data is defined by M rows and N columns. A visualization of this data is termed a table visualization. We define the columns to be the dimensions or variates (also called fields or attributes), and the rows to be the data records. The data records are sometimes called n-dimensional points, or cases. For a more thorough discussion of the table model, see [Car99]. This very general definition only rules out some structured or hierarchical data. In the most general case, a visualization maps certain dimensions to certain features in the visualization. In geographical, scientific, and imaging visualizations, the spatial dimensions are normally assigned to the appropriate x, y, or z spatial dimension. In a typical information visualization, there is no inherent spatial dimension, but quite often the dimension mapped to height and width on the screen has a dominating effect. For example, in a scatter plot of 4D data, you could map two features to the X and Y axis and the other two features to the color and shape of the plotted points. The dimensions assigned to the X and Y axis would dominate many aspects of analysis, such as clustering and outlier detection. Some table visualizations—such as parallel coordinates, survey plots, and radviz—treat all data dimensions equally. We call these *regular table visualizations* (RTVs).

The data in a table visualization is discrete. The data can be represented by different types, such as integer, real, categorical, nominal, and so on. In most visualizations, all data is converted to a real type before rendering the visualization. We are concerned with issues that arise from the various types of data, and use the more general term *table visualization*. These visualizations can also be called array visualizations because all the data is of the same type.

Table visualization data is not hierarchical. It does not explicitly contain internal structure or links. The data has a finite size (N and M are bounded). The data can be viewed as M points having N dimensions or features. The order of the table can sometimes be considered another dimension, which is an ordered sequence of integer values from 1 to M. If the table represents points in some other sequence, such as a time series, that information should be represented as another column.

2.3 Terms

Key terms associated with this topic are defined in the following.

Table versus array ■ At times we may use the term *array* when discussing tabular data at the final visualization stage, where it is usually converted to array data.

Multidimensional, multivariate ■ In many data mining data sets, it is unknown whether a particular attribute or feature is independent of any other attributes. The more appropriate term is *multidimensional multivariate information visualizations*, because dependent attributes should be termed *variates* and independent attributes should be termed *dimensions*. At times, we may use the word *dimension* when it could be either dimension or variate. See [Won97] for additional discussion on terminology.

Dimensional brushing ■ A technique [Bec87] for highlighting a particular *n*-dimensional subspace in a table visualization. Each dimension has an active range, and points within this active range can be colored or highlighted with a particular value. The visualization area of this brush is colored differently.

Class points or the classification dimension ■ In data mining or machine learning, a special categorical dimension is often designated for particular classifications. For example, in a data set called "cars," there might be three classifications: American, Japanese, and European. Additional dimensions might be horsepower, weight, mpg, acceleration, cylinders, and year. Although any dimension can be used for classification, data mining algorithms work better if the range of values of the classification dimension is small. Points with different classifications, such as brushed points, can be colored with different values.

Jittering or agitating ■ A technique [Cle93] whereby data points in a visualization are randomly moved a small distance, to improve the display, or to reveal obscured (overlapped) data points.

Splatting ■ A technique for allowing 3D scatter-plot points to have some transparency and get more points on the screen.

Local normalization ■ Each dimensional range is scaled to be between 0 and 1, thus giving each dimension equal weight.

Global normalization ■ All data values are scaled to be between the maximum and minimum of all data values. The dimension that has the highest data values may have greater weight or impact in some visualizations.

Table 2.1

Local versus global normalization.

Raw Data			After Local Normalization			After Global Normalization		
Mpg	*Weight*	*Cylinders*	*Mpg*	*Weight*	*Cylinders*	*Mpg*	*Weight*	*Cylinders*
10	3000	8	0.0	1.0	1.0	0.0020	1.0000	0.0013
30	2000	4	1.0	0.0	0.0	0.0087	0.6666	0.0000
20	2500	6	0.5	0.5	0.5	0.0053	0.8333	0.0007

In many visualizations, this will have the same effect as not scaling the data at all. Typically, for some visualizations or data mining algorithms it is better to scale the data to a range between 0 and 1 or −1 and 1. Table 2.1 shows the difference between local and global normalization for three records similar to the Car data set.

Weighted normalization ■ In most cases, local normalization is used for visualization. When many columns of a data set are the same type, it is convenient for those columns to have the same normalization. For full flexibility, it should be possible to transform each column with a different "weighted" normalization.

Flattening ■ Expanding a categorical (or nominal) dimension in a data set by creating a new unique category value, with the data values becoming 0 or 1, based on the original category value of that record. For example, for a data set with one dimension, the origin of the car, three records might be:

```
MPG  Origin
---  ------
12   American
13   Japanese
14   European
```

Flattened, the records become:

```
MPG  American  Japanese  European
---  --------  --------  --------
12   1         0         0
13   0         1         0
14   0         0         1
```

Data probing ■ An interaction often implemented by clicking or brushing on a particular point in a visualization to display some or all of the pertinent information about the data record represented by that point.

Random dimensional layout ■ In most visualizations, the layout of the dimensions affects the visualization. Even in a simple scatter plot, the dimension chosen for the X axis or the Y axis changes the visualization. In higher-dimensional visualizations, the problem becomes more severe. A technique we have used for detecting patterns in some visualizations is to randomly change the layout of the dimensions. In some visualizations, such as radviz (described later), this helps determine whether there is some possible structure to the data.

2.4 Line Graphs/Multiple Line Graphs

Line graphs are used for displaying single-valued or piecewise continuous functions of one variable. They are normally used for 2D data (x, y) where the x value is not repeated. A background grid can be used to help determine the absolute values of the points. Multiple line graphs can be used or overlaid to show more than two dimensions. $(x, y1, y2, y3,$ and so on) The fact that the first dimension or the independent variable is unique gives this dimension special significance. This dimension typically represents the ordering of the table (a number from 1 to M). Often this initial ordering of the table is correlated to one of the dimensions of the data, such as time.

There are, however, problems with using overlaid multiple line graphs. Different types of continuous lines (colored, dashed, and so on) have to be used to distinguish each dimension. Each dimension may have a different scale that should be shown. For more than three dimensions, multiple line graphs can become confusing, depending on the scale and whether or not an offset is used to separate the dimensions. If a distinctly colored line is used to identify each dimension, brushing with color cannot be used to distinguish classification points. For noting interdimensional correlation, a survey plot (see Section 2.9) might be more suitable. If you are analyzing one or two continuous functions in detail, a line graph is appropriate. Figure 2.1 is a multiline graph of the Car data set, where the X axis orders the data records by type (American, Japanese, and European). Within each type, the records are sorted by year. The Y axis represents the various dimensions (locally normalized), and the line plots are colored by the type of car. The offsets between line plots are the same because the range of each line plot is the same after the normalization.

Figure 2.1

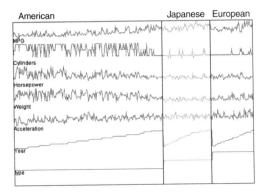

Multiline graph of the Car data set. (See also color plate.)

2.5 Scatter Plots

The scatter plot is probably the most popular data mining visualization tool. It helps find clusters, outliers, trends, and correlations. Brushing and colored class points are used to gain additional insights on the data. Zooming, panning, and jittering can be used to improve the visualization when too many points overlap or the resolution of the data causes many data points to lie at the same (x, y) coordinate. Glyphs, icons, color, and splatting are additional features or techniques that have been used to extend the usefulness of the scatter plot. The 3D scatter plot with animation, different colors, different shapes, and interaction can extend the data mining capabilities to three, four, five, or more dimensions. Depending on the user interface, the insight into the higher dimensions is rarely as good as with the standard 2D plot. One reason is that after two dimensions are used for the X and Y axes, the other dimensions (Z axis, color, shape, animation, and so on.) do not have equal affect on the visualization.

2.5.1 Scatter-Plot Matrix

A grid of 2D scatter plots is the standard means of extending the scatter plot to higher dimensions. If you have 10-dimensional data, a 10×10 array of scatter plots is used to provide a visualization of each dimension versus every other dimension. This is useful for looking at all possible two-way interactions or correlations between dimensions. The standard display quickly becomes inadequate for high dimensions, and user interactions of

Figure 2.2

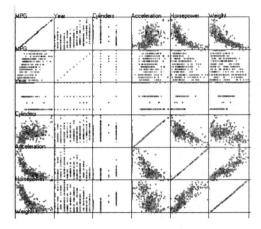

A scatter-plot matrix of the Car data set.

zooming and panning are needed to interpret the scatter plots effectively. Figure 2.2 shows a scatter-plot matrix for the Car data set. Data for American cars is red, Japanese green, and European blue. Positive correlations can be seen between horsepower and weight. Negative correlations can be seen between mpg and horsepower and weight.

2.6 Variations on the Scatter-Plot Matrix

There are several variations on the scatter-plot matrix theme. The Hyper-Slice [Van93] is a matrix of panels where "slices" of a multivariate function are shown at a certain focal point of interest ($c1$, $c2$, $c3$, and so on to cn) (Figure 2.3). This is similar to N-vision [Fei90]. The matrix panel allows you to interactively explore a multivariate function. Another similar technique, more suitable for data mining, is called prosection [Spe95]. Instead of all points being projected onto the $N \times N$ scatter-plot matrix, only points within a certain range of each dimension are shown. This is similar to brushing and dynamic queries [Ahl92].

The HyperBox [Alp91] also uses pairwise projections of the data. The projections are onto panels of an n-dimensional box, where each panel has a different orientation. Additionally, dimensions can be cut so that histograms can be shown on the panels according to ranges of the dimensions being cut. Figure 2.4 shows an example of a HyperBox.

Figure 2.3

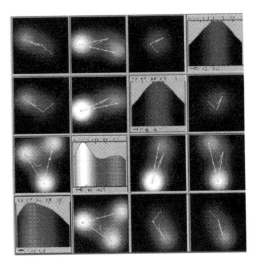

HyperSlice matrix of a multivariate function.

Figure 2.4

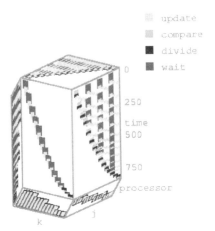

HyperBox display. (See also color plate.)

2.7 Bar Charts and Histograms

Bar charts are normally used for presentation purposes. They are related to histograms and survey plots (see Section 2.9), which are used frequently in

Figure 2.5

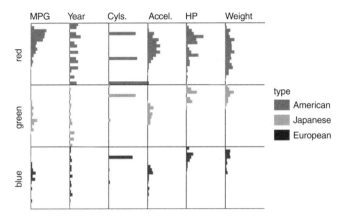

Histogram matrix of the Car data set. (See also color plate.)

data mining. Bar charts are line graphs with the area under the line filled in. Data points are usually repeated to widen the bar. Histograms are bar charts (or graphs) where the value for the bar represents a sum of data points. Histograms visualize discrete probability density functions. Multiple bar graphs and histograms can be used effectively (see "Survey Plots") in data mining. You can use an array of histograms to approximate the density functions of all dimensions of the data. Figure 2.5 is a histogram matrix of the Car data set dimensions for each class.

2.8 Permutation Matrix

In the 1960s, Jacques Bertin [Ber83] introduced the permutation matrix, an example of which is shown in Figure 2.6. This interactive plot is very similar to the survey plot (see Section 2.9), whereby the heights of bars correspond to data values. By permuting or sorting the rows or columns, depending on how the data is oriented, patterns in the data can be seen quite easily. In one of the modes of the permutation matrix, all data values below the average value are colored black, and all data values above the average are colored white. A green dashed bar corresponding to the average data value for each dimension is also displayed through the data. One implementation, Visulab [Hin93], has an automatic permutation mode, which looks for patterns in the data and permutes the matrix according to any patterns it finds.

Figure 2.6

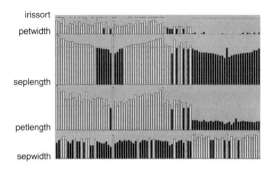

Permutation matrix of the Iris Flower data set.

2.9 Survey Plots

A simple technique of extending a point in a line graph (like a bar graph) down to an axis has been used in many systems (table lens [Rao94]). A simple variation of this extends a line from a center point, where the length of the line corresponds to the dimensional value. Another way of describing this is as follows: rotate a permutation matrix 90 degrees, shorten each bar graph by 50%, and extend an equal bar graph on the other side of the axis. This visualization has been called a survey plot in the program Inspect [Loh94], and is obviously similar to a permutation matrix. This particular visualization of *n*-dimensional data allows you to see correlations between any two variables, especially when the data is sorted according to a particular dimension. When color is used for different classifications, you can sometimes see (using a sort) which dimensions are best at classifying data. The survey plot is one of the visualizations evaluated that can find exact rules in a machine-learning data set (see Chapter 11, "Benchmark Development for the Evaluation of Visualization for Data Mining"). The survey plot shown in Figure 2.7 plots American (red), Japanese (green), and European cars. The data is sorted by number of cylinders and then by miles per gallon.

2.10 Grand Tour and Projection Pursuit

In scatter plots of data with more than two dimensions, there is a projection of the data down to two dimensions. The scatter-plot matrix makes the projections orthogonal to all possible pairs of the original dimensions. These

Figure 2.7

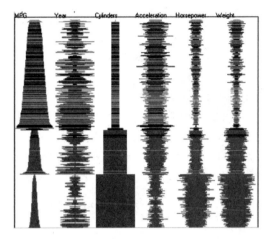

Survey plot of the Car data set sorted by cylinders and mpg.

$N \times (N-1)/2$ projections do not, however, guarantee the "best" view of the data. This "best" view of the data may be some projection that allows a linear discrimination of two classes of data. The Grand Tour [Asi85] is a method of showing or animating these projections. The Grand Tour is typically applied to a single scatter plot (or a 3D scatter plot), where the X and Y axes represent linear combinations of the N dimensions. Projection pursuit also produces projections of the data where a particular goal, such as discriminating between two data classes, drives the projections. These methods require time and animation. Depending on the display techniques, if a useful projection is found, it is not always clear how to get useful information from the linear combinations of the dimensions. Principal component analysis can be used for a 2D layout using only the two most important components, but this also suffers from a lack of easy interpretation of the X and Y axes.

2.11 Andrews's Curves

Andrews's curves [And72] plot each n-dimensional point as a curved line, using the function where the n-dimensional point is $X = (x1, x2, \ldots, xn)$. The function is usually plotted in the interval $-Pi < t < Pi$. This is similar to a Fourier transform of a data point. One advantage of this visualization is that it can represent many dimensions. A disadvantage is the computational time

Figure 2.8

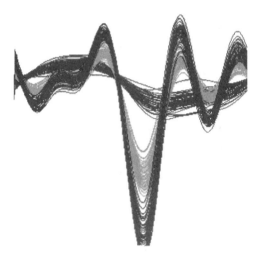

Andrews's curves of the Iris data set (three types of flowers).
(See also color plate.)

required to display each n-dimensional point for large data sets. The Iris Flower data set is plotted using Andrews's curves, an example of which is shown in Figure 2.8.

$$f(t) = x1/sqrt(2) + x2 \cdot \sin(t) + x3 \cdot \cos(t) + x4 \cdot \sin(2t) + x5 \cdot \cos(2t) + \dots \quad (1)$$

2.12 Glyphs and Icons

There are two types of visualization based on glyphs and icons. In each case, certain features of the glyph or icon are mapped to certain dimensions of an n-dimensional data point. Probably the most famous are the Chernoff [Che71] faces (Figure 2.9), where data dimensions can be mapped to facial features such as the angle of the eyes and the width of the nose (the effectiveness of this technique is widely debated). The star glyph (plot) [Cha83] is probably the most widely used glyph. In the star plot, the dimensions are represented as equal angular spokes radiating from the center of a circle. The outer end of each spoke (axis) represents the maximum value of the dimension, and the center of the circle represents the minimum dimensional value. An outer line or perimeter is drawn to connect all the data value points on each dimensional radius. This is similar to plotting points in polar coordi-

Figure 2.9

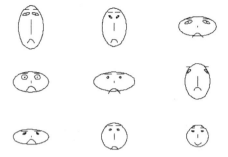

Chernoff faces (courtesty of Matt Ward, Worcester Polytechnic Institute).

Figure 2.10

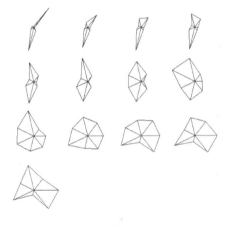

Star glyphs from Xmdv.

nates (a polar chart), which use the length of the spokes and the angle, instead of the familiar X-Y axis in Cartesian coordinates. In a typical display, there is a star glyph for every n-dimensional data point. As shown in Figure 2.10, one problem [War98] is how to organize all star glyphs on the screen in a meaningful manner.

The second type of glyph and icon visualization is when icons are packed together in a dense display. Features in the data set can be mapped to textures that are perceived by the visual system [Pic88]. This method has been used successfully for visualizing many dimensions of imaging data and is starting to be applied to information visualizations [Pin99]. Figure 2.11 shows a basic icon. Normally, various data dimension values are mapped to the

Figure 2.11

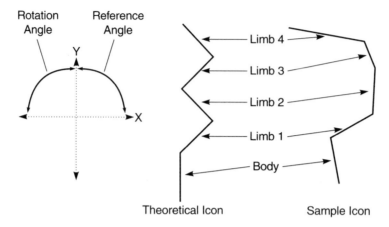

Theoretical Icon   Sample Icon

Stick figure icon.

Figure 2.12

	Low Job Married	High Job Married	Low Job Single	High Job Single
Male Low Education				
Male High Education				
Female Low Education				
Female High Education				

Mapping Census data onto an icon.

parameters of the icon, such as length of a limb or rotation angle of a limb. Figure 2.12 shows an icon mapping of several parameters from a Census data set of New England technicians and engineers, and Figure 2.13 shows icons plotted in a scatter plot of Age versus Income. The texture patterns of male and female, and high and low education, can be seen. Some other icon visualizations are shape coding [Bed90], color icons [Lev91, Kei94, Erb95] and tilebars [Hea95].

Figure 2.13

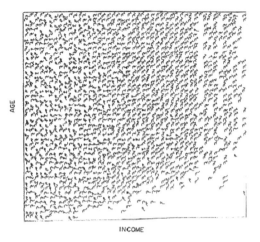

AGE

INCOME

Iconographic plot of Census data.

2.13 Recursive Table Visualizations

The following group of visualizations is termed *recursive* because the displays they create impose a hierarchical structure on the data such that some dimensional values are "embedded" in displays of other dimensions. These visualizations have also been called hierarchical axes in Wong and Bergeron [Won97].

2.14 Dimensional Stacking

General logic diagrams (dimensional stacking) were first described in Michalski [Mic78] and displayed only Boolean data values (binary). The Boolean inputs were extended to discrete categorical values (or binned ordinal values) and used for general data exploration by Matt Ward [War94a]. The technique is more generally called dimensional stacking and is implemented in the packages Xmdv [War94] and MLC++[Koh97], as well as the latest version of MineSet [Bru97]. Autoglyph [Bed90] produces a display similar to dimensional stacking but is not recursive in nature. A 2D grid is divided into sets of embedded rectangles representing the categorical dimensions or attributes of the data. There are two outer dimensions along the X and Y axes, and each additional pair of dimensions is embedded into the outer-level rectangles.

This recursive embedding continues until all dimensions or features are used. Ward and LeBlanc [War94a] call the successive embeddings "speeds."

Displaying more than nine dimensions with this technique is difficult. Each dimension should be categorical or binned (discretized), with not much more than four or five categories or bins. These are artificial limitations imposed by the display resolution. Panning or zooming techniques could avoid the need for limitations, but then you are never getting the "entire" picture at once. A final dependent dimension or classification is usually used to color or fill the smallest embedded rectangle. The outer dimensions or lower speeds have a different (more important?) effect than the inner or higher-speed dimensions. Hence, the mapping problem of which dimensions to choose for outer and inner representations becomes significant. Because of the nested dimensions on the horizontal and vertical axes, labeling becomes problematic in the visualization. Differently sized grid lines should be used to emphasize the difference between a new nested dimension and the separate bins of a dimension.

The method of binning or discretization has a strong effect on the visualization. Not only is the number of bins important but also how you divide the bins. Entropy-based binning [Koh96] helps separate the classes while keeping the number of bins small. This can also reduce the number of data points with mixed classifications in the final embedded rectangle. Dimensional stacking can be used for finding clusters, outliers, and patterns or rules in data. Depending on the dimensional layout and binning, dimensional stacking can be an important analysis tool. Figure 2.14 shows a dimensional stacking of the Iris Flower data set (three colors representing three types of flowers, with some squares having mixed classifications). The outer X axis is the binned *petal width* dimension, the inner X axis is the binned *petal length* dimension. The outer Y axis is the binned *sepal width*, and the inner Y axis is the binned *sepal length*. The concentrations of the three flower types are represented by the squares colored with three colors.

2.15 Temple MVV

In the Temple MVV system, the dimensional stacking idea has been extended and combined with the ideas of histograms and treemaps [Joh91] to produce a unique visualization. Treemaps are a hierarchical visualization where the size of nested rectangles represents data such as the size and location of files on a disk operating system. In a Temple MVV, Ted Mihalisin

Figure 2.14

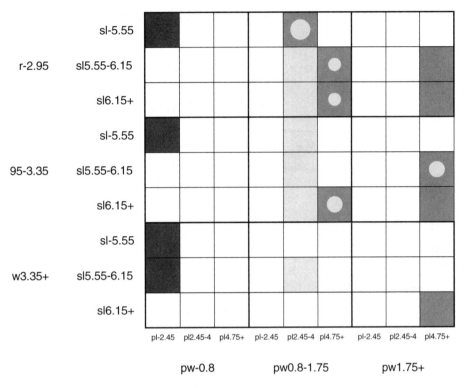

Dimensional stacking of the Iris Flower data set (from the MLC++ program).

[Mih90 and Mih91] uses a similar idea, with histograms nested within each other along the horizontal and vertical axes. Combined with binning, nested labeling, and some of the ideas of dimensional stacking, this visualization helps us see dimensional interaction (such as two- and three-way) that is difficult to see in most visualizations. Like dimensional stacking, this visualization is difficult for initial users to understand. With the interaction, data probing, and good labeling available in MVV, it has been our experience that you can learn to understand this visualization. As an example, see Figure 2.15, a 4D view of the Car data set, and Figure 2.16, a 5D view of the DNA Exon/Intron data set. The X and Y axes on the left and bottom in both displays show the nested, binned dimensions, whereas the legends on the right side of the display show how each dimension is binned.

Figure 2.15

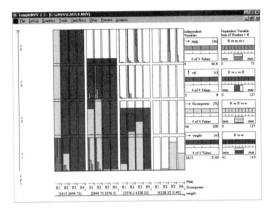

Temple MVV display of the Car data set using four dimensions.
(See also color plate.)

Figure 2.16

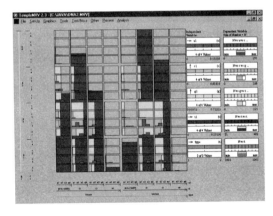

Temple MVV of a DNA data set using five dimensions.
(See also color plate.)

2.16 N-vision (Worlds Within Worlds)

When interactive 3D rendering became available, it was quickly applied to visual data analysis. If you take the dimensional stacking paradigm and extend it to an interactive, 3D environment, you might get a system similar to Feiner and Beshers's N-vision system [Fei90]. This system allows the

Figure 2.17

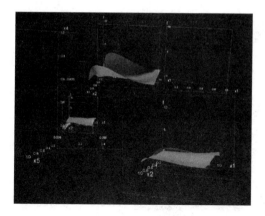

A five-variable function in N-vision.

exploration of *n*-dimensional functional spaces, but it could be adapted to *n*-dimensional data sets. To explore an *n*-dimensional function with this system, you recursively nest dimensions three at a time from outer to inner cubes (similar to dimensional stacking). The outer dimensions get fixed to constant values, whereas the inner dimensions are used to display a 3D function as a surface. A dipstick (measuring) device on the screen probes values on the surface. The outer fixed dimensions and the inner variable dimensions can be resized and manipulated for navigation. It is not clear whether this nested dimensional navigation is better than other interactive techniques, such as a guided Grand Tour or zooming and panning on a scatterplot matrix for visual data mining. It is likely that the data would have to be binned, and the inner three dimensions would be similar to standard 3D scatter plots (sometimes called spin plots in statistics). MineSet [Bru97] now has a decision table visualization that has some of the features of N-vision and dimensional stacking. Sample displays from N-vision are shown in Figures 2.17 and 2.18.

2.17 Fractal Foam

Fractal foam, a multidimensional visualization in SPSS Diamond [Sps98], represents the correlation between dimensions recursively. You choose a starting dimension that is represented as a colored circle. The other dimensions are represented as smaller circles running counterclockwise around

Figure 2.18

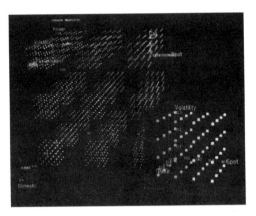

Another multidimensional function displayed with N-vision.

the main circle. The size of the surrounding circles represents the correlation coefficient between the first dimension and the surrounding dimensions. This process is then repeated, with smaller circles around each of the other circles representing their paired correlations. Dimensions that are highly correlated will have larger circles. Other statistical features (such as standard deviation, skew, and Kurtosis) can be mapped to the roughness, tilt, and flatness of the circles. This visualization is not of the data itself but of some of the statistical features of the data. This visualization suggests how other "features" of data can be used in visual data analysis. Figure 2.19 shows an example of fractal foam.

2.18 Clustering Visualizations

Several multidimensional visualizations attempt to show possible clusters in a data set. Two of these are dendograms and Kohonen neural networks, described in the sections that follow.

2.18.1 Dendograms

Dendograms are tree diagrams based on how close individual data elements cluster. The clustering usually starts by defining a metric between the data elements and clustering the closest elements first. Defining the metric,

Figure 2.19

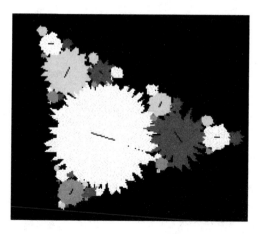

Fractal foam display: sepal length (center), petal length
(right), petal width (top), sepal width (bottom).

especially for categorical data, can be complicated. When elements are clustered in the dendogram, a horizontal and two vertical lines connect the two elements or clusters. The distance between elements or clusters is increased until all elements are connected. This "bottom-up" or agglomerative method is the usual method of creating a dendogram. There are several methods of calculating distances between clusters, with different methods producing different clusterings. The number of clusters created can be increased or decreased by setting a threshold at a particular distance. Various interactions such as data probing and class coloring or brushing can also increase the usefulness of this visualization. Figure 2.20 shows a dendogram clustering of the Iris Flower data set. The three types of flowers are colored and correspond well to the clustering from the dendogram.

2.18.2 Kohonen Nets

Another clustering technique that can be used as a visualization is a Kohonen neural network (also called a self-organized map, SOM) [Koh82]. An n-dimensional data set is used to train a neural network. The n dimensions are used as n-input nodes to the net. The output nodes of the net are arranged in a rectilinear grid (for example, a 5×6 grid would contain 30 output nodes). All input nodes are connected to all output nodes. The training and the weights are adjusted so that only one output node is turned on for a

Figure 2.20

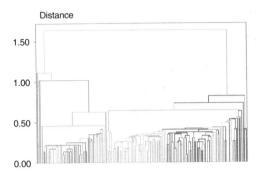

Dendogram clustering of the Iris Flower data set
(from the Inspect program). (See also color plate.)

given input (one record of the n-dimensional data set). Input vectors that are "closer" (via input values and neuron weights) to an output node will have the weights reinforced, whereas input vectors further away will turn on other output nodes. The training stops after a fixed time has elapsed or when the output nodes become stable for all inputs. The output nodes of the network generate x and y coordinates for each input vector. The x and y coordinates correspond to one output node turned on, which can be used for a 2D display. The design of the net is such that similar data elements are mapped to similar x and y coordinates. The data elements can be plotted (usually with jittering) on a scatter plot using the x and y coordinates generated from the Kohonen network. The disadvantage (as with most neural nets) is that the clusters created are not usually easily described in terms of the original data features or dimensions. The Kohonen net can also be considered a type of nonlinear data projection onto two dimensions. In this way, it is similar to multidimensional scaling techniques, such as a Sammon plot (see Section 2.21). The Kohonen SOM is somewhat similar to a K-means clustering algorithm. The differences are that the output of a Kohonen SOM is topological and clusters near each other are similar. In Figure 2.21, a Kohonen net is generated from the Iris Flower data set and used to map the data points. The 150 data points map to an X-Y grid of 5 × 6. The 5 × 6 grid (30 clusters) is the default Kohonen size in the Clementine program used to build the SOM. The points are jittered to show multiple mappings. Notice that four grid points have overlapping classifications, as compared with the five overlapping squares from the dimensional stacking (Figure 2.14). However, with the dimensional stacking the meaning of the x and y coordinates is known. The

Figure 2.21

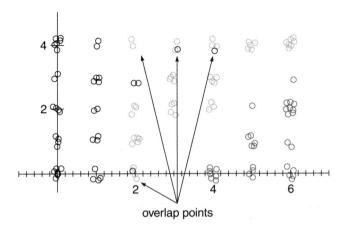

overlap points

Kohonen map of the Iris Flower data set (four overlapping squares).
(See also color plate.)

Kohonen net and plot was done using the Clementine data mining package
[Cle98].

2.19 Nonlinear Projection Visualizations: Sammon Plots and Multidimensional Scaling

In higher-dimensional spaces, clustering and patterns can exist based on distances between the data points. When these points are projected linearly, as in a scatter-plot matrix, the true distance between points is often lost in the projection. Multidimensional scaling is a technique that projects data down to two dimensions while trying to preserve the distances between all points. The Sammon [Sam69] plot was one of the first techniques. This type of visualization is similar to Kohonen maps, which can also be considered a nonlinear projection. The underlying creation methods are quite different, and therefore we have kept them in separate categories. These techniques could also be classified as "data pre-processing" and "dimensional reduction" [Kei97]. In Figure 2.22 the Iris Flower data set is plotted using a Sammon plot from the Tooldiag [Rau98] package. The three types of flowers (blue, red, and green) are clearly clustered using this nonlinear projection.

Figure 2.22

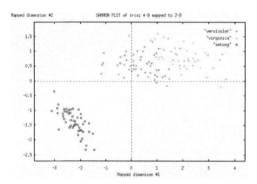

A Sammon dimensional reduction of the Iris Flower data set.

2.20 Virtual Reality: PITS (Populated Information Terrains) Visualizations

A number of virtual reality (VR) paradigms have been applied to information visualization. Sometimes called Benediktine [Ben91] spaces (coined by William Gibson in a science fiction story [Gib93]), these visualizations have the same types of problems as mapping higher dimensions to two dimensions. Benedikt talked about the mapping problem in terms of extrinsic dimensions (three spatial coordinates, one time) and intrinsic dimensions such as shape, color, and texture when creating worlds in cyberspace. This mapping problem is even greater in three dimensions when there are no obvious extrinsic dimensions of the data to map to the three spatial dimensions. Interaction (movement in three dimensions) is a necessary part of any VR visualization, and this requires learning on the part of the user. It is not clear whether the fast 3D graphics and a VR environment produce better visualizations for data mining. SGI's MineSet 3D scatter plot with animation is one of the better examples, and does seem to give insights into the data. Vineta, a VR display for document retrieval, is shown in Figure 2.23. The natural scene paradigm is another visualization technique that attempts to exploit the human visual system by mapping data onto natural scenes. The term *natural scenes* refers to scenes you might see in nature, such as trees, landscapes, and mountains. The human visual system evolved in nature and the assumption is that it is optimized for extracting and identifying features in a natural environment. This technique is not currently used in virtual reality,

Figure 2.23

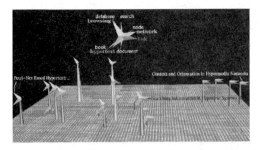

Vineta virtual reality world for document retrieval.
(See also color plate.)

Figure 2.24

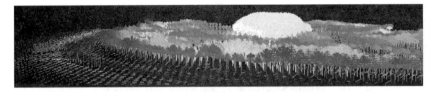

Iconographic natural scene paradigm (brain tumor).

but it could evolve in that direction. In Figure 2.24, iconographics is extended to a natural scene from a brain tumor image [Pin99].

2.21 Parallel Coordinates

First described by Al Inselberg [Ins85], parallel coordinates represent multi-dimensional data using lines. A vertical line represents each dimension or attribute. The maximum and minimum values of that dimension are usually scaled to the upper and lower points on these vertical lines. $N - 1$ lines connected to each vertical line at the appropriate dimensional value represent an n-dimensional point. In Figure 2.25, the Iris Flower data set is displayed using parallel coordinates, where the three types of flowers are represented with red, green, and purple lines.

Figure 2.25

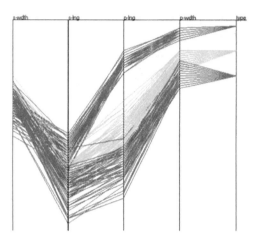

Parallel coordinates of the Iris Flower data set
(global normalization). (See also color plate)

2.22 Pixel Techniques, Circle Segments, and Recursive Pattern

The pixel techniques by Keim [Kei97] are visualizations used with large amounts of data and many dimensions. These visualizations arrange the display in areas according to the size and number of dimensions of the data. The arrangements are based on the distance of the data records from some origin (query). Each attribute (or dimension) is usually assigned one pixel, and its value is based on some color scale. Various arrangements of the data (such as recursive pattern, spiral technique, or circle segments) produce different visualizations. We have modified the circle segment technique so that an interspersed colored classification lies between a grayscale representation of the data values. Each arc represents one data value of one dimension. In Keim's original idea, the arc would represent many data values, one for each pixel in the arc. Variations of the circle segment visualizations use straight lines instead of arcs. Similar to the survey plot, the order of the data (inner to outer arcs) is very important in the visualization. When sorted by classification, the circle segment visualization can be used to determine which features (dimensions) are important for the classification of the data. Figure 2.26 is a modified circle segment display of the Car data set. Newly emerging techniques in this category include heatmaps and patchgrid.

Figure 2.26

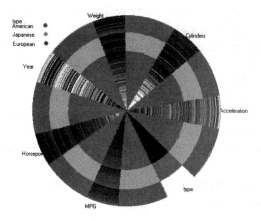

Circle segment (modified) of the Car data set.

2.23 Recently Developed Visualizations

Several new visualizations were developed during research at the Institute for Visualizations and Perception Research at the University of Massachusetts, Lowell: radviz [Hof97], circular parallel coordinates, gridviz, and the modified circle segment visualization (previously described). Comparing these visualizations with more classic visualizations (such as parallel coordinates and the survey plot) identified many common features. One key element was that all dimensions contributed equally to the visualization (thus evolved the concept of regular table visualizations, RTVs).

2.23.1 Radial Coordinate Visualization (Radviz)

The spring paradigm for the display of data has been quite successful [Hof97, Ols93, Bru98, The98]. We developed an n-dimensional radial visualization (radviz) similar in spirit to parallel coordinates, in which n lines emanate radially from the center of the circle and terminate at the perimeter, where there are special endpoints. The equally spaced points are called dimensional anchors (DAs) [Hof00]. One end of a spring is attached to each DA. The other end of each spring is attached to a data point. The spring constant K_i has the value of the i-th coordinate of the data point. The data point values are typically normalized to have local normalization. Each data point is then displayed at the position that produces a spring force sum of 0. If global normalization is used or the data values have their original values, a dimension with a larger magnitude than the others will dominate the spring visualization. For example, in the Car data set visualization, all data points would be pulled to the weight dimension, because this dimension has much larger values than the others. If all n coordinates have the same value, the data point lies exactly in the center of the circle. If the point is a unit vector point, it lies exactly at the fixed point on the edge of the circle, where the spring for that dimension is fixed. Many points can map to the same position. This mapping represents a nonlinear transformation of the data that preserves certain symmetries. The following are features of this visualization.

- Points with approximately equal dimensional values (after normalization) lie close to the center.
- Points with similar dimensional values, whose dimensions are opposite each other on the circle, lie near the center.
- Points that have one or two coordinate values greater than the others lie closer to the dimensional anchors (fixed points) of those dimensions.
- The position of a point depends on the layout of the particular dimensions around the circle.
- Radviz is easy to compute, as $O(M \times N)$ times the cost of computation, where N is the number of dimensions and M is the number of records.

The following are hypotheses that appear to be true from experimental data:

- An n-dimensional line maps to a line.
- A sphere maps to an ellipse.
- An n-dimensional plane maps to a bounded polygon.

Figure 2.27 shows a radviz visualization of the Car data set.

2.23.2 Circular Parallel Coordinates (Overlapping Star Plots)

A simple variation of parallel coordinates is a circular version, in which the axes radiate from the center of a circle and extend to the perimeter. The line segments are longer on the outer part of the circle, where higher data values are typically mapped, whereas inner dimensional values toward the center

Figure 2.27

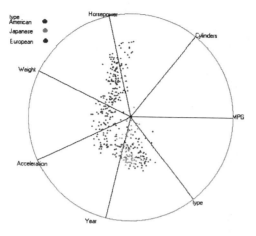

*Radial coordinate visualization (radviz) of the Car
data set. (See also color plate.)*

of the circle are more cluttered. This visualization is actually star glyphs
(plots) of the data superimposed on one another. Because of the asymmetry
of lower (inner) data values from higher ones, certain patterns may be easier
to detect with this visualization. Figure 2.28 shows a circular parallel coordinate display of the Iris Flower data set.

2.23.3 Gridviz and Other Force Field Visualizations

Gridviz is a simple extension of radviz that places the dimensional anchors
(fixed spring points) on a rectangular grid instead of on the perimeter of a
circle. The spring forces work the same as in radviz: data points are plotted
where the sum of the spring forces is zero. Dimensional labeling is difficult,
but the number of dimensions that can be displayed increases significantly.
For example, in a typical radviz display, you are limited to the points around
a circle (50 to 100 seems to be a reasonable limit). However, in a grid layout
you can easily fit 50×50 (2500) grid points or dimensions into the same area.
Assigning 2500 dimension labels at each grid point is impossible. An obvious
variation of both radviz and gridviz is to use other types of forces between
the data points and the dimensional anchor endpoints. Figure 2.29 shows a
gridviz of a 48-dimension data set, contrasted with the same data set displayed with radviz (Figure 2.30).

Figure 2.28

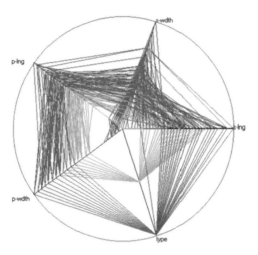

Circular parallel coordinates of the Iris Flower data set (local normalization). (See also color plate.)

Figure 2.29

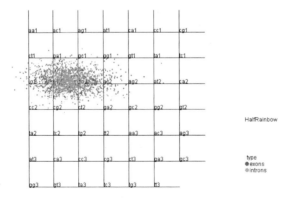

Gridviz of a 48-dimension Exon/Intron data set. (See also color plate.)

2.23.4 Dimensional Anchor Visualizations

A more formal visualization representation encompasses many of the previously described visualizations into a model we call dimensional anchor visualizations. This model allows you to produce visualizations that have fea-

Figure 2.30

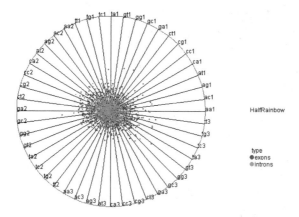

Radviz of a 48-dimension Exon/Intron data set.
(See also color plate.)

tures of parallel coordinates, radviz, survey plots, and scatter plots. It also
allows you to take a Grand Tour in the visualization space of these four visualizations. For more information about dimensional anchor visualizations,
see [Hof00]. An example of these visualizations is polyviz, described in the
following section.

2.23.5 Expanded Radviz (Polyviz)

One of the problems with radviz is that *n*-dimensional points with quite different values can get mapped to the same spot on the display. If the fixed
spring points (dimensional anchors) for each dimension are expanded as a
distribution spread out along an axis, the overlap problem is greatly reduced.
This distribution of points along an axis is quite common in visualizations,
being used in scatter plots and parallel coordinates. In Figure 2.31, the distribution for each dimension is shown by lines emanating from an axis (dimensional anchors), arranged in a *spread polygon* configuration. We have named
this visualization *polyviz*. In this visualization, you get the clustering/outlier
capability of radviz, as well as the ability to see the distribution of the data in
each dimension (similar to parallel coordinates). The polygon is spread out
to distinguish the distribution lines at the adjacent ends of the dimensional
anchors (axis). With higher dimensions, the polygon becomes more like a
circle, and the polyviz spring mappings become more similar to radviz.

Figure 2.31

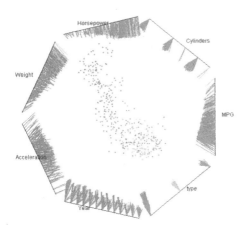

Polyviz on the Car data set.

2.26 Conclusion

No single visualization is best for high-dimensional data exploration: some visualizations are better for showing clusters or outliers, whereas others can display two- and three-way correlations. Some visualizations handle more data records than others. Some can handle quite large data sets, whereas others are most suited for smaller data sets. In all cases, this implies that data mining packages should contain an arsenal of visualizations.

References

[Ahl92]   C. Ahlberg, C.Williamson, and B. Shneiderman. "Dynamic Queries for Information Exploration: An Implementation and Evaluation," *Proceedings of the ACM CHI Conference*, ACM Press, pp. 619–626, 1992.

[Alp91]   B. Alpern and L. Carter. "Hyperbox," *IEEE Visualization '91 Proceedings*, San Diego, pp. 133–139, 1991.

[And72]   D. F. Andrews. "Plots of High-Dimensional Data," *Biometrics*, pp. 69–97, March 1972.

[Asi85]   D. Asimov. "The Grand Tour: A Tool for Viewing Multidimensional Data," *SIAM Journal on Scientific and Statistical Computing*, 6, pp. 128–143, 1985.

[Bed90]   J. Beddow. "Shape Coding of Multidimensional Data on a Microcomputer Display," *IEEE Visualization '90*, San Francisco, pp. 238–246, 1990.

[Ben91]   M. Benedikt. "Cyberspace: Some Proposals," *Cyberspace: First Steps*. Cambridge, MA. MIT Press, pp. 273–302, 1991.

[Ber83]   J. Bertin. *Semiology of Graphics*, W. J. Berg (translator), from *Sémiologie Graphique* (Editions Gauthier-Villars, Paris, 1967). Madison, WI. The University of Wisconsin Press, 1983.

[Bru97]   C. Brunk, J. Kelly, and R. Kohavi. "MineSet: An Integrated System for Data Mining," *Third International Conference on Knowledge Discovery and Data Mining*, 1997.

[Bru98]   C. Brunsdon, A. S. Fotheringham, and M. E. Charlton. "An Investigation of Methods for Visualizing Highly Multivariate Datasets," *www.agocg.ac.uk/sosci/casestudies/contents.html*.

[Car99]   S. K. Card, J. MacKinlay, and B. Shneiderman. *Readings in Information Visualization: Using Vsion to Think*. San Francisco. Morgan Kaufmann Publishers, 1999.

[Cha83]   J. M. Chambers, W. S. Cleveland, B. Kleiner, and P. A. Tukey. *Graphical Methods for Data Analysis*. Belmont, CA. Wadsworth Press, 1983.

[Che71]   H. Chernoff. "The Use of Faces to Represent Points in n-Dimensional Space Graphically," Technical Report No. 71, Department of Statistics, Stanford University, Stanford, CA, 1971.

[Cle93]   W. S. Cleveland. *Visualizing Data*. Summit, NJ. Hobart Press, 1993.

[Cle98]   Clementine. *www.isl.co.uk/clem.html*.

[Fei90]   S. Feiner and C. Beshers. "Worlds Within Worlds: Metaphors for Exploring n-Dimensional Virtual Worlds," *ACM Proceedings Conference on User Interface Software Design*, pp. 76–83, 1990.

[Gib93]   W. Gibson. "Burning Chrome," *Science Fiction Fantasy*. New York. Harper-Collins, 1993. ISBN 0-586-07461-9.

[Hea95]   M. A. Hearst. "Tilebars: Visualization of Term Distribution Information in Full Text Information Access," *Proceedings of Human Factors in Computing Systems*, CHI'95, Denver, CO, ACM, pp. 59–66, 1995.

[Hin93]   H. H. Hinterberger and C. Schmid. "Reducing the Influence of Biased Graphical Perception with Automatic Permutation Matrices, SoftStat 93," *Proceedings of the Seventh Conference on the Scientific Use of Statistic-Software*, March 14–18, 1993.

[Hof97]   P. E. Hoffman, G. G. Grinstein, K. Marx, I. Grosse, and E. Stanley. "DNA Visual and Analytic Data Mining," *IEEE Visualization '97*, Phoenix, AZ, pp. 437–441, 1997.

[Hof00]   P. E. Hoffman and G. Grinstein. "Dimensional Anchors: A Graphic Primitive for Multidimensional Multivariate Information," Workshop on New Paradigms in Information Visualization and Manipulation, in conjunction with the ACM Conference on Information and Knowledge Management (CIKM'99). To be published in 2000.

[Ins85]   A. Inselberg. "The Plane with Parallel Coordinates," Special Issue on Computational Geometry, *The Visual Computer* 1: 69–91, 1985.

[Joh91]   B. Johnson and B. Shneiderman. "Treemaps: A Space-Filling Approach to the Visualization of Hierarchical Information," *IEEE Visualization '91*, pp. 284–291, 1991.

[Kei94]   D. A. Keim and H.-P. Kriegel. "VisDB: Database Exploration Using Multidimensional Visualization," *Computer Graphics & Applications*, pp. 40–49, September 1994.

[Kei97]   D. A. Keim. "Visual Techniques for Exploring Databases," invited tutorial, *Conference on Knowledge Discovery in Databases* (KDD'97), Newport Beach, CA, 1997.

[Koh82]   T. Kohonen. "Self-Organized Formation of Topologically Correct Feature Maps," *Biological Cybernetics* 43, 59–69, 1988.

[Koh96]   R. Kohavi and M. Sahami. "Error-Based and Entropy-Based Discretization of Continuous Features." *Conference on Knowledge Discovery in Databases* KDD'96, 1996.

[Koh97]   R. Kohavi, D. Sommerfield, and J. Dougherty. "Data Mining Using MLC++, a Machine Learning Library in C++," *International Journal of Artificial Intelligence Tools*, 6:4, pp. 537–566, 1997.

[Lev91]   H. Levkowitz. "Color Icons: Merging Color and Texture Perception for Integrated Visualization of Multiple Parameters," *IEEE Visualization '91*, San Diego, October 1991.

[Loh94]   H. Lohninger. "INSPECT: A Program System to Visualize and Interpret Chemical Data," Chemometrics and Intelligent Laboratory System 22, 147–153 (*www.lohninger.com/inspect.html*), 1994.

[Mic78]   R. S. Michalski. "A Planar Geometric Model for Representing Multidimensional Discrete Spaces and Multiple-Valued Logic Functions," Technical Report UIUCDCS-R-78-897, University of Illinois at Urbana-Champaign, 1978.

[Mih90] T. Mihalisin, E. Gawlinski, J. Timlin, and J. Schwegler. "Visualizing Scalar Field on a Dimensional Lattice," *IEEE Visualization '90*, IEEE CS Press, pp. 255–262, 1990.

[Mih91] T. Mihalisin, J. Timlin, and J. Schwegler. "Visualizing Multivariate Functions, Data, and Distributions," *IEEE Computer Graphics & Applications*, 11:3, 28–34, 1991.

[Ols93] K. A. Olsen, R. R. Korfhage, K. M. Sochats, M. B. Spring, and J. G. Williams. "Visualisation of a Document Collection: The VIBE System," *Information Processing and Management*, 29:1, Pergamon Press, pp. 69–81, 1993.

[Pic88] R. M. Pickett and G. G Grinstein. "Iconographic Displays for Visualizing Multidimensional Data," *Proceedings of the IEEE Conference on Systems, Man, and Cybernetics*, vol. I, pp. 514–519, 1988.

[Pin99] D. Pinkney. "A Framework for Iconographics: A Formal Model of Icons, Interactions, and Interpolations." Doctoral thesis, University of Massachusetts, Lowell, Computer Science Dept., 1999.

[Rao94] R. Rao and S. K. Card. "The Table Lens: Merging Graphical and Symbolic Representations in an Interactive Focus + Context Visualization for Tabular Information," *Proceedings of CHI'94*. Boston. ACM Press, pp. 318–322, 1994.

[Rau98] T. W. Rauber. "Tooldiag," Universidade de Lisboa, Dept. of Electrical Engineering. *www.uninova.pt/~tr/home/tooldiag.html*.

[Sam69] J. W. Sammon, Jr. "A Nonlinear Mapping for Data Structure Analysis," *IEEE Transactions on Computers*, C-18(5), pp. 401–409, May 1969.

[Spe95] R. Spence, L. Tweedie, H. Dawkes, and H. Su. "Visualisation for Functional Design," *IEEE Visualization '95 Information Visualization Symposium '95*, pp. 4–10, 1995.

[Sps98] SPSS Diamond, *www.spss.com/software/diamond*.

[The98] H. Theisel and M. Kreuseler. "An Enhanced Spring Model for Information Visualization," *Computer Graphics Forum*, 17:3, Conference Issue, *The International Journal of the Eurographics Association*, 1998.

[Uci97] *www.ics.uci.edu/AI/ML/MLDBRepository.html*.

[Van93] J. J. van Wijk and R. van Liere. "HyperSlice," *IEEE Visualization '93*, G. M. Nielson and R. D. Bergeron (editors). Los Alamitos, CA. IEEE Computer Society Press, pp. 119–125, 1993.

[War94a] M. O. Ward, J. LeBlanc, and R. Tipnis. "N-Land: A Graphical Tool for Exploring N-Dimensional Data," *Proceedings of Computer Graphics International Conference*, 1994.

[War94b] M. O. Ward. "XmdvTool: Integrating Multiple Methods for Visualizing Multi-variate Data," *IEEE Visualization '94*, 1994.

[War98]   M. O. Ward. "Glyph Placement for Effective Information Display," *cs.wpi. edu/~matt/courses/cs563/talks/glyph_place.html*.

[Won97]   P. Wong and R. D. Bergeron. "30 Years of Multidimensional Multivariate Visu-alization," *Scientific Visualization: Overviews, Methodologies & Techniques*, IEEE Computer Society Press, pp. 3–33, 1997.

Chapter 3

Evaluation of Visualization Systems

RONALD M. PICKETT
GEORGES G. GRINSTEIN

University of Massachusetts, Lowell

3.1 Need for Evaluation

The current approach to evaluation and enhancement of visualization displays and visualization systems is largely a matter of qualitative judgment of how well we are doing and trial and error in efforts to do better. Predictable and efficient progress requires that we develop quantitative methods of evaluation. We need to determine quantitatively the relative merits of competing displays or systems and be able to tell, when we adjust parameters, whether we have made it better or worse. With sufficiently sensitive tracking of the effects of our adjustments, we might even hope to gain some basis for modeling what we are doing.

3.2 Basic Approach Required

We need to develop tests whereby each display or system under study can be subjected to a standardized test of its capacity to make visible each of a well-selected set of standard test patterns. The first requirement is for visualization scientists in conjunction with statisticians to develop those test patterns. What these test patterns should be will obviously vary from one type of visualization technique to another, and what would constitute an appropriate set for any given technique would no doubt vary with the changing spectrum of databases being analyzed. The secret to success, we think, will be to proceed in a well-focused way, dealing with just one basic technique at a time, and developing test patterns for just a few key types of data structure. The second requirement is to devise appropriately the testing procedures and apply them to systematic programs of study.

3.3 Creating a Set of Discriminating Test Patterns

The first line of attack would be to survey among the databases for which a display or system would be applied the types of target structures known to occur and are commonly sought. If, for example, you are working with multi-spectral image databases in a medical context, test patterns might be devised that mimic certain types of lesions; or, if in a weather prediction context, targets that mimic tropical storm systems. To test a display or visualization system's effectiveness in finding structure of interest in financial data, you might seek to devise test patterns that mimic failing businesses or incipient market crashes. Alternatively, you might go out into the various domains and collect actual specimens of the target structures of interest, provided of course that you can obtain gold standard "ground truths." This general approach, whether with actual or simulated specimens, presumes that you know what you are looking for. Devising test patterns that can test a system for its truly exploratory visualization capability (i.e., to reveal structures for which you have no prior specification) is another problem altogether, and perhaps an extremely difficult one. As a practical matter, you might hope to approach that type of generalized test with a set of test patterns for key structures from several different domains. Beyond that, you might hope to approach the problem of devising a generalized set of test patterns in an abstract way—in terms of purely statistical definitions and operations on numerical arrays. But here, you would need some type of system, starting, we think, with a taxonomy of statistical structures that can be imposed on different types of data arrays.

3.4 Devising Testing Procedures

We are talking here about conducting tests with human observers of the perceptibility of complex test patterns—complex visual patterns for the most part, but quite possibly auditory patterns as well. The data in which the test pattern is immersed is typically noisy. The observer's task may be to determine whether the pattern is present or absent in the data array or whether the pattern in array 1 is the same as in array 2, or perhaps the task is to scale some property of the pattern. Procedures well developed in the area of experimental psychology are available for conducting such tests to ensure obtaining precise, reliable, and objective measures of the observer's performance. These measures of performance when obtained with different displays or systems under controlled conditions can serve in turn as precise, reliable, and objective measures of each system's effectiveness in revealing test patterns. One class of testing procedures is available for tests with real target structures—structures that come inextricably immersed in their naturally noisy arrays. Other procedures, typically more powerful and flexible, are available for tests that employ synthetic target structures—structures in which you can manipulate not just the structure itself but the noise, and in particular the signal-to-noise ratio.

3.5 Suggestion for an Initial Program of Work

An initial program of work should be aimed at clarifying the general need for an approach to evaluation and providing some clear illustrations. It would probably be best to concentrate on one main visualization system supporting a variety of display techniques, and so the first step would be to select it. The second step would be to survey the various domains in which that system would be applied and identify a set of key target structures, many of which would come from domain experts and data mining known structures. The third step would be to assemble, for each of these key structures, a reasonably large number of independently generated tokens that would serve as the items that constitute the test. The fourth step would be to conduct a series of tests in which one or another parameter of the display or system is manipulated to determine whether it has a beneficial or detrimental effect. Measures of the observer's accuracy in perceiving the tokens for each type of test pattern under each of the parameter settings would constitute the figures of merit for each of the system variants under study.

Chapter 4

The Data Visualization Environment

MIKE FOSTER

Jet Propulsion Laboratory

ALEXANDER G. GEE

University of Massachusetts, Lowell

Introduction

Presented here are the issues for the development of visualization and interaction techniques within exploration environments. Discussions include the requirements for supporting users and the possible addition of computer-assisted techniques. The development of a taxonomy for visualization techniques and interaction methods is recommended. Finally, a generalized collaborative exploration environment that supports multiple users and various computers is introduced, providing a look at future data mining and visualization systems.

The knowledge discovery in databases (KDD) process is not a black box based on some searching algorithms that return information about the data, but rather an interactive process involving a human user. Consequently, the design of applications and tools for the mining and visualization of databases must take into consideration the user. Users will require systems that support numerous mining algorithms, various visualization techniques, direct interactions between the algorithms and visualizations, and possibly computer guidance. Future data exploration tools will evolve from single-user applications running on computers to collaborative human-computer environments. These new exploratory systems will share the discovery workload with the user in a process that incorporates data mining algorithms and data visualization displays combined through interactive controls. By providing appropriate connection mechanisms between computer and user exploration activities, the resulting knowledge will have greater value.

First, what are the requirements of users involved in an interactive-guided KDD process? Next, what are the defining characteristics of the various visualization techniques and interaction tools? Finally, what is needed to help multiple computers and several individuals collaborate in data explorations?

4.1 User Requirements

The development of any interactive system requires a close look at the user requirements for such systems. Users are the individuals who are interactively using the computers to explore data. We need to understand what users require for exploring data sets, small and large. What types of visualization tools and interaction methods are useful in a human-computer exploratory environment?

The understanding of user requirements helps in the development of exploration systems. The sharing of tasks between users and computers to enhance the exploration process is established by the needs of users. If a mapping could be defined between a user's model and the computer's model for the exploration environment, interactive support from both machines could be defined. The suggestion of a formal grammar to define such a mapping between users and computer was one solution. It was also conjectured that this mapping might be defined in such a way as to be domain independent. The specifics of an exploration, such as the type of data under observation, could be kept very general. This development of an underlying language for both user and computer could provide the connection for a cooperative exploration system.

One of the most difficult problems of dealing with large data sets is how to present the data to the user. Current data sets have many attributes, with a large number of cases. Typically, it is impossible to present a user with a general picture of the entire data set. How then can a user understand the scope of a problem with a narrow view of the data? In answer to this question, we have devised a data presentation method based on multiple levels of abstraction. Each level will compress the information contained in the next lower level, where the base level contains the raw data. As with all compression techniques, the higher the compression the larger the summary of information presented. Such a presentation method must also provide evidence to support such a compression, in order to maintain the user's confidence that the display is faithful to the underlying data presented. Users should be able to trust the validity of any visual display of data in an exploratory process, hence providing valid knowledge about the data. These levels of abstraction can be generated by several methods, including scales, clustering, and even through data mining algorithms. One suggestion for producing the levels included the use of hexagonal bins. The procedure for generating these levels could be computed when the data was obtained or dynamically created during the exploration process. With such hierarchical data representations, it should be possible to visualize each level and interactively visualize slices down through these levels.

Another requirement imposed by users of an exploration environment is the need to support several different visualization displays with their various interactions. In dealing with this support, developers need to factor in response time as well. Caching and pre-fetching will help provide an application with the necessary speed and responsiveness. For caching to be effective, a means of persistent data storage must be developed. This way, anything that has been computed can be stored so that it would not need to be computed again. Instead of performing a possible time-consuming calculation, the algorithm can simply read the result from disk. Including the cache within the exploration system will allow users to move quickly back and forth between different views without having to recalculate anything. Whereas caching eliminates the need to recompute anything, pre-fetching will perform the calculations in advance, placing them in the cache for when the user needs them. In a multithreaded graphical environment, system idle times can be used to run a pre-fetch thread that will attempt to predict actions the users might take, and prepare the results of those calculations so that they can be accessed quickly. Aggressively prefetching either the next zoom level down or the next screenful of data are just two methods that will provide a noticeable improvement in the speed in which data is displayed.

Consequently, it is important for any interactive environment to take into consideration the user's requirements. These requirements include visualization and interaction issues directly related to the user, the design of system models for both the user and the computer, and the construction of the underlying system architecture.

4.2 Computer Support

Given such a wide selection of data visualization tools and interaction techniques, how does a user know when one technique is better suited for a given problem? Future exploration systems will likely provide knowledge-based support to reduce the number of choices the user has, at least initially. Computer assistance can be applied in two ways. First, the computer could provide logical choices to the user that are appropriate for various situations. Second, the system might automatically perform certain common tasks. Through such computations, the computer will better support the exploration process and the user.

An important activity for the previously described computer support is the development of a taxonomy of visualizations and interactions. A useful mapping of techniques to problems would help computer-guided explorations by suggesting visualization techniques appropriate for data queries or computational results. It would be beneficial for a visualization system to have knowledge about each visualization method, to provide mining and interaction techniques that are representative of such a display. Similar to the taxonomy of visualization techniques would be the taxonomy of visualization interactions for the optimized support of exploration activities.

Researchers are now starting to work on taxonomies for interactive visualizations, including a group at Carnegie Mellon University who have developed an initial framework for classifying interactive visualizations [Chu96]. Similar to the work performed by the human-computer interaction community, these individuals have developed a classification system based on primitive functional components. They further present rules for the composition and structure of these primitives. Their goal is the development of toolkits for "assembling visualization interfaces both interactively and automatically" [Chu96].

Thus, the development of taxonomies for both visualization techniques and interaction methods will be important for the next generation of exploration systems. The result of such work will elevate the general conception of computers to exploratory assistants. Through active participation, the computer assists the work of its user.

4.3 Collaboration Tools

An important addition to an exploration environment would be the support of multiuser collaboration. This involves a scale-up from the individual exploration sessions to group collaborative exploration efforts. As data sets increase in size, one computer and one user would no longer have the power or the time to handle the amount of new super-large data sets. Current efforts need to address how groups of users can interactively explore data sets in a collaborative manor with multiple machines. Data collection, exploration, analysis, and collaborative working will appear in the next decade brought forth by "widespread, networked, multimedia interpersonal collaborative computing" [Pea94]. Depending on the domain, future KDD applications will need to support several people working independently or several people working together, possibly on the same data.

The standard approach for scientific research involving several scientists usually means sitting in front of a single workstation, where they visualize results. Currently aimed at individuals separated geographically, collaborative environments push to have individuals working together via remote machines providing identical displays. An example project in Europe, PAGEIN (Pilot Applications on Gigabit European Integrated Network), provides an experimental test bed for remote supercomputing, heterogeneous cooperative computing, and group work in applied research [Ruh93]. This also represents the need to combine different types of resources for one project. It should be possible to integrate the computational power of supercomputers with the graphical capabilities of scientific workstations [Wie93]. Collaborative environments range from joint student projects to industrial cooperative experiments, such as PAGEIN. The CoVis project, sponsored by the National Science Foundation, provides K–12 students with a collaboration system for scientific research [Gom94]. This second example provides individuals with a shared multimedia database application called the Collaboration Notebook, a software support that includes a scientific visualization package [Ede95, Gom94].

The first step to providing multiuser support is to record user exploration sessions, or what some call audit trails. This logging system would provide a record of all the work done, allowing it to be repeated in the future or analyzed at a later data. Undo capabilities could also be factored into the design of the log. Each entry could be a representation of an *action* class, where each object would have perform and reverse methods. Perform would be the action, whereas reverse would return the system to the previous state. Keeping these actions inside a queue, you could later step through the analytical process, either as a demo or a review.

The next step is to provide a mechanism to view the data space and to display those sections of the data space that have been covered for analysis versus those sections that still need to be looked at. It could be worthwhile to provide an automatic partitioning mechanism that would divide the data space among users and machines. This is a visualization problem of the working data space with user involvement and the various available machines.

Finally, there is the issue of real-time collaboration explorations. Such issues as system synchronization, data read-write requirements, and interactive visualization updates become important research topics. Synchronization techniques also need to be addressed when dealing with collaboration systems. If several people are looking at the same data display from different remote sites, something must be done so that two people do not make incompatible changes to the display. For example, if two people are looking at one week's worth of data out of an entire month, one user may try to zoom in to the first data, whereas another user may try to scroll forward one screen. Depending on the order, they could be looking at either the second day of data or the first day of the second week. In most cases, such as this, it would merely be a minor annoyance. However, if two other users receive the instructions in a different order, they would be looking at completely different data sets. One easy way to resolve this would be to think of the data set as a whiteboard with only one pen. If someone wants to modify the data, they would need to grab the pen in order to make the change. This could lead to a *lock starvation* type of problem if someone were to keep the pen, but because the users would be collaborating, it would probably be safe to assume that everyone would be willing to take the pen, use it, and then return it when through. Everyone who wants to use the pen could be placed in a queue and notified when it is their turn. This pen and queue could trivially be maintained through a network program either running as a separate application or as part of the graphical user interface of the project leader.

Consequently, there are many issues in developing group collaboration tools for the data exploration process. The power of collaboration is not just for remote groups but also within departments, possibly even in the same room. It is standard practice to have teams working on projects, which is no less true to data exploration groups. Hence, the development of exploration environments that support several individuals and various computers should increase the resulting knowledge.

4.4 Conclusion

The development of data exploration environments requires research from several areas, including data visualization and interaction techniques. From the need to understand user requirements to the generalization of exploration systems, there are many issues still left unanswered. The importance of a taxonomy for visualization techniques and interaction methods is self-evident, as it could be used in many applications involving visualization.

References

[Chu96]   M. C. Chuah and S. F. Roth. "On the Semantics of Interative Visualizations," *Proceedings of the IEEE Symposium on Information Visualization*, October 28–29, 1996, pp. 29–36.

[Ede95]   D. Edelson, D. O'Neill, L. Gomez, and L. D'Amico. "A Design for Effective Support of Inquiry and Collaboration," *Proceedings of the Conference on Computer Support for Collaborative Learning*, 1995, pp. 107–111.

[Gom94]   L. Gomez, B. Fishman, J. Polman, R. Fish, S. Bly, Y. Andres, and S. Canetti. "Media Spaces and Their Application in K–12 and College Learning Communities," Panel conducted at the Annual Meeting of the Computer Human Interaction Special Interest Group of the Association for Computing Machinery, Boston, 1994, pp. 185–186.

[Pea94]   R. Pea, D. Edelson, and L. Gomez. "Distributed Collaboration Science Learning Using Scientific Visualization and Wideband Telecommunications," Symposium of Multimedia Information Systems for Science and Engineering Education: Harnessing Technologies at the 160th Meeting of the American Association for the Advancement of Science, February 22, 1994.

[Ruh93]   R. Ruhle, U. Lang, and A. Wierse. "Cooperative Visualization and Simulation in a Supercomputer Environment," Proceedings of the Joint International Conference on Mathematical Methods and Supercomputing in Nuclear Applications," vol. 2, April 19–23, 1993, pp. 530–541.

[Wie93]   A. Wierse, U. Lang, and R. Ruhle. "Architectures of Distributed Visualization Systems and Their Enhancements," Eurographics Workshop on Visualization in Scientific Computing, Abingdon, UK, 1993.

Chapter 5

Visualizing Massive Multivariate Time-Series Data

DENNIS DECOSTE

Jet Propulsion Laboratory and
California Institute of Technology

Introduction

This chapter summarizes our experience and philosophy in developing tools for mining and visualizing massive multivariate time-series data. Our primary task is discovering nominal relationships among sensors from large-scale historic data sets of NASA spacecraft, such as the Space Shuttle, typically consisting of thousands of sensors, each sampled over millions of time points. Our work focuses on discovering context-sensitive high- and low-envelope functions particularly useful for detecting future abnormalities and faults during health monitoring operations. However, we believe the visualization issues being addressed in our work are applicable to general large-scale time-series data mining tasks and are relatively underexplored to date in the data mining community.

We have been developing a visualization system for exploring massive time-series data, summarizing discoveries, and interactively guiding the KDD process. One of the key goals driving our work has been to scale up effectively to temporal databases on the order of years of data (i.e., 1 sample/ sec) over tens of thousands of raw (sensor) and derived (transformed) features, for a variety of engineering sensor data from both deep space and earth-orbiting spacecraft, such as the Space Shuttle.

Our Java-based prototype, which we call HyperCells, essentially builds upon the paradigm of a multi-windowed row/column spreadsheet, with which most users are already comfortable. The key difference is that our cells routinely contain 2D scrollable strip charts (with each X axis representing a time range and each Y axis representing a value range). In addition, we allow for intercell annotations, such as color-coded causal arrows, to summarize discovered relationships, such as a hypothesized cause of some circled hypothesized anomalous event in time.

We argue that getting your "hands around the data and results" can require displaying and navigating potentially hundreds of cells at once. In scientific and academic report plots, annotations such as axis tick marks, text labelings, and plot-separating space typically consume much of the limited number of display pixels—and in fact often simply "get in the way." In contrast, our cells typically contain only the plot lines themselves, enabling hundreds of cells to be usably visualized on a single display. Specific labeling and time/value coordinate information can be effectively obtained dynamically only as requested. Indeed, we strongly believe that effective visualization of massive time-series discoveries must focus on such dynamic interaction, navigation, and explanation, rather than on static layouts typical of hardcopy reports.

We have found that as long as annotations are available temporarily (via interactive requests), users often have little difficulty keeping track of which unlabeled plot represents what (based on visual cues such as cell location and quickly accumulated experience about the basic waveform characteristics that generally distinguishes particular sensors from one another). Furthermore, to minimize wasteful white space, we have found that automatic scaling of the data to span the full height of each plot cell works well in conjunction with what we call "synchronized cursors." The main cursor displays in the cell the mouse pointer is currently over, indicating the sensor value range and time range corresponding to the pointer's current X and Y screen position within that cell. Additional synchronized cursors display at the X and Y positions within any other user-selected cells, with those positions corresponding to the same value and time ranges as the main cursor. By moving the main cursor to a visual landmark in the current cell, users can easily visually compare its sensor value or time point against that of other landmarks visible in other selected cells. For example, this conveniently shows whether plots of two cells peak at about the same value for the same time point, without requiring traditional tick marks or uniform scaling.

Effective visualization and navigation of massive time series introduces special requirements for efficient indexing and caching of the archived data, over multiple time scales and time windows. Even million-pixel displays cannot display all of the data in full resolution, nor would that be an effective means of summarization. In addition, all of the archived data typically cannot be stored in RAM, requiring effective indexing, caching, and pre-fetching. For example, during a typical navigation to walk through a set of newly discovered anomalies and hypothesized causes, the mapping relations from data times/values to *x/y* pixels for each plot cell typically changes for each discovery summarization. Discovered relations involving weeks or months of data (representing millions of time samples) can often be summarized as min/max/mean *y* values across the X axis using a cell width of mere tens or hundreds of pixels, but that will only be effective for interactive KDD if context switching among those time periods to perform the necessary pixel binning of archived data can be done in real time (or intelligently anticipated and precomputed during human visualization/navigation of earlier contexts).

Such concerns of scalability and effective dynamic navigation relate to several key research issues for integrating visualization with KDD. In our current work, we have been investigating front-end computation steering, primarily to invoke our KDD engine to discover input-conditional envelopes (i.e., hi/lo bounds) on historic time-series data, in terms of input and target features refined by humans based on visualization-inspired intuitions. Some of the details of our KDD engine, called Envelope Learning and Monitoring Using Error Relaxation (ELMER), are described in [DeC97]. Such front-end steering is very much in the spirit of the "what-if" nature of the spreadsheet model we are generalizing in our visualization work.

We have also found it very productive to view visualization as a separate and distinct engine of the larger KDD process, with its own visualization language within which discovery and summarization engines can explain their results. This includes not only the static property information typical of such languages (such as colors, annotations, and layout information) but dynamic information, such as sequencing of navigation events, which correspond to the sort of mouse and keyboard navigation commands a user might invoke manually. Explaining temporal discoveries can, for example, require showing dynamic evolution or jumping between several similar cases scattered across various months. Indeed, we believe that work toward portable or common subsets of dynamic visualization languages/concepts would be a particularly worthy goal for the KDD and visualization community at large.

References

[DeC97]   D. DeCoste. "Mining Multivariate Time-Series Sensor Data to Discover Behavior Envelopes," *Proceedings of the Third Conference on Knowledge Discovery and Data Mining (KDD-97)*, Newport Beach, CA, August 1997.

Chapter 6

Portable Document Indexes

JOHN LIGHT

Intel Architecture Labs

6.1 Background

I have constructed a system that allows desktop visualization of any document set. The system is detailed in [Lig96] and is fully functional at this time.

My primary interest is the effective use of the desktop computer in document exploration. Too much emphasis has been placed on server functionality, relegating the desktop computer to textual input and output, acting as little more than a dumb terminal.

Interactive document exploration on the desktop requires that the exploration process be scalable in both storage and processing requirements. Scalable storage requires compact representations of documents. Scalable processing means $N \times \log_N$ processing at worst, with linear processing preferable. My system provides compact document representations (~1% of original size) and linear processing.

The system represents each document as a vector of topic strengths. The topic strengths are calculated relative to a pre-authored list of topics. Authorship of the topics is both the greatest strength and greatest weakness of my system. The weakness results from the early binding of semantic content. Once calculated, the definition of a topic is forever embodied in the topic strength value throughout later processing steps. The strength of the approach is that this early binding provides the desired storage and processing scalability and allows the user to exploit expert knowledge about the document set.

The availability of a vector of topic strengths about each document lends itself to many types of visualization. The one I have chosen to pursue is a Cartesian graph of a subset of the topic space. One to three topics can be chosen as axes for the Cartesian graph, resulting in a 2D or 3D graph of the documents.

(The visualization is implemented in OpenGL, allowing the unified use of 2D and 3D presentation.)

6.2 My Corner of Data Mining

Data mining, or what we did before the term was invented, has historically been the province of experts in the subject area being mined. The expertise was needed to understand the encoding and format of the data, as well as the context and meaning of the data. The KDD community is trying to provide automated means of exploring data mines, reducing or eliminating any need for the expert.

My interest in data mining is limited to unstructured collections of textual material, which I refer to as document sets. I leave databases, spreadsheets, and other structured sources to others. This corner of data mining has traditionally been left to various text indexing techniques, including full text indexing, Boolean query, or subset indexing schemes such as Glimpse.

A further benefit of the construction of the topic is that they can act as filters, to further reduce processing and storage for focused exploration. Because most documents are not about most topics, and the mechanism minimizes false positives, the topic vector for most documents is sparse, allowing them to be used in filtering operations without loss of generality.

My approach works on any document set, whether it is a document archive (such as the Tipster archives of news articles) or a Web site, both of which I have demonstrated working with my system. Just as likely a target is the set of text files on a desktop machine or file server.

I feel my major contribution in this area is that my system empowers the expert rather than eliminates him. The expert needs to identify the fundamental topics, or *dimensions*, of the document set. Then he must describe the topics using the terms and phrases normally used to talk about each topic. This allows the expert's knowledge to be used in exploring the document set without requiring the expert's personal intervention in any transaction. This is the proper role of the expert, involved indirectly in the process, not relegated to the sideline.

6.3 **My Take on Visualization**

My primary interest is visualization. I had to dabble in information retrieval technology to provide the quantifications necessary to support interesting visualizations. Visualization is the payoff.

Rather than create visualizations to present results to the user, I believe that visualization should be a means of involving the user in a search for results. Too much visualization attempts to create, either directly or indirectly, a single picture that shows *the answer*. Instead, the visuals should be part of a process that allows the user to find the answer in his own mind. This is a place where print visuals diverge from computer visuals: print visuals can only just sit there, whereas computer visuals can always respond.

To involve the user, we must stop trying to put print visuals on the computer screen and instead ask ourselves how we can empower users to find answers themselves. This means that our computer visuals must be simpler and more interactive. They must communicate a lot of raw information rather than small amounts of cooked information. To do this we must recognize the difference between left-brain and right-brain activity.

Left-brain/right-brain theory is controversial, but regardless of the actual brain mechanism, there is evidence that two visual channels connect our brains to the world. One (to the left brain) is good at symbolic, coded information such as text, but is able to deal with only limited complexity (this is where the *hrare* limit (7 ± 2) comes from). The other (to the right brain) deals best with concrete, uninterpreted information of nearly any complexity. Your right brain cannot recognize words, and your left brain cannot recognize faces.

I believe that at any one time we can only get useful input from one visual channel at a time. On the other hand, our brains are able to switch between channels quite well. Furthermore, the channel used is not under our conscious control without significant training. By carefully constructing our visualizations to appeal (at different times) to different channels, we can aid the user in adapting appropriately. On the other hand, when we are not careful about constructing our visualizations, we can make it very difficult for users to glean the data we present. By engaging the user's right brain in high bandwidth visualizations, we can make a place for the user in the exploration process.

6.4 Summary

I see effective document set exploration as a collaboration between the software developer, experts in the documents being explored, and the user. Most document exploration tries to place the entire burden on the software, ignoring two potential contributors. My system is a first step in fully exploiting all of the available resources.

Reference

[Lig96]   J. Light. "A Distributed, Graphical, Topic-Oriented Document Search System," *Proceedings of Visual Data Exploration and Analysis IV*, 1996, SPIE Volume 3017, pp. 129–135.

Character-Based Data Visualization for Data Mining

Michel Pilote
Madeleine Fillion

Livetech Research International, Inc.

Introduction

Is the use of high-quality graphics an essential ingredient of data visualization? We identify some core mechanisms that will benefit any data visualization system, independently of the degree of graphical sophistication. Limited graphics can even prove advantageous at times, such as at the exploration analysis stage of data mining for large data sets.

In the context of improving the integration of data mining and knowledge discovery systems with visualization, are graphical user interfaces (GUIs) absolutely necessary for visualization and data mining? In the commercial sector, and possibly in the mind of many researchers, data visualization is often equated with the use of high-quality graphics. But an effective data visualization system requires the combination of many components, many of which are independent of the visual presentation of information. These same underlying mechanisms can still prove very useful and effective when used by themselves, with highly simplified and restricted syntactic means.

To better uncover these underlying principles and mechanisms, this chapter explores the feasibility and potential of concentrating on character-based displays and interaction to support data visualization for data mining, without the benefits of the familiar point-and-click GUIs and bitmapped displays. In many cases, we have been able to find ways to sustain comparable usability and effectiveness, while simplifying the development and support tasks.

In the context of visualization techniques, we particularly focus on the initial *exploration analysis* phase, typically defined as using interaction, as well as undirected search for structures and trends, to provide hypotheses about some data [Bro97]. Very limited graphical means can prove especially useful at this data exploration stage, to equip someone to rapidly navigate and make sense of large amounts of new information with unknown structure.

7.1 Motivation

This research evolved from earlier projects in building "classification systems," in which we found that relying on automated mechanisms such as rules could be detrimental both for their users as well as their technical support [Der97]. We achieved greater effectiveness, productivity, reliability, and manageability by replacing rules with "partitions" of the relevant data domains, together with the means of "navigating" among various data slices and levels of detail. Users reported feeling "inside" their data and becoming able to "sense" the presence of interesting or abnormal combinations [Hub97]. These early applications showed many of the characteristics that now motivate the integration of data visualization and data mining.

Although we had initially used a GUI front end to achieve these effects, we noticed that most of the screen content of interest to these users was basically textual and numerical information. Furthermore, the functionality we had built into this GUI turned out to be the most difficult part to adapt to new situations. These factors motivated us to investigate the consequences of removing any dependency on bitmapped technology. We selected an application domain that is particularly dependent on sophisticated graphical means: the world of market trading and financial derivatives. This domain is also especially challenging because it involves matching a high volume of constantly updated time series from unreliable data sources.

7.2 Underlying Semantic Components

This section defines, analyzes, and illustrates a number of operations we found useful to support data visualization for the purpose of data mining, independently of the degree of graphical sophistication used to package this information. The next section presents examples of these operations, applied to a test database of financial market activity.

Any *classification* mechanism will partition a set of records into a number of *classes*. The operations discussed in the following proved most useful to manipulate these classes of records.

Structural operations work on attributes (at the metadata level) to vary the number of subclasses and their respective cardinality. These operations can be subdivided into products, unions, and mappings. *Product* operations combine attributes to increase the number of subclasses, and thus reduce the cardinality of each of these subclasses. *Union* operations (often called generalization) group possible values of the selected attribute(s) to end up with fewer data subclasses of higher cardinality. *Mapping* operations take subclasses as separate entities, with attributes corresponding to "aggregates" of lower-level attributes, or link separate data sets according to a common key.

Navigation operations allow us to filter in and out some of these subsets, to zoom in and out at different levels of detail. We use the *select* or *delete* operation to control the number of selected data records, either by restricting the cardinality of subsets or by restricting attribute values. We sometimes need to *hide* some data records, as opposed to deleting them, in the context of overlapping subclasses induced by multivalued attributes and by mappings. The *expand* operation allows us to bring back all records holding some value. We can *undo* any of these operations, which are kept in a command history.

Presentation operations are used to consider a given set of records from different points of view and in various formats. These operations include adding totals, averages, and percentages of various types. Other "presentation" operations will vary the number of dimensions, from lists to tables, cubes, and so on (these are actually alternative ways of visualizing the effects of "product" operations). Another option is to vary the attributes displayed for each combination and their format.

Data transformation operations are used to add computed attributes. Their values are computed as needed, as opposed to being stored in the database.

Annotation operations allow us to record user input to be used for further selections. Such operations can be used, for example, to flag data errors observed while navigating among data records using the previously described operations. These flags and notes can then be used to select or remove as needed these entities, as part of further navigation.

7.3 **Examples**

Figure 7.1 shows the type of data that underlies our examples. We have a database of market quotes, taken at various intervals, presenting the price activity and volume during this period. Records of "intra-day" activity also include a "time" value. Futures market quotes can be given for different contract expiry months. Figure 7.2 presents a simplistic example of a classification, according to the "period" attribute. The entire set of records has been divided into five classes. Each cell shows the number of records, with a corresponding value.

Figure 7.3 depicts the result of a product operation combining the "date" and "period" attributes. It shows the bottom portion of a cross-reference table between these two attributes. We now have many more classes, each containing a smaller number of records. Conversely, Figure 7.4 shows the result of a union operation, where we have joined all "date" values according to their first two positions, representing the "year" involved. This has reduced the number of classes, and increased the number of records in each of these classes.

Figure 7.5 shows some time series resulting from a mapping operation, grouping all records with the same "label," contract expiry month ("exp"), and "period." In addition to inheriting these values from individual quotes, the new entities will carry attributes, such as the number of quotes in each of these time series ("card"), and starting date. Figure 7.6 classifies these time series according to the year portion of their starting dates and their sampling periods. Figure 7.7(a) illustrates a navigation operation, where we focus on time series starting in 1997 by selecting the "97" value of the vertical axis. Then, in Figure 7.7(b), we perform a "product" operation, adding the middle two positions of the starting date to split the resulting row according to distinct starting months.

Figure 7.8 shows portions of translation tables that can support different presentations of classifications involving ticker labels and contract expiry codes. As an example of a data presentation operation, Figure 7.9(a) shows a portion of a 2D breakdown between sticker labels and sampling periods for futures market quotes. Labels have been grouped in this figure by their category, and then replaced by their description, using the first translation table shown in the previous figure. We would have previously used the "equity" attribute of this translation table to select only the "futures" quotes. To further illustrate how structural and navigational operations can be combined to achieve a desired effect, Figure 7.9(b) presents the result of mapping individual quotes in the current figure to their corresponding time series. From this

Figure 7.1

per	id	exp	date	open	high	low	close	vol	time
1s	sp	7h	970115	772.	772.25	771.9	772.25	8	1510
1s	sp	7h	970115	772.3	772.4	772.15	772.2	14	1511
1s	sp	7h	970115	772.3	772.3	771.6	771.6	15	1512
1s	sp	7h	970115	771.7	771.8	771.4	771.6	10	1513
1s	sp	7h	970115	771.7	771.8	771.3	771.7	10	1514
1s	sp	7h	970115	771.8	771.8	771.5	771.65	9	1515
30s	xon		970115	105.	105.125	103.875	104.125	2422	1500
30s	z		970115	20.875	21.	20.75	20.75	239	1500
5s	oex		970115	753.09	753.97	752.99	753.86	50	1500
5s	sp	7m	970115	779.75	779.75	779.75	779.75	1	1505
5s	sp	7m	970115	778.7	778.7	778.7	778.7	1	1510
5s	sp	7m	970115	778.8	778.85	778.8	778.85	2	1515
ds	sp	7z	970115	797.6	799.	791.25	794.65	15	
ds	xon		970115	102.75	105.5	102.625	104.125	16503	
ds	z		970115	21.	21.125	20.75	20.75	1355	

Sample entries in our quotes database, showing the sampling frequency (period), ticker label (id), contract expiry code (exp), price activity, volume, and time of data. Period codes indicate each 1-, 5-, and 30-minute period (1s, 5s, 30s) as well as a "daily" component (ds).

Figure 7.2

PERIOD	Quotes
0s:	698
1s:	292
30s:	57294
5s:	5661
ds:	93847

Classification of our entire database according to the different values of the "period" attribute: tick-by-tick; 1, 5, and 30 minutes; and daily.

Figure 7.3

```
DATE x PERIOD            Quotes
-------------            ------
          0s   1s  30s   5s  ds
          --   --  ---   --  --
971215:    -   - 1113   - 324
971216:    -   - 1128   - 325
971217:    -   - 1132   1 325
971218:    -   - 1138   1 325
971219:    -   - 1145   - 325
971222:    -   -  907  49 344
971223:    -   - 1156  11 335
971224:    -   -  505  70  -
971229:    -   - 1208 185 350
971230:    -   - 1316 248 345
971231:    -   - 1312 210 346
980102:    -   - 1274 282 345
980105:    -   - 1288 308 346
980106:    -   - 1293 313 346
980107:    -   - 1094 467 352
980108:    -   - 1278 778 350
980109:    -   - 1262 699 350
980112:    -   - 1294 632 349
980113:    -   - 1310 455 354
980114:    -   - 1315 274 353
980115:    - 165 1313 255 352
980116: 292 127 1302 248 352
980119:    -   -  821 175  -
```

*Bottom portion of the cross-reference table
resulting from the product operation between
quote date and sampling period, for all quotes.*

point of view, selecting the US Dollar row will give us the list of time series shown in Figure 7.5.

Examples of data transformations include attributes such as "description," "card," and "start" attached to the mapping-based time series shown in Figure 7.5. Values for these attributes are computed from the individual quotes involved in these time series. The "description" attribute is produced

Figure 7.4

```
YEAR x PERIOD              Quotes
-------------             ------
       0s  1s   30s   5s    ds
       --  --   ---   --    --
91:    -   -     -    -    173
92:    -   -   174    -    280
93:  406   -     -    -    508
94:    -   -     -    -    506
95:    -   -     -    -    524
96:    -   -     -    -   9901
97:    -   - 42276  775 78106
98:  292 292 14844 4886  3849
```

Cross-reference table resulting from the union of quote dates by year, for our entire database.

Figure 7.5

```
description                                        label exp per card start
-----------                                        ----- --- --- ---- -----
US Dollar (March 98 contract; 30 min quotes)       dx 7h 30s 211  971219
US Dollar (March 98 contract; daily quotes)        dx 7h ds  16   971219
US Dollar (June 98 contract; 30 min quotes)        dx 7m 30s 57   971219
US Dollar (June 98 contract; 5 min quotes)         dx 7m 5s  65   971219
US Dollar (June 98 contract; daily quotes)         dx 7m ds  16   971219
US Dollar (September 98 contract; 30 min quotes)   dx 7u 30s 11   971217
US Dollar (September 98 contract; 5 min quotes)    dx 7u 5s  2    971217
US Dollar (September 98 contract; daily quotes)    dx 7u ds  20   971216
US Dollar (December 98 contract; 30 min quotes)    dx 7z 30s 10   971223
US Dollar (December 98 contract; daily quotes)     dx 7z ds  16   971219
US Dollar (Current contract; 30 min quotes)        dx y  30s 580  971112
US Dollar (Current contract; 5 min quotes)         dx y  5s  292  980107
US Dollar (Current contract; daily quotes)         dx y  ds  298  961120
```

Selected time series in futures markets, showing the description corresponding to particular labels, expiration month code (exp), sampling periods (daily, 30 and 5 minutes), as well as the number of data points in each of these time series (card) and the date of the first of these points (start).

Figure 7.6

```
FIRST_YEAR x PERIOD  Symbols
-------------------  -------

     0s 1s 30s 5s  ds
     -- -- --- --  --
91:  -  -   -  -    2
92:  -  -   1  -    1
93:  1  -   -  -    -
95:  -  -   -  -    4
96:  -  -   -  -  293
97:  -  - 177 32   91
98:  1  1   8 10    5
```

*Classification of all time series
(a mapping) by the product of their
starting year (a union) and period.*

Figure 7.7

```
FIRST_YEAR x PERIOD  Symbols          FIRST_MONTH x PERIOD  Symbols
-------------------  -------          --------------------  -------

     0s 1s 30s 5s ds                         30s 5s ds
     -- -- --- -- --                         --- -- --
97:  -  - 177 32 91               9703:    -  -  1
                                  9709:    1  -  1
                                  9710:   10  -  -
                                  9711:   85  -  -
                                  9712:   81 32 89
```

(a)   (b)

*(a) Result of selecting the "97" row in the previous Figure (a navigation opera-
tion), and (b) splitting this row by starting month (a further product).*

by raising the "id" and "exp" attribute values from individual quotes up to the
time series, respectively matching them with the key of the tables TICKER
and CONTRACT shown in Figure 7.8, replacing these values with the corresponding "description" from these tables, and combining the results with
the "period" values also raised from the individual quotes. Figure 7.10 shows
another type of data transformation, where the stock quotes are classified

Figure 7.8

```
TICKER:   id  description    equity  category     exchange
======    --  -----------    ------  --------     --------
          cr  CRB            Futures Indexes      CBOT
          dx  US Dollar      Futures Indexes      FINEX
          mb  Muni Bond      Futures Indexes      CBOT
          sp  S&P 500        Futures Indexes      CME
          oex S&P 100        Stocks  Indexes      CBOE
          an  Amoco Corp     Stocks  Petroleum    NYSE
          ash Ashland Inc    Stocks  Petroleum    NYSE
          chv Chevron Corp   Stocks  Petroleum    NYSE
          mob Mobil Corp     Stocks  Petroleum    NYSE
          tx  Texaco Inc     Stocks  Petroleum    NYSE
          xon Exxon Corp     Stocks  Petroleum    NYSE
          z   Woolworth Corp Stocks  Drug/Discount NYSE

CONTRACT: exp description    month      year
========  --- -----------    -----      ----
          7f  January 97     January    97
          7g  February 97    February   97
          7h  March 97       March      97
          7j  April 97       April      97
          7k  May 97         May        97
          7m  June 97        June       97
          7n  July 97        July       97
          7q  August 97      August     97
          7u  September 97   September  97
          7v  October 97     October    97
          7x  November 97    November   97
          7z  December 97    December   97
```

Sample translation records for ticker labels and contract expiry codes. Ticker labels (id) can be shown by their description, and grouped by equity type, category, or exchange. Contract expiry codes (exp) can also be replaced by their description, and grouped by month or year.

Figure 7.9

(a)

```
    TICKER [category, description] x PERIOD     Futures Quotes
    ----------------------------------------    --------------
                                            0s  1s 30s  5s   ds
                                            --  -- ---  --   --
    GRAINS/OILSEEDS             corn:        -   -  90   -  594
            "               soybean oil:     -   -  23   -  332
            "              soybean meal:     -   - 146 292  332
            "                 soybeans:      -   -  70   -  867
            "                   wheat:       -   - 106   -  611
    INDEXES                      CRB:        -   - 331   -  403
            "                 Muni Bond:     -   -  22   -  304
            "                 S&P 500:     698 292 318 576 1924
            "                US Dollar:      -   - 869 359  648
    INTEREST RATES      T-bills(90-day):     -   -  25   -  256
            "                 T-bonds:       -   -  13  41  312
            "            T-notes(6.5-10yr):  -   -  30  17  318
```

(b)

```
    TICKER [category, description] x PERIOD     Futures Symbols
    ----------------------------------------    ---------------
                                            0s 1s 30s 5s ds
                                            -- -- --- -- --
    GRAINS/OILSEEDS             corn:        -  -  1   -  3
            "               soybean oil:     -  -  1   -  3
            "              soybean meal:     -  -  2   1  3
            "                 soybeans:      -  -  2   -  5
            "                   wheat:       -  -  3   -  5
    INDEXES                      CRB:        -  -  3   -  4
            "                 Muni Bond:     -  -  1   -  3
            "                 S&P 500:       -  1  3   2  5
            "                US Dollar:      -  -  5   3  6
    INTEREST RATES      T-bills(90-day):     -  -  1   -  2
            "                 T-bonds:       -  -  1   1  2
            "            T-notes(6.5-10yr):  -  -  2   1  2
```

(a) Portion of a cross-reference table between sticker labels and sampling period for futures market quotes. Labels are grouped first by category and then by description. (b) Portion of the cross-reference table resulting from mapping the individual quotes in Figure 7.9(a) into their corresponding time series.

Figure 7.10

```
SPREAD%LOG x PERIOD  Stocks Quotes
------------------   -------------
            30s   5s     ds
            ---   --     --
>=10000:     -     -      1
>=3162:      -     -      -
>=1000:      -     -      -
>=316:       2     -      1
>=100:       -     -      3
>=31:        2     -      6
>=10:       12     -    397
>=3:      1003     -  24548
>=0:     51241   921  42793
Total:   52260   921  67749
```

*Stock quotes classified according to the spreads
between their "high" and "low" values, as a percentage
of these lows, on a logarithmic scale.*

according to the difference between their "high" and "low" values, as a percentage of the low value, along a logarithmic scale. Notice that the top rows in this figure most likely reflect data errors.

To illustrate the use of "annotation" operations, Figure 7.11 lists the individual stock quotes underlying the fourth row of the previous figure, where the "high" value seems out of line with the corresponding "low" value. Figure 7.12(a) further details the third of these quotes, from which we can conclude that the "open" and "low" values are in error for this 9:00 AM "961119" record. Figure 7.12(b) shows the result of replacing these offending values with "n/a," as well as attaching a "note" to the entire time series. Other examples of using structural and navigational operations to identify data errors would include similarly visualizing the relative differences between values for numerical attributes (such as "open," "high," "low," and "close") for consecutive quotes according to their "date" and "hour" values. A further option to locate data errors would be to match daily values with those from intra-day samples. This last strategy provides an example of the second type of mapping operations, linking different entities according to some common key; in this case, "date."

Figure 7.11

```
date    open    high    low    close    volume  hour  description
----    ----    ----    ---    -----    ------  ----  -----------
961210   3.00   24.00   3.00   23.625   1548    930   Genl Instrument
960701  18.75  150.00  18.50   18.625   12681   0     Westinghouse Elec
961119 123.39  666.13 123.39  665.360   37      900   Major Market Index
```

Stock quotes records where "(high – low) / low" falls in the "316–999" percentage range (fourth row in Figure 7.10).

Figure 7.12

(a)
```
label:       xmi
period:      30s
description: Major Market Index (30 min quotes)

date:    961118  961118  961119  961119  961119
open:    665.69  664.09  123.39  665.36  664.97
high:    665.97  665.08  666.13  666.08  667.3
low:     664.14  662.98  123.39  664.8   664.75
close:   664.14  663.42  665.36  664.97  667.24
volume:  68      105     37      66      61
hour:    1430    1500    900     930     1000
```

(b)
```
label:       xmi
period:      30s
note:        bad data @ 961119:900
description: Major Market Index (30 min quotes)

date:    961118  961118  961119  961119  961119
open:    665.69  664.09  n/a     665.36  664.97
high:    665.97  665.08  666.13  666.08  667.3
low:     664.14  662.98  n/a     664.8   664.75
close:   664.14  663.42  665.36  664.97  667.24
volume:  68      105     37      66      61
hour:    1430    1500    900     930     1000
```

(a) Stock quotes surrounding the third entry in Figure 7.11, and (b) annotations to flag data errors, both on the actual data record involved and on the entire time series.

7.4 **Discussion**

Series of frozen figures, such as those in the previous illustrations, do not even come close to conveying a feel for the effectiveness that this set of operations can support, in the hands of an experienced operator. Such a person will zip from one view to the next, often glancing at one for less than a second, while deciding which other view to explore next. Processing speed is paramount to support this performance. This represents a means of capturing user commands with a maximal economy of hand and eye movement. Locating choices within pull-down menus is not the fastest way for such an experienced user to operate. Typing textual commands, often abbreviated, although requiring more education and practice, generally supports a faster navigation.

The semantic mechanisms previously described still fall under the area of data visualization, because they require and support a close interaction with a person using this information to control their operation. They represent one end in the spectrum of data mining approaches, the other end including the more familiar alternative of *automatic* data mining, in which visualization is traditionally used in the last phase—result presentation.

A successful automated classification system might reduce to 10%, or even 5%, the number of cases needing to be manually reviewed. We can achieve a productivity gain of the same "order of magnitude" by capitalizing on visualization instead of classification. The semantic operations previously described provide the means for business workers to identify and review such subsets of most interest to them, in the same amount of time as they would have taken to review the cases flagged by a typical automated classification system.

This approach simplifies development and support tasks. In comparison, automated systems require significant design, programming, and testing. These systems need to be reprogrammed as soon as circumstances change. Such reprogramming often introduces errors, as testing is reduced under the pressure of tight deadlines. Performance of automated systems thus tends to degrade over time. Significant new cases remain temporarily ignored, and therefore wily operators can take advantage of these holes to outwit the system, until they are recognized and plugged.

On the contrary, users of a visualization system based on the semantic operations previously described can bypass all of these problems. Instead, they get a feeling of completeness, where nothing escapes their attention. This feeling builds confidence in their opinions and decisions. They can back up these decisions with their own analysis and statistics. They develop a "feel" for the entire domain under their supervision. They can immediately detect new trends, and can focus on the most critical cases first. They can quickly skip cases that are not a problem anymore. They do not depend on anyone else to define criteria or reprogram their system. Nor do they need to wait for anyone to deal with new situations.

7.5 Related Work

Some researchers experimenting with interaction and visualization techniques have recognized that "the overhead of interpretation and first-class graphical objects limits the data set size that can be manipulated rapidly" [Der97]. However, their most typical reaction is to focus on manipulating small samples to attain initial intuitions about large data sets. The dangers of such parceling out are well detailed in the keynote address to KDD'97 attendees [Hub97]. This seasoned statistician argues against attempting to circumvent human inability to inspect large data sets by automating some aspects of exploratory analysis. Instead, he describes the machine assistance needed to step from large to huge data sets as "an integrated computing environment that allows easy improvisation and retooling." He sees such a system as aiding with the improvisation of search tools and with keeping track of the progress of an analysis. Our visualization approach supports this vision, not only in the flexibility in which it can be guided by a human operator but in its ability to keep track of the status of the analysis at every step.

The division of "structural" semantic mechanisms into product, union, and mapping operations was inspired by the field of pure mathematics called category theory. This theoretical foundation also holds intriguing promise toward organizing and monitoring some of the most recent financial instruments, such as complex derivative products, as these can be decomposed into simpler, standard components. These components in turn could be organized and analyzed in large numbers with the semantic operations we have identified.

7.6 Conclusion

We found that we could remove the GUI aspects of a data visualization system and still retain a very rich and fruitful functionality. This simplification actually helps to better understand useful underlying "semantic" capabilities that will benefit any visualization system. These basic building blocks can be combined to provide a rich and flexible exploration environment, which has proven able to match the productivity gains produced by some familiar data mining classification mechanisms. We identified how they also provided a number of further advantages, which illustrate how the synergy between human strengths and machine capabilities can provide the ultimate *adaptive* systems.

References

[Bro97] P. L. Brooks. "Visualizing Data," *DBMS Magazine*, Special Issue: Data Warehousing, Miller Freeman 10:9, August 1997, pp. 38–47.

[Der97] M. Derthick, J. Kolojejchick, and S. F. Roth. "An Interactive Visualization Environment for Data Exploration," *Proceedings of the Third International Conference on Knowledge Discovery and Data Mining* (KDD'97), Newport Beach, CA, August 1997, pp. 2–9.

[Hub97] P. J. Huber. "From Large to Huge: A Statistician's Reactions to KDD and DM," Keynote Address, *Proceedings of the Third International Conference on Knowledge Discovery and Data Mining* (KDD'97), Newport Beach, CA, August 1997, pp. 304–308.

[Kei97] D. Keim. "Visual Techniques for Exploring Databases," Tutorial T6, *Third International Conference on Knowledge Discovery and Data Mining*, Newport Beach, CA, August 14, 1997.

[Pil91] M. Pilote and M. Fillion. "Automated Underwriting at Continental Canada: Results and Major Obstacles," *Proceedings of the First AI Conference on Wall Street*, New York, October 1991, R. S. Freedman (editor), pp. 168–173. Los Alamitos, CA. IEEE Computer Society Press.

[Pil93] M. Pilote and M. Fillion. "Man-Machine Synergy in Action," *Adaptive Intelligent Systems: Proceedings of the BANKAI Workshop*, Brussels, Belgium, October 1992, pp. 43–58. Amsterdam. Elsevier Science, 1993.

Part II

KDD AND MODEL VISUALIZATION

Chapter 8

Visualization in the Knowledge Discovery Process

KEN COLLIER
MURALIDHAR MEDIDI
DONALD SAUTTER

Northern Arizona University

The Center for Data Insight (CDI) was established in January of 1997 as a clearinghouse of information about current data mining tools and methods, a point source of comparative and benchmark data about the various tools, and a knowledge discovery support service for corporate members of the CDI. One research area under way in the CDI involves data visualization. Although this research effort remains in its infancy, there are several focus areas and the publication of results is imminent.

Although current visualization techniques have progressed dramatically in the past decade, this technology still largely resides at the end of the knowledge discovery process. Furthermore, most current data mining tools do not yet take full advantage of the effectiveness of advanced visualization techniques. We believe that two things must happen to see a substantial improvement in the usefulness of data visualization:

- A metric must be developed to quantitatively evaluate and compare the effectiveness of the variety of visualization techniques toward guiding data visualization technology.

- Data visualization must permeate the knowledge discovery process from data cleansing and warehousing through data mining and exploration. This advance is likely to improve the understanding that users have about their data, thereby increasing the likelihood that new and useful insights about the data will be gained.

We are currently actively involved in research into the first of the previously listed items, with plans to begin exploring the second item in the near future. Our research into visualization effectiveness metrics involves conducting a thorough analysis of visualization techniques. We hope to identify and understand the key characteristics that impact the effectiveness of a particular technique. It is not likely that we will be able to say that method X is twice as good as method Y. However, we expect to be able to suggest that certain characteristics contribute significantly to how well a particular method enhances end-user understanding, whereas other characteristics may actually deter that understanding.

Chapter 9

What Can Visualization Do for Data Mining?

ANDREAS WIERSE

University of Stuttgart, Germany

Contributions to the literature have dealt with the question of how visualization can benefit from the integration with databases (visualization here mostly has meant scientific visualization). The introduction of visualization to the database community is another topic that has received attention, working in the opposite direction. Although there is no question about the usefulness of both directions, it can easily be seen that in both parts the base domains still dominate clearly. There is no system available that integrates a full-featured DBMS (database management system) with a complete visualization tool: either a full-blown database management system is supplemented with a visualization front end, or a complete visualization toolkit is given the ability to access databases.

In the first case, the visualization functionality is usually limited to some rather simple display routines, either for the data itself or for the relations between the data sets; rarely are these visualizations 3D (where the third dimension is more than an optical polish). This may be related to the fact that most database-accessing workplaces are historically text based. With the wide availability of PCs, reasonably fast 2D graphics were possible, but 3D graphics capabilities can hardly be seen in database-oriented workplaces. If 3D graphics for database-related activities were really convincing, this could be proven by the number of workplaces for which the additional cost has been spent.

In the case of visualization tools, usually an interface to a DBMS is provided, allowing you to send queries. In the field of scientific visualization, however, the data that is displayed rarely fits into the structures of these

DBMSs. In size and in structure, scientific data differs significantly from the standard relational database entries. Object-oriented approaches are better suited, but today they are not as far developed as the DBMS. The COVISE visualization environment developed by the Computing Center of the University of Stuttgart tries to significantly integrate the data management in the base architecture of the visualization system; but compared with a real-world DBMS, the data management is rather simple. In the environment of visualization systems, usually file servers can be found instead of database servers.

To which of these two cases belongs data mining? Obviously the first case: data mining is a technology that is closely coupled to databases. Visualization comes in when the results of such mining are analyzed; the iteration of visualization and mining makes it easier for users to find the interesting patterns. However, the visualization techniques applied to such results are simple compared to the algorithms used in scientific visualization. This of course leaves ample space for improvements: new visualization techniques should be developed that fit the needs of the users of data mining. However, it is in question whether the need for complex 3D visualization really exists or whether a few simple algorithms will be sufficient for successful data mining.

Chapter 10

Multidimensional Information Visualizations for Data Mining

PATRICK E. HOFFMAN
GEORGES G. GRINSTEIN

University of Massachusetts, Lowell

Introduction

Visualization represents an underutilized and often ineffectively utilized data mining technique. Many modern visualizations invented in the past few years have not yet been integrated with the blossoming data mining tools of neural networks, rule-based classifiers, and other exciting machine-learning algorithms. This chapter identifies visualizations that can be used to help understand the "black box" functions learned with neural nets and complex rule-based classifiers.

10.1 Background

Computer graphics is widely abundant today. Almost every new software product has a reasonably developed graphical user interface (GUI), where the important and key "visual" aspects of user interaction and information are displayed. The trend continues toward higher resolution. For example, high-definition television (HDTV) will provide a larger display surface. However, this will have little impact on the fundamental problem, which is limited display resources: finite space, finite color selections, and finite number of pixels.

Most visualization systems are focused for a specific domain, such as weather, scientific computation, information retrieval, software analysis, network analysis, and so on. Flexible and general-purpose multidimensional information visualizations (MIVs) are not very abundant and clearly are needed for today's data mining problems for which experimentation is still the fundamental paradigm. Some newer data mining packages are realizing the importance of these new visualization techniques and are starting to incorporate them in their products.

10.2 Multidimensional Information Visualizations

The following are some of the MIVs we believe are valuable:

- 2D and 3D scatter plots, bar charts, histograms (with shape, color, and animation)
- Composite, box, and whisker charts
- Contour plots
- Virtual reality (N-vision, QPIT), scientific visualization
- Grids of scatter plots for multidimensional displays (Xmdv, etc.)
- Parallel coordinates [Ins87]
- Icons, glyphs (dimensional stacking, Chernoff faces)
- Projection pursuit [Fri74], Grand Tour [Asi85]
- Polar charts
- Circle segments [Ank96]
- Radviz, radial coordinates [Hof01]
- Table lens [Rao94], survey plots, array histograms
- Sammon plots [Sam69]
- Kohonen nets for clustering [Koh82] [Koh84]
- Other multidimensional scaling
- Polyviz
- Heatmap
- Patchgrid

10.3 Integration with Data Mining Tools

Many of the previously listed techniques can be found in stand-alone packages, but no package or tool currently includes most of these techniques. Additionally, when these techniques are included, there is little help in knowing when to best apply the visualization technique. Most packages concentrate either on machine learning or a specific subset of visualization techniques. Few packages effectively integrate both visualization and machine learning.

10.4 Visualizing Neural Nets, and Other Classifiers

It seems that many neural net packages provide means of visualizing the weights in the network to possibly give some insight as to which input features are most important in that network. Some packages try to visualize the learned network function by mapping the network down to two dimensions [Kli01, Mor95]. Visualization methods selected from the preceding list need to be applied to a learned network. In this manner, the function learned by the network could be "visualized" using any visualization method. If we assume that some visualizations work better than others for certain functions, the proposed method is only limited by the particular visualization selected and not by the neural network. In the same manner, complicated rule-based classifications could also be visualized [Cle01].

References

[Ank96]   M. Ankerst, D. A. Keim, H.-P. Kriegel. "Circle Segments: A Technique for Visually Exploring Large Multidimensional Data Sets," *IEEE Visualization'96 Proceedings, Hot Topic*, San Francisco, 1996.

[Asi85]   D. Asimov. "The Grand Tour: A Tool for Viewing Multidimensional Data," *SIAM Journal on Scientific and Statistical Computing*, 6(1):128–143, 1985.

[Cle01]   Clementine. *www.isl.co.uk/clem.html*.

[Fri74]   J. H. Friedman and J. W. Tukey. "A Projection Pursuit Algorithm for Exploratory Data Analysis," *IEEE Transactions on Computers*, C-23:881–890,1974.

[Hof01]   P. Hoffman. "Radviz," *www.cs.uml.edu/~phoffman/viz*.

[Icn95]   *www.io.org/~causal/c_p/icnn95/nn95s419.htm#p2085.*

[Ins87]   A. Inselberg and B. Dimsdale. "Parallel Coordinates for Visualizing Multi-dimensional Geometry." In T. L. Kunii (editor), *Proceedings of Computer Graphics International '87*, Tokyo. Berlin. Springer-Verlag, 1987.

[Kli01]   S. Klinke. "Visualization of Feedforward Neural Networks via Multidimensional Scaling in XploRe," *www.wiwi.hu-berlin.de/~sigbert/wias.html.*

[Koh82]   T. Kohonen. "Self-Organized Formation of Topologically Correct Feature Maps," *Biological Cybernetics* 43,59–69, 1982.

[Koh89]   T. Kohonen. *Self-Organization and Associative Memory*, Third Edition. New York. Springer-Verlag, 1989.

[Mar95]   A. R. Martin and M. O. Ward. "High Dimensional Brushing for Interactive Exploration of Multivariate Data," *Proceedings of the IEEE Conference on Visualization* (*Visualization'95*), pp. 271–278, Atlanta, 1995.

[Mor95]   N. Morch, U. Kjems, L. K. Hansen, C. Svarer, I. Law, B. Lautsup, S. Strother, and K. Rehm. "Visualization of Neural Networks Using Saliency Maps," *Proceedings of the 1995 IEEE International Conference on Neural Networks*, vol. 4, pp. 2085–2090.

[Ols93]   K. A. Olsen, R. R. Korfhage, K. M. Sochats, M. B. Spring, and J. G. Williams. "Visualisation of a Document Collection: The VIBE System," *Information Processing and Management*, 29:1, pp. 69–81. Tarrytown, NY. Pergamon Press, 1993.

[Rao94]   R. Rao, S. K. Card. "Table Lens: Merging Graphical and Symbolic Representations in an Interactive Focus Plus Context Visualization for Tabular Information." In *Proceedings of the ACM Conference on Human Factors in Computing Systems* (CHI'94), pp. 318–322, Boston, April 1994.

[Sam69]   J. A. Sammon. "A Nonlinear Mapping for Data Structure Analysis," *IEEE Transactions on Computers*, C-18(5):401–409, May 1969.

[Vuu93]   L. G. Vuurpij and T. E. Schouten. "Convis: A Distributed Environment for Control and Visualization Neural Networks," *Proceedings of the International Conference on Artificial Neural Networks*, pp. 1078–1081, Amsterdam, 1993.

[Wil93]   P. Wilke. "Visualization of Neural Networks Using NeuroGraph," *Proceedings of the IFIP Working Group 3.2 Working Conference on Visualization in Scientific Computing: Uses in University Education*, UC California, Irvine, S. D. Franklin (editor), 1993.

Chapter 11

Benchmark Development for the Evaluation of Visualization for Data Mining

Georges G. Grinstein*
Patrick E. Hoffman*
Ronald M. Pickett

University of Massachusetts, Lowell

Sharon J. Laskowski

The National Institute of Standards and Technology

Introduction

We are currently seeing a rapid growth in the development of tools and techniques for supporting knowledge discovery in databases (KDD). New sets of powerful data visualization tools have appeared in the marketplace and in the research community. This, combined with readily available computer memory, speed, and graphics capabilities makes it possible to explore larger and larger data sets. Although this trend has served to increase the interest and effort of corporations in exploring their data for hidden nuggets of information, these visualization tools are not well integrated with data mining software, and it is difficult to judge the effectiveness of either the visualizations or the data mining. To remedy the situation, it is becoming increasingly important to develop appropriate data sets and reproducible benchmark

* This work was funded in part with research funding from the National Institute of Standards and Technology.

tests to identify the current best practices and to steer development of future systems.

In this chapter, we discuss some of the issues that need to be addressed in order to provide benchmark testing and evaluation to the visualization and data mining communities. We survey evaluation approaches that have been applied in other information technology domains and then describe a basic framework in which to perform evaluations. We conclude with a discussion and examples of various visualization techniques, each exercised on several different data sets. These examples illustrate the type of environment for testing that is critically needed to advance the development of visualization for data mining. Such an environment, when fully developed, should provide a broad array of tests for comparative evaluation on a common set of criteria and provide for comparisons across systems on the same data and tasks.

11.1 Background

In a Meta Group, Inc., survey, "Data Mining: Trends, Technology, and Implementation Imperatives," it was found that the data mining market will grow 150% to $8.4 billion by 2000. Half of 120 companies surveyed believe that data mining will be critical for their businesses in the next two years [Won97]. Some expect that visualization software will proliferate even on Wall Street over the next few years [Yra96], in response to its special needs to comprehend complex data. What is often missing in all this talk, however, is a recognition of the difficulties to be faced. Without the appropriate visualization techniques, these data mining approaches will remain difficult to use and will require a great deal of expertise. Corporations understand the promise of data mining to wade through large amounts of data, but they are not adequately aware of the human limitation in grasping what the analyses show [Mar96], and many are finding that the tools just cannot handle the volume of data they are gathering [Ste97].

It is clear that no one general set of visualization tools will be suitable to address all problems. Different tools must be chosen based on the task and data. Currently, there is little guidance for these choices. The only way to address this problem is through the development of evaluation methodologies and benchmarks that show the strong and weak features of specific classes of visualizations. Then we can begin to answer the question "How do we effectively slice, dice, plot, color, and interact with data in a visualization?"

A recent special advertisement in *Computer World* describing a data mining "face-off" provides a good example of the need for such guidance. Five companies participated in a "competition" in which they described how they would respond to two hypothetical requests for proposals that could be solved by a data mining and/or data warehouse solution. The solutions varied widely, from a total data management strategy to the data mining alone, and ranged in cost from $150,000 to over $1 million. This wide discrepancy in approach and cost makes clear the importance of being able to sharply evaluate the solutions toward selecting the best.

Usama Fayyad, in a recent editorial [Fay97], makes the point that the database and information retrieval communities have met with great success in advancing algorithm performance by establishing benchmark data sets, and he believes that the KDD community could benefit as well.

Evaluations that produce clear benchmarks are also needed to steer development toward optimal solutions, models, and theory. In other areas of information technology—such as speech recognition, image recognition, and information retrieval—benchmarks and evaluation metrics have clearly helped to move new technology into useful, reliable, and predictable products. We believe they are critical in this research area as well. Before we specifically address the question of evaluation for visualization in the context of data mining, we first look at some of the successful approaches to evaluation in these other areas of information technology.

11.1.1 Benchmarking and Evaluation for Information Technology

The Information Technology Laboratory at the National Institute of Standards and Technology (NIST) [NIS97] has been supporting and contributing to the development of tools to measure the effectiveness of information technology applications. The goal is to provide researchers, developers, and users objective criteria for understanding how products and techniques perform and for assessing their quality. These tools include test and evaluation methods, metrics, and reference data sets. For example, NIST provides large unstructured text collections and uniform scoring procedures for the Text Retrieval Conference (TREC) [TRE97]. This annual event, now in its sixth year, has proven to be an invaluable resource to the information retrieval research and development community. Its activities have enabled great strides in improving the search engines and in speeding the transfer of this technology. Large test corpora, queries, and associated pooled evaluations are made available to participants who are required to submit the output of their search engines for evaluation before the actual workshop. [Voo97] contains an overview and proceedings from the 1997 conference. TREC has encouraged research in text retrieval; increased communication among industry, academia, and government; sped the transfer of technology from research labs into commercial products by demonstrating improvements in retrieval methodologies; and increased the availability of appropriate evaluation techniques.

A similar effort by NIST has been the development of test corpora and evaluation methods for spoken language recognition. NIST has been involved in the creation and distribution of speech corpora—nearly 30 of them—and associated benchmark evaluations. These evaluations have proved to be critical in the recent commercialization of speech recognition. Details are contained in [NIS98a].

These efforts and others, in such areas as fingerprint recognition and optical character recognition [NIS98b], have been very successful. Hence, it is reasonable to assume that such an approach can also be applied to improving the quality of the next generation of tools that integrates data visualization into the KDD process.

11.1.2 State of the Art in Benchmarking and Test Data Sets for KDD

There has already been a substantial amount of effort in the area of benchmarking and test data sets for KDD. See, for example, the data sets identified in the knowledge discovery nuggets Web site [Kdn98], such as those in the machine learning database repository and the neural networks benchmarking Web sites, which provide good starting points for reproducible experiments, especially for neural net algorithms. However, these sets suffer a variety of limitations. Many are very small or are limited to very specific learning algorithms. Some of these collections are synthetic; that is, they were designed a priori to stress prediction algorithms in predetermined ways. Many of the large sets are from the statistical community, rather than the visualization community, and typically do not include benchmarks.

The Information Exploration Shootout [IES97], developed at the University of Massachusetts at Lowell and the MITRE Corporation, has begun to address the need for more serious comparative evaluations of the various data exploration techniques. The first two data sets, network intrusion and on-line daily news archives of Web pages, were chosen because of their timely subject matter and for their size (200 Mb and 1.2 Gb, respectively), as well as for their potential to have synthetic (planted) intrusions and to deal with "free-form" patterns of information (typical news and large amounts of other unstructured data). However, there has been no agreed-upon set of metrics or evaluation criteria on which to judge and compare approaches to exploring these data sets visually.

Finally, in 1997, the Knowledge Discovery in Databases Conference organized its first knowledge discovery and data mining tools competition, the KDD Cup. This competition was aimed at demonstrating and comparing the effectiveness of tools in the area of supervised learning. The winners were determined on the basis of a weighted combination of classification accuracy (predictive power, or "lift"), software novelty, efficiency, and the data mining methodology used. Note that to properly evaluate the competition, entered data sets had to be analyzed ahead of time. For large data sets, this is very time consuming. The emphasis here was more on data mining algorithms than on visualization. It is easier to measure accuracy of the classifications than to measure and compare one visualization with another. Visualization has a number of dimensions to be measured and is highly dependent on the user, the task, and the structure of the data. It is difficult to pull these out to identify an optimal method.

11.2 Issues in Benchmarking and Evaluation

In this section we discuss three major issues that contribute to the difficulty of creating benchmarks and evaluation methodologies for visualization techniques aimed at supporting data mining of large data sets.

11.2.1 Dependence of Performance on User Knowledge and Expertise

To illustrate the importance of factoring user knowledge and expertise into a benchmarking effort, we relate some of our experiences with the Information Exploration Shootout's first exercise [Gri97], which involved the detection of intrusions into a computer network. The two major challenges for the participants were the complexity of the problem domain and the size of the database. Details of the Internet protocol and Internet operations are arcane, and to adequately address, let alone solve the problem, an expert in the field is necessary. The central need for a domain expert is typically a common feature of real-world knowledge discovery problems. The skills we found to be required in our approach were (1) domain knowledge of computer network security, (2) experience with visualization software, and (3) statistical expertise.

The first task of the shootout was a large pre-processing activity. We grouped the individual packet records into natural clusters of communications sessions. The resulting reduction in size was substantial. For example, the baseline data set contains over 350,000 records. The corresponding session-level data set contains approximately 16,000 records. We then analyzed the processed data sets predominantly with visualization techniques. For many we used parallel coordinate plots and conditioning. Even in this step, the visualization is driven by domain knowledge. With this approach, several anomalies were identified, and these turned out to be network intrusions when interpreted by a system administrator aware of various network attacks.

This experience showed that there are a number of aspects of the process that have to be evaluated, and that much depends on domain expertise and on the amount of data involved. Even with this large but not huge set, the visualization required a scaling down of the problem. Any benchmark testing methodology must consider these complex requirements. Testing must also include a good understanding of the perceptual issues involved, as discussed in the next section.

11.2.2 Perceptual Issues in the Evaluation of Visualization Systems

The challenge in conducting an evaluation of any system is to ensure that the evaluation is both valid and discriminating, and, where one system is to be compared to another, that the comparison is fair. By fair, we mean that testing must occur under controlled conditions: the challenges put to the systems must be equivalent and each system (or system variant, if incremental tuning or adjustment is being investigated) must be operated under similar conditions. In the case of comparing system speed of performance, obviously the systems must run on platforms with equivalent speed so that ensuring fairness with respect to purely computational operation of a visualization system is a non-issue. It is also assumed that a system performs deterministically; that is, in exactly the same way computationally every time it operates on the same data. However, that is definitely not the case with respect to those aspects of the operation of a visualization system that involve human sensory, perceptual, and cognitive processes. These can vary widely in their operation from one test of the system to another, and the fairness of comparisons can be undermined, unless care is taken to ensure comparable operation from test to test. We propose there are three basic ways in which comparability must be protected.

There is first the need to ensure comparability of performance at the sensory level. Several factors have to be considered, including display calibration, control of lighting and other viewing conditions, and adequate testing and selection of observers, particularly with respect to such critical aspects as color vision and stereoscopic vision where that might apply. Comparability at the level of perceptual processing must also be ensured, and that will depend in large part on whether the required perceptual processing of the visualization is preattentive or not. By preattentive, we mean that the process runs off automatically; that is, it requires no conscious analysis, only that the observer attends to the display. The possibility of encoding data into forms that elicit such automatic processing has been demonstrated in several exploratory visualization systems [Pic95]. To the extent that a visualization system depends on purely preattentive perceptual processing, the problem of ensuring comparability from test to test devolves to ensuring only that the various determinants of comparable sensory processing mentioned previously are adequately controlled. But it is not likely we will ever be able to depend entirely on preattentive perceptual processing in visualization systems.

We should aim to exploit preattentive perceptual processing as much as possible, but visualization will probably always have to depend on perceptions that require a large component of consciously controlled, deliberate analysis. This implies that, to a large degree, the effectiveness of the perceptual processes will depend on what is termed *perceptual learning*. The effectiveness is related to the degree to which the observer can learn how to look at, how to see, and how to assemble the various components and features of structures potentially visible in the display before they are adequately perceived. Perceptual learning has received extensive attention in the psychology literature; see [Gib69], for example. Perhaps the best examples of dependence on perceptual learning for effective performance come from fields of medical image analysis, where, for example, the pathologist in training only slowly learns with coaching to differentiate, say, the malignant from the benign specimen under the microscope, yet when experienced sees the difference instantly. Many visualization systems will depend on the observer's having learned how to perceive what is there. This means that when competing systems are tested and compared, the evaluators must ensure that the observers in each test have had adequate perceptual training and experience.

A third area important to consider in protecting comparability among visualization systems has to do with the methodology provided for the observers to conduct their analyses and report their findings. Alternative methods for laboratory testing of sensory and perceptual performance have received extensive development in experimental psychology; see, for example, Chapter 2 in [Sch96]. The strengths and weaknesses of these alternatives have also received extensive study, as have the implications for their use in evaluating systems in real-world settings. A good case in point has been the extensive debate and development of techniques appropriate for testing medical imaging and diagnostic systems; see, for example, [Swe82]. The particular methodology not only will affect the richness and precision of the analyses conducted and the reports produced but can shape the basic nature of the game the observer plays. It is vastly important in comparing one system to another not just that the same methodology be applied but that it be one that ensures, within its own operation, comparable figures of merit from test to test.

The best way to ensure that testing is comparable among the different systems to be evaluated is to have the evaluations done together in the same laboratory and, with appropriate protections for independence of the tests, on the same observers. This would suggest that ultimately you would like to develop a central testing laboratory. However, it would be possible, and perhaps more practical, to develop standard procedures that provide for testing in different settings. Either approach would require a potentially large investment. But the payback could be very high. The potential value of visualization techniques will continue to grow as the capability for gathering and exploring large amounts of data continues to expand, and the development of approaches that can make those techniques as effective as possible will be well worth the investment.

11.2.3 Issues in Acceptance by the KDD Community

Grinstein et al. [Gri98] suggest other thorny issues that must be addressed. One is that any benchmarking effort has to produce credible subjective measures of effectiveness and reconcile them with an adequately broad spectrum of objective measures. Another is that the effectiveness, and in turn the broad acceptance and use of, the benchmarking enterprise will depend on how well it can support modeling and steer development of improved techniques. The entire enterprise depends on consensus in the visualization and KDD communities to cooperate and participate in the process, and that in turn depends on building up its credibility to produce sensible measures and ultimately more and more effective systems.

11.3 Proposed Characteristics of an Evaluation Environment

An evaluation methodology for data visualization techniques within the KDD process is different than pure (non-applied) visualization. The visualization community recognizes that good visualizations are those that are designed for the task and domain. Similarly, any specific visualization or visualization technique must be judged in the context of the step in the KDD process and the domain in which it is being applied. However, even in the visualization community there is no ongoing, comprehensive evaluation effort, and therefore we cannot look to that community for any systematic collection of tasks, data sets, or benchmarks on which to base KDD visualization evaluation.

In order to develop an evaluation methodology, we must, then, develop a taxonomy of tasks and data sets that supports evaluation of a specific visualization system or approach in the context of tasks and data sets that have some relevance to the steps in the KDD process and application. We envision an evaluation environment that contains numerous data sets and application-based tasks that feed into a repository of evaluation outcomes and guidelines. This environment would support an ongoing effort to systematically develop benchmark data sets and outcomes against which evaluation methods and sets could be validated and visualization techniques tested. Figure 11.1 outlines the structure of such an environment.

This approach does require the development of tasks that have outcomes that can be evaluated. Although the KDD process has been described in terms of tasks such as data warehousing, target data selection, cleaning, preprocessing, transformation and reduction, data mining, model selection, interpretation, and so on, the granularity of these processes is too large to be useful in defining such tasks. In the sections that follow, we attempt to define a set of testing criteria, and then describe a preliminary set of lower-level tasks we think have been useful in prototyping an evaluation environment.

11.3.1 Basic Testing Criteria and Measures

In this section we discuss some basic features of measurement in the context of visualization that could possibly lead to an evaluation methodology that allows for controlled, repeatable test and evaluation.

Figure 11.1

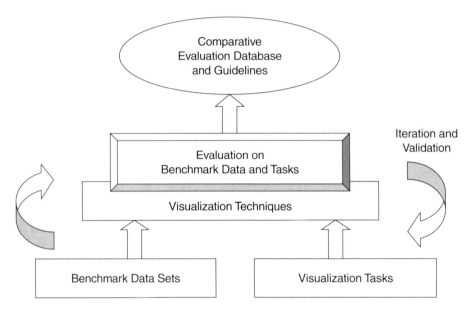

Evaluation environment for visualization.

11.3.2 Basic Testing Criteria

Visualization techniques can be judged on a number of criteria across the data with respect to the types and amounts of data that can be handled and with respect to the type and quantity of human interactions it can support. Across the data, these include scalability, dimensionality, structure, and noise. Across the human interactions, these include various aspects of the techniques' capabilities to support interaction with the system and with the data at various stages in the visualization process. These include degree of interactivity, flexibility, ease of expression, and query functionality. Each of these requires some sort of metric assignment so that these features can be compared across visualizations. Furthermore, a systematic, controlled approach is required to take into consideration not just the algorithms but the interactive qualities of a particular visualization and the perceptual capabilities of the users. To summarize, any benchmark testing for visualization in the data mining process needs to address criteria such as the following:

■ Scalability, time to process, and time to visualize large amounts of data

■ Ease of expressing and integrating domain knowledge

- Dealing with uncertain or incorrect, "dirty" data
- Ease of classification and categorization
- High dimensionality
- Flexibility of visualization
- Query and database functionality
- Summarization of results

Visualization techniques need to be characterized according to a set of features derived from these criteria. Only then can they be evaluated against data sets and associated tasks that explicitly exercise them against these criteria. This approach to "benchmark" testing ensures that the results of evaluations can be compared across different visualization techniques or systems. We are assuming, however, that there has been some control for different user populations and usability of the tools themselves. This can be addressed in several ways. Either users must be trained on the systems, or the demographics of the users (for example, whether novices or experts in the domain) must be controlled for and specified. It should be noted that although we have used some of these criteria informally in the prototype environment, integrating them in a systematic way for use in evaluation is an open problem. We also have not specified the human interaction and perception characteristics needed for collection for the repository and guidelines.

11.4 Measures

There are a number of different types of measures to consider in an evaluation. Technology-based measures look at the degree to which a system can handle data sets of varying sizes. This could be tested with a series of data sets of increasing size. Task-based measures depend on the task for the domain and KDD process. For example, you could measure the output of the task of finding the outliers in a set. These measures must be designed for each task category. User-based measures include items such as time to set up and run a data set and degree of user satisfaction.

In Section 11.5, a basic set of measures—such as ability to identify outliers and clusters—has been applied in the comparative evaluations done for the prototype. Once again, these have not been formalized in any systematic manner, but are simply used as a proof of concept for the approach to evaluation suggested here. They are based on the known features of the benchmark data sets.

11.4.1 Common Test Data Sets and Tasks

A key component of this evaluation approach is the construction of test data sets. The data sets alone are not sufficient; they must be accompanied by tasks so that the evaluation measures can be applied. This invites a trade-off in using synthetic versus real data. Synthetic data is more difficult to construct, but the "correct" answers are known. Real data is easier to collect, but it is more difficult to evaluate performance, because it is nearly impossible to "know" the correct output to a task in any reasonably sized data set.

One idea that has been applied in the TREC conference to address this problem is that of "pooling" results to estimate the correct answers. The "findings" over the course of multiple evaluations could be collected and pooled to create a set of "best" answers. Alternatively, the group that constructs a data set could be assigned to find the answers before the release of the data, but this is quite resource intense for any one group.

11.5 Implementing a Prototype Evaluation Environment

Any evaluation methodology needs to provide cheap, reproducible metrics-based evaluation methods and tools plus common data sets and tasks. It is difficult to measure across low-level support technology (e.g., database capabilities), visualization capability, user interaction, and data mining component interaction simultaneously.

One solution is to develop some basic test data sets and start with some single component tasks. This can form the basis on which to develop a set of validated measures. Having such data sets and measures should support repeatable experiments. Such collective measures, developed for each system, would allow for comparative evaluation.

Ultimately, such an environment would build up a comprehensive record, composed of results collected over time on different sets and systems, that would eventually yield some guidelines for choosing visualization techniques.

In an effort to formalize a benchmark environment for visualization and data mining, a prototype effort has begun at the University of Massachusetts at Lowell. Several machine-learning data sets (primarily from UC Irvine Machine Learning Repository [UCI97]) are used as input to a range of multi-dimensional visualizations. The data sets are ordered by increasing size and complexity. The following five visualizations, described in detail in the next section, were chosen for their apparent usefulness in exploring large data sets:

- Parallel coordinates
- Scatter-plot matrix
- Survey plot
- Circle segments
- Radviz

By using specific data set examples with known features, various limitations of the visualizations can be demonstrated. These data sets can also be used to test various data mining algorithms, such as classification or clustering. Most data mining software packages include some of these data sets as examples or demos to illustrate the features of the package. More and much larger data sets will have to be included in a full evaluation environment. The data sets, the visualizations, and the Java application used in the analysis can be accessed from [Hof98a].

11.5.1 Overview of the Visualizations to Be Compared

We begin with short descriptions of the five chosen visualization techniques. The examples shown are meant to be representative of the output of these techniques. However, for the purposes of this chapter, they are not meant to be analyzed in detail. In particular, color obviously cannot be used to discriminate among the sample data if you are reading a black-and-white copy of this paper.

Parallel Coordinates

First described by Al Inselberg [Ins85], parallel coordinates are a simple but powerful way to represent multidimensional data. Each dimension or attribute is represented by a vertical line. The maximum and minimum value of that dimension is usually scaled to the upper and lower points on these vertical lines. An n-dimensional point is represented by $N-1$ line segments connected to each vertical line at the appropriate dimensional value.

In Figure 11.2, automobile data is displayed using parallel coordinates, with the American cars represented with red lines, the Japanese cars with green lines, and the European cars with blue lines. (Again, note color is not observable in a black-and-white copy of the paper. Red shows up darker; hence, the higher weights among the American cars, showing darker lines toward the bottom of the *weight* coordinate.)

Figure 11.2

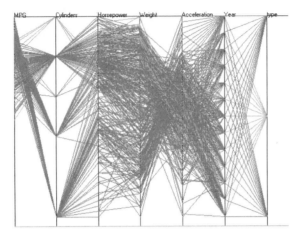

Parallel coordinates, Car data set. (See also color plate.)

Scatter-Plot Matrices

Grids of 2D scatter plots are the standard way of extending the scatter plot to higher dimensions. For example, if you have 10-dimensional data, a 10×10 array of scatter plots is used to look at each dimension versus every other dimension. This is useful for looking at all possible two-way interactions or correlations between dimensions. Figure 11.3 shows a scatter-plot matrix of the Iris Flower data set.

Survey Plots

A simple technique of extending a point in a line graph (like a bar graph) down to an axis has been used in many systems, such as the table lens at Xerox PARC [Rao94]. A simple variation of this extends a line around a center point, where the length of the line corresponds to the dimensional value. This has been called a survey plot in the program Inspect [Loh94]. It is a visualization of n-dimensional data that allows you to quickly see correlations between any two variables, especially when the data is sorted on a particular dimension. When color is used for different classifications, a sort can sometimes make it easy to see which dimensions are best at classifying the data.

The survey plot in Figure 11.4 shows American (red, darkest), Japanese (green, lightest) and European (blue) cars. The data is sorted by cylinders and miles per gallon.

Figure 11.3

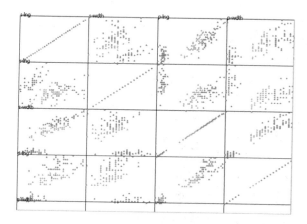

Scatter-plot matrix, Iris Flower data set. (See also color plate.)

Figure 11.4

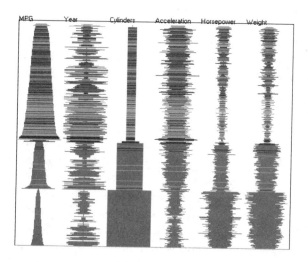

Survey plot, Car data set. (See also color plate.)

Circle Segments

The idea of circle segments originated from Ankerst and Keim [Ank96]. It is similar to the survey plot. However, the data starts from the center of a circle and radiates to the perimeter. A grayscale is used to show the value of a particular dimension, whereas the class value is colored in pie segments

Figure 11.5

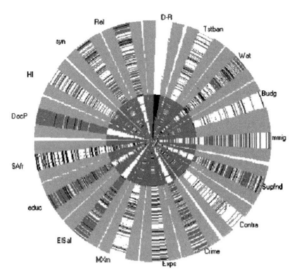

Circle segments, Congress Voting data set.

sandwiched around the dimensional values. (This idea of grayscale between class colors is different from the original circle segments.) In Figure 11.5, a circle segments visualization of the Congress Voting data set is shown.

Radviz

Spring constants can be used to represent relational values between points [Ols93]. [Hof97] developed a radial visualization (radviz), similar in spirit to parallel coordinates (lossless visualization), in which n-dimensional data points are laid out as points equally spaced around the perimeter of a circle. The ends of each of n springs are attached to these n perimeter points. The other ends of the springs are attached to a data point. The spring constant K_i equals the values of the i-th coordinate of the fixed point. Each data point is then displayed where the sum of the spring forces equals 0. All the data point values are usually normalized to have values between 0 and 1.

For example, if all n coordinates have the same value, the data point will lie exactly in the center of the circle. If the point is a unit vector, that point will lie exactly at the fixed point on the edge of the circle (where the spring for that dimension is fixed). Many points can map to the same position. This represents a nonlinear transformation of the data, which preserves certain symmetries and which produces an intuitive display. Some features of this visualization are:

Figure 11.6

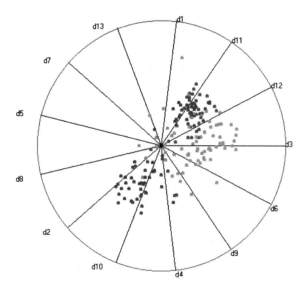

Radviz, Wine data set. (See also color plate.)

- Points with approximately equal coordinate values will lie close to the center.
- Points with similar values whose dimensions are opposite each other on the circle will lie near the center.
- Points that have one or two coordinate values greater than the others lie closer to those dimensions.
- An *n*-dimensional line will map to a line.
- A sphere will map to an ellipse.
- An *n*-dimensional plane maps to a bounded polygon.

In Figure 11.6, an example of the radviz visualization is shown using the Wine data set. Three types of wine can be seen.

11.5.2 Overview of the Data Sets Used in the Comparisons

The 10 data sets (Simple Seven, Balloons, Contact Lenses, Shuttle O-rings, Monks problem, Iris Flower, Congress Voting, Liver Disorders, Cars, and

Wines) were analyzed with the data mining tool Clementine [Cle98], as well as the five visualizations. The Clementine results and the data sets can be accessed from the Web site [Hof98b]. Two rule-based classifiers (based on Quinlan's C4.5 algorithm), a neural net, and statistical tools were used on the data sets for comparisons with the visualizations.

Description of the Data Sets

All of the data sets except the Simple Seven set are from the UC Irvine Machine Learning Repository [UCI97]. The first seven-point data set was created to illustrate the features of radviz compared with the other visualizations. However, it is a useful data set to show the basic features of a visualization. Two of the data sets—Car and Iris Flower—were used because of their familiarity. Nearly every data mining package comes with at least one of these two data sets. The other seven data sets were chosen by increasing complexity from the UC Irvine collection. A short description follows, with some detail provided later when comparing the visualizations.

Simple Seven ■ Seven data points used to show point overlap and normalization

Balloons ■ Data for demonstrating a rule for inflating balloons

Contact Lenses ■ Data illustrating a complicated rule for prescribing what types of contact lenses to wear

Shuttle O-rings ■ Data concerning the Challenger shuttle failure

Monks Problems ■ Several data sets implementing rules to test machine-learning algorithms (designed specifically to be difficult for the algorithms)

Iris Plant Flowers ■ From Fischer [1936], physical measurements from three types of flowers

Congressional Voting Records ■ Democrat and Republican votes on 16 issues from 1984

Liver Disorders ■ Data set that can possibly predict liver disease from blood tests and consumption of alcohol

Car (Automobile) ■ Data concerning cars manufactured in America, Japan, and Europe from 1970 to 1982

Wine Recognition ■ Data of 13 chemical attributes measuring three types of wines

Complexity of Data Sets

The complexity of a data set depends on many factors, including the number of records, the number of dimensions (or attributes), the cardinality of each dimension, the independence of each dimension, and the underlying function or model that produces the data.

One measure of complexity, the algorithmic measure [Cha66, Kol65, Sol64], says the complexity is reduced to the size of whatever algorithm can be used to create the data set. In data mining, this becomes the "model" used to describe the data set, and finding this model (such as a rule or a neural net) is often the main problem.

One idea of complexity would then be "how difficult is it to find a rule explaining the data set?" Another definition could be simply the "information content" or entropy of the data set. If certain fields or dimensions can be used to predict other fields, what is the highest classification achieved from a machine classification algorithm? How long and how much memory does it take for certain data mining algorithms to operate on the data set? Answering the last question may be the most practical measure of the complexity of a data set used in data mining. Building a statistical model of the data set has the problem of "the curse of dimensionality," where the joint probability calculation is related to the product of the cardinality for each dimension. Many data mining packages automatically bin continuous fields to reduce the cardinality of each dimension. As one possible measure of complexity, we have included the log of product of the cardinality (PoC) in the data set description.

Although the data sets are listed in order of increasing complexity, there does not seem to be much correlation with how well a visualization performs. Larger data sets would probably start showing a correlation, but this needs to be investigated.

11.5.3 Comparisons of Different Visualizations for Each Data Set

In this section, we compare the visualizations across the 10 data sets described in the previous section.

Simple Seven Data Set

This is a very simple data set that can be used to illustrate several features of multidimensional visualizations. It was created to show specific differences

Table 11.1

Simple Seven data set.

Dim1	Dim2	Dim3	Dim4	Class
10	10	10	10	P1
5	5	5	5	P2
1	1	1	1	P3
1	0	0	0	P4
0	20	0	0	P5
1	1	0	0	P6
1	2	3	0	P7

in various visualizations. It contains seven instances, seven classes, and four numeric attributes. There are four dimensions (Dim1, Dim2, Dim3, Dim4) and a class. Dimension cardinality is 4, 6, 5, 4, 7, respectively (number of cases). The PoC is 3360; log of PoC is 8.12. The seven points are listed in Table 11.1. The features this data set can illustrate are:

- Global/local normalization (see description in material following)
- Point overlap
- Jittering features
- Categorical-to-numerical mapping (seven class attributes)

Figure 11.7 shows the radviz visualization on the Simple Seven data set. Points P1, P2, and P3 lie exactly in the same spot (center) on the display. Jittering the position helps this point-overlap problem. Alternatively, by using different colors and shapes we can just notice the point-overlap problem. In a standard scatter-plot display, jittering is a standard visualization technique to help show that many points might have the same exact value, or that they map to the same display point. In the radviz display, notice that points 4 and 5 lie on the circle, because only one dimension has a non-zero value (the springs pull the data point to the edge). In the current spring paradigm, there is no distinction between the value of 1 and 20 (if no other dimensional values exist). Points 6 and 7 (light blue and dark blue) lie in spots where the combined spring forces are zero.

In Figure 11.8, the Simple Seven data set is shown using local normalization instead of global normalization. Local normalization means that each dimension is scaled from its maximum and minimum to between 1 and 0. Global normalization scales all values from an overall maximum and mini-

Figure 11.7

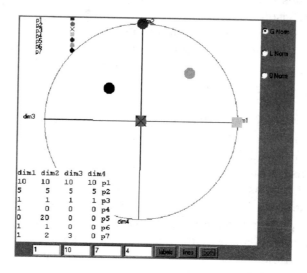

Simple Seven, radviz—global normalization. (See also color plate.)

Figure 11.8

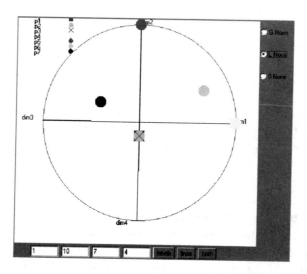

Simple Seven, radviz—local normalization.

mum to values between 1 and 0. Clearly this changes the location of the points in this visualization.

The global/local normalization problem is clearly seen in all visualizations: radviz, parallel coordinates, survey plot, and circle segments (see Figures 11.7 through 11.14.). In circle segments only the tones of the grayscale change with local/global normalization.

When the class dimension is used in the visualization, it can sometimes have a powerful effect. In the next group of figures (11.15 to 11.18), the categorical variable (p1. . . p7) is converted to a number and used as part of the visualization. In radviz, it has the effect of pulling the latter points to the "type dimensional radius." Obviously, in many data analysis activities (such as clustering by class), removing the "class dimension" in radviz would be desirable. However, in parallel coordinates and survey plot, it actually seems to enhance the visual data analysis process.

Thus, in visual data mining, it is desirable to have the ability to remove one or more dimensions from the visualization. Visualizations should have various jittering and normalization options, and visualizing a particular dimension or class attribute by means of color, or as one of the normal dimensions, is also a desirable visualization feature.

This data set is not applicable to any data mining algorithm, because there is no underlying model of the data. In the rest of the data sets, the visualization techniques will be compared with some data mining algorithm (such as C4.5 and a neural net from Clementine).

Balloons, Inflated or Not Inflated

The Balloon database is a good example of purely categorical data. Each attribute can take on only one of two values: stretched or dipped, adult or child, yellow or purple, large or small. The class or the value to be predicted is whether the balloon can be inflated or not. There are actually four data sets corresponding to four rules on how a balloon is inflated. The data set used in the examples uses the following rule: if an "adult" and "stretched," the balloon is inflated. There are twenty instances (four repeated), two classes, and four binary categorical attributes. The data set is number 9 in the UCI collection. The dimensions are color, size, act, age, and inflated. The cardinality is 2, 2, 2, 2, 20, respectively, with the PoC equal to 640, and the log of PoC equal to 6.46. The features this data set can illustrate are:

■ Properties of an all-categorical data set

■ Categorical (binary) to numerical mapping

■ Visual "rule discovery"

Figure 11.9

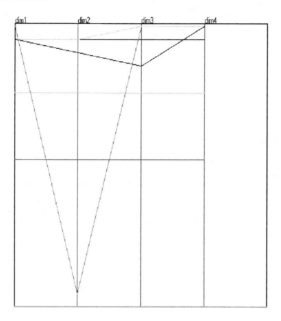

Simple Seven, parallel coordinates—global normalization.

Figure 11.10

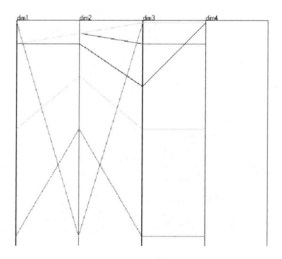

Simple Seven, parallel coordinates—local normalization.

Figure 11.11

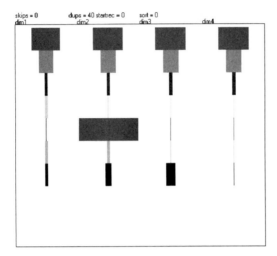

Simple Seven, survey plot—global normalization.

Figure 11.12

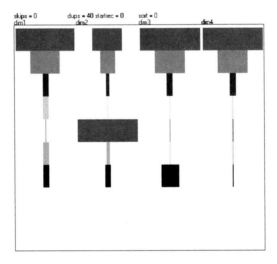

Simple Seven, survey plot—local normalization.

Figure 11.13

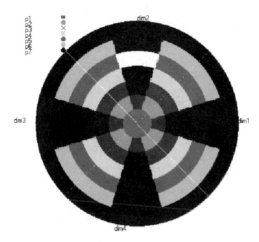

Simple Seven, circle segments—global normalization.

Figure 11.14

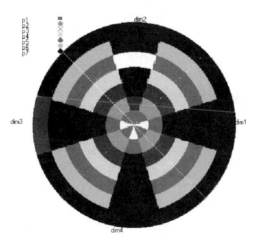

Simple Seven, circle segments—local normalization.

Figure 11.15

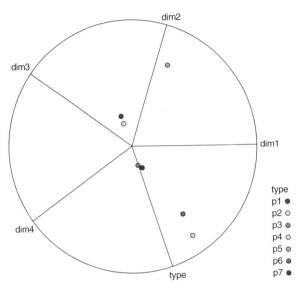

Simple Seven, radviz, using type *as a dimension.*
(See also color plate.)

Figure 11.16

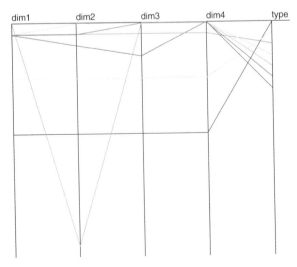

Simple Seven, parallel coordinates, using type
as a dimension. (See also color plate.)

Figure 11.17

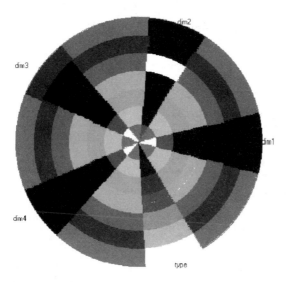

Simple Seven, circle segments, using type *as a dimension.*

Figure 11.18

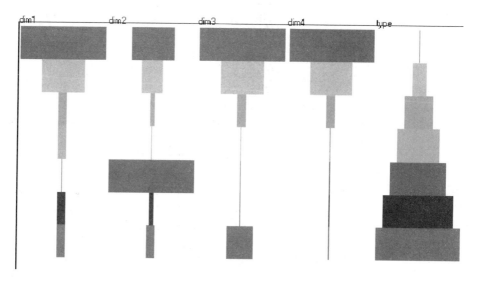

Simple Seven, survey plot, using type *as a dimension.*

Table 11.2

Balloon data set.

Color	Size	Act	Age	Inflated
YELLOW	SMALL	STRETCH	ADULT	T
YELLOW	SMALL	STRETCH	ADULT	T
YELLOW	SMALL	STRETCH	CHILD	F
YELLOW	SMALL	DIP	ADULT	F
YELLOW	SMALL	DIP	CHILD	F
YELLOW	LARGE	STRETCH	ADULT	T
YELLOW	LARGE	STRETCH	ADULT	T
YELLOW	LARGE	STRETCH	CHILD	F
YELLOW	LARGE	DIP	ADULT	F
YELLOW	LARGE	DIP	CHILD	F
PURPLE	SMALL	STRETCH	ADULT	T
PURPLE	SMALL	STRETCH	ADULT	T
PURPLE	SMALL	STRETCH	CHILD	F
PURPLE	SMALL	DIP	ADULT	F
PURPLE	SMALL	DIP	CHILD	F
PURPLE	LARGE	STRETCH	ADULT	T
PURPLE	LARGE	STRETCH	ADULT	T
PURPLE	LARGE	STRETCH	CHILD	F
PURPLE	LARGE	DIP	ADULT	F
PURPLE	LARGE	DIP	CHILD	F

This data set also illustrates how a categorical dimension should/could be expanded or flattened to a new dimension for each value the categorical dimension can take. Each dimension can be two values, but when this is visualized, it is not clear what "number" represents yellow/purple, stretch/dip, and so on. The original Balloon data set is shown in Table 11.2.

The data set can be expanded (or flattened), as shown in Table 11.3. The number of dimensions has doubled. However, some visualizations (radviz) can better illustrate the categorical nature of the data set. Clusters and rules can sometimes be easier to find with this "dimensional expansion." In Figure 11.19, a cluster or possible rule seems evident in the radviz display. In the survey plot (Figure 11.20) with flattening, the rule for inflation can be seen. Hence, "categorical expansion" or flattening should be a standard feature of visual data mining. As will be shown in other data set examples, some visualizations (e.g., radviz) can demonstrate that patterns exist, but other visualizations (e.g., survey plot) or data mining algorithms are needed to find the exact

Table 11.3

Expanded (flattened) Balloon data set.

Yellow	Purple	Small	Large	Stretch	Dip	Adult	Child	True	False
1	0	1	0	1	0	1	0	1	0
1	0	1	0	1	0	1	0	1	0
1	0	1	0	1	0	0	1	0	1
1	0	1	0	0	1	1	0	0	1
1	0	1	0	0	1	0	1	0	1
1	0	0	1	1	0	1	0	1	0
1	0	0	1	1	0	1	0	1	0
1	0	0	1	1	0	0	1	0	1
1	0	0	1	0	1	1	0	0	1
1	0	0	1	0	1	0	1	0	1
0	1	1	0	1	0	1	0	1	0
0	1	1	0	1	0	1	0	1	0
0	1	1	0	1	0	0	1	0	1
0	1	1	0	0	1	1	0	0	1
0	1	1	0	0	1	0	1	0	1
0	1	0	1	1	0	1	0	1	0
0	1	0	1	1	0	1	0	1	0
0	1	0	1	1	0	0	1	0	1
0	1	0	1	0	1	1	0	0	1
0	1	0	1	0	1	0	1	0	1

rule or pattern. In the data mining program Clementine, a simple rule and neural net was easily found to classify the data. However, the C4.5 rule found was not quite as simple as it could be.

Contact Lenses

This data set has some complicated rules on prescribing whether a person should wear hard, soft, or no contact lenses. The description of the database does not list the rules.

There are 24 instances, three classes, and four discrete attributes. The data set is number 52 in the UCI collection. The dimensions are age, prescription, astigmatism, tear production rate, and class (hard, soft, no). The cardinality is 3, 2, 2, 2, 3, 24 (cases), respectively, with the PoC equal to 1728 and the log of PoC equal to 7.45. The mapping of categorical data for each dimension is as follows:

Figure 11.19

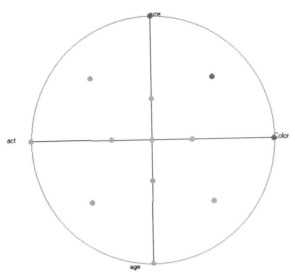

Balloons, radviz, inflated points in red (dark).

Figure 11.20

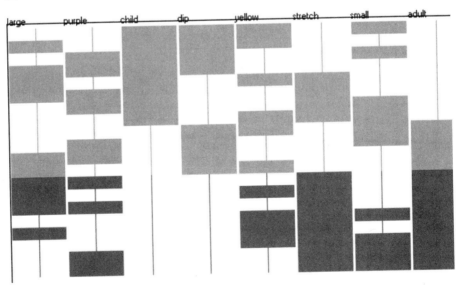

Balloons (flattened), shows Adult and Stretch = Inflated *(red, dark).*

Classes

1. Patient should be fitted with hard contact lenses
2. Patient should be fitted with soft contact lenses
3. Patient should not be fitted with contact lenses

Attributes

1. Age of the patient: (1) young, (2) pre-presbyopic, (3) presbyopic
2. Spectacle prescription: (1) myope, (2) hypermetrope
3. Astigmatism: (1) no, (2) yes
4. Tear production rate: (1) reduced, (2) normal

The features this data set can illustrate are:

- Properties of a categorical data set
- Categorical (binary and tertiary) to numerical mapping
- Partial visual "rule discovery" from a complicated rule

Using the survey plot visualization (with appropriate sorting), it is fairly easy to find a few rules:

- If the tear production rate is reduced, do not prescribe contact lenses.
- If the patient is astigmatic, prescribe hard or no contact lenses.

With the radviz visualization, and using random dimensional layout, you can find some nonlinear clustering of the three classes (hard, soft, no). (See Figure 11.21.)

However, the documentation says there are nine rules covering the data set. Clementine's neural net and C4.5 only achieved accuracy of 73 and 81%, respectively, with simple default settings. The original data set maps the categorical dimensions to numeric values (probably for some "numerical" data mining algorithms). When the "categorical" dimensions are expanded (flattened), the visualizations become more meaningful. In this data set, the radviz visualization hinted at the classification rule, and the survey plot visualization came closer to finding the rule. However, machine learning (C4.5) did best at finding this complicated rule.

Figure 11.21

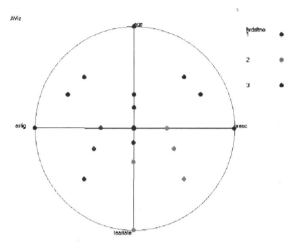

Contact lenses, radviz (the pattern suggests some rules are present).

Shuttle O-rings

This is the infamous data set concerning the Shuttle disaster. Does the data set allow you to predict the failure of the O-ring? It contains 23 instances and five numerical attributes (only four with different values). The data set is number 81 in the UCI collection. The dimensions are number of O-rings, number of O-rings with thermal distress, launch temperature, leak check pressure, and flight number. The cardinality is 1, 3, 1, 6, 3, 23 (cases), respectively, with the PoC equal to 3312 and the log of PoC equal to 8.11. The features this data set can illustrate are:

- Simple regression prediction on one variable
- Outlier versus part of the model
- Trying to make predictions from too little data

In various visualizations (parallel coordinates, radviz, survey plot—Figures 11.22 through 11.24), it is easy to see a correlation with lower temperature and an increase in number of O-rings under thermal distress.

Figure 11.22

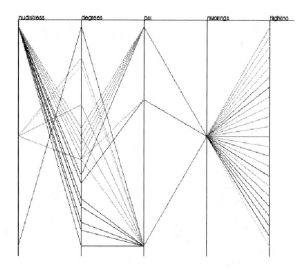

Shuttle O-rings, parallel coordinates. (See also color plate.)

Figure 11.23

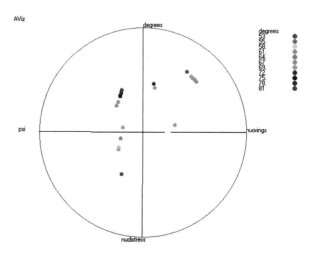

Shuttle O-rings, radviz. (See also color plate.)

Figure 11.24

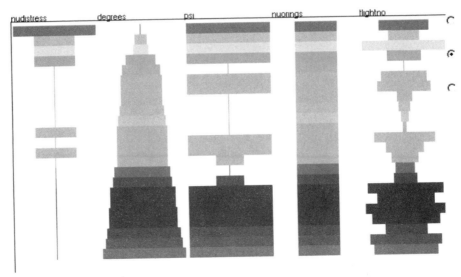

Shuttle O-rings, survey plot. (See also color plate.)

Monks Problems

This data set (Monks training set 1) was specifically created to test induction algorithms and has sometimes been encoded as monks wearing six different articles of clothing with various colors. There are 24 instances, one class (0, 1), and six nominal attributes. The data set is number 65 in the UCI collection. The dimensions are class (0, 1), a1, a2, a3, a4, a5, and a6. The cardinality is, respectively, 2, 3, 3, 2, 3, 4, 2, 124 (cases), with the PoC equal to 107,136 and the log of PoC equal to 11.58. The dimension information is as follows:

    class: 0, 1
    a1: 1, 2, 3
    a2: 1, 2, 3
    a3: 1, 2
    a4: 1, 2, 3
    a5: 1, 2, 3, 4
    a6: 1, 2

Figure 11.25

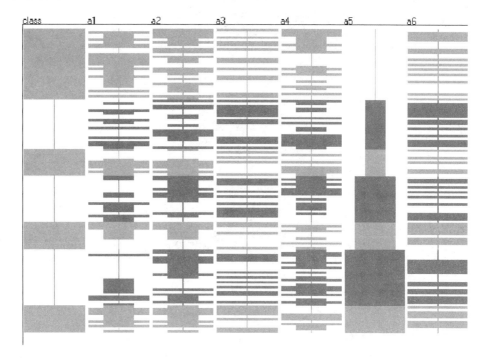

Monks training set 1, survey plot, rule on (green light).

The features this data set can illustrate are:

- Visual "rule discovery"
- Properties of a categorical data set
- Categorical-to-numerical mapping

There are actually three data sets, which implement three different rules. Each data set contains a training and test set. In Figures 11.25 through 11.27, we are looking at the first training set. The rule for the first data set can be found in a survey plot visualization (Figure 11.25), where the attributes are sorted by a5 and then the class value. It is clear that the rule (green values) is when a5 is at its smallest value or when the values of a1 = a2. This rule was difficult to find visually. However, in some layouts of radviz it was hinted that a rule might involve a5 and a1/a2. (See Figure 11.26.) The rule was also evident in some layouts of parallel coordinates. (See Figure 11.27.)

Figure 11.26

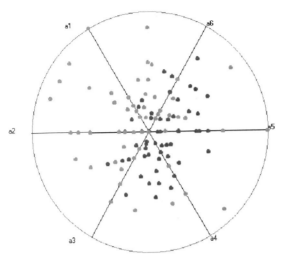

Monks training set 1, radviz.

Figure 11.27

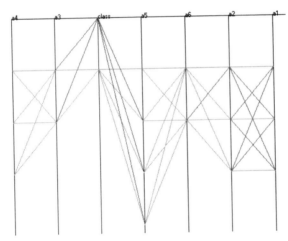

Monks training set 1, parallel coordinates.

The simple default values of Clementine (C4.5 and NN algorithms) found a rule and net that were, respectively, only 92% and 97% accurate, and the C4.5 rule was more complicated than a5 = 1 or a1 = a2. To design a visualization that would help you easily find such rules is a challenge.

Figure 11.28

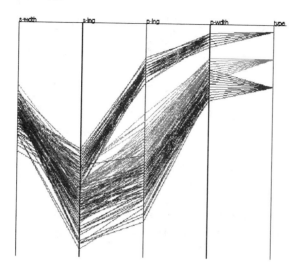

Iris Flowers, parallel coordinates. (See also color plate.)

Iris Plant (Fischer 1936—Flowers) Database

The Iris Flower database is perhaps the most often used data set in pattern recognition, statistics, data analysis, and machine learning. The task is to predict the class of the flower based on the four physical attribute measurements. There are 150 instances, three classes, and four numeric attributes. The data set is number 46 in the UCI collection. The dimensions are class (Setosa, Versicolor, Virginica), sepal length, sepal width, petal length, and petal width. The cardinality is 35, 23, 43, 22, 3, 150 (cases), respectively, the PoC is equal to 342,688,500, and the log of PoC equals 19.65. One class is linearly separable from the other two, but the other two are not linearly separable from each other. The features this data set can illustrate are:

- Cluster detection
- Outlier detection
- Important feature detection
- Find class clusters

In most of the visualizations, you can see the three clusters of flower types, and in many of them (Figures 11.28 and 11.29) it can be seen that petal length and petal width are very good discriminators of the three classes.

Figure 11.29

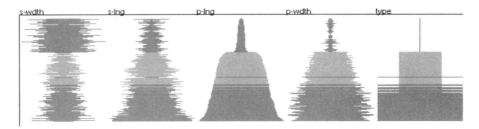

Iris Flowers, survey plot. (See also color plate.)

Several points could be considered "outliers," which show up clearly in several visualizations, as in the scatter-plot matrix of Figure 11.3.

Congressional Voting Records (Republican or Democrat)

This is a data set that many people can relate to easily. The data set is the voting record of Democrats and Republicans on 16 issues in 1984. There are 435 instances and 17 variables. The data set is number 106 in the UCI collection. The first dimension, primary classification, identifies the parts, Republican or Democrat. The remaining 16 dimensions represent Boolean (yes or no) votes, including numerous missing values, are listed as follows:

1. handicapped-infants
2. water-project-cost-sharing
3. adoption-of-the-budget-resolution
4. physician-fee-freeze
5. El-Salvador-aid
6. religious-groups-in-schools
7. anti-satellite-test-ban
8. aid-to-Nicaraguan-contras
9. mx-missile
10. immigration
11. synfuels-corporation-cutback
12. education-spending

13. superfund-right-to-sue
14. crime
15. duty-free-exports
16. export-administration-act-South-Africa

The cardinality is, respectively, 2, 3, 3, 3, 3, 3, 3, 3, 3, 3, 3, 3, 3, 3, 3, 3, 435 (cases), with the PoC equal to 37,450,647,270 and the log of PoC equal to 24.35. The features this data set can illustrate are:

- Cluster detection
- Outlier detection
- Important feature detection (for class distinction)
- Find class clusters (specific clusters that separate classes)
- Usefulness of circle segments
- Difficulties of parallel coordinates, scatter-plot matrix

Most issues segregate Democrats and Republicans to a certain extent, and this was seen in the visualizations. Radviz points out some interesting outliers based on combinations of issues. The survey plot with sorting on each issue can show which individual issues predict political parties best. The circle segment visualization showed which issues went mostly according to party lines (see Figure 11.5; mostly dark or mostly white segments). These types of categorical (y/n/?) dimensions pose difficulties for some types of visualizations (parallel coordinates, scatter-plot matrix). It is possible that a different encoding method could make them more useful. Clementine algorithms had prediction accuracies greater than 95%, and could quickly list the best discriminators. An interesting question is whether it is possible for someone trained in the various visualizations to predict classification accuracies.

Liver Disorders (Bupa Medical Research)

This data set is concerned with factors that may contribute to liver disease. The first five attributes are blood tests thought to be sensitive to liver disorders that might arise from excessive alcohol consumption.

There are 345 instances (male patients), two classes (1, 2), six numeric attributes. The data set is number 54 in the UCI collection. The dimensions are mcv (mean corpuscular volume), alkphos (alkaline phosphotase), sgpt

Figure 11.30

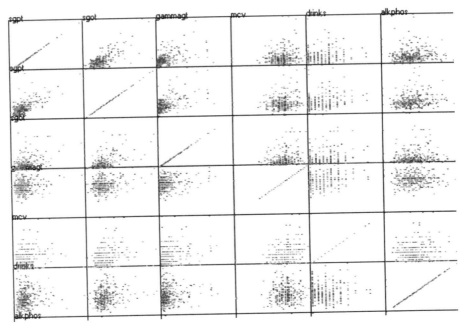

Bupa liver disorders, scatter-plot matrix.

(alamine aminotransferase), sgot (aspartate aminotransferase), gammagt (gamma-glutamyl transpeptidase), drinks, and type (class). The cardinality is 26, 78, 67, 47, 94, 16, 2, 345 (cases), respectively, with the PoC equal to 6,627,313,854,720 and the log of PoC equal to 29.52. The features this data set can illustrate are:

- Outlier detection
- Difficulties of visual data mining

This seems to be the most difficult data set in which to discern any patterns. The description seems to imply that the seventh attribute (dimension) was a selector on the data set (liver disease or not). The documentation implies that only "drinks > 5" seems to correlate with anything. Visually, this seems difficult to observe. The scatter-plot matrix in Figure 11.30 seems to show that clustering the red and green points (different types) is difficult. Clementine's data mining tools seem to be able to discriminate better than

70% (see Web page [Hof98a]). However, the "drinks" attribute does not seem to be a factor based on the neural net sensitivity analysis.

Car Data Set

This data set is included in many data mining and visualization packages. It has been modified from the original CMU Statlib Library. Five instances have been taken out because of missing values. The original problem was to predict the miles per gallon for a type of car. The different characteristics of American, European, and Japanese cars from 1970 to 1982 are demonstrated in this data set.

There are 393 instances, seven attributes, six numeric attributes, and one categorical. The data set is number 5 in the UCI collection. The dimensions are mpg, cylinders, horsepower, weight, acceleration, year, and type. The cardinality is 128, 5, 93, 346, 95, 13, 3, 393 (cases), respectively, with the PoC equal to 29,986,086,124,800 and the log of PoC equal to 31.03. The features this data set can illustrate are:

- Outlier detection
- Cluster detection
- Class cluster detection (type of car)
- Important feature detection

In many visualizations you can see the clustering of American cars with increased horsepower, weight, cylinders, and acceleration. The Japanese cars have high mpg, low weight, smaller number of cylinders, and lower acceleration. The European cars have more intermediate values, but seem to have the best acceleration. (See Figures 11.2 and 11.4.) This is an excellent data set to show a wide range of facts and features using the visualizations. There are several versions of this data set. The one used in Figures 11.2 and 11.4 has only six dimensions and one class attribute. It is interesting that the data mining algorithms cannot seem to classify car type at much better than 70% accuracy for American, Japanese, or European.

Wine Recognition Database

Three types of wine are characterized by 13 (continuous) chemical attributes. There are 178 instances, three classes (1, 2, and 3), and 13 numeric attributes. The data set is number 110 in the UCI collection. The dimensions are class

Figure 11.31

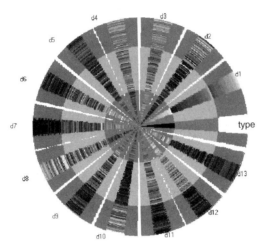

Wine data set, circle segments.

and 13 unknown continuous variables. The cardinality is 3, 126, 133, 79, 63, 53, 97, 132, 39, 101, 132, 78, 122, 121, 178 (cases), respectively, with the PoC equal to 1.80e+028 and the log of PoC equal to 65.07. The features this data set can illustrate are:

■ Outlier detection

■ Cluster detection

■ Class cluster detection (type of wine)

■ Important feature detection (which helps predict type of wine)

Several visualizations (scatter plot, parallel coordinates, and radviz) show that many of the 13 dimensions can approximately separate the classes of wines. Some features can discriminate all three, and some just two of the three types of wine. Circle segments again quickly shows which features are good discriminators (Figure 11.31) of the two and three types of wine. From the data set description, the three wine types are 100% separable, but this is not easy to show using standard visualizations (radviz, Figure 11.6). Possibly a projection (radviz or Grand Tour) could show a better linear separation. The neural net in Clementine had predicted accuracy of 100%. However, the C4.5 algorithm only had 94.4%, using cross-validation. This data set demonstrates that statistical and classification algorithms are needed for a full data mining analysis.

Table 11.4

Parallel coordinates.

DATA SET/TASK	See Outliers	See Clusters	Find Class Clusters	See All Important Features	See Some Important Features	See Possible Rule/Model	See Exact Rule/Model
Balloons							
Balloons—flattened							
Lenses							
Lenses—flattened							
O-rings	Y	Y	Y	Y	Y	Y	
Monks1—training		Y		Y	Y	Y	Y
Iris	Y	Y	Y	Y	Y	Y	
Congress							
Liver	Y	Y					
Cars	Y	Y	Y		Y	Y	
Wine	Y	Y	Y		Y	Y	

11.5.4 Summary of Results

In Tables 11.4 through 11.8, we provide a summary of the results of the visualization comparisons. Each table represents one of the visualization techniques evaluated on nine of the data sets (two of which where flattened for an additional two sets). Each column represents one of the seven features or "tasks." A "Y" in a column signifies that yes, the visualization can be used to detect that feature satisfactorily. A blank signifies a "no" or "Not Applicable." The data is a rather fascinating overview of strengths and weaknesses across an interesting set of visualization, data sets, and tasks. For example, the survey plot is clearly superior to the other visualizations in finding the exact rule or model. Circle segments is rather specialized for finding important features. The charts not only provide a powerful way of comparing this particular set of visualization techniques. They also illustrate a potentially very powerful general tool. That general tool could help researchers gain broad insights regarding strengths and weaknesses of different types and classes of visualization techniques. It can form a basis for developing new techniques and models, and for guiding the evolution and improvement of visualization technology.

Table 11.5
Radviz.

DATA SET/TASK	See Outliers	See Clusters	Find Class Clusters	See All Important Features	See Some Important Features	See Possible Rule/Model	See Exact Rule/Model
Balloons		Y	Y			Y	
Balloons—flattened		Y	Y		Y	Y	
Lenses		Y	Y		Y		
Lenses—flattened		Y	Y		Y		
O-rings	Y	Y	Y	Y	Y	Y	
Monks1—training		Y					
Iris	Y	Y	Y			Y	
Congress	Y	Y	Y		Y		
Liver	Y	Y					
Cars	Y	Y	Y		Y	Y	
Wine	Y	Y	Y		Y	Y	

Table 11.6
Survey plot.

DATA SET/TASK	See Outliers	See Clusters	Find Class Clusters	See All Important Features	See Some Important Features	See Possible Rule/Model	See Exact Rule/Model
Balloons				Y	Y		Y
Balloons—flattened				Y	Y		Y
Lenses				Y	Y		
Lenses—flattened				Y	Y		
O-rings	Y			Y	Y	Y	
Monks1—training				Y	Y	Y	Y
Iris	Y	Y	Y	Y	Y	Y	
Congress				Y	Y		
Liver							
Cars				Y	Y	Y	
Wine				Y	Y	Y	

Table 11.7

Circle segments.

DATA SET/TASK	See Outliers	See Clusters	Find Class Clusters	See All Important Features	See Some Important Features	See Possible Rule/Model	See Exact Rule/ Model
Balloons							
Balloons—flattened							
Lenses							
Lenses—flattened							
O-rings							
Monks1—training							
Iris				Y	Y		
Congress				Y	Y		
Liver							
Cars				Y	Y	Y	
Wine				Y	Y	Y	

Table 11.8

Scatter-plot matrix.

DATA SET/TASK	See Outliers	See Clusters	Find Class Clusters	See All Important Features	See Some Important Features	See Possible Rule/Model	See Exact Rule/ Model
Balloons							
Balloons—flattened							
Lenses							
Lenses—flattened							
O-rings	Y	Y	Y	Y	Y	Y	
Monks1—training							
Iris	Y	Y	Y		Y	Y	
Congress							
Liver	Y	Y					
Cars	Y	Y	Y		Y	Y	
Wine	Y	Y	Y		Y	Y	

11.6 Future Work

We believe that test and evaluation methods can contribute significantly to the development of the next generation of information exploration and KDD tools. We hope that the feedback from researchers and developers who study this chapter will serve to guide us in future work to expand and enrich a much needed environment that we have only been able to illustrate here. With help from the research community and industry, we would like to develop the taxonomy of visualizations and some benchmark data sets.

We have designed an architecture to support task/feature-based benchmarking. A system is evaluated on a set of tasks and data sets, based on KDD/visualization process tasks and representative data. For each system, a capability matrix can be formed. As evaluations are performed for many systems, a technology matrix can be created, charting algorithms versus features.

Acknowledgments

This chapter is the result of discussions by the working group on requirements for benchmarking formed during the workshops on Issues in the Integration of Data Mining and Data Visualization held at the 1997 Conference on Knowledge Discovery and Data Mining and at the 1997 Visualization Conference. The authors would like to thank those who participated in the discussions held at the workshops on this topic. To Mark Levenson, Mohammed Shahbaz Anwar, Ken Collier, and Donald Sautter, thank you for your insightful comments.

References

[Ank96]   M. Ankerst, D. A. Keim, and H.-P. Kriegel. "Circle Segments: A Technique for Visually Exploring Large Multidimensional Data Sets, *IEEE Visualization '96 Proceedings, Hot Topic*, San Francisco, 1996.

[Cha66]   G. J. Chaitin. "On the Length of Programs for Computing Finite Binary Sequences," *Journal of the ACM*, 13(4): 547–569, October 1966.

[Cle98]   Clementine. *www.isl.co.uk/clem.html.*

[Fay97]   U. Fayyad. "Editorial," *Data Mining and Knowledge Discovery*, 1:3, pp. 237–239, 1997.

[Fis36]   R. A. Fischer. "The User of Multiple Measurements in Axonomic Problems," *Annals of Eugenics* 7:179–188, 1936.

[Gib69]   E. J. Gibson. *Principles of Perceptual Learning.* New York. Appleton-Century-Crofts, 1969.

[Gri97]   G. Grinstein, S. Laskowski, B. Rogowitz, and G. Wills. "Panel: Information Exploration Shootout Project and Benchmark Data Sets," *IEEE Visualization '97 Proceedings*, pp. 511–513, Phoenix, 1997. *www.cs.uml.edu/~phoffman.*

[Gri98]   G. Grinstein, A. Inselberg, and S. Laskowski. "Panel: Key Problems and Thorny Issues in Multidimensional Visualization," *IEEE Visualization '98 Proceedings*, Research Triangle Park, NC, 1998.

[Hof97]   P. Hoffman, G. Grinstein, K. Marx, I. Grosse, and E. Stanley. "DNA Visual and Analytic Data Mining," *IEEE Visualization '97 Proceedings*, pp. 437–441, Phoenix, 1997. *www.cs.uml.edu/~phoffman/viz.*

[Hof98a]   *www.cs.uml.edu/~phoffman.*

[Hof98b]   *ivpr1.cs.uml.edu/shootout/vizdatasets/.*

[IES97]   *iris.cs.uml.edu:8080.*

[Ins85]   A. Inselberg. "The Plane with Parallel Coordinates," *The Visual Computer* 1, pp. 69–91, 1985.

[Kdn98]   *www.kdnuggets.com/data sets.html.*

[Kol65]   A. N. Kolmogorov. "Three Approaches to the Quantitive Definition of Information," *Problems of Information Transmission* 1, pp. 1–17, 1965.

[Loh94]   H. Lohninger. "INSPECT: A Program System to Visualize and Interpret Chemical Data,"*Chemomet. Intell. Lab. Syst.* 22, 147–153, 1994.

[Mar96]   J. Martin. "Beyond Pie Charts and Spreadsheets," *Computer World*, May 27, 1996.

[NIS97]   *www.nist.gov/itl.*

[NIS98a]   *www.nist.gov/itl/div894/894.01/slp.htm.*

[NIS98b]   *www.nist.gov/itl/div894.03/vip.html.*

[Ols93]   K. A. Olsen, R. R. Korfhage, K. M. Sochats, M. B. Spring, and J. G. Williams. "Visualisation of a Document Collection: The VIBE System," *Information Processing and Management*, vol. 29, no. 1, pp. 69–81. Tarrytown, NY. Pergamon Press, 1993.

[Pic95]   R. M. Pickett, G. G. Grinstein, H. Levkowitz, and S. Smith. "Harnessing Pre-attentive Perceptual Processes in Visualization," *Perceptual Issues in Visualization*, G. Grinstein and H. Levkowitz, (editors). New York. Springer-Verlag, 1995.

[Rao94] R. Rao and S. K. Card. "The Table Lens: Merging Graphical and Symbolic Representations in an Interactive Focus + Context Visualization for Tabular Information," *Proceedings of CHI'94*, pp. 318–322. Boston. ACM Press, 1994.

[Sch96] H. R. Schiffman. *Sensation and Perception*, New York, John Wiley and Sons, 1996.

[Sol64] R. J. Solomonoff. "A Formal Theory of Inductive Inference," Information and Control 7:122, 224–254, 1964.

[Ste97] C. Stedman. "Users Want Data Mining Tools to Scale Up," *Computer World*, September 1997.

[Swe82] J. A. Swets and R. M. Pickett. *Evaluation of Diagnostic Systems: Methods from Signal Detection Theory*. New York. Academic Press, 1982.

[TRE97] *trec.nist.gov.*

[UCI97] *www.ics.uci.edu/AI/ML/MLDBRepository.html.*

[Voo97] E. M. Voorhees and D. K. Harman. *The Fifth Text Retrieval Conference (TREC-5)*, NIST Special Publication 500-238, National Institute of Standards and Technology, Gaithersburg, MD, 1997.

[Won97] W. Wong. "Study: Data Mining Market at $8.4B by 2000," *Computer World*, October 1997.

[Yra96] T. Yrastorza. "The Big Picture," *Computer World*, August 1996.

Chapter 12

Data Visualization for Decision Support Activities

HENRY S. GERTZMAN

High Summit Consulting

MCI Telecommunications Corporation is one of the largest and fastest-growing telecommunications companies in the world, and is internationally recognized for its innovative marketing techniques. MCI has been quick to capitalize on developing technologies in support of its marketing and sales activities. MCI was one of the first commercial companies to develop and successfully implement data warehousing involving multi-terabytes of data for decision support activities. In recognition of this work, MCI was honored to receive the Computerworld Smithsonian Award "for heroic achievement in information technology in recognition of your visionary use of information technology," and the Data Warehousing Institute recognized MCI as a winner in the 1996 Best Practices Awards program.

To leverage this investment in data, databases, and data warehousing hardware and software, MCI is looking closely at new methods of data modeling, data mining, KDD, and data visualization to support innovative marketing and decision support activities. As a part of this effort, we are heading up a data discovery initiative within MCI. We are particularly interested in exploring methods of mining very large amounts of data, measured in terabytes and stored in relational databases within massively parallel processing (MPP) data warehousing systems. In one of our own warehouses, we have over 200 million records, each containing upward of 1200 attributes, comprising several terabytes of raw data. To complicate matters, some of this data is quite sparsely populated.

Unfortunately, most of the data mining and data discovery tools currently available will *not* operate effectively on such large amounts of data nor on MPP platforms. Because of the large number of attributes and because of data sparsity issues, we need the ability to "mine" this data *without sampling*, or at least to develop data reduction techniques that will not destroy the patterns for which we are searching, if we are to effectively uncover previously unknown patterns among these attributes. Once these patterns are "discovered," much of the original data can be filtered down to manageable sizes, and traditional data mining tools can be applied.

To effectively "mine" such data, we need processes, techniques, and algorithms that can be used to initially identify all of the promising data combinations that are candidates for further analysis. With such large amounts of data, visualization, as part of the exploration process, becomes imperative. Yet, it is not obvious how to effectively visualize the results of mining large amounts of data in n dimensions, where n can be as large as 1200! We are particularly interested in the following topics:

- Visualization as a part of the exploration process
- Scalability issues, especially scalability both in data and in the number of parallel processors (both with SMP and MPP computer architectures)
- How visualization can help in the initial "survey" of data in order to help drive further data mining activities
- Open systems issues

In addition, we are interested in the following topics:

- The requirements that visualization places on knowledge discovery systems
- How to model the user, including tasks, processes, and support issues
- Advanced user interfaces for data mining
- System integration issues
- Computational steering for data mining
- Scalability to large databases
- Data and computation sharing
- Applications of integrated systems

There are related issues that can be helped by appropriate data visualization techniques. For example, consider semicompact data clusters in k space. If you were to add an additional uncorrelated dimension, these "spheroids" of clustered data would be transformed into "tubes" or "ribbons" in $(k + 1)$

space. Data visualization might be used to quickly help identify such "dimensions of non-correlation."

A second area of interest is how to recognize and exploit any "natural ordering" of categorical data as part of the data preparation process. When this ordering exists and is properly employed, it can improve the results of many KDD processes. Visualization should be able to help identify such natural orderings.

A third area of interest is how to effectively visualize data embedded in a large number of dimensions. At the very least, you would desire visualization techniques that scale linearly (even sublinearly) in the number of attributes, bypassing the sometimes combinatorial explosions that can occur with multiple dimensionality. "Dimensional compatification" is needed, whereby the "less important" dimensions can be projected onto a single hybrid dimension, or even eliminated entirely. Innovative data visualization techniques can help in all of these areas, as a part of the overall KDD process.

Chapter 13

A Visualization-Driven Approach for Strategic Knowledge Discovery

DAVID LAW YUH FOONG*

National University of Singapore

Introduction

This chapter describes an interactive visualization approach for knowledge discovery. The pivotal roles of visualization in the KDD process, particularly in the data pre-processing and data mining phases, are highlighted. We have demonstrated empirically the strategic importance of establishing a visualization platform with dual objectives: first as a channel for the infusion of human cognitive inputs and relevant domain knowledge to guide the KDD process, and second as an effective front-end tool in synergy with other types of data mining techniques. We propose that the strategic use of domain knowledge, the formalization of a three-step human-centered loop (data exploration, hypothesis formulation, and hypothesis testing), and the cooperative use of data mining techniques are critical success factors in any real-world KDD application.

In the face of rapid technological advancement and competitiveness in industry and research, two major trends have emerged. First, there is an increase in organizational complexity in terms of functionality and operations, as these organizational activities become more knowledge intensive. This gives rise to a second trend in which the volume and dimension of

* This research was initiated at the Centre for Natural Product Research, Institute of Molecular and Cell Biology (Singapore).

organizational data escalates at a fast pace. To make better and more informed decisions at various stages of an organization's business and operations, there is a need to discover and extract relevant, useful, crucial information and knowledge from the growing data repositories. Knowledge discovery in databases (KDD), commonly known as database mining, has emerged to meet this need. KDD is defined as the "non-trivial process of identifying valid, novel, potentially useful, and ultimately understandable patterns in data" [Fra91]. This could be achieved through a multistep KDD process, and it is defined as "using the database along with any required selection, pre-processing, sub-sampling, and transformations of it; to apply data mining methods (algorithms) to enumerate patterns from it; and to evaluate the products of data mining to identify the subset of the enumerated patterns deemed 'knowledge'" [Fay96].

In this chapter, we address the issue of how data visualization can function as an effective front-end tool, in synergy with other data mining techniques, and how it can serve as an interactive platform to exploit domain knowledge and human cognitive capabilities through user participation within the KDD process. In particular, we highlight the role of visualization in the KDD process, especially in the steps involving KDD planning, data pre-processing, and data mining. We present a visualization-driven KDD approach that it is hoped will provide a clear strategy for the integration of KDD and visualization.

13.1 Motivation and Related Work

Before a KDD process can be successfully implemented, there are many issues to address and limitations to overcome. These issues arise at different stages of the KDD process in relation to the nature and complexity of the activities associated with the respective stages. The major tasks in the KDD process include initial overall KDD planning (establishing goals and formulating hypotheses), data attribute selection, data sampling, data dimensional reduction and summarization, data verification, data transformation, selection of suitable data mining techniques or tools to support the discovery process, and the presentation and interpretation of results. Ideally, all of these steps could be fully automated, but this is very difficult in reality. You should realize that KDD is very much a human-centered and domain-centered process. The need for human direction and domain knowledge guidance is clearly evident, especially if the application domain environment is complex. Human experts possess visual and cognitive abilities, as well as domain knowledge that combined could augment the KDD process. However, human expertise and resources are scarce, which limits the involvement of humans in KDD. One approach to lessen this constraint is to find ways of summarizing data sets or data mining results and to present them to the human analyst in an intuitive manner for easy comprehension.

Most of the current KDD researchers and practitioners tend to focus on technical issues, such as the automation of various KDD steps or the development and optimization of data mining algorithms, using techniques from statistics, artificial intelligence, and database and high-performance computing. However, some researchers have realized the important roles of humans within the KDD process [Bra96, Gri96] and the potential support capabilities of interactive visualization in KDD [Kei95, Gri92, Han97]. Recently there is an increased emphasis on the development of interactive visualization-based KDD applications, using a variety of novel approaches and techniques [Bru97, Der97, Fel97, Lee95, Mih97, Sub97]. We concur with the general view that visualization is an effective and intuitive method for knowledge discovery. Human perceptual and cognitive capabilities can be exploited through visualization. Together with inputs from domain knowledge, experience, and heuristics, we regard these elements as essential in KDD. The strategic use of domain knowledge in the KDD process [Foo97] and the maintenance of a high degree of interactivity—first between humans and computers and second between different data mining techniques in a cooperative fashion [Foo01]—are critical success factors in any real-world KDD application. Visualization is poised to facilitate such practices.

We recognize that visualization is a very effective means of incorporating in human participation. This will open up channels for the infusion of domain knowledge into the KDD process whereby relevant, useful, and important background business information and domain heuristics can be fully exploited to guide KDD. Visualization can be used as a data mining technique on its own, or it can be an effective front-end tool in synergy with other data mining methods, within a hybrid, interactive, and cooperative KDD framework. Visualization has its place in all key phases of the KDD process, beginning with initial overall KDD planning, data pre-processing, and data mining to results presentation. In the following sections, we briefly discuss our visualization-driven KDD approach, in particular, its strategic roles in data pre-processing and data mining. Some successful applications of this approach to data analysis and exploration in pharmaceutical drug discovery research are illustrated.

13.2 Integrating KDD and Visualization

The KDD process serves as a systematic framework to guide information exploration and knowledge discovery tasks. Visualization has played a pivotal role in KDD. The two-tier objective of our strategy is to maintain a high degree of user interactivity and feedback, while at the same time tapping the benefits of using more than one type of data mining technique in synergy. Using application examples from a natural product drug-screening domain, we highlight, empirically, the benefits of this strategy in the data pre-processing and data mining phases of KDD.

13.2.1 Using Visualization in Data Pre-processing

Before data mining, the pre-processing and preparation of raw data sets is necessary. Visualization can also be used as a summarization tool for the human user to gain an overview of data sets. This enables him to formulate accurate hypotheses and objectives for KDD, and to select carefully only the relevant and useful data to be sampled and extracted for data pre-processing. During data pre-processing, visualization can be used to verify data sets, and to check for data discrepancies, errors, missing data, duplication, and inconsistencies. This helps filter off nonrelevant data, increasing the accuracy and efficiency of data mining. A beneficial side effect of this is the opportunity to perform data verification and validation of the transactional databases and data warehouses from which data is extracted and sampled for data mining. Thus, visualization could serve as a channel for the inflow of relevant domain knowledge and human decisions, which could help optimize these otherwise laborious data pre-processing activities.

Figures 13.1 and 13.2 are examples of 2D graphical box plots of an experimental data set from biological drug screening. Data from certain attributes of interest is used for the plots. Figure 13.1 illustrates the usefulness of visualization for data integrity checks. From the figure, incomplete or missing values can be detected instantly along the Y axis (e.g., those attribute values with "?" symbols or blanks). Errors in certain attribute values are visible along the X axis, which could possibly be a result of human errors during the data entry process (e.g., attribute value YMPGV was incorrectly entered as YMPGVc). Figure 13.2 summarizes the distribution of data points of a categorical attribute (X axis) along the range of a numeric attribute (Y axis). This is very useful for data selection and sampling. The human analyst is able to inspect the data set visually in order to assess its suitability for data mining. If the data set is appropriate, the next step is to determine which portions may

Figure 13.1

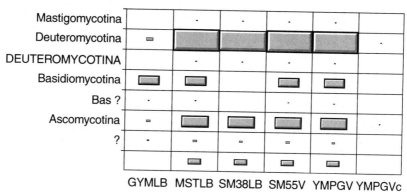

Using visualization for data verification and validation.

Figure 13.2

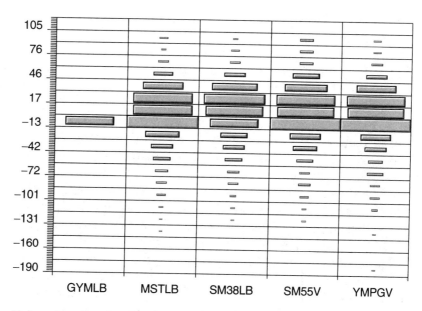

Using visualization for data selection and sampling.

be interesting or useful for further analysis, and subsequently extract a sub-set of data from the original set for data mining (e.g., the human analyst may choose to select all data points above a certain cutoff value on the Y axis, ignoring all other data with values below this cutoff point). In this way, a human analyst could rely on visualization to plan and carry out data pre-processing tasks.

13.2.2 Using Visualization in Data Mining

The data mining step within the KDD process involves the application of suitable algorithms, tools, and techniques to pre-processed data sets in order to facilitate data exploration and useful pattern extraction. Generally, visualization is a good technique for providing a summary and overview of a data set. However, visualization would not be an appropriate technique if the objective of a data analysis session were to find more detailed correlation and patterns among a large number of data attributes. In other words, visualization will be less useful for sifting specific patterns from high-dimensional data sets and data with a large number of categorical attribute values. On the other hand, nonvisualization-based data mining techniques such as machine-learning algorithms are able to analyze a data set (possibly with a large number of attributes) and generate detailed patterns and correlation in the form of decision trees or rules.

One of the limitations of these algorithms is that very often the results generated are far too detailed for the purpose of initial data exploration and overall data summarization. Moreover, most of these algorithms are highly susceptible to various forms of errors and noise in the data. Hence, there is a need to find means of overcoming the potential limitation of any particular technique while at the same time combining the strengths of visualization with other data mining techniques, to cope with the needs of real-world KDD applications. Figure 13.3 illustrates a hybrid data mining approach of using more than one technique. Clusters, distribution patterns, and anomalies in data sets can be detected and compared by applying various types of data mining techniques, in a complementary and strategic manner. The data mining capabilities and requirements within the three-step iterative data analysis loop, at different stages of the data mining process, could be met with techniques such as visualization of graphical plots and generation of more detailed types of correlation and patterns (such as classification rules, association rules, and decision trees) using suitable algorithms.

Visualization can be used either as a stand-alone data mining technique or as a front-end input to other data mining tools, in a complementary fashion. This results in a more powerful and synergistic approach to data exploration and discovery. Intermediate results generated by one data mining technique will be analyzed by a human analyst, who will subsequently decide how to proceed, perhaps using a second technique. This may involve

Figure 13.3

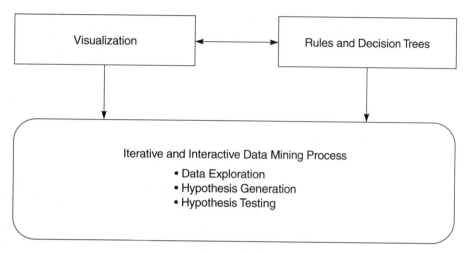

Hybrid techniques used cooperatively in data mining.

iterative reselection of data sets and attributes, and any pre-processing steps necessary. New human hypotheses may be postulated along the way, based on initial rounds of data mining results, which may require further verification and testing through subsequent sessions of mining. The iterative processes will terminate when the results are deemed satisfactory.

13.3 Conclusion

Indeed, visualization plays a pivotal role in the KDD process. It provides an excellent platform for human-computer interaction by narrowing the gap between human and computer during data analysis, and consequently tightens the three-step iterative loop of data exploration, hypothesis formulation, and hypothesis testing. The proposed two-tier strategy for the integration of knowledge discovery and visualization emphasizes the strategic role of visualization as a front-end technique in the KDD process. During data pre-processing, visualization serves as a front-end data verification tool that allows for the prompt detection of errors inherent in data sets. At the data mining step, visualization serves as a front-end data mining tool, providing first-level data exploration and analysis for the human analyst, whose output serves as input to other data mining techniques. Through visualization we are able to combine the strategies of human participation effectively with domain knowledge guidance, in a unified manner, enhancing the KDD process. By identifying and formalizing the role of visualization in the KDD process, future KDD systems developed to facilitate one or more KDD steps could incorporate visualization as a necessary key component in enabling appropriate human intervention.

References

[Bra96]   R. J. Brachman and T. Anand. "The Process of Knowledge Discovery in Databases," *Advances in Knowledge Discovery and Data Mining*, G. Piatetsky-Shapiro and W. J. Frawley (editors), pp. 37–57. Cambridge, MA. AAAI Press/MIT Press. 1996.

[Bru97]   C. Brunk, J. Kelly, and R. Kohavi. "MineSet: An Integrated System for Data Mining," *Proceedings of the Third International Conference on Knowledge Discovery and Data Mining* (KDD'97), pp. 135–138. Menlo Park, CA. AAAI Press, 1997.

[Der97]   M. Derthick, J. Kolojejchick, and S. F. Roth. "An Interactive Visualization Environment for Data Exploration," *Proceedings of the Third International Conference on Knowledge Discovery and Data Mining* (KDD'97), pp. 2–9. Menlo Park, CA. AAAI Press, 1997.

[Foo97]   D.L.Y. Foong. "The Role of Exogenous Knowledge in the Knowledge Discovery Process," *International Conference on Artificial Intelligence and Soft Computing*, pp. 5–8. IASTED ACTA Press, 1997.

[Foo01]   D.L.Y. Foong. "An Interactive Data Mining Strategy for Drug Screening," submitted to *Informatica: An International Journal of Computing and Informatics*, 2001.

[Fay96]   U. M. Fayyad, G. Piatetsky-Shapiro, and P. Smyth. "Knowledge Discovery and Data Mining: Towards a Unifying Framework," *Proceedings of the Second International Conference on Knowledge Discovery and Data Mining* (KDD'96), pp. 82–88. Menlo Park, CA. AAAI Press, 1996.

[Fel97]   R. Feldman, W. Klosgen, and A. Zilberstein. "Visualization Techniques to Explore Data Mining Results for Document Collections," *Proceedings of the Third International Conference on Knowledge Discovery and Data Mining* (KDD'97), pp. 16–23. Menlo Park, CA. AAAI Press, 1997.

[Fra91]   W. J. Frawley, G. Piatetsky-Shapiro, and C. J. Matheuse. "Knowledge Discovery in Databases: An Overview," *Knowledge Discovery in Databases*. Cambridge, MA. AAAI Press/MIT Press, 1991.

[Gri92]   G. G. Grinstein, J. C. Sieg, S. Smith, and M. G. Williams. "Visualization for Knowledge Discovery," *International Journal of Intelligent Systems*, 7:7, 1992, pp. 637–648.

[Gri96]   G. G. Grinstein. "Harnessing the Human in Knowledge Discovery," *Proceedings of the Second International Conference on Knowledge Discovery and Data Mining* (KDD'96), pp. 384–385. Menlo Park, CA. AAAI Press, 1996.

[Han97]   D. J. Hand. "Intelligent Data Analysis: Issues and Opportunities," *Advances in Intelligent Data Analysis: Reasoning About Data, Lecture Notes in Computer Science*, X. Liu, P. Cohen, M. Berthold (editors), vol. 1280, pp. 1–14. Berlin/ Heidelberg. Springer-Verlag, 1997.

[Kei95]   D. Keim. *Visual Support for Query Specification and Data Mining*. Aachen. Verlag Shaker, 1995.

[Lee95]   H. Y. Lee, H. L. Ong, and L. H. Quek. "Exploiting Visualization in Knowledge Discovery," *Proceedings of the First International Conference on Knowledge Discovery and Data Mining* (KDD'95), pp. 198–203. Menlo Park, CA. AAAI Press, 1995.

[Mih97]   T. Mihalisin and J. Timlin. "Fast Robust Visual Data Mining," *Proceedings of the Third International Conference on Knowledge Discovery and Data Mining* (KDD'97), pp. 231–234. Menlo Park, CA. AAAI Press, 1997.

[Sub97]   R. Subramonian, R. Venkata, and J. Chen. "A Visual Interactive Framework for Attribute Discretization," *Proceedings of the Third International Conference on Knowledge Discovery and Data Mining* (KDD'97), pp. 82–88. Menlo Park, CA. AAAI Press, 1997.

Chapter 14

A Visual Metaphor
for Knowledge Discovery
An Integrated Approach
to Visualizing the Task,
Data, and Results

PETER DOCHERTY
ALLAN BECK

Compression Sciences Ltd.

Introduction

This chapter investigates the following two main areas in an attempt to formulate an integrated approach to visualizing the knowledge discovery (KD) task, the data required within that task, and the results of the task:

- How to describe a complete KD task in an intuitive visual manner
- How to visualize the actual data being mined, the transformation process, and the data mining algorithms

There are a number of issues related to the successful execution of a KD process requiring human interaction. A framework of integrated visualization techniques enables a user to better solve these issues:

Data preparation ■ Providing an overview of large volumes of data

Data modeling ■ Providing a visual model of the source domain data set

Data selection ■ Identifying rough areas of interest in the data (i.e., directed sampling of the original data set)

Data cleansing ■ Identifying areas within the data population that require cleansing

Task visualization ■ Providing a view of a KD task as it is put together, along with visual feedback from a task as it executes

Results visualization ■ Providing a visual view of the task results

The output from a KD (or data mining) task can be of a wide variety of types, and the selection of a particular data mining algorithm can affect the visualization technique used (and vice versa). There are also a number of other issues that cut across several of the previously listed areas, including:

Scalability ■ How to handle both small and large volumes of data in a consistent and efficient manner

Static versus dynamic data ■ What are the different techniques that should be used and what techniques can be applied to both types of data?

Utilization of a combination of techniques in an integrated manner ■ How can several visualization methods be combined to improve the overall results?

14.1 Knowledge Discovery Framework

This section outlines the requirements of a framework for the KD system based on a series of interconnected KD components. A framework is a set of related operations that can be configured to solve a set of problems in a particular domain. In this case, the framework will be used to serve KD applications. For example, the framework could be used for a very general-purpose KD system, supplying a broad range of KD components to the user. The same framework, however, could be configured as a very specific application, providing only the essential components to solve a particular problem. By modeling the KD process as a framework, the system can support both of these scenarios.

Each component implements a single KD task. For example, a data source component will be used to retrieve a data set from a database. A data mining component will be responsible for finding patterns from its input data set. By linking these components, the user will be able to describe each step in

Figure 14.1

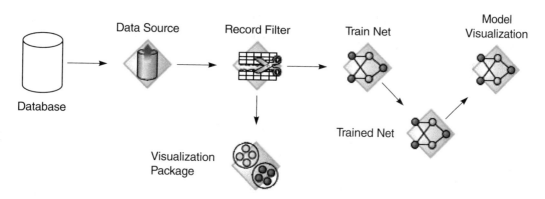

Example KD process plan.

the KD process plan, outlined in the following, from data selection through results generation (Figure 14.1):

- Records are extracted from a database using a data source component.

- These records then pass through a record filter component. This component will reduce the record set based on some user-specified criteria (e.g., sample 10% of the data at random).

- There are now two paths out of the record filter component: One path passes the remaining records to a visualization component. This component will allow the user to inspect the data set at this point in the process. The second path leads to a neural network training component. This will use the records it receives as input to produce a trained model of the data.

- The trained neural network model can then be visualized to aid the user's understanding of the model that has been produced.

It is not known in advance all of the KD components the framework will have to support. The framework will therefore be extensible to all new components to be available as plug-ins. So that the development of components is separated from the development of the framework, components will be wrapped in an open API. This means that components will conform to a well-defined and public interface. Any component that provides that interface will plug into the framework (Figure 14.2). The framework will not make assumptions about the internal processing of any component, and the component does not make calls to the framework. Instead, the component is passive until the framework calls it via the API. The framework takes care of

Figure 14.2

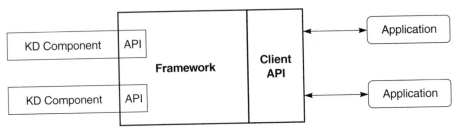

KD framework.

structure, flow of control, and calls to the system API. The framework exports a client API, which is used by application programmers to develop systems based on the framework (Figure 14.2).

14.1.1 KD Framework Requirements

A KD system must provide support for all stages in the KD process. It must also support the loops and iterations that occur during the execution of a KD process plan.

The richer the set of algorithms and tools that can be made available to the user, the more powerful the system will be in terms of the number and complexity of problems that can be solved. This, however, must be balanced against the increased learning curve required for such a system. The solution is to make the system a framework based on plug-in components.

Appropriate visualization techniques can help reduce the complexity of such a system by providing the user with mechanisms to increase her understanding of the KD process plan, the models being produced, and the data being analyzed. For example, the ability to dynamically add a component to visualize the data flowing between two components while the plan is being executed allows the user to monitor the effectiveness of the data transformation methods while developing the plan.

The system must also integrate with the tools that are already used by the analyst (but fall outside the scope of the system). For example, visualization tools are used at almost every stage of the KD process, and it would be a major advantage if such tools integrated seamlessly with the KD system. Statistical packages and database report writers are other examples of such "third-party" tools.

Color Plates

Figure 1.2(a)

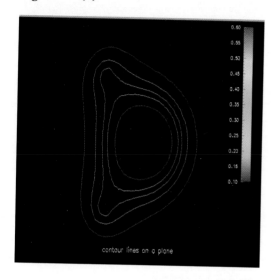

contour lines on a plane

Figure 1.3(b)

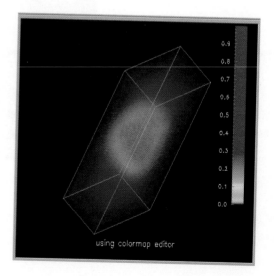

using colormap editor

Figure 1.4(a)

Figure 1.4(b)

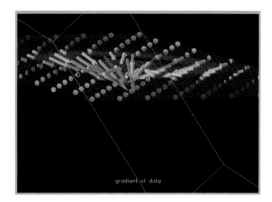

Figure 1.6 (b)

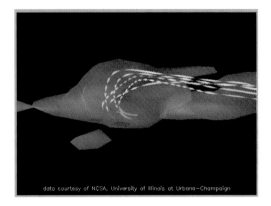

Figure 1.7 (b)

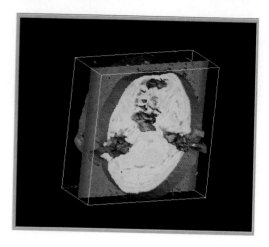

Figure 2.1

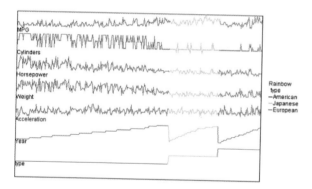

Figure 2.4

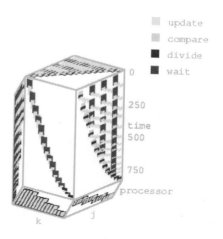

Figure 2.5

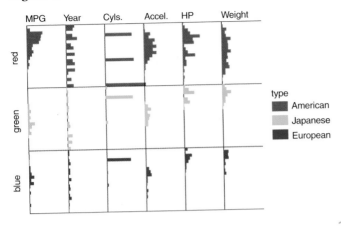

Figure 2.8

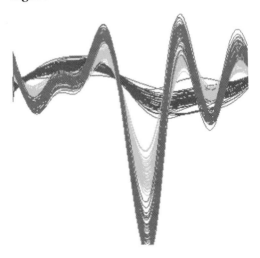

Figure 2.15

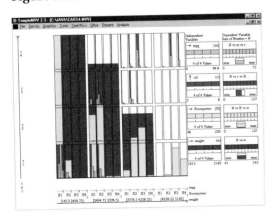

Figure 2.16

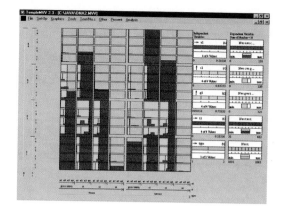

Figure 2.20

Figure 2.21

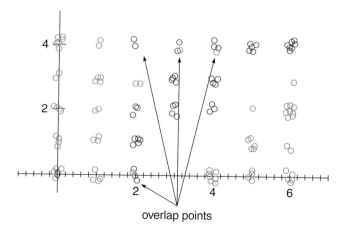

overlap points

Figure 2.23

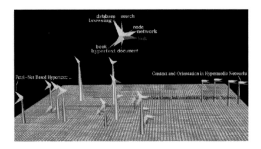

Figure 2.25

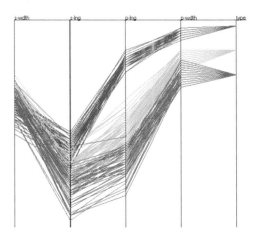

Figure 2.27

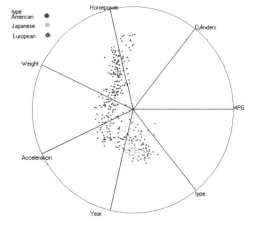

Figure 2.28

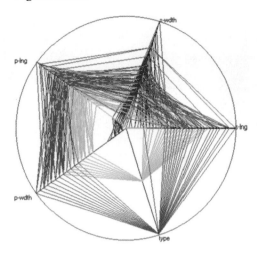

Figure 2.29

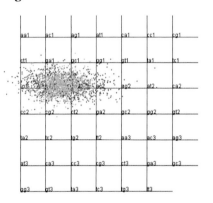

Figure 2.30

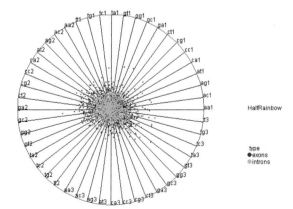

Figure 11.2

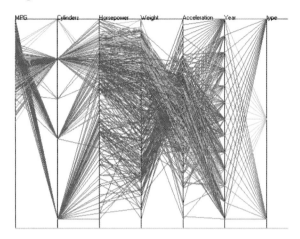

Figure 11.3

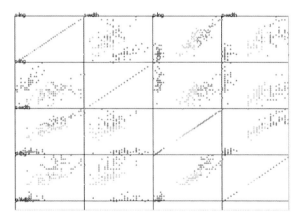

Figure 11.4

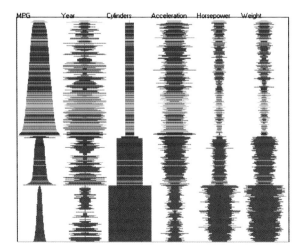

Figure 11.6

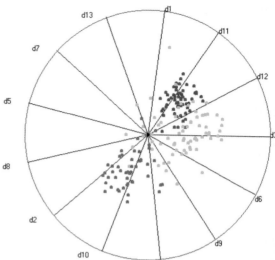

Figure 11.7

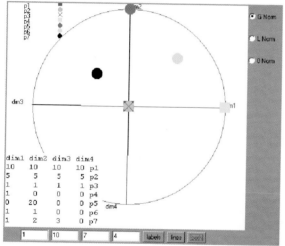

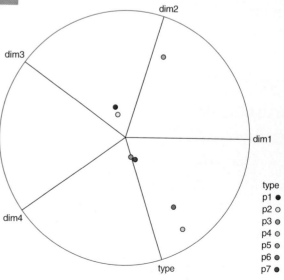

Figure 11.15

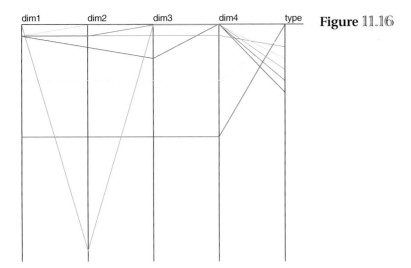

Figure 11.16

Figure 11.22

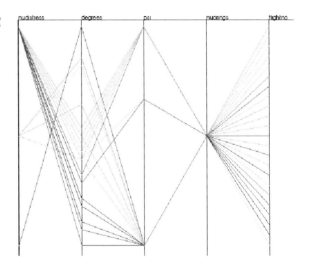

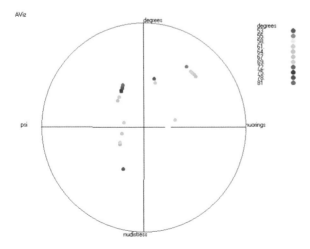

Figure 11.23

Figure 11.24

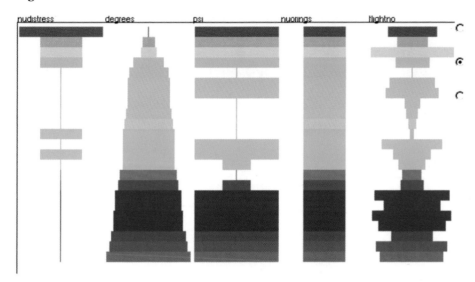

Figure 11.28

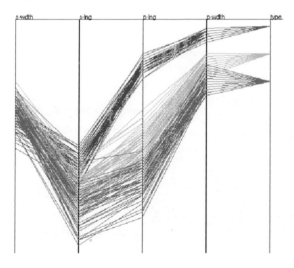

Figure 11.29

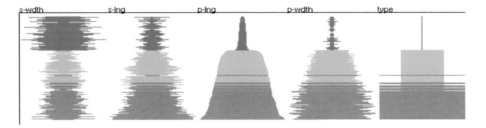

Figure 15.4

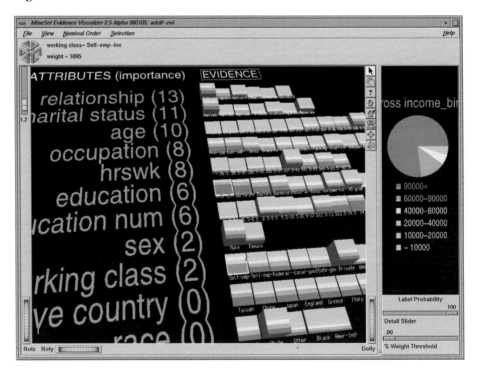

Figure 18.3

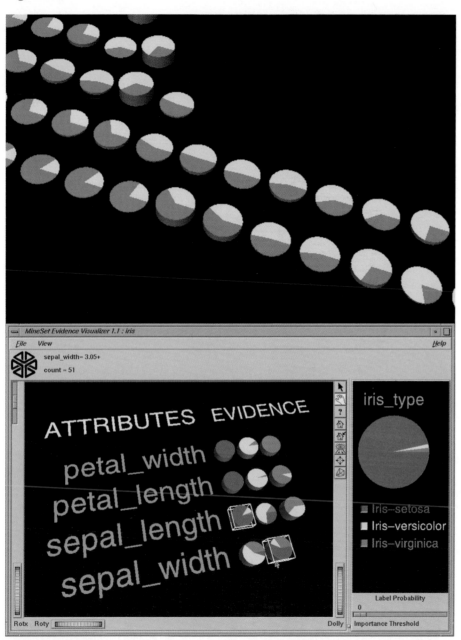

Figure 18.4

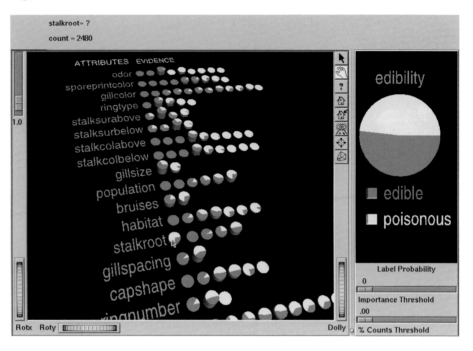

Figure 18.5

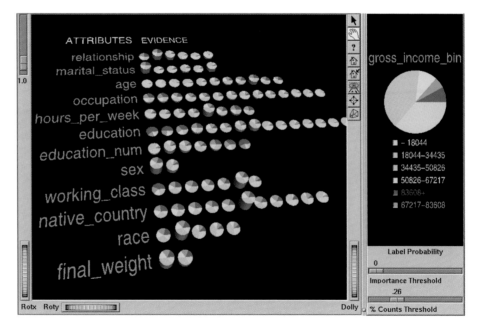

Figure 19.6

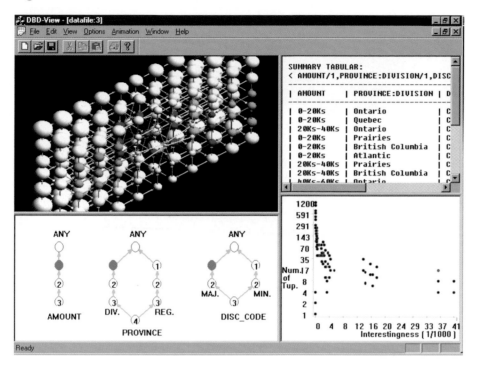

Figure 31.1

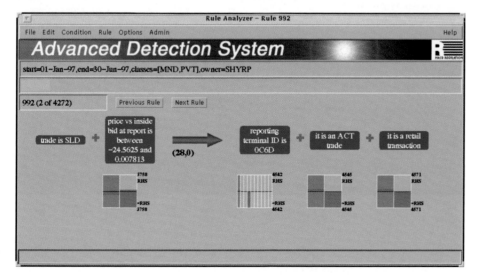

Figure 31.5

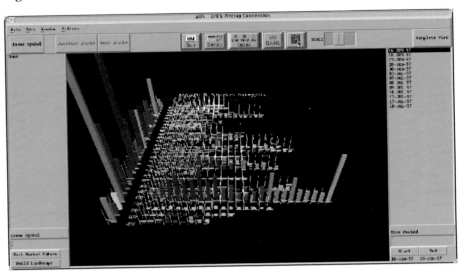

Figure 31.6

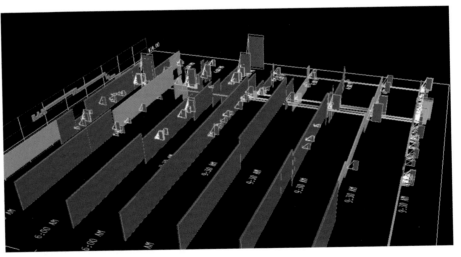

14.2 KD Toolkit

The KD framework provides a flexible and extensible platform for KD. The KD toolkit builds on the platform provided by the KD framework and provides a graphical interface to the functionality delivered by the framework and the components within that framework. The main goals of the visualizations provided within the KD toolkit are:

- Integration of visualization into the KD process
- Visualization of information at every step in the KD process
- Visualization as a step within the KD process (i.e., visualization as a component)
- Information visualization
- Provision of "before and after" views of information
- Multiple views of the same information
- Visualization of the models produced by the KD process

14.3 Integrating Visualization

The key role visualization plays in the KD process can be seen immediately from the diagram in Figure 14.3, with visualization taking a central role throughout the KD process.

By facilitating the immediate feedback of progress from the KD task, visualization allows a swift iteration through the various stages, with new information discovered at each stage being fed back to the user using a variety of appropriate techniques.

14.3.1 The Traditional Approach

Traditionally, visualization within the KD process is performed at the beginning and the end of the process, as shown in Figure 14.4. At the beginning of the process—problem definition and data selection—visualization can be used to investigate the available data and select appropriate data sets. Visualization at the end of the process—results interpretation—usually consists of visualization or presentation of the result set.

Figure 14.3

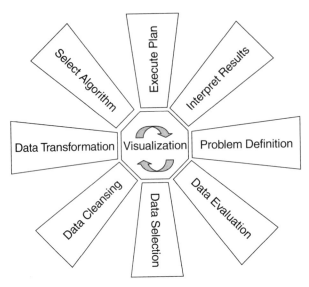

The KD process.

Figure 14.4

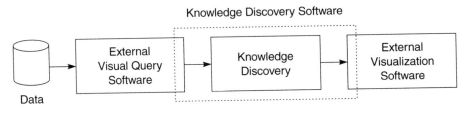

"Traditional" approach to KD and visualization.

The visualization capability provided within KD software varies. Often software solutions concentrate on the KD task or a particular step, rather than the KD process as a whole. Such tools expect the necessary input data set to be preselected and in a compatible format, or that discovered results will be output in a format compatible with the available external visualization software. There is often little or no visualization possible within the KD process itself.

Figure 14.5

An example process plan.

14.3.2 The Integrated Solution

The KD toolkit will allow the user to visualize the input data set and result set of a KD task without the use of third-party or external visualization software. The user will be able to visually build queries to select appropriate data for a KD task. The KD toolkit will also provide a selection of popular business visualizations for use in analyzing and presenting results. The user will be able to print a visualization and copy a snapshot of the visualization to the system clipboard.

The KD toolkit will also allow interaction with external visualization software. The user will have access to storage *components*, such as the CSV Sink component, which will store data in common file formats, compatible with external software packages.

14.4 Visualization of the Process

Allowing the user to easily and intuitively create and perform a KD task is one of the main goals of the KD toolkit, as is the provision of a visual design and execution environment for KD tasks. To this end, the KD toolkit will allow the user to visually create, edit, and execute process plans. The user will also be given a visual indication of the state (running, stopped, error, and so on) of components, links, and the process plan itself.

The user will be able to create new process plans—either manually or through the guidance of a plan wizard. The user will be able to add components into the plan, link them, configure them as appropriate for the given task, and finally execute the plan. The example plan in Figure 14.5 shows a simple KD task to read data from a database and scale the data as appropriate for the decision tree, which then performs a classification task on the data and writes the results to a CSV file.

Figure 14.6

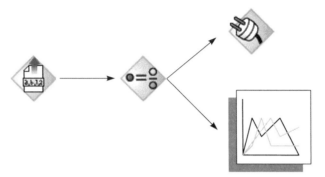

Visualization within the KD process.

The user can also be given feedback as to the progress of the process plan as it is executing; for example, how many data records have passed along the various links between the components, a plot of the error rate from a given algorithm training component, and so on. This type of visual feedback from a running plan combines to give a greater understanding of the plan itself and the dynamic behavior it exhibits.

14.4.1 Visualization Within the Process

Although the traditional approach uses visualization as the first and last steps of the KD process, it fails to take advantage of visualization within the KD process. The KD toolkit integrates visualization into every step within the KD process (Figure 14.6).

The user will have access to drop-in visualization components that can be added into process plans to allow visualization at every step of the KD process.

14.4.2 Visualization as a Step in the Process

As well as being a useful tool when integrated into the KD process, visualization can itself be a step within the process. For example, in the cluster visualization in Figure 14.7, the user could select a particular cluster of interest (shown in gray) and pass the selected cluster on to the next step in the KD process.

Figure 14.7

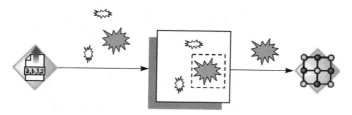

Visualization as a step in the KD process.

The KD toolkit will enable visualization to be used as a step within the KD process. The user will be able to select data items within a visualization for use by components within the same process plan.

14.5 Information Visualization

Information visualization is the visualization of information, or data used within the KD process. Information visualization in this sense is the visualization of nonspatial data or information and does not include scientific visualization.

14.5.1 Before and After Visualization

It is often useful to visualize the effect a particular step in the KD process has on data. For example, it may be useful to visualize data after a clustering algorithm has been applied, to allow the user to identify clusters and remove outliers. It may also be useful to view the "before and after" effects on data when acted upon by a component, as in Figure 14.8. The user will be able to visualize information at every step within a process plan and add information visualizations into a process plan.

14.5.2 Dynamic Data Visualization

Dynamic visualizations, or snoopers, are useful tools to help the user quickly understand and evaluate the data within a KD task. Snoopers (Figure 14.9) can be dynamically added and removed to any link within a process plan, to visualize the data passing along the link.

Figure 14.8

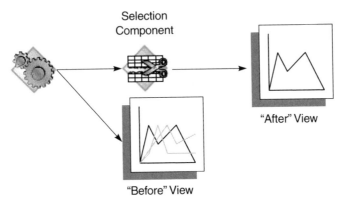

Visualizing before and after a component.

Figure 14.9

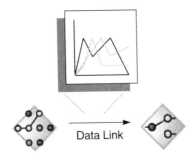

Example snooper.

Snoopers will attempt to select an appropriate visualization based on the given data, such as a data table view for textual data. The user will be able to add and remove snoopers, configure the snooper view type, and select the data dimensions to display within the visualization.

14.5.3 Multiple Views

The understanding gained by the visual representation of information can be greatly enhanced by visualizing the same information in different ways.

Figure 14.10

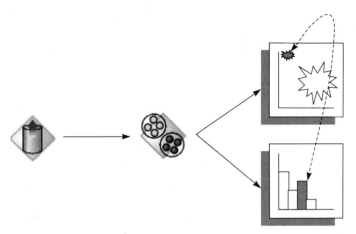

Multiple views of the same data set.

Figure 14.10 shows two example visualizations—a bar chart and a scatter plot—of the same data set. Each view provides the user with useful information: the bar chart view is displaying the yearly customer product sales, whereas the scatter plot is displaying customer information. From the information presented in the scatter plot, it appears that there are two distinct groups of customers, identified by the two clusters of data items. The KD toolkit will allow the user to select multiple views of the same data set.

Visual Interaction

Visual interaction with the data can also enhance understanding. The user will be able to highlight data items within a visualization and see the same data items highlighted in other views of the same data set. In Figure 14.10, the user has highlighted a particular cluster of data items within the scatter plot. The data items within the highlighted cluster are also automatically highlighted with the bar chart. From the example, it can be seen that one of the identified customer groups is exclusively buying a particular product.

The user will also be able to view information on selected data items (Figure 14.11). For example, if the user selects a bar within the bar chart view, they will be presented with information about the data items that make up the bar.

Figure 14.11

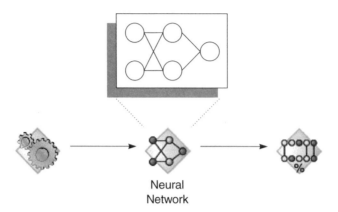

Neural
Network

Neural network model visualization.

14.6 Model Visualization

It is important that the user has confidence in the knowledge discovered by a process plan. To help increase the user's confidence in results and to reduce the risk of wrong decisions or incorrect assumptions made during the KD task, the user will be able to visualize the algorithm data models used within a process plan. It may be useful to steer the learning of the algorithm by visualizing the model as it is produced. In this way, incorrect or invalid decisions made by the algorithm trainer can be corrected before the final model is generated. It should also be possible to view any relevant output statistics from the algorithm, such as the error rate, or to animate the algorithm as it classifies a given data record, showing the paths used in the particular case and the key factors the algorithm is using to determine its prediction.

For example, if the user is using a neural network to classify customers likely to default on a loan, it may be helpful if the user were able to view how the classifications were determined. Providing a visualization of the topology and associated weights of the neural network data model could help increase confidence in the accuracy of the results. The user will be able to view the internal data models of many types of algorithms, such as neural networks, decision trees, naive Bayes, and so on.

14.7 Terms and Definitions

Component ■ A processing component of a *process plan* used to perform a given task within the plan

Data link ■ A link from an output on a *component* to an input of another *component*

KD framework ■ The KD framework used to provide the KD functionality

KD toolkit ■ The KD application built on top of the *KD framework* (combination of *KD framework* and user interface)

Process plan ■ A combination of *components* linked to undertake a given KD task.

Chapter 15

Visualizing Data Mining Models

KURT THEARLING

Exchange Applications

BARRY BECKER

Silicon Graphics, Inc.

DENNIS DeCOSTE

Jet Propulsion Laboratory

WILLIAM D. MAWBY

Michelin Tire Corporation

MICHEL PILOTE

Livetech Research International, Inc.

DAN SOMMERFIELD

Silicon Graphics, Inc.

Introduction

The purpose of data visualization is to give the user an understanding of what is going on. Because data mining usually involves extracting "hidden" information from a database, this understanding process can get somewhat complicated. In most standard database operations, nearly everything the user sees is something he knew existed in the database already. A report showing the breakdown of sales by product and region is straightforward for the user to understand, because he intuitively knows that this type of information already exists in the database. If the company sells different products in different regions of the county, there is no problem translating a display of this information into a relevant understanding of the business process.

Data mining, on the other hand, extracts information from a database that the user did not already know about. Useful relationships between variables that are nonintuitive are the jewels that data mining hopes to locate. Because the user does not know beforehand what the data mining process has discovered, it is a much bigger leap to take the output of the system and translate it into an actionable solution to a business problem. In addition, because there are usually many ways to graphically represent a model, the visualizations used should be chosen to maximize the value to the viewer. This requires that we understand the viewer's needs and design the visualization with that end user in mind. If we assume that the viewer is an expert in the subject area, but not in data modeling, we must translate the model into a more natural representation. For this purpose we suggest the use of "orienteering" principles as a template for our visualizations.

15.1 Orienteering

Orienteering is typically accomplished by two chief approaches: maps and landmarks. Imagine yourself set down in an unknown city with instructions to find a given hotel. The usual method is to obtain a map showing the large-scale areas of the city. Once the "hotel district" is located, you will then walk along, looking for landmarks such as street names until you arrive at your location. If the landmarks do not match the map, you will re-consult the map and even replace one map with another. If the landmarks do not appear correct, usually you will backtrack, try a short side journey, or ask for further landmarks from people on the street. The degree to which you will follow the landmark chain or trust the map depends on the match between the landmarks and the map. It will be reinforced by unexpected matches (happening along a unique landmark for which you were not looking), by finding the landmark by two different routes, and by noting that variations are small. Your experience with cities and maps and the urgency of your journey will also affect your confidence.

The combination of a global coordinate system (the map analogy) and the local coordinate system (the landmarks) must fit together and must instill confidence as the journey is traversed. The concept of a manifold is relevant in that the global coordinates must be realizable, as a combination of local coordinate systems in some sense. To develop trust on the part of the user, we should

- Show that nearby paths (small distances in the model) do not lead to widely different ends
- Show, on demand, the effect different perspectives (change of variables or inclusion probabilities) have on model structure
- Make dynamic changes in coloring, shading, edge definition, and viewpoint (dynamic dithering)
- Sprinkle known relationships (landmarks) throughout the model landscape
- Allow interaction that provides more detail and that answers queries on demand

The advantages of this manifold approach include the ability to explore it in some optimal way (such as projection pursuit), the ability to reduce the models to an independent coordinate set, and the ability to measure model adequacy in a more natural manner.

15.2 Why Visualize a Data Mining Model?

The driving forces behind visualizing data mining models can be broken down into two key areas: understanding and trust. Understanding is undoubtedly the most fundamental motivation behind visualizing the model. Although the simplest way to deal with a data mining model is to leave the output in the form of a black box, the user will not necessarily gain an understanding of the underlying behavior in which she is interested. If she takes the black box model and scores a database, she can get a list of customers to target (send them a catalog, increase their credit limit, and so on). There is not much for the user to do other than sit back and watch the envelopes go out. This can be a very effective approach. Mailing costs can often be reduced by an order of magnitude without significantly reducing the response rate.

The more interesting way to use a data mining model is to get the user to actually understand what is going on, so that she can take action directly. Visualizing a model should allow a user to discuss and explain the logic behind the model with colleagues, customers, and other users. Getting buy-in on the logic or rationale is part of building users' trust in the results. For example, if the user is responsible for ordering a print advertising campaign, understanding customer demographics is critical. Decisions about where to put advertising dollars are a direct result of understanding data mining models of customer behavior. There is no automated way to do this. It is all in the marketing manager's head. Unless the output of the data mining system can be understood qualitatively, it will not be of any use. In addition, the model needs to be understood so that the actions taken as a result can be justified to others.

Understanding means more than just comprehension; it also involves context. If the user can understand what has been discovered in the context of business issues, he will trust it and put it into use. There are two parts to this problem: (1) visualization of the data mining output in a meaningful way, and (2) allowing the user to interact with the visualization so that simple questions can be answered. Creative solutions to the first part have recently been incorporated into a number of commercial data mining products, such as MineSet [Bru97]. Graphing lift, response, and (probably most importantly) financial indicators (e.g., profit, cost, ROI) gives the user a sense of context that can quickly ground the results in reality. After that, simple representations of the data mining results allow the user to see the data mining results. Graphically displaying a decision tree (CART, CHAID, and C4.5) can significantly change the way in which the data mining software is used. Some algorithms can pose more problems than others (e.g., neural networks), but novel solutions are starting to appear.

It is the second part that has yet to be addressed fully. Interaction is, for many users, the Holy Grail of visualization in data mining. Manipulation of the data and viewing the results dynamically allow the user to get a feel for the dynamics and to test whether something really counterintuitive is going on. The interactivity helps achieve this, and the easier this is to do, the better. Seeing a decision tree is nice, but what users really want to do is drag and drop the best segments onto a map of the United States in order to see if there are sales regions that are neglected. The number of "what if" questions that can be asked is endless: How do the most likely customers break down by gender? What is the average balance for the predicted defaulters? What are the characteristics of mail order responders? The interaction will continue until the user understands what is going on with his customers. Users also often desire drill-through, so that they can see the actual data behind a model (or some piece of the model), although it is probably more a matter of perceptions rather than actual usefulness. Finally, integrating with other decision support tools (e.g., OLAP) will let users view the data mining results in a manner they are already using for the purpose of understanding customer behavior. By incorporating interaction into the process, a user will be able to connect the data mining results with his customers.

15.3 Trusting the Model

Attributing the appropriate amount of trust to data mining models is essential to using them wisely. Good quantitative measures of "trust" must ultimately reflect the probability that the model's predictions would match future test targets. However, due to the exploratory and large-scale nature of most data mining tasks, fully articulating all of the potential factors toward achieving this would seem generally intractable. Thus, instead of focusing on trying to boil "trust" down to one probabilistic quantity, it is typically most useful to visualize along many dimensions some of the key factors that contribute to trust (and distrust) in models. Furthermore, as with any scientific model, because you can ultimately only disprove a model, visualizing the limitations of the model is of prime importance. Indeed, you might best view the overall goal of "visualizing trust" as that of understanding the limitations of the model, as opposed to understanding the model itself.

Because data mining relies heavily on training data, it is important to understand the limitations given data sets put on future application of the resulting model. One class of standard visualization tools involves probability density estimation and clustering over the training data. Especially interesting would be regions of state space that are uncommon in the training data yet do not violate known domain constraints. You would tend to trust a model less if it acts more confident when presented with uncommon data as future inputs. For time-series data, visualizing indicators of non-stationarity is also important.

15.3.1 Assessing Trust in a Model

Assessing model trustworthiness is typically much more straightforward than the Holy Grail of model understanding per se—essentially because the former is largely deconstructive, whereas the latter is constructive. For example, without a deep understanding of a given model, you can still use general domain knowledge to detect that it violates expected qualitative principles. A well-known example is that you would be concerned if your model employed a (presumably spurious) statistical correlation between shoe size

Figure 15.1

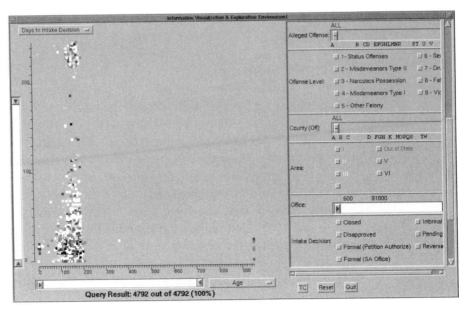

Age (in months) versus "days to intake decision" for juvenile crime offenders, Maryland Department of Juvenile Services. Note the 80-year-old "children" on the right side of the graph.

and IQ. Of course, there are still very significant challenges in declaring such knowledge as completely and consistently as possible.

Domain knowledge is also critical for outlier detection needed to clean data and avoid classic problems, such as a juvenile crime committed by an 80-year-old "child." If a data mining model were built using the data in Figure 15.1, it is possible that outliers (most likely caused by incorrect data entry) will skew the resulting model (especially the 0-year-old children, which are more reasonable than 80-year-old children). The common role of visualization here is largely in terms of annotating model structures with the domain knowledge they violate.

Not all assessments of trust are negative in nature, however. In particular, you can also increase your trust in a model if other reasonable models seem worse. In this sense, assessing trust is also closely related to model comparison. In particular, it is very useful to understand the sensitivity of model predictions and quality to changes in parameters and/or structure of the given model. There are many ways to visualize such sensitivity, often in terms of local and global (conditional) probability densities—with special interest in determining whether multiple modes of high probability exist for some parameters and combinations. Such relative measures of trust can be considerably less demanding to formulate than attempts at more absolute measures, but they do place special demands on the visualization engine, which must support quick and non-disorienting navigation through neighboring regions in model space.

Statistical summaries of all sorts are also common and useful for gathering insights for assessing model trust. Pairwise scatter plots and low-dimensional density estimates are especially common. Summaries can be particularly useful for assessing the relative trust of two models, by allowing analysis to focus on subsets of features for which their interrelationships differ most significantly between two models.

It is often useful to combine summaries with the interactive ability to drill through to the actual data. Many forms of visual summary actually display multiple scales of data along the raw to abstract continuum, making visual drill-through a natural recursive operation. For example, compressing millions of samples into a time-series strip chart that is only 1000 pixels wide allows you to quickly see the global highest and lowest points across the entire time range, as well as the local high and low points occurring within each horizontal pixel.

Most useful are models that qualify their own trustworthiness to some degree, such as in quantifying the expected variance in the error of their predictions.

In practice, such models tend to be relatively rare. Heavy emphasis on expected-case rather than worst-case performance is generally not all that inappropriate, in that you are typically ultimately interested in concepts such as expected cumulative payoff.

There are important classes of tasks, such as novelty detection (e.g., fraud detection), for which quantified variance is essential. Standard techniques are learning confidence intervals (e.g., error bars for neural networks) and general probability density estimation. A promising recent approach [Sgi01], called bounds estimation, attempts to find a balance between the complexity of general probability density estimation and the simplicity of the mean estimation plus variance estimation approach to error bars.

Finally, it is important, though rather rare in practice to date, to consider many transformations of the data during visual exploration of model sensitivities. For example, a model that robustly predicts well the internal pressure of some engineering device should probably also be able to do well predicting related quantities, such as its derivative, power spectrum, and other relevant quantities (such as nearby or redundant pressures). Checking for such internal consistency is perhaps ultimately one of the most important ways of judging the trustworthiness of a model, beyond standard cross-validation error. Automated and interactive means of exploring and visualizing the space (and degrees) of inconsistencies a model entails seems to be a particularly important direction for future research on assessing model trustworthiness.

15.4 Understanding the Model

A model that can be understood is a model that can be trusted. Although statistical methods build some trust in a model by assessing its accuracy, they cannot assess the model's semantic validity—its applicability to the real world. A data mining algorithm that uses a human-understandable model can be checked easily by domain experts, providing much needed semantic validity to the model. Unfortunately, users are often forced to trade off accuracy of a model for understandability.

Advanced visualization techniques can greatly expand the range of models that can be understood by domain experts, thereby easing the accuracy/understandability trade-off. Three components are essential for understanding a model: representation, interaction, and integration. Representation refers to the visual form in which the model appears. A good representation displays the model in terms of visual components that are already familiar to the user. Interaction refers to the ability to see the model in action in real time, to let the user play with the model as if it were a machine. Integration refers to the ability to display relationships between the model and alternate views of the data on which it is based. Integration provides the user context.

The rest of this section focuses on understanding classification models. Specifically, we examine three models built using Silicon Graphic's MineSet: decision tree, simple Bayesian, and decision table classifiers [DeC97]. Each of these tools provides a unique form of understanding based on representation, interaction, and integration.

The graphical representation should be simple enough to be easily understood, but complete enough to reveal all information present in the model. This is a difficult balance because simplicity usually trades off against completeness. 3D visualizations have the potential to show far more information than 2D visualizations while retaining their simplicity. Navigation in such a scene lets you focus on an element of interest while keeping the rest of the structure in context. It is critical, however, that the user be able to navigate through a 3D visualization in real time. An image of a 3D scene is merely a 2D projection and is usually more difficult to understand than a scene built in two dimensions.

Figure 15.2

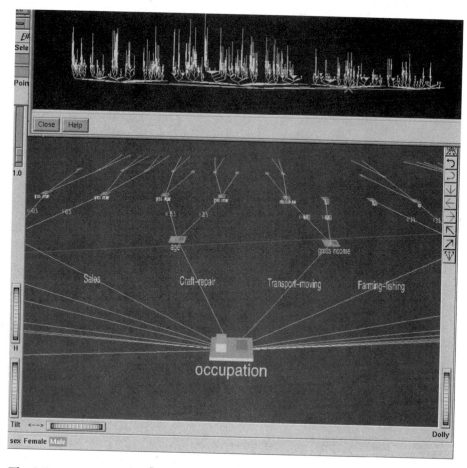

The MineSet Tree Visualizer shows only that portion of the model close to the viewer.

Even with three dimensions, many models still contain far too much information to display simply. In these cases, the visualization must simplify the representation as it is displayed. The MineSet decision tree and decision table visualizers use the principle of hierarchical simplification to present a large amount of information to the user.

Decision trees are easy to understand but can become overwhelmingly large when automatically induced. The SGI MineSet Tree Visualizer uses a detail-hiding approach to simplify the visualization. In Figure 15.2, only the first few levels of the tree are initially displayed, despite the fact that the tree is extensive. The user can gain a basic understanding of the tree by following

Figure 15.3

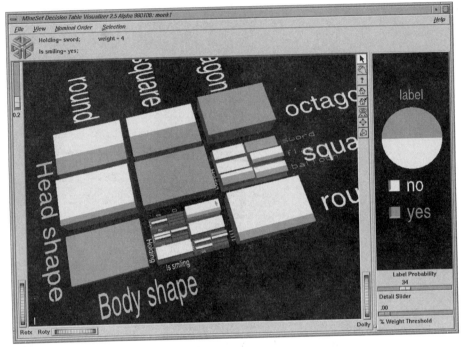

The MineSet Decision Table Visualizer shows additional pairs of attributes as the user drills down into the model.

the branches of these levels. Additional levels of detail are revealed only when the user navigates to a deeper level, providing more information only as needed.

Using decision tables as a model representation generates a simple but large model. A full decision table theoretically contains the entire data set, which may be very large. Therefore, simplification is essential. The MineSet decision table arranges the model into levels based on the importance of each feature in the table. The data is automatically aggregated to provide a summary using only the most important features. When the user desires more information, he can drill down as many levels as needed to answer his question. The visualization automatically changes the aggregation of the data to display the desired level of detail. In Figure 15.3, a decision table shows the well-known correlation between head shape and body shape in the Monk data set. The visualization also shows that the classification is ambiguous in cases where head shape does not equal body shape. For these cases, the user can drill down to see that the attribute jacket color determines the class.

Although a good representation can greatly aid the user's understanding, in many cases the model contains too much information to provide a representation that is both complete and understandable. In these cases, we exploit the brain's ability to reason about cause and effect and let the user interact with the more complex model. Interaction can be thought of as "understanding by doing," as opposed to "understanding by seeing."

Common forms of interaction are interactive classification, interactive model building, drill-up, drill-down, animation, searching, filtering, and level-of-detail manipulation. The fundamental techniques of searching, filtering, drill-up, and drill-down make the task of finding information hidden within a complex model easier. However, they do not help overall understanding much. More extensive techniques (interactive classification, interactive model building) are required to help the user understand a model too complicated to show with a static image or table. These advanced methods aid understanding by visually showing the answer to a user query while maintaining a simplified representation of the model for context.

The MineSet Evidence Visualizer allows the user to interact with a simple Bayesian classifier (Figure 15.4). Even simple Bayesian models are based on multiplying arrays of probabilities that are difficult to understand by themselves. However, by allowing the user to select values for features and see the effects, the visualization provides cause-and-effect insight into the operation of the classifier. The user can play with the model to understand exactly how much each feature affects the classification and ultimately decide to accept or reject the result. In the example in the figure, the user selects the value of "working class" to be "self-employed-incorporated," and the value of "education" to be "professional-school." The pie chart on the right displays the expected distribution of incomes for people with these characteristics.

Beyond interactive classification, interactively guiding the model-building process provides additional control and understanding to the user. Angoss [Ang01] provides a decision tree tool that gives the user full control over when and how the tree is built. The user may suggest splits, perform pruning, or manually construct sections of the tree. This facility can boost understanding greatly. Figure 15.5(a) shows a decision tree split on a car's brand attribute. Whereas the default behavior of the tree is to form a separate branch on the tree for each categorical value, a better approach is often to group similar values together and produce only a few branches. The result shown in Figure 15.5(b) is easier to understand, and can sometimes give better accuracy. Interactive models allow the user to make changes such as this as the situation warrants.

Figure 15.4

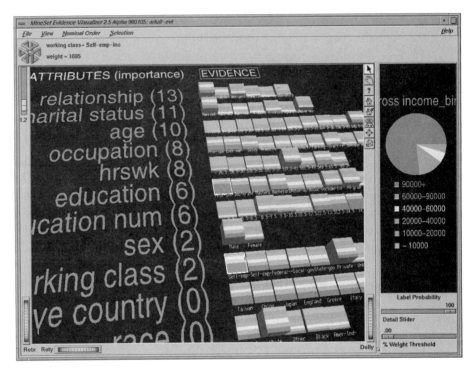

Specific attribute values are selected in the Evidence Visualizer in order to pre-dict income for people with these characteristics. (See also color plate.)

Interactive techniques and simplified representations can produce models that can be understood within their own context. However, for a user to truly understand a model, she must understand how the model relates to the data from which it was derived. For this goal, tool integration is essential.

Few tools on the market today use integration techniques. The techniques that are used come in three forms: drill-through, brushing, and coordinated visualizations. Drill-through refers to the ability to select a piece of a model and gain access to the original data upon which that piece of the model was derived. For example, the decision tree visualizer allows selection and drill-through on individual branches of the tree. This will provide access to the original data used to construct those branches, leaving out the data represented by other parts of the tree. Brushing refers to the ability to select pieces of a model and have the selections appear in an alternate representation. Coordinated visualizations generalize both techniques by showing multiple representations of the same model, combined with representations of the original data. Interactive actions that affect the model affect other

Figure 15.5

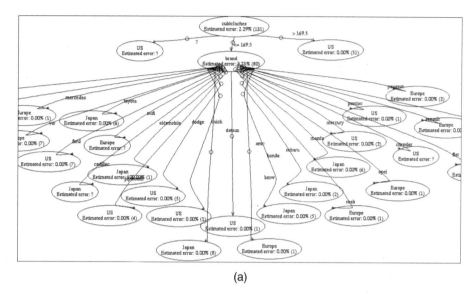

(a)

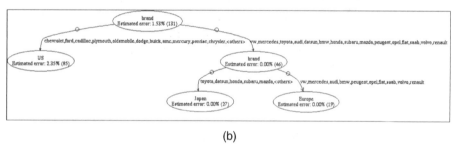

(b)

(a) A decision tree having branches for every value of the brand attribute, and (b) a decision tree that groups values of brand to produce a simpler structure.

visualizations. All three of these techniques help the user understand how the model relates to the original data. This provides an external context for the model and helps establish semantic validity.

As data mining becomes more extensive in industry applications, and as the number of automated techniques employed increases, there is a natural tendency for models to become increasingly complex. To prevent these models from becoming mysterious oracles, whose dictates must be accepted on faith, it is essential to develop more sophisticated visualization techniques to keep pace with the increasing model complexity. Otherwise, there is a danger that we will make decisions without understanding the reasoning behind them.

15.5 Comparing Different Models Using Visualization

Model comparison requires the creation of an appropriate metric for the space of models under consideration. To visualize the model comparison, these metrics must be interpretable by a human observer through her visual system. The first step is to create a mapping from input to output of the modeling process. The second step is to map this process to the human visual space.

15.5.1 Meanings of the Term *Model*

It is important to recognize that the term *model* can connote several meanings. Common usage often associates the term *model* with the data modeling process. For example, we might talk of applying a neural network model to a particular problem. In this case, the term *model* refers to the generic type of model known as a neural network. Another use of the term *model* is associated with the result of the modeling process. In the neural network example, the model could be the specific set of weights, topology, and node types that produces an output given a set of inputs. In still another use, the term *model* refers to the input/output mapping associated with a "black box." Such a mapping necessarily places emphasis on careful identification of the input and output spaces.

15.5.2 Comparing Models as Input/Output Mappings

The input/output approach to model comparison simply considers the mapping from a defined input space to a defined output space. For example, we might consider a specific 1-gigabyte database with 25 variables (columns). The input space is simply the Cartesian product of the database's 25 variables. Any actions inside the model, such as creation of new variables, are hidden in the "black box" and are not interpreted. At the end of the modeling process, an output is generated. This output could be a number, a prioritized list, or even a set of rules about the system. The crucial issue is that we can define the output space in some consistent manner to derive an input-to-output mapping.

It is the space generated by the mappings that is of primary importance to the model comparison. For most applications the mapping space will be well defined once the input and output spaces are well defined. For example, two classifiers could be described by a set of input/output pairs, such as (obs1, class a), (obs2, class b), and so on. The comparison metric could then be defined on these pairs as a count of the number differing, GINI indices, classification cost, and so on. The resulting set of pairs could be visualized by simple plotting of points on a 2D graph. The two models could be indexed by color or symbol codes, or you could focus on the difference between each model directly and plot this. This approach should prove adequate as long as we restrict attention to a well-defined input/output structure.

15.5.3 Comparing Models as Algorithms

In the view of a model as a static algorithm, again there seems to be a reasonable way of approaching the model comparison problem. For example, a neural network model and an adaptive nonlinear regression model might be compared. These models would be expressed as a series of algorithmic steps. Each model's algorithm could then be analyzed by standard methods for measurement of algorithmic performance, such as complexity, the finite word length, and the stability of the algorithm. The investigator could also include measures on the physical implementation of the algorithm, such as computation time or computation size. Using these metrics, the visualization could take the form of bar charts across the metrics. Again, different models could be encoded by color or symbol, and a graph of only difference between the two models on each metric could be provided. Each comparison would be for a static snapshot, but certainly dynamic behavior could be exploited through a series of snapshots (i.e., a motion picture).

15.5.4 Comparing Models as Processes

The view of the model as a process is the most ill defined and therefore most intractable of the three views, but this should not minimize its importance. Indeed, its sheer complexity might make it the most important view for the application of visualization. It is precisely in this area that we encounter the subject area expert for whom these systems should offer the most benefit (such as confidence and trust).

The modeling process includes everything in and around the modeling activity, such as the methods, the users, the database, the support resources, and constraints such as knowledge, time, and analysis implementation. Clearly, this scope is too large for us to consider. Let us narrow our scope by assuming that the model comparison is being applied for one user on one database over a short time period. This implies that user differences, database differences, and knowledge difference can be neglected. We are left with analysis methods and implementation issues. For most subject area experts the implementation and the analysis are not separable, and so we will make the additional assumption that this issue can be ignored as well. With these simplifying assumptions we are essentially defining model comparison to be the comparison of modeling method and implementation simultaneously.

Imagine two models that are available in some concrete implemented form. These could be different general methods such as neural networks versus tree-based classifiers, or they could be different levels of sophistication within a class of models such as CART versus CHAID tree structures. Remember that we are now focusing only on the modeling process and not on its input/output or algorithmic structure. It seems that reasonable metrics can be defined in this situation. For example, the running time could be such a metric, or the interpretability of instructions, or the number of tuning parameters that must be chosen by the user at run time. The key here is that these metrics must be tailored to the user who is the target of the application. Thus, whereas the input/output view focused on these spaces, and the algorithmic view focused on the properties of the algorithm independently of the user, now we must focus in great detail on the user's needs and perceptions.

Once a set of metrics is chosen, we appear to be in a similar situation to that described under the algorithmic comparison. We should be able to show the distances between models in each of the defined metrics in a bar chart or other standard display. Color or symbol coding can be used to show the results from each model on the same chart as well.

There will be many possible metrics for the model-building process, at least one per user. Since it is unlikely we can choose a set of "one-size-fits-all" metrics, it is more useful to establish properties of good metrics and create methods to establish them in novel situations. The metrics chosen by an academic researcher would likely be very different from those chosen by a business user. Some properties of good metrics for the modeling process should be

- that they are expressed in direct risk/benefit to the user.
- that they evaluate their sensitivity to model input and assumptions.
- that they can be audited (open to questioning at any point).
- that they are dynamic.
- that they can be summarized in the sense of an overall map.
- that they allow reference to landmarks and markers.

Some aspects of the visualization process will take on added importance. One such aspect is the sequential behavior of the modeling process. For example, it is common to plot frequently the updated fit between the data and the model predictions as a neural network learns. Human beings will probably give more trust to a method that mimics their own learning behavior (i.e., a learning curve that starts with a few isolated details, then grows quickly to broad generalizations, and then makes only incremental gains after that in the typical S shape). Unstable behavior or large swings should count against the modeling process.

Another aspect of importance should be a visual track of the sensitivity of the modeling process to small changes in the data and modeling process parameters. For example, you might make several random starts with different random weights in a neural network model. These should be plotted versus one another showing their convergence patterns, again perhaps against a theoretical S-shaped convergence.

The model must also be auditable, meaning that inquiries may be made at any reasonable place in the modeling process. For a neural network we should be able to interrupt it and examine individual weights at any step in the modeling process. Likewise for a tree-based model we should be able to see subtrees at will. Ideally, there could be several scales in which this interruption could occur.

Because most humans operate on a system of local and global coordinates, it will be important to be able to supplement visualizations with markers and a general map structure. For example, even though the direct comparison is between two neural nets with different structures, it would be good to have the same distances plotted for another method with which the user is familiar (such as discriminant analysis), even if that method is inadequate. If the same model could be used on a known input, the user could establish trust with the new results. It might also be useful to have simultaneously a detailed and a summarized model displayed. For example, the full tree-based classifier might have 25 branches, but the summarized tree might show the broad limbs only. Finally, if the output is a rule, it might be useful to drive (through logical manipulation) other results or statements of results as a test of reasonableness.

15.6 Conclusion

In this chapter we have discussed a number of methods of visualizing data mining models. Because data mining models typically generate results that were previously unknown to the user, it is important that any model visual-ization provide the user with sufficient levels of understanding and trust.

Acknowledgments

The authors would like to thank Professor Ben Shneiderman and his col-leagues at the Human-Computer Interaction Laboratory, University of Mary-land, College Park, for providing Figure 16.1. It was created using an early version of the Spotfire visualization software (*www.ivee.com*).

References

[Ang01]   *www.angoss.com.*

[Bru97]   C. Brunk, J. Kelly, and R. Kohavi. "MineSet: An Integrated System for Data Access, Visual Data Mining, and Analytical Data Mining," *Proceedings of the Third Conference on Knowledge Discovery and Data Mining* (KDD'97), New-port Beach, CA, August 1997.

[DeC97]   D. DeCoste. "Mining Multivariate Time-Series Sensor Data to Discover Be-havior Envelopes," *Proceedings of the Third Conference on Knowledge Dis-covery and Data Mining* (KDD'97), Newport Beach, CA, August 1997.

[Rat97]   D. Rathjens. *MineSet User's Guide.* Mountain View, CA. Silicon Graphics, 1997.

[Sgi01]   *www.sgi.com/Products/software/MineSet.*

Chapter 16

Model Visualization

WESLEY JOHNSTON

Chevron Information Technology Company

Introduction

I come to the discussion as a data miner, working in a corporate setting with domain experts who have considerable analytical expertise. I do not know much about the state of the art of data-related visualization, or what clever extensions might be feasible in the near future. My experience with data visualization tools has been that they have been helpful at exploring hunches and in presenting results. For example, a relevant scatter plot (either 2D or 3D) can be extremely insightful—if the relevant axes can be easily discovered. However, my experience has been that data visualization was the wrong primary tool when the goal was to find a good classifier model in a complex situation. Although visual exploration can be interesting and sometimes insightful, without sound insight or without data mining's power to more thoroughly explore the space, data visualization may be merely a waste of time.

This chapter is basically a wish list of what I would like to have from data visualization to support the knowledge discovery process. In it I offer two key thoughts:

- Emphasize "model visualization." The knowledge discovery (KD) process is an iterative search through the space of models, trying to find one or more models that provide the best solution to a business problem. Current focus is on "data visualization." The best solution is to have both model and data visualization and to integrate them well.

- Aid improvement of spatial and temporal data mining.

16.1 Emphasize "Model Visualization"

Although visualization of the data along axes of the independent variables (or transformations thereof) is a useful step for exploration, the main effort in the evaluation phase is the comparative exploration of the various models, as applied to various data sets. Rather than merely thinking of "data visualization," we should also be thinking about "model visualization," as well as the visualization of linkages of the model to the data. There are several implications for visualization in the evaluation phase, which is a precursor to the next iteration of the KDD process.

16.1.1 Support Individual Mode Evaluation

Visualization should support the detailed evaluation of individual models. Business problems usually require measurement of more than just a single number representing the overall accuracy of a model. For example, confusion matrices are an important demand from most of our users, who are often interested in the worst-case accuracy more than the overall accuracy. Visualization of "rich" confusion matrices would be beneficial.

A "rich" confusion matrix would be one that used 3D graphics to represent the cells of the matrix. For example, a row in the confusion matrix represents one of the actual classes. A base across the entire row could represent the overall accuracy of all of the actual class, using color to scale the accuracy. On top of the base could be a vertical symbol for each cell to show both accuracy and relative number of cases in the data set, using size, color, or shape. Optionally, the orientation could be toggled to show the accuracy as a percentage of the predicted classes, instead of as a percentage of the actual classes. Such a confusion matrix would give a rich insight into how well the model is doing in the "nooks and crannies" of the data.

16.1.2 Support Simultaneous Evaluation of Candidate Models

Visualization should support the simultaneous comparative evaluation of several candidate models. The search for a "silver bullet" model is usually a waste of time. Too much past work (particularly with neural networks) has focused on building *a* model. Our experience is that the data usually supports a very large number of models of roughly equal accuracy. The task then is best seen as how to distinguish all of these data-supported models, so that we choose the best one (or more) to satisfy business problems. For example, put the "rich" confusion matrices of several models on screen at the same time, allowing easy pointing to any one of a number of data sets. When you point the collection of models at a particular data set, the screen shows at a glance all of the confusion matrices.

16.1.3 Provide Viewing of Multiple Models and Data Sets

Visualization should easily allow pointing to any of a group of data sets. Too often, visualization is restricted to one model on one data set. We need to be able to easily view the effect of multiple models on any one or more of a number of data sets, in order to fully evaluate the models. Whatever visual tools exist should provide an easy means of keeping the model evaluation environment on screen and simply pointing to a different data set to see how things look there. It may also be that one or more data sets need to be viewed temporarily as a single snapshot, and this capability too needs to be supported.

16.1.4 Provide Graphic Representation of Model Space and Data Point Distinctions

Visualization should show how the model splits up the space and should tie the data points to the model(s). Beyond accuracy, there is the credibility of models. The more easily models can be represented and evaluated, particularly for "what if" analysis, the more confidence there is in the models. Visualization can also be helpful here. For example, it would be very helpful to graphically illustrate how the space of the two or three most important independent variables is split up by a model, as well as where the individual data points for any given data set fall within those split regions. Color the regions by class and then plot the data points on the same graph, using shape, size, or color to represent classes. Then tie all of this into the rules or decision tree, so that a specific rule can be chosen and highlighted on the graph, in order to quickly see the scope of that rule.

16.1.5 Support Model Sensitivity Analysis and Fine-Tuning

Finally, visualization should support sensitivity analysis and fine-tuning of models. For the chosen model(s), graphical support of sensitivity analysis can help determine the limits of applicability of the model(s). Every model has specific splits, but those are just numbers within a range between two training cases. Therefore, what are the implications of moving the split within the range, both on the training data and the test data? What are the critical cases for the model, those that could have given a different model with just a small change in value? Where is the model going to fall off a cliff? Where is it on solid ground? Visualization could be a great help in this area.

For a very simple example, a tool that ties the rules to a visual form of the space, showing the regions the rules create, could allow interactive modification of the rule with corresponding changes to the graph, as well as to a pair (a "before" and an "after") of on-screen "rich" confusion matrices showing the impact of the change. Another example might be a graphical tool to show the actual ranges of values around the model's splits, both in the training and the test data. There are probably many more creative ways of applying visualization toward strong support of sensitivity analysis.

16.2 Aid Improvement of Spatial and Temporal Data Mining

Within the data mining community, spatial and temporal data mining represents a small minority of applications. Development of techniques in these areas thus proceeds more slowly. Moving windows still seem to be the representation of choice. It seems that a scenario such as the following might somehow be possible.

Consider a highly complex 3D spatial data set on which humans can easily recognize intricate shapes, when viewing the data in a 2D or 3D image. The shapes may even have some discontinuities. Representation of the data in 3D and having data mining tools still recognize such shapes is a problem. Might there be some carryover from data visualization methods that would help with the representational issue?

There might also be some interactive tool for having a human highlight a series of these shapes on different images, so that data mining could build a model. This would require that the tool somehow capture such highlights and turn them into data. Data mining could then build models, provided there were enough consistency in the shapes. Such a tool would need to be general enough to apply to whatever type of data was involved in the current project.

Some of these issues have been resolved in specific applications. The Sky Catalog application, for example, is somewhat similar, although it is able to leverage the point-like nature of the objects it is classifying without dealing with tracing the entire shape or with discontinuities. It seems that some clever integration of data mining and visualization could help a lot with spatial data, as well as be extended somehow to temporal data.

Chapter 17

Issues in Time-Series and Categorical Data Exploration

NANCY GRADY
RAYMOND FLANERY, JR.
JUNE DONATO
JACK SCHRYVER

Oak Ridge National Laboratory

Introduction

Data mining techniques are becoming increasingly critical in handling large data sets of rapidly accumulating data from different types of sources. Although it is vital to develop automated techniques that can filter and categorize data, it is equally important to take the final step to communicate and understand the process and results using visual techniques. Data exploration has traditionally been considered in terms of user interface issues for interactive browsing. As the quantity of data to be examined increases, however, it becomes even more important to blend the boundaries between the visual presentation of a data mining process and user-driven data exploration. As many classes of data are being collected, it also becomes important to explore the integration of different mining techniques to address the overall problem. To illustrate these ideas, we discuss two projects in which we have addressed issues in large-scale data exploration and in data mining from disparate sources.

17.1 Interactive Exploration of Streaming Time-Series Data

Data creators (such as computational science models of large-scale phenomena, image collection satellites, and national scientific user facilities) and business processes (such as credit card transactions or retail sales) can generate enormous amounts of data. The difficulties in storing and examining this data are readily apparent. It is impossible to manually scan these huge input streams to locate the regions of interest. In many situations, tools are needed to greatly reduce the amount of data to be examined by the analyst. Once this reduction has occurred, it must be possible to interactively browse the remaining data to pinpoint regions of interest. We need tools to help bring the science out of scientific data sets.

Time-series data streams present three major challenge areas for a generalized data exploration system: providing algorithms for the analysis and creation of metadata, filtering out data that is uninteresting, and interactive exploration of the regions of interest. Further operational constraints are based on the size of the data set and the speed with which the analysis must take place.

One approach to the exploration of time-series numeric data [Fla96] uses statistical filters to test the changing characteristics of the data as it is streaming in. When the filters determine that a region in the data no longer fits the general trends, that region would benefit from examination by the scientist. By saving that point and a sample region around it, the amount of data to be examined manually can be greatly reduced.

A visual browsing system [Fla96] was developed within the visualization package AVS [AVS01] to allow interactive viewing and examination of the data regions of interest in an input stream. Through the use of feature extraction techniques [Dow95], interesting regions in the data can be identified. These techniques are implemented as AVS modules, which operate on the incoming data stream. Histograms and box plots of the raw data sections are displayed, allowing the user to tailor parameters to better reduce or filter the resulting data representation. The browsing system then selects a data window around a region of interest determined by the filters, storing the data along with the statistically determined metadata in a Postgres [Sto01] database. The strengths of Postgres are that it allows back-end functions to better utilize the CPUs of the host machine, and provides object-oriented extensions that allow useful large objects to be stored with the data.

For the data exploration phase, a 2D graphical representation of the metadata guides the user through the data. Selection of an interesting point in the display retrieves the raw data for viewing. This approach works very well for user exploration of 1D streams of time-series data.

17.2 Integrating Different Mining Algorithms

The Oak Ridge National Laboratory has recently developed a data mining approach to predict bankruptcy in personal credit card accounts [Don01]. Although the transaction patterns are time-series data streams, there are both numeric and character data attributes for each account, resulting in a number of more complex factors to be considered in communicating the knowledge content within this data. In the data mining phase of this work, decision trees have been used to partition the accounts within the database into groups of good, bankrupt, or delinquent, based on attributes signifying their current status. The transactions for the accounts within each group are then used to train a partially recurrent neural network to recognize the behavior pattern in the running balance. When tested against a new set of accounts, the system does indicate a predictive power for bankruptcy.

The difficulty in handling a multi-staged approach such as this centers on the lack of interoperability between systems. All data flows must be handled manually, as there is no standard data representation to share between tools. The standardization of data definition languages for mining algorithms would greatly ease the programming burden on researchers wishing to integrate tools for a larger problem-solving environment.

Proper evaluation of this methodology for bankruptcy prediction requires the integration of visual representations for both the account information and the transaction data in the database. The separation of accounts through a decision tree provides its own natural representation, shown in Figure 17.1.

However, a simple enhancement over merely presenting the hierarchical structure of the tree could use size and color for the nodes to indicate the predicted status of the represented accounts. This visual representation can convey a sense of the number of accounts (given by the width of the box) and the type of classification (given by the color). Likewise, the splitting nodes could be colored by the variable being split (shown in white in Figure 17.2).

Another representation, shown in Figure 17.3, would indicate the percentages of correctly classified records in each leaf node to get a sense of the accuracy of the prediction. Like the tree diagram, this representation is difficult to handle for large decision trees. A circular presentation serves to

Figure 17.1

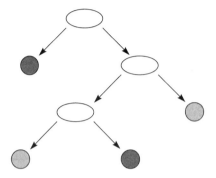

Tree diagram for decision tree output.

Figure 17.2

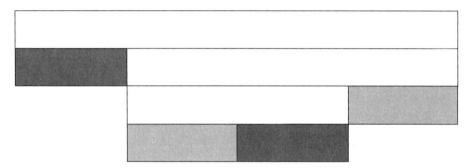

Tabular view of decision tree classifications.

increase the area of the lower branches while maintaining a sense of proportion of records through the angular display. The space-filling mode shown in Figure 17.3(a) adds a great deal of weight to nodes higher in the tree. The non-space-filling mode shown in Figure 17.3(b) gives a better sense of proportion for the numbers of records in the nodes.

Although better, this representation would still suffer for larger trees. The table and pie representations would, however, be more compact than the actual tree diagram. Differing representations may provide insight into the records being split. Having standard representational forms for this decision tree's metadata files would allow users to switch between representations for those most instructive. In addition, these views should link to images better suited for large structures as the decision trees grow in complexity.

Figure 17.3

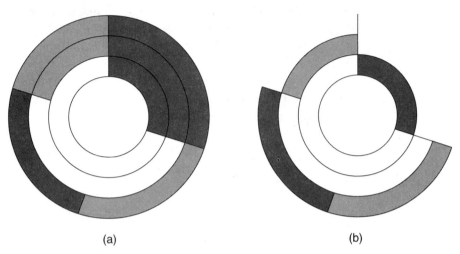

(a)   (b)

Pie chart view of decision tree classifications in (a) space-filling and (b) non-space-filling modes.

For the bankruptcy problem, the decision tree also would provide an appropriate interface for accessing the grouped accounts' transaction data. Selection of the "leaf" could easily link to other displays for the accounts or transaction patterns represented by that class of accounts. The challenge is in the representation of multiple transaction data streams of differing data types. These temporal sequences represent multidimensional data and a noisy level of detail, and the transactions are not all at the same behavioral point at a given calendar time (i.e., the remaining time until the onset of bankruptcy would be a more appropriate temporal scale for the analysis). The transaction pattern must be processed to present varying degrees of detail to bring out the broad features in the continuous data, to provide dimensional reduction for the discrete data, and to allow some modification to the time origin in order to align the data to a future point in time (at the declaration of bankruptcy).

The next visualization challenge is in the animation of the status of the neural network. Artificial neural networks are an excellent data mining tool for learning a pattern of behavior. Hidden layers of feed-forward networks are also capable of learning the important "features" of an input representation. As nonlinear systems, however, they make human interpretation of the learned "features" quite difficult. Presentation of the knowledge contained in the artificial neural network will require connections between the predicted value of the network (probability of bankruptcy), the trajectory of the hidden/context layers in reduced dimensions, and the raw transaction patterns. Another useful representation would show the trajectory taken by each account as it moves through the high-dimensional hidden/context layer "space" from good to bankrupt status. These visual representations would be of great assistance in understanding the interrelationship between the analysis of the account records through the decision tree and the transaction patterns through a neural network.

17.3 Conclusion

These two exploratory projects have dealt with technical issues for the creation of visual data exploration systems for both time-series and categorical data and for the integration of mining algorithms dealing with these data types. The data mining project for predicting personal bankruptcy is a work in progress that will require unique solutions for data exploration and interpretation on a massive data set, including the comparison of a large number of sliding origin temporal transaction patterns and the animation of the algorithms being used to analyze them. Developers of data exploration systems would greatly benefit from the availability of standard data structures and of interchangeable visual representations for this data.

Acknowledgments

These projects were funded under the laboratory director's research and development program at the Oak Ridge National Laboratory. ORNL is managed by Lockheed Martin Energy Research Corporation for the U.S. Department of Energy under contract no. DE-AC05-96OR22464.

References

[AVS01]   AVS, Application Visualization System, Advanced Visualization Systems, Inc.

[Don01]   J. M. Donato, J. C. Schryver, N. W. Grady, R. L. Schmoyer, and G. C. Hinkel. "A Data Mining Approach to Personal Bankruptcy Prediction" (unpublished).

[Dow95]   D. J. Downing, W. F. Lawkins, M. D. Morris, and G. Ostrouchov. "A Method for Detecting Changes in Long Time Series." Anonymous ORNL/TM-12879, September. 1995, Oak Ridge National Laboratory, Oak Ridge, TN.

[Fla96]   R.E.J. Flanery and J. M. Donato. "Large-Scale Data Analysis Using AVS5 and POSTGRES," A. Wierse, G. Grinstein, and U. Lang (editors). Anonymous 1183, *Lecture Notes in Computer Science*. New York. Springer-Verlag, 1996.

[Sto01]   M. Stonebraker and G. Kemnitz. "The POSTGRES Next Generation DBMS," EECS Department, University of California, Berkeley.

Chapter 18

Visualizing the Simple Bayesian Classifier

BARRY BECKER
RON KOHAVI
DAN SOMMERFIELD

Silicon Graphics, Inc.

Introduction

The simple Bayesian classifier (SBC), sometimes called naive Bayes, is built based on a conditional independence model of each attribute, given the class. The model was previously shown to be surprisingly robust to obvious violations of this independence assumption, yielding accurate classification models even when there were clear conditional dependencies. The SBC can serve as an excellent tool for initial exploratory data analysis when coupled with a visualizer that makes its structure comprehensible. We describe such a visual representation of the SBC model that has been successfully implemented. We also describe the requirements we had for such a visualization and the design decisions we made to satisfy them.

18.1 The Simple Bayesian Classifier

In supervised classification learning, a labeled training set is presented to the learning algorithm. The learner uses the training set to build a model that maps unlabeled instances to class labels. The model serves two purposes: use in prediction of labels of unlabeled instances and provision of valuable insight for people trying to understand the domain. Simple models are especially useful if the model is to be understood by nonexperts in machine learning.

The SBC is built, as previously mentioned, based on a conditional independence model of each attribute, given the class [Goo65, Dud73, Lan92]. Formally, the probability of a class label value C_i for an unlabeled instance $X = \langle A_1, \ldots, A_n \rangle$ consisting of n attribute values is given by

$P(C_i|X)$

$$= P(X|C_i) \cdot P(C_i)/P(X) \qquad \text{by Bayes rule}$$

$$\propto P(A_1, \ldots, A_n|C_i) \cdot P(C_i) \qquad P(X) \text{ is the same for all label values}$$

$$= \prod_{j=1}^{n} P(A_j|C_i) \cdot P(C_i) \qquad \text{by conditional independence assumption}$$

This probability is computed for each class, and the prediction is made for the class with the largest posterior probability. The probabilities in the foregoing formulas must be estimated from the training set. This model is very robust and continues to perform well even in the face of obvious violations of this independence assumption [Dom96, Koh95].

We begin with a discussion of our motivation and requirements for the SBC visualization. We then describe it in detail and explain why we made certain design decisions.

18.2 Motivation and Requirements for Visualization

The ability to describe the structure of a classifier in a way that people can easily understand transforms classifiers from incomprehensible black boxes to useful tools that convert the data into knowledge. One advantage of the SBC is that it uses a fairly simple model that users can easily understand. The following describes the visual representation of the SBC model that has been successfully implemented in SGI's MineSet data mining product under the name Evidence Visualizer.

Classification of data without any explanation of the underlying model reduces the trust of users in the system and does not help the knowledge discovery process. For example, Spiegelhalter and Knill-Jones [Spi84] reported that physicians would reject a system that gave insufficient explanation, even though it had good accuracy. A visualization accompanying an induced classifier provides a way for users to understand the model used in the classi-fication. A human may choose to reject a classification, or the entire model, if he realizes that the classifier is basing its decision on factors that are not significant or relevant, or that the classifier is ignoring crucial factors.

In constructing our visualization of the structure of the SBC, we incorpo-rated the following design requirements:

- Users with very little knowledge of statistics should be able to quickly grasp the primary factors (attributes and values) influencing classification.

- Users should be able to see the entire model and understand how it ap-plies to records, rather than the visualization being specific to every record, as was done in the evidence balance sheets described in Spiegel-halter and Knill-Jones ([Spi84], Tukey's discussion) and Madigan, Mosurski, and Almond [Mad97]. Showing users the complete model provides a much more powerful knowledge discovery tool.

- Users should be able to compare the relative evidence contributed by every value of every attribute.

- Users should be able to see a *characterization* of a given class. We define a characterization for a class as being a list of attribute values or ranges that differentiates that class from others. (Some SAS users we talked to claimed that CROSSTAB, a procedure for generating cross-tabulated counts, was probably the most frequently used procedure in SAS; the SBC provides a similar function. We believe the visualization may be far more useful than textual tables.)

- Users should be able to infer record counts and confidence in the shown probabilities so that the reliability of the classifier's prediction for spe-cific values can be assessed quickly from the graphics. The precise num-bers can always be made accessible through interaction with the visual-ization, but most of the time a visual cue should be what prompts a user to desire such a number.

- The system should handle many attributes (on the order of hundreds), including attributes with hundreds of values, without creating an incom-prehensible visualization or a scene that is impractical to manipulate.

- Users should be able to interact with the visualization to perform classifi-cations. Specifically, users should be able to classify data directly in the visualizer and watch the predictions change as they select values for attributes.

Given the foregoing desiderata, we constructed a visualization called Evidence Visualizer.

18.3 Proposed Visualization

The Evidence Visualizer displays the structure of the SBC and allows users to interact with it, examine specific values, show probabilities of picked objects, and ask what-if questions. Figure 18.1 and 18.2 show the two possible displays users see.

There are two panes in the Evidence Visualizer. The right pane shows a large pie with prior probabilities for the possible label values. As the user interacts with the visualization by choosing values for attributes, the slices update to show the posterior probabilities. The left pane consists of rows of pie charts, one for each attribute. The attributes are sorted in order of importance, computed as the conditional entropy [Cov91] of each attribute and label. The left pane switches to a bar chart representation of evidence for a label once a specific label is selected. There is one pie chart or bar for each discrete value or range of the attribute.

18.3.1 The Pie Chart Representation

In the pie chart representation on the left, the height of a pie is proportional to the number of instances having that attribute value. The sum of the pie heights for every row is constant. The slices of the pies represent the *evidence*, defined as the normalized conditional probabilities of an attribute value (or range) A, given a class label C_i of n possible classes. Specifically, the size of each slice for an attribute representing class label value C_i is

$$P(A|C_i)/\sum_{i=1}^{n}P(A|C_i)$$

The size of a pie slice indicates the amount of evidence to "add" to the class label matching the slice if we know that an instance has the given attribute value that matches the specific pie. If the slices are of equal size for an attribute value, knowing that an instance has this specific attribute value adds equal evidence to all classes, indicating that the posterior probability will not change, and thus this attribute value is irrelevant according to the SBC model.

Figure 18.1

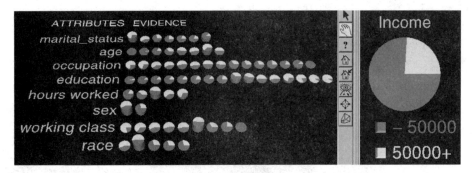

Evidence Visualizer's pie chart display of the SBC model. The height of each pie represents the number of instances for that value or range.

Figure 18.2

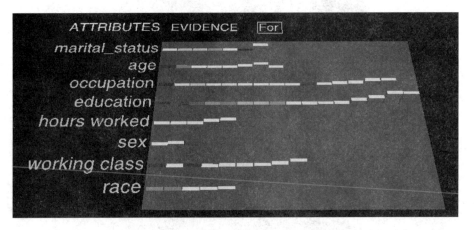

Evidence Visualizer's bar chart display of the SBC model. The height shows evidence for the selected class. The bars become less saturated as the number of instances decreases, signifying a wider confidence interval.

Users may interact with the visualization by selecting values for the attributes and observing how the posterior probability (pie chart on the right) changes. For example, selecting the pie for *sepal length* < 5.45 inches and the pie for *sepal width* > 3.05 inches shows that an iris with these characteristics is probably an iris-setosa (Figure 18.3).

Figure 18.3

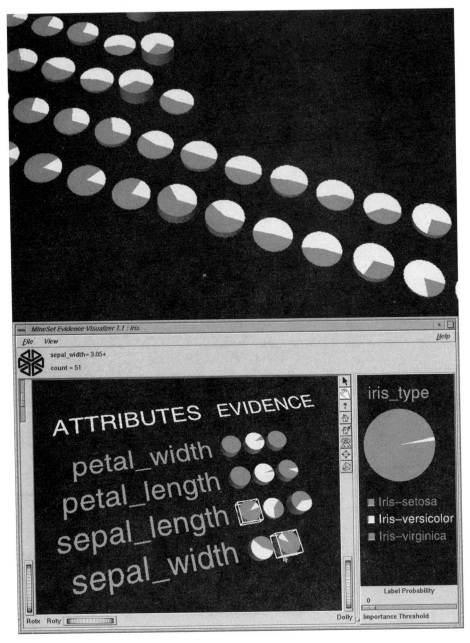

*Close-up on some attribute values (top) and selection of specific value ranges
to see the posterior probability (bottom). (See also color plate for Figure 18.3.)*

18.3.2 The Bar Chart Representation

The bars representation gives evidence that is *additive* as opposed to multiplicative. Formally repeated as follows:

$$P(C_i|X) \propto \prod_{j=1}^{n} P(A_j|C_i) \cdot P(C_i)$$

we can take negative logs of each side (a small epsilon is added to avoid logs of zero if a Laplace correction is not applied). Class i with the smallest value of $-\log(P(C_i|X))$ is predicted, which is equivalent to the class i with the smallest value of the following expression:

$$-\sum_{j=1}^{n} \log(P(A_j|C_i)) - \log(P(C_i))$$

In this mode of the Evidence Visualizer, which displays evidence against the selected class, each bar's height is proportional to $-\log(P(A_j|C_i))$ and the base height (representing the prior evidence) on which all bars stand as proportional to $\log(P(C_i))$. This shows evidence *against* each class because the class with the smallest sum is predicted. In a complementary mode, showing evidence for the selected class, the bar height shows the sum of the log evidence against *all other* classes, as shown in Figure 18.2. A bar for class i is then proportional to

$$-\log(1 - P(A_j|C_i))$$

and the base is proportional to $\log(1 - P(C_i))$. This mode was found to be more intuitive to users.

This type of representation is excellent for characterizing a class of interest. If you select a different class, the heights and colors of the bars change to represent the new class. The colors become less saturated (i.e., grayer) if the confidence interval for the estimated evidence is large, signifying that the estimate is based on a small number of instances. The tool is interactive and users can highlight a bar by moving the cursor over it. Once a bar representing A_i is highlighted, statistical information is shown, including $P(C_j|A_i)$, $P(A_i|C_j)$, the additive evidence, 95% confidence intervals for the probabilities, and the instance count.

The additive evidence can be interpreted as the information content in bits [Cov91]. High-evidence values will increase the class posterior probability more. This evidence can be summed in order to determine which class is being predicted by the model (unlike probabilities, which must be multiplied). This is analogous to a race between runners, each representing a class. Each time an attribute value is selected, each runner for each class is advanced by the corresponding amount of evidence. The predicted class is represented by the runner that advanced the furthest.

Because only the relative distances are important, we found it useful to subtract the evidence of the class with the smallest evidence from the rest. This is analogous to measuring relative distances from the slowest runner. When there are values that add similar evidence to all classes, the bar heights will be low. In two class problems, every attribute value will have at most one bar with a positive height. This method accentuates the importance of differences in evidence, as opposed to absolute values.

The visualizer orders the values (or ranges) depending on the attribute type. If the attribute is ordered (continuous ranges are commonly discretized), there is a natural order defined. If the attribute is nominal, there are a variety of methods the visualizer provides to order the values, as follows:

- The values could be sorted alphabetically. Sorting values alphabetically can aid in locating specific values when many are present; for example, when an attribute describes the country of birth.

- The values can be sorted by decreasing number of instances, with the leftmost values having the greatest height and decreasing to the right. The values further to the right would have less statistical significance and can be ignored by the user or not drawn below some threshold count.

- The values can be sorted by decreasing size of conditional probability value for a specified label value. This makes the values that give the most evidence for the given class toward the left. As can be seen for the education attribute shown in Figures 18.1 and 18.3 (left), this often has the effect of ordering an attribute in a natural way. The user selects the class value to use for sorting, with a default to the value with the largest prior probability.

- A method we have not yet implemented involves automatic grouping of values. If certain values result in similar conditional probabilities, we can group them in a single pie.

We have found the visualizer to be very useful in aiding knowledge discovery and in understanding patterns. Customers of MineSet reported that end users find it useful and easy to understand.

18.4 Design Decisions

Our proposed visualization satisfies the requirements outlined in Section 18.2. The following describes in detail some of the choices made and the reasons for making them.

We found that a 3D representation is the best way to accommodate large numbers of attributes and values. 3D navigation combined with perspective allows the user to closely examine an area of interest while maintaining context in the entire visualization. The predicted distribution of classes was included in a separate 2D pane to make it readily accessible.

We display probabilities as both pies and bars because each representation has distinct advantages in helping a user understand the operation of the SBC. We found that a pie chart was optimal for showing probabilities because the angles subtended by the slices and representing relative conditional probabilities always sum to one. This allows us to easily display a full probability distribution in a small space. We recognize some of the drawbacks of pie charts noted by Tufte [Tuf83, p. 178], but in our case they have several advantages that outweigh their disadvantages. Pie charts are used pervasively in magazines and newspapers to represent distributions, making them understood and recognized by everyone. The use of pie charts allows many probability distributions to be displayed simultaneously, something we have not been able to achieve with other graphical representations.

Because the pie charts are of the same size and laid out on a line, they are similar to charts used by *Consumer Reports* to represent product quality through a set of circles filled with varying amounts of green and black to signify good and bad aspects, respectively. Tufte [Tuf83, p. 174] lauded this approach as "a particularly ingenious mix of table and graphic."

The use of the third dimension allows us to show the number of records underlying a particular distribution as the height (z coordinate) of the pie chart. This display gives users a quick means of gauging the reliability of any given distribution by rotating the scene.

The pie representation is strongest when the user is interested in distributions over all classes. The alternate representation, using bars, is more useful when the user is interested in properties of a specific class, and its use during interactive classification closely parallels the use of an evidence balance sheet to explain a result [Spi84]. The use of log probabilities for the bars coupled with subtracting the minimum bar height from all bars makes this representation ideal for understanding the effect each attribute value has on the final prediction. Prediction is accomplished simply by adding bar heights (evidence) corresponding to the user's choices for each class and picking the class with the highest total evidence.

Nominal attributes with many values pose problems because they flood the visualization with a large number of pies, which may be difficult to interpret or compare. We provide two mechanisms for solving this problem. First, we order the values based on user preference (alphabetical, counts, probabilities). Second, we provide an option to remove values based on less than a user-specified small percentage of the data, typically 1% or less, thus eliminating the least significant portions of the scene. These two mechanisms combined make it easier for users to focus on the key values.

It is very important to display reliability of the probability estimates through the visualization. The pie chart display accomplishes this by showing the number of records behind each distribution as the height; higher pies are more reliable. The bars mode uses height to show evidence; therefore, we had to choose an alternate method. We lower the saturation of a bar as its confidence worsens, effectively graying out bars with little support. This display of confidence is essential in the bars mode because probability distributions estimated from little data tend to be heavily skewed, resulting in large bars that pop out during visualization. Making these bars gray prevents them from heavily influencing the user.

If there are many classes, it can be difficult to locate the name of the class that is predicted. For this reason, the class labels listed on the right pane are ordered by decreasing prior probabilities (Figure 18.4). The exact probabilities can be determined by moving the cursor over a particular class label.

Our visualization is also designed to handle unknown (null) values. Because nulls are handled differently in the classification process, probability distribution pies representing null attribute values appear in a special leftmost column, offset slightly from the other values. They also may not be selected by the user; to leave an attribute's value undefined, the user simply leaves all attribute values in a specific row unselected. For an example of unknown handling, see the first value of attribute *stalkroot* in Figure 18.4. You can see that *odor* on the top was ranked as an excellent discriminator; the values are perfect discriminators except for the value *none*, which is represented by the third pie from the left. The pointer points to the first value of *stalkroot*, which is slightly offset to help the user understand that the first value is a missing (null) value.

In some cases, the classes are an ordered list. This usually occurs as a result of binning a continuous variable in order to use it as a class label. In this case, the class colors are not assigned randomly: a continuum is used to indicate the low to high ordering of the classes. Users can hence easily identify values that lend strong evidence for predicting a class at one end of the range or the other, as shown in Figure 18.5. Because the label *gross income*

Figure 18.4

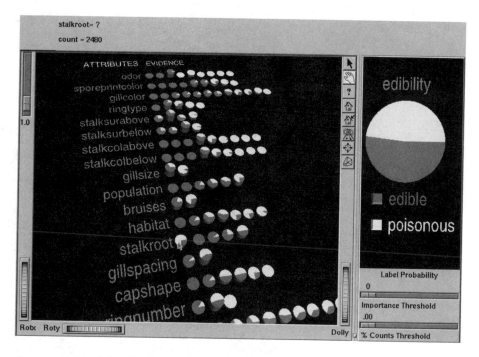

An example of the Evidence Visualizer for the Mushroom data set, where the goal is to determine mushroom edibility. (See also color plate.)

was binned and has a natural ordering, the colors assigned form a continuous spectrum from green to red, where red is the highest range. Also note that the class labels on the right are arranged according to their proportion of the expected probability distribution, the largest slice appearing at the top. You can quickly see that salary rises with age.

To allow the user to see data sets with hundreds of attributes, we compute the *importance* of each attribute and display them in the scene ordered by this measure. Technically, the importance value is the conditional entropy [Cov91] of each attribute and the label. Attributes with low conditional entropy have little effect on the posterior probability. A slider button on the bottom right (Figure 18.1) allows users to remove lower-ranked attributes from the visualization.

To aid understanding with respect to the actual data used to build the classifier, it is possible to *drill through* to the instances that produced certain graphics. For example, a user may select the pies corresponding to

Figure 18.5

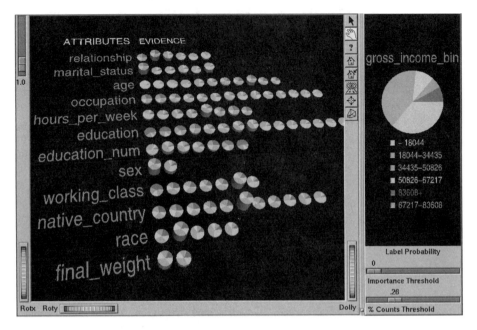

An example of a binned attribute used as a label. The goal is to understand factors affecting income. (See also color plate.)

education = masters and *occupation = clerical* and see the instances in the data set that have these two values.

18.5 Summary

We described a visual representation of the SBC model that has been successfully implemented and can help you to understand the underlying model and the importance of specific attributes and attribute values in the classification process. The visualization gives insight into how classification is done, as well as allowing users to answer what-if questions through interactions with the visualization, something we found very useful. We also described the desiderata for such a visualization and the specific design decisions that we made to meet the requirements.

Acknowledgments

We would like to thank everyone on the SGI MineSet team, especially Joel Tesler and Gerald Sangudi, who helped with the conception of the Evidence Visualizer.

References

[Cov91] T. M. Cover and J. A. Thomas. *Elements of Information Theory*. New York. John Wiley & Sons, 1991.

[Dom96] P. Domingos and M. Pazzani. "Beyond Independence: Conditions for the Optimality of the Simple Bayesian Classifier," L. Saitta (editor), *Machine Learning: Proceedings of the Thirteenth International Conference*, pp. 105–112. San Francisco. Morgan Kaufmann, 1996.

[Dud73] R. Duda and P. Hart. *Pattern Classification and Scene Analysis*. New York. John Wiley & Sons, 1973.

[Goo65] I. J. Good. *The Estimation of Probabilities: An Essay on Modern Bayesian Methods*. Cambridge, MA. M.I.T. Press, 1965.

[Koh95] R. Kohavi and D. Sommerfield. "Feature Subset Selection Using the Wrapper Model: Overfitting and Dynamic Search Space Topology," *The First International Conference on Knowledge Discovery and Data Mining*, pp. 192–197, 1995.

[Lan92] P. Langley, W. Iba, and K. Thompson. "An Analysis of Bayesian Classifiers," *Proceedings of the Tenth National Conference on Artificial Intelligence*, pp. 223–228. Cambridge, MA. AAAI Press/MIT Press, 1992.

[Mad97] D. Madigan, K. Mosurski, and R. G. Almond. "Graphical Explanation in Belief Networks," *Journal of Comparative and Graphical Statistics*, 1997.

[Spi84] D. J. Spiegelhalter and R. P. Knill-Jones. "Statistical and Knowledge-Based Approaches to Clinical Decision-support Systems, with an Application in Gastroenterology," *Journal of the Royal Statistical Society*, 147, pp. 35–77, 1984.

[Tuf83] E. R. Tufte. *The Visual Display of Quantitative Information*. Cheshire, CT. Graphics Press, 1983.

Chapter 19

Visualizing Data Mining Results with Domain Generalization Graphs

ROBERT J. HILDERMAN
LIANGCHUN LI
HOWARD J. HAMILTON

University of Regina, Canada

Introduction

The DB-Discover system is a research software tool for knowledge discovery from databases. Utilizing an efficient attribute-oriented induction algorithm based on the climbing tree and dropping condition methods, called multi-attribute generalization, it generates many possible summaries of data from a database. In this chapter, we present the design of the data visualization capabilities of DB-Discover. We describe how our data visualization techniques help us manage the many possible summaries and how potentially interesting summaries are selected from them. A prototype system has been implemented that allows many alternative visualizations of the summaries. The results of our work enable a domain expert to quickly and efficiently analyze the content of a database from many different perspectives.

This chapter describes the design of the data visualization capabilities of the DB-Discover system. *DB-Discover* is a research software tool for knowledge discovery from databases (KDD), developed at the University of Regina from 1992 to date [Bru97, Der97, and Car97]. Data visualization can be used in a KDD system (1) to guide discovery, (2) to guide the presentation of the results, and (3) to present the results themselves. Here we focus on the second stage.

KDD algorithms can be broadly classified into two general areas: summarization and anomaly detection. *Summarization algorithms* find concise descriptions of data, such as high-level summaries, sets of rules, or decision trees. *Anomaly detection algorithms* identify unusual features of data, such as combinations that occur with greater or lesser frequency than expected. DB-Discover produces many possible summaries of data retrieved from a database. We describe techniques for (1) managing the many possible summaries available for output, and (2) selecting the anomalous (and potentially interesting) summaries among them. As well, techniques for guiding the discovery process are described.

The remainder of this chapter is organized as follows. In the following section, we describe DB-Discover. In Section 19.2, we show how data visualization can help a domain expert efficiently manage and analyze discovered information. In Section 19.3, we summarize our results and suggest future research.

19.1 The DB-Discover System

The DB-Discover system is based on *multi-attribute generalization*, an enhanced version of a well-known data mining technique called attribute-oriented induction [Cai91]. *Attribute-oriented induction* summarizes data in a database according to user-defined concept hierarchies associated with relevant attributes. In this section, we describe in general terms how DB-Discover works to generate summaries from data in a database. First, in Section 19.1.1, we informally describe attribute-oriented induction and present an example showing how a concept hierarchy can be ascended to produce a summary. Then in Section 19.1.2, we describe domain generalization graphs, the primary data structure used in multi-attribute generalization, and show how they are used to extend the scope of the attribute-oriented induction methodology. Finally, in Section 19.1.3, we describe the process of multi-attribute generalization, whereby domain generalization graphs are used to guide the generalization of a set of attributes.

19.1.1 Attribute-Oriented Induction

Transforming a specific data description into a more general one is called *generalization*. Generalization techniques include the dropping condition and climbing tree methods [Mic83]. The *climbing tree method* transforms

Figure 19.1

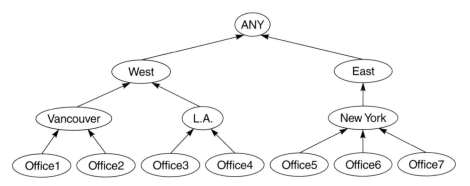

CH for the office *attribute.*

the data in a database by repeatedly replacing specific attribute values with more general concepts according to user-defined concept hierarchies. A *concept hierarchy* (CH) associated with an attribute in a database is represented as a tree in which leaf nodes correspond to actual domain values in the database, intermediate nodes correspond to a more general representation of the domain values, and the root node corresponds to the most general representation of the domain values. For example, a CH for the *office* attribute in a sales database is shown in Figure 19.1. Knowledge about the higher-level concepts (i.e., non-leaf nodes) can be discovered by generating the summaries corresponding to each level of the CH.

The *dropping condition method* transforms the data in a database by removing a condition from a conjunction of conditions, so that the remaining conjunction of conditions is more general. For example, assume the conjunction of conditions (*shape* = "round" ∧ *size* = "large" ∧ *color* = "white") describes the concept *ball*. Removing the condition *color* = "white," which is equivalent to generalizing the *color* attribute to *ANY*, yields the conjunction of conditions (*shape* = "round" ∧ *size* = "large"). The concept *ball* is now more general because it encompasses large round objects of any color.

Attribute-oriented induction (AOI) [Han92, Han93, Han94] is a summarization algorithm that integrates the climbing tree and dropping condition methods for generalizing data in a database. An efficient variant of the AOI algorithm has been incorporated into DB-Discover. By associating a CH with an attribute, DB-Discover can generalize and summarize the domain values for the attribute in many different ways. An attractive feature of DB-Discover is that it is possible to obtain many different summaries for an attribute by

Table 19.1

The sales database.

Office	Shape	Size	Color	Quantity	Amount
2	Round	Small	White	2	$50.00
5	Square	Medium	Black	3	$75.00
3	Round	Large	White	1	$25.00
7	Round	X-Large	Black	4	$100.00
1	Square	X-Large	White	3	$75.00
6	Round	Medium	Black	4	$100.00
4	Square	Small	White	2	$50.00

Table 19.2

An example sales summary.

Office	Quantity	Amount	Count
West	8	$200.00	4
East	11	$275.00	3

simply changing the structure of the associated CH, and these new summaries can be obtained without modifying the underlying data.

For example, consider the database shown in Table 19.1. Using the CH from Figure 19.1 to guide the generalization, one of the many possible summaries that can be generated is shown in Table 19.2, where the *office, quantity,* and *amount* attributes have been selected for generalization, and the actual values for the *office* attribute in each tuple have been generalized to the level of *west* and *east*. The values in the *quantity* and *amount* attributes have been accumulated accordingly, and a new attribute, called *count*, shows the number of specific tuples accumulated in each generalized tuple.

As a result of recent research, the AOI variant in DB-Discover is among the most efficient of KDD methods [Car95a, Car95b, Car95c, Car97, Han94, Hwa95]. In particular, algorithms for generalizing relational databases are presented in [Car97] that run in $O(n)$ time, where n is the number of tuples in the input relation, and require $O(p)$ space, where p is the number of tuples in the generalized relation (typically $p \ll n$), while producing exactly the same output as created by previous algorithms. In [Car97], it is also proven that an AOI algorithm that runs in $O(n)$ time is optimal for the defined generalization problem.

Figure 19.2

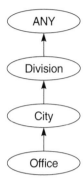

DGG for the office *attribute.*

19.1.2 Domain Generalization Graphs

A fundamental problem with AOI methods is that they are limited in scope. That is, where multiple CHs are associated with an attribute, the user is required to select just one during a discovery task. Consequently, only those summaries that can be generated from the chosen CH are presented to the user, ignoring the relative merits of other possible summaries that could be generated from the other CHs.

To facilitate the generation of other possible summaries, *domain generalization graphs* (DGGs) are used to augment CHs and expand the scope of our AOI methods [Ham96, Hil97, Pan96]. Informally, a DGG associated with a CH defines a partial order that represents a set of generalization relations for the attribute. A DGG always includes a single source (i.e., the node at the lowest level corresponding to the domain of the attribute) and a single sink (i.e., the node at the highest level corresponding to the most general representation of the domain and that contains the value *ANY*). The node at each level in a DGG is a general description of the nodes at the same level in the corresponding CH. For example, the nodes at each level of the CH in Figure 19.1 correspond to the nodes at the same level in the more general representation of the DGG in Figure 19.2. That is, *west* and *east* correspond to *division; Vancouver, L. A.,* and *New York* correspond to *city,* and *office1* to *office7* correspond to *office*. Note that a CH always corresponds to a single-path DGG.

When there are multiple CHs associated with a single attribute, knowledge of the meaning of an attribute can be expressed in many different ways, and a multipath DGG can be constructed from single-path DGGs. Figure

Figure 19.3

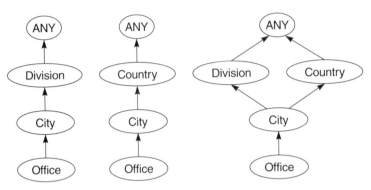

Multipath DGG for the office *attribute.*

19.3 shows a multipath DGG on the right that has been constructed from the two single-path DGGs on the left. Here, we assume that a common name used in the single-path DGGs associated with the attribute represents the same partition of the domain in the associated CHs. For example, in Figure 19.3, the *ANY, city,* and *office* nodes in the single-path DGGs on the left represent the same partition of the domain in the associated CHs. Consequently, the like-named nodes can be combined in the multipath DGG.

DB-Discover traverses a multipath DGG to generate the minimum number of summaries for an attribute in a space-efficient manner. For example, assume we want to generate a summary at the *city* level of the multipath DGG in Figure 19.3. The *office* node represents the domain for the *office* attribute. To generate this summary, either of the CHs associated with the original single-path DGGs could be selected to guide the generalization. Because the *city* node represents the same partition of the domain in the associated CHs, it does not matter to DB-Discover which CH is chosen to obtain this summary. If DB-Discover generated summaries by following the two single-path DGGs independently, six summaries would be generated, of which two would be duplicate summaries corresponding to the *city* and *ANY* nodes. The other two summaries would correspond to the *division* and *country* nodes. However, by following the multipath DGG, it only generates four summaries, corresponding to the *city, division, country,* and *ANY* nodes.

19.1.3 Multi-Attribute Generalization

A typical discovery task usually involves generalization of a set of attributes, where each attribute is associated with a multipath DGG. When generalizing

Table 19.3

Domains for the shape, size, *and* color *attributes.*

Shape	Size	Color
Round	Small	Black
Square	Medium	White
	Large	
	X-Large	

Table 19.4

Domain for the compound attribute shape-size-color.

Shape-size-color

Round-small-black
Round-small-white
Round-medium-black
Round-medium-white
Round-large-black
Round-large-white
Round-x-large-black
Round-x-large-white
Square-small-black
Square-small-white
Square-medium-black
Square-medium-white
Square-large-black
Square-large-white
Square-x-large-black
Square-x-large-white

a set of attributes, the set can be considered a single attribute whose domain is the cross product of the individual attribute domains. For example, given the domains for the attributes *shape, size,* and *color* shown in Table 19.3, the domain for the compound attribute *shape-size-color* is as shown in Table 19.4.

A generalization from the domain for the *shape-size-color* attribute is a combination of nodes from the DGGs associated with the individual attributes, taking one node from the DGG for each attribute. For example, consider again the database shown in Table 19.1. The *shape, size, color,* and *quantity* attributes have been selected for generalization. Using the CHs from Figure 19.4 for the *shape, size,* and *color* attributes, where two CHs are

Figure 19.4

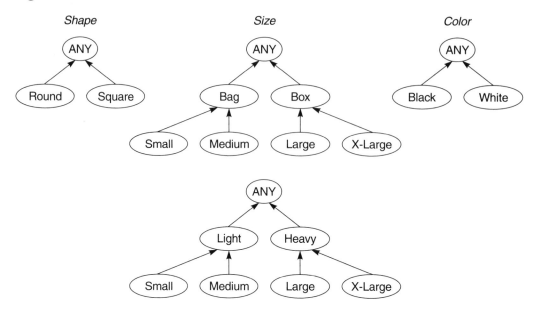

CHs for the shape, size, *and* color *attributes.*

shown for the *size* attribute, and the associated DGGs shown in Figure 19.5, one of the many possible summaries that can be obtained by generalizing to the DGG node combination *ANY-package-color* is shown in Table 19.5. We use the climbing tree method to obtain the generalized values for the *shape* and *size* attributes. Because the value for the *shape* attribute now covers all possible values, we could use the dropping condition method to remove the *shape* column from our summary without losing any meaningful information.

The *generalization state space* consists of all possible summaries that can be generated from the DGGs associated with the set of attributes. This space is more general than a version space [Mit78] because we allow more complex generalizations than value-to-ANY, and our summaries contain a relation rather than a single conjunctive description. On the other hand, it is more constricted than a Galois lattice [God95] because not every possible subset is included in the lattice. The generalization state space is obtained by determining all possible combinations of nodes from the DGGs, and then generating the summary that corresponds to each node combination. For example, the generalization state space for the compound attribute *shape-*

Figure 19.5

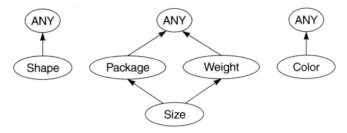

DGGs for the shape, size, *and* color *attributes.*

Table 19.5

Summary for the DGG node combination ANY-package-color.

Shape	Size	Color	Quantity	Count
ANY	Bag	White	4	2
ANY	Bag	Black	7	2
ANY	Box	White	4	2
ANY	Box	Black	4	1

size-color example consists of $2 \times 4 \times 2 = 16$ summaries, where 2, 4, and 2 are the number of nodes in the DGG associated with the *shape, size*, and *color* attributes, respectively. The two summaries corresponding to the node combinations *shape-size-color* and *ANY-ANY-ANY* are considered trivial. In the *shape-size-color* summary, all of the attributes are ungeneralized (as in the original database), and in the *ANY-ANY-ANY* summary, all of the attribute values are generalized to the value *ANY.* The size of the generalization state space depends only on the number of nodes in the associated DGGs; it is not dependent on the number of tuples in the input relation. For *m* attributes, a database of *n* tuples, and an $O(n)$ generalization algorithm, creating all possible summaries requires

$$O\left(n\prod_{i=1}^{m}|D^i| \right)$$

time, where $|D^i|$ is the number of nodes in DGG D^i. We have developed and implemented practical serial and parallel algorithms for traversing the generalization state space where *m* is small (≤ 5) and *n* is large ($> 1,000,000$).

19.2 Data Visualization in DB-Discover

In the example in the previous section, the DGGs used were of low complexity, and few summaries were generated. In practical cases, multi-attribute generalization has the potential to generate many summaries. This is because the number of attributes to be generalized could be large or the DGGs associated with the attributes could be complex. Our experience in applying data mining techniques to the databases of our commercial partners has shown that domain experts typically perform AOI on a few attributes for which considerable domain knowledge has been accumulated. This domain knowledge can be translated into a complex set of multipath DGGs.

To assist the domain expert, we propose a tool, with a GUI, called DBD-View. *DBD-View* ranks and arranges summaries, according to various user-defined criteria, so that they can be quickly and efficiently analyzed. Our approach is based on a simple, yet powerful, architecture that uses different views for visualizing the summaries generated by a discovery task. In this section, we describe DBD-View and show how it works to manage summaries. In Section 19.2.1, we describe the window upon which views are placed, known as the *viewspace*. In Section 19.2.2, we describe the method used for ranking summaries according to their size and interestingness. In Section 19.2.3, we describe the global view. The *global view* is a visualization that shows a representation of the complete generalization state space. In Section 19.2.4, we describe the local view. The *local view* is a visualization that shows a representation of the generalization state space that allows it to be broken down into smaller components. In Section 19.2.5, we describe the summary view. The *summary view* is a visualization that shows a representation of a single summary. Finally, in Section 19.2.6, we describe other functionality provided by DBD-View that allows a domain expert to change the default settings.

19.2.1 The Viewspace

The viewspace is a window upon which up to three different views may be placed. The screen snapshot in Figure 19.6 shows a viewspace that has been filled with a global view (top left), a local view (bottom left), and a summary view (right). We describe the options available for displaying these views in the sections that follow.

Figure 19.6

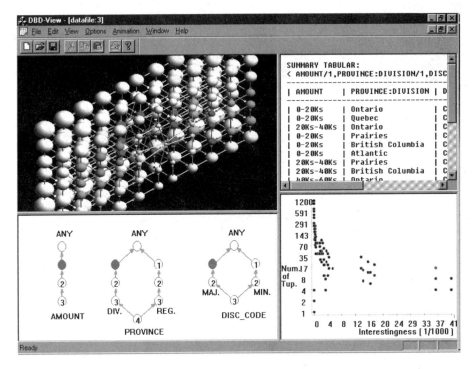

Viewspace showing global, local, and summary views. (See also color plate.)

19.2.2 Ranking Summaries

We rank the interestingness of the summaries generated by DB-Discover using measures based on relative entropy and variance. *Relative entropy,* also known as the *Kullback-Leibler (KL) distance,* has been suggested as an appropriate measure for comparing data distributions in unstructured textual databases [Fel95]. Here, we use KL distance to compare the distribution defined by the structured data in a summary to that of a model distribution of the data. *Variance,* the most common measure of variability used in statistics, is used to compare the distribution defined by the data in a summary to that of a uniform or expected distribution of the data. Ranking summaries using these interestingness heuristics allows us to reduce, or prune, the number of summaries that must be considered by the domain expert.

Figure 19.7

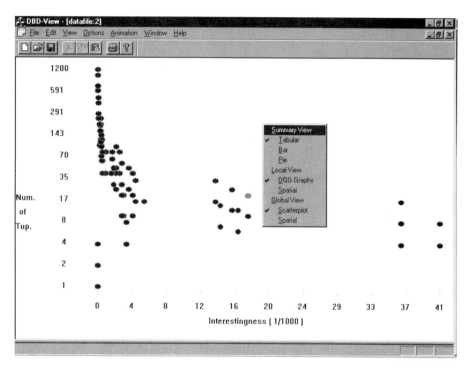

Scatter-plot global view.

As a result of previous work [Ham96], we believe that an important property of interestingness measures should be to rank summaries of low complexity (i.e., those with few attributes and/or few tuples) as more interesting. The variance heuristic has this property. Low-complexity summaries are attractive because they are more concise and intuitively easier to analyze and understand.

19.2.3 The Global View

There are two types of global views used to represent the complete generalization state space: a scatter-plot global view and a spatial global view. The *scatter-plot global view* represents the generalization state space as a 2D graph, where the number of tuples in a summary is plotted against the interestingness of the summary. For example, Figure 19.7 shows the scatter-plot global view of the complete generalization state space for a small discovery

Figure 19.8

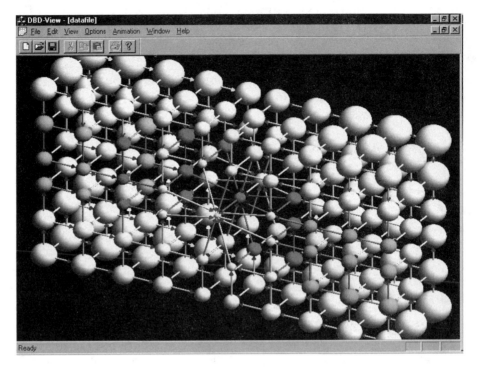

Spatial global view.

task. Each dot on the graph corresponds to one of the summaries in the generalization state space. A summary corresponding to a dot to the left of the graph is considered less interesting than one to the right of the graph. A summary corresponding to a dot near the top of the graph contains more tuples than one near the bottom of the graph.

The *spatial global view* represents the generalization state space as a directed graph consisting of nodes of various sizes and colors, connected by edges. The relative size of a node is representative of the number of tuples in the corresponding summary. That is, the larger the node, the larger the corresponding summary. Similarly, the color of a node is representative of the interestingness of the corresponding summary. For example, Figure 19.8 shows the spatial global view of the complete generalization state space for a small discovery task. Because node $D2$ is larger than node $D3$, node $D2$ corresponds to a summary containing more tuples. In addition, because node $D3$ is lighter than node $D2$, node $D3$ corresponds to a summary of higher interest.

The domain expert can utilize the scatter-plot and spatial global views to obtain an easy-to-understand, initial overview analysis of the summaries in the generalization state space. If a particular summary seems interesting, he can left click on a dot (in scatter-plot global view) or node (in spatial global view) to make the corresponding summary the active summary. When a summary becomes the *active summary*, the local and summary views are also updated to coincide with the new global view. If the domain expert wants to save a particular summary, he can left double click on a dot or node to display the corresponding summary in a new summary view window that is separate from the viewspace. The summary view shown in this window is displayed unchanged until the window is closed by the domain expert (i.e., it does not change when the active summary changes).

19.2.4 The Local View

There are two types of local views used to dissect the generalization state space: a separate graphs local view and a spatial local view. The *separate graphs local view* represents a summary in the generalization state space as a combination of nodes from the DGGs associated with the attributes being generalized. For example, Figure 19.9 shows the three DGGs from which the summaries in the generalization state space were generated. There is one solid (highlighted) node in each of these DGGs where the DGG node combination coincides with the active summary in the global and summary views.

The domain expert can navigate throughout the generalization state space by selecting different combinations of nodes from the separate graphs local view. If a particular summary seems interesting, he can left click one node in each DGG to highlight it and change the active summary to that which corresponds to the selected DGG node combination. When a summary becomes the active summary, the global and summary views are also updated to coincide with the new local view.

The *spatial local view* represents a logically connected group of summaries in the generalization state space. For example, Figure 19.10 shows a neighborhood in the generalization state space immediately surrounding the node corresponding to the active summary. The node corresponding to the active summary is the single highlighted node at the center of the view, and is called the *current node*. Below the current node are all nodes in the generalization state space from which it is possible to reach the current node by generalizing one attribute up one level in the associated DGG. These nodes are a more specific representation of the current node. Above the cur-

Figure 19.9

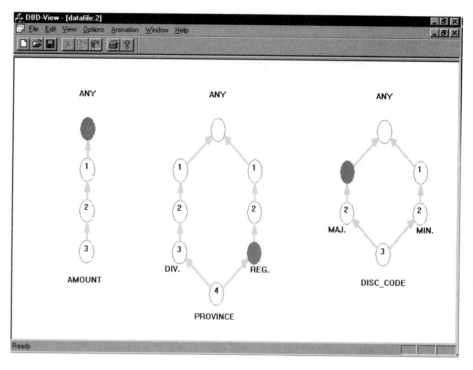

Separate graphs local view.

rent node are all nodes in the generalization state space that can be reached from the current node by generalizing one attribute up one level in the associated DGG. These nodes are a more general representation of the current node. The labels in the nodes identify the attribute that has been generalized (for those nodes below the current node) or that will be generalized (for those nodes above the current node).

The domain expert can navigate throughout the generalization state space by selecting a node from the spatial local view. If a particular summary seems interesting, she can left click on the corresponding node to highlight it and change the active summary to that which corresponds to the active node. The spatial local view is then updated to show the selected node as the current node (by moving it to the center of the view). When a node becomes the active node, the global and summary views are also updated to coincide with the new local view.

Figure 19.10

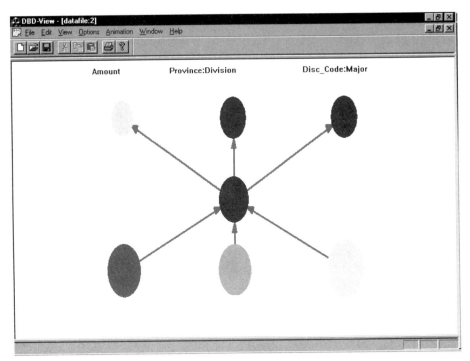

Spatial local view.

19.2.5 The Summary View

The default output format for displaying the summary view is to display it as a table. A sample table is shown in Figure 19.11. Alternative output formats include bar charts, column charts, line charts, pie charts, comma-delimited files, and tab-delimited files. Comma- and tab-delimited files allow the output to be used as input to commonly used spreadsheet packages.

19.2.6 Changing Default Settings

The default view settings for displaying the results of a discovery task are *scatter plot*, *separate graphs*, and *tabular* for the global, local, and summary views, respectively. The default interestingness heuristic is *variance from uniform*, with *pruning up and down* using the *less than or equal* comparator. The domain expert can change the default settings for DBD-View to change

Figure 19.11

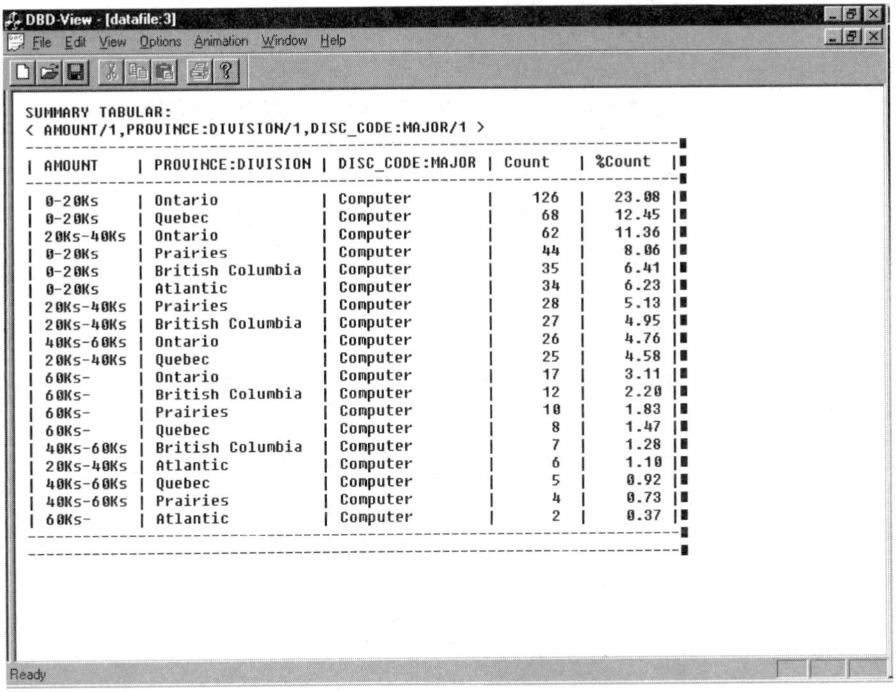

```
DBD-View - [datafile:3]                                                    _ 8 X
File  Edit  View  Options  Animation  Window  Help                         _ 8 X

SUMMARY TABULAR:
< AMOUNT/1,PROVINCE:DIVISION/1,DISC_CODE:MAJOR/1 >
--------------------------------------------------------------------------------
| AMOUNT     | PROVINCE:DIVISION | DISC_CODE:MAJOR | Count | %Count |
--------------------------------------------------------------------------------
| 0-20Ks     | Ontario           | Computer        |   126 |  23.08 |
| 0-20Ks     | Quebec            | Computer        |    68 |  12.45 |
| 20Ks-40Ks  | Ontario           | Computer        |    62 |  11.36 |
| 0-20Ks     | Prairies          | Computer        |    44 |   8.06 |
| 0-20Ks     | British Columbia  | Computer        |    35 |   6.41 |
| 0-20Ks     | Atlantic          | Computer        |    34 |   6.23 |
| 20Ks-40Ks  | Prairies          | Computer        |    28 |   5.13 |
| 20Ks-40Ks  | British Columbia  | Computer        |    27 |   4.95 |
| 40Ks-60Ks  | Ontario           | Computer        |    26 |   4.76 |
| 20Ks-40Ks  | Quebec            | Computer        |    25 |   4.58 |
| 60Ks-      | Ontario           | Computer        |    17 |   3.11 |
| 60Ks-      | British Columbia  | Computer        |    12 |   2.20 |
| 60Ks-      | Prairies          | Computer        |    10 |   1.83 |
| 60Ks-      | Quebec            | Computer        |     8 |   1.47 |
| 40Ks-60Ks  | British Columbia  | Computer        |     7 |   1.28 |
| 20Ks-40Ks  | Atlantic          | Computer        |     6 |   1.10 |
| 40Ks-60Ks  | Quebec            | Computer        |     5 |   0.92 |
| 40Ks-60Ks  | Prairies          | Computer        |     4 |   0.73 |
| 60Ks-      | Atlantic          | Computer        |     2 |   0.37 |
--------------------------------------------------------------------------------
--------------------------------------------------------------------------------

Ready
```

Tabular summary view.

the way in which views are displayed and summaries are ranked. These settings can be accessed through the View and Options drop-down menus shown on the menu bar of Figure 19.6. The View drop-down menu is also available as a context-sensitive menu by right clicking anywhere in the viewspace, as shown on the scatter-plot global view in Figure 19.7. The Options menu is not shown.

The View menu has settings for the three views corresponding to the summary, local, and global views. Currently selected settings are indicated by a check mark. To change a view setting, double click the mouse pointer on the required setting. This removes the check mark from the previously selected setting and places a check mark at the newly selected setting. A check mark can be toggled off and on by clicking the mouse pointer on the currently selected setting. If no setting is selected for a particular view, that view will be removed from the viewspace. If no setting was previously selected for a particular view, that view will be added to the viewspace.

The Options menu has settings for the interestingness heuristic, the pruning direction, and the pruning comparator. These settings can be changed in the same manner as the View menu settings described previously.

Interestingness heuristics settings include *variance from uniform, relative entropy,* and *variance from expected.* When an alternative interestingness heuristic is selected, the summaries do not need to be regenerated. The views are simply redisplayed according to the chosen heuristic. That is, no additional recalculation is required because the ranking for each interestingness heuristic is calculated and stored at the time a summary is generated.

The pruning direction settings include *pruning up, pruning down,* and *pruning up and down.* The pruning comparator settings include *none, less than,* and *less than or equal.* Pruning reduces the number of summaries that must be considered by the domain expert in some circumstances. For example, if a node is a direct descendant of some other node in the generalization state space, but the corresponding summary has higher interest, the ancestor can be eliminated from further consideration. For example, nodes $D2$, $D3$, and $D4$ are all direct descendants of node $D1$. Because $D2$, $D3$, and $D4$ also have higher interest according to the present measure, $D1$ can be ignored. Similar pruning can be done in the situation in which a node is a direct descendant of a node that has higher interest. For example, node $D5$ is a direct descendant of node $D2$. Because $D2$ has higher interest, $D5$ can be ignored.

Pruning can also be done based on the table threshold, attribute threshold, and interest threshold. When pruning using the table threshold, all nodes whose corresponding summaries contain more tuples than the table threshold will be pruned. When pruning using the attribute threshold, all nodes whose corresponding summaries contain an attribute where the number of distinct values remains greater than the attribute threshold will be pruned. Finally, when pruning using the interest threshold, all nodes whose corresponding summaries have interestingness less than the interest threshold will be pruned.

19.3 Conclusion and Future Work

We have presented the design of the data visualization capabilities of the DB-Discover system. Utilizing multi-attribute generalization, DB-Discover generates all possible summaries from the DGGs associated with a set of attributes. We showed how data visualization techniques can be used in a KDD system to manage the summaries generated and to select potentially interesting summaries for further analysis. The primary benefit from our approach is that a domain expert can quickly and efficiently analyze the content of a database from many different perspectives.

Our experience has shown that this is a promising approach toward greater understanding of discovered knowledge. However, future work will involve enhancing the data visualization capabilities of DB-Discover. For example, more work needs to be done to refine the interestingness and pruning heuristics. In addition, techniques for displaying and navigating extremely large generalization state spaces are required. Finally, techniques for allowing the domain expert to interactively guide a discovery task require further investigation.

References

[Cai91]   Y. Cai, N. Cercone, and J. Han. "Attribute-Oriented Induction in Relational Databases," G. Piatetsky-Shapiro and W. Frawley (editors), *Knowledge Discovery in Databases*, pp. 213–228. Cambridge, MA. AAAI/MIT Press, 1991.

[Car95a]   C. L. Carter and H. J. Hamilton. "A Fast, On-Line Generalization Algorithm for Knowledge Discovery," *Applied Mathematics Letters*, 8:2, pp. 5–11, 1995.

[Car95b]   C. L. Carter and H. J. Hamilton. "Performance Evaluation of Attribute-Oriented Algorithms for Knowledge Discovery from Databases," *Proceedings of the Seventh IEEE International Conference on Tools with Artificial Intelligence (ICTAI'95)*, Washington, DC, November 1995, pp. 486–489.

[Car95c]   C. L. Carter and H. J. Hamilton. "Fast, Incremental Generalization and Re-generalization for Knowledge Discovery from Databases," *Proceedings of the 8th Florida Artificial Intelligence Symposium*, Melbourne, FL, April 1995, pp. 319–323.

[Car97]   C. L. Carter and H. J. Hamilton. "Efficient Attribute-Oriented Algorithms for Knowledge Discovery from Large Databases," *IEEE Transactions on Knowledge and Data Engineering*, 1997.

[Fel95]   R. Feldman and I. Dagan. "Knowledge Discovery in Textual Databases (KDT)," *Proceedings of the First International Conference on Knowledge Discovery and Data Mining (KDD'95)*, Montreal, August 1995, pp. 112–117.

[God95]   R. Godin, R. Missaoui, and H. Alaoui. "Incremental Concept Formation Algorithms Based on Galois (Concept) Lattices," *Computational Intelligence*, 11:2, pp. 246–267, 1995.

[Ham96]   H. J. Hamilton, R. J. Hilderman, and N. Cercone. "Attribute-Oriented Induction Using Domain Generalization Graphs," *Proceedings of the Eighth IEEE International Conference on Tools with Artificial Intelligence (ICTAI'96)*, Toulouse, France, November 1996, pp. 246–253.

[Han92]   J. Han, Y. Cai, and N. Cercone. "Knowledge Discovery in Databases: An Attribute-Oriented Approach," *Proceedings of the 18th International Conference on Very Large Data Bases*, Vancouver, August 1992, pp. 547–559.

[Han93]   J. Han, Y. Cai, and N. Cercone. "Data-Driven Discovery of Quantitative Rules in Relational Databases," *IEEE Transactions on Knowledge and Data Engineering*, 5:1, February 1993, pp. 29–40.

[Han94]   J. Han. "Towards Efficient Induction Mechanisms in Database Systems," *Theoretical Computer Science*, vol. 133, October 1994, pp. 361–385.

[Hil97]   R. J. Hilderman, H. J. Hamilton, R. J. Kowalchuk, and N. Cercone. "Parallel Knowledge Discovery Using Domain Generalization Graphs," J. Komorowski and J. Zytkow (editors), *Proceedings of the First European Conference on the Principles of Data Mining and Knowledge Discovery*, Trondheim, Norway, June 1997, pp. 25–35.

[Hwa95]   H.-Y. Hwang and W.-C. Fu. "Efficient Algorithms for Attribute-Oriented Induction," *Proceedings of the First International Conference on Knowledge Discovery and Data Mining (KDD-95)*, Montreal, August 1995, pp. 168–173.

[Mic83]   R. S. Michalski. "A Theory and Methodology of Inductive Learning," R. S. Michalski, J. G. Carbonell, and T. M. Mitchell (editors), *Machine Learning: An Artificial Intelligence Approach*, pp. 83–134. Palo Alto, CA. Tioga Publishing Company, 1983.

[Mit78]   T. M. Mitchell. *Version Spaces: An Approach to Concept Learning*. Stanford, CA. Stanford University Press, 1978.

[Pan96]   W. Pang, R. J. Hilderman, H. J. Hamilton, and S.D. Goodwin. "Data Mining with Concept Generalization Graphs," *Proceedings of the Ninth Annual Florida AI Research Symposium*, Key West, FL, May 1996, pp. 390–394.

Chapter 20

An Adaptive Interface Approach for Real-Time Data Exploration

MARTIN R. STYTZ
SHEILA B. BANKS

Air Force Institute of Technology

A model large-scale database (LSDB) synthetic data environment (SDE) interface would enable the user to perform a wide variety of useful work and aid the user's visualization, exploration, and comprehension of the SDE. The interface would give the user convenient access to synthetic environment display parameters, analysis reports, conferencing and collaboration capabilities, intelligent agents, recording devices, and situation awareness aids. The interface would also allow the user to directly manipulate objects within the SDE and provide means for the user to perform manipulations using common interface mechanisms.

The current state for users within an LSDB places an unmanageable cognitive burden on the user. The user must attempt to understand the environment, extract relevant information, analyze the information, and make decisions based on the relevant information. Because of the sheer volume of the data and because relevant information is difficult to locate, human decision making necessarily suffers. Although advances in user interface design can alleviate some of this problem, the basic problem of information overload cannot be addressed simply through development of a better interface or with the use of ad hoc decision support tools.

Current SDE tools only provide motion control through the data space. However, the user has limited control to data presentation and content. The current tools only emphasize these shortfalls and the requirement to provide additional capability to help the user by locating important data, highlighting it for the user, and focusing the user on the relevant aspects of the data. This realization led us to the approach and techniques of the Symbiotic Information Reasoning and Decision Support (SIRDS) project.

Our goal is to develop a comprehensive software engineering, knowledge engineering, and knowledge acquisition methodology for symbiotic information reasoning and decision support (SIRDS). The name for the methodology is descriptive of our intent. The interface should be symbiotic; that is, work tasks should be appropriately partitioned between the computer and the user. The computer looks to the user to provide guidance and insight into the information necessary to draw complex, or high-level, inferences from the data, and to guide the data mining effort. The user, on the other hand, looks to the computer to perform data acquisition and management, perform quantitative and qualitative data analysis, perform the data mining and extend the data discovery, perform routine inference to enable decision support, and manage the data and its display. A symbiotic approach is necessary because the objective is to let the user and the computer share the task load; therefore, we use a human-centered approach to task partitioning. The information reasoning component of the interface deals with the issues related primarily to abstracting and analyzing information. The decision support aspect of the approach relates to the need to enable the user to understand the relevant data and to perform necessary analysis to allow the system to provide information highlighting and user focus of attention activities.

SIRDS requires the development of an adaptive, intelligent, learning man-machine interface. SIRDS addresses a wide range of issues, including data mining, data fusion, ambiguity resolution, representational mapping, user intent inferencing, mixed initiative dialogue, and other agent and data visualization factors that must be considered in the formation of a self-consistent, adaptive, learning interface system. Construction of the interface requires a mix of traditional human-computer interaction, data visualization, and intelligent agents within a software engineering framework. The framework supports the symbiosis of human cognition and computational power required to deal with complex data environments. Intelligent agents are a key aspect of SIRDS, and they perform information fusion, analysis, and abstraction, as well as deriving information requirements and controlling information display. These agents within SIRDS are necessarily of two different types: one type for the task of reasoning to direct system data acquisition, assessment, and information synthesis; the other for reasoning about information display. However, the same software architecture and development methodology is employed to realize both types of agents.

In addition to performing information retrieval and analysis, SIRDS uses information visualization techniques to enable the user to understand the derived information, synthesis operations, and available processing options. However, to maximize user effectiveness in an information-dense environment, SIRDS must operate in anticipation of user information needs. To do so, SIRDS must first ascertain user information requirements based on the current situation and a history of required information. SIRDS then mitigates data retrieval operations and provides focus on and analysis of the resulting relevant information.

The first step toward realizing this vision is the development of a design methodology for intelligent agents for the control of information display and for assistance in the integration and access to information. The display of information should be performed by agents of human-computer interaction and information presentation, whether the interface be a 2D or 3D representation. To be comprehensive, the methodology must address information representation and visualization by the interface agents, the software design of these agents, usability criteria for agents, and metrics for determining the necessary agents for interface control. Our initial design methodology for intelligent agents for the control of information display is based on research into decision networks that incorporate uncertainty reasoning with previous user performance and profiles to anticipate future user behavior and needs for information presentation. These networks employ a general user support profile and possess the capability to support specific users by learning information requirements and refining the general network to accommodate these specific needs. As user-specific profiles are generated, this information is used to refine the general support network. We believe this approach is scalable in breadth across all interface elements and in depth toward ever smaller units of information.

Initial development in the area of intelligent agents for information management and display is demonstrated by our Intelligent Interface Agent (IIA). IIA supports effective user intent prediction by incorporating the ability to model both the uncertainty in user intent and dynamic user behavior within its knowledge representation. To effectively predict user intent, an accurate cognitive model of the user is necessary. The problem with most cognitive models for intelligent user interfaces is that they rely on knowledge representations that lack flexibility and power in two key areas: the representation of uncertainty and dynamic user modeling. Employing a knowledge representation that correctly captures and models uncertainty in human-computer interaction can improve the modeling of the user and the user interface behavior. One representation that is ideal for representing uncertainty are Bayesian networks (BNs). Bayesian techniques have attractive properties for developing interface intelligence because they can capture uncertainty, which is required to model human intent. Bayesian techniques are also extremely useful in predicting future events.

The initial design methodology for agents is based on research in decision support and data abstraction performed while developing the Sentinel in our lab. The Sentinel ties together several disjoint data gathering systems to present a clear and consistent insight into the action within an SDE.

The Sentinel project's goal was to address the information space situation-awareness problem by providing an information consolidation and analysis capability. By providing these capabilities, each Sentinel gives the user an indication of the importance of the activity within its information space. The user is thereby relieved of having to determine the important areas of the information space from raw data. Initial assessments are based on the ratings provided by Sentinels, each Sentinel providing a consolidated assessment of the total activity within its information space.

Synthetic data environments provide a potentially revolutionary means for humans to interact with each other and with information. However, to achieve this potential, techniques that allow users to accomplish a wide variety of work and communication within a synthetic data environment must be developed. Our approach to an adaptive user interface for synthetic data environments, SIRDS, provides one means to allow users effective access to and use of the SDE and its data. SIRDS has begun to develop capabilities in a wide range of issues, including user intent inferencing, mixed initiative dialogue, data visualization, data mining, and information fusion factors that form the basis of a self-consistent, adaptive, learning interface system for synthetic data environments.

There are a multitude of issues remaining to be addressed to achieve our vision for exploration of LSDBs. However, in our view there are six issues that are of critical importance. These issues are (1) development of a user-centered joint design approach for the user interface and intelligent agents, (2) development of usability metrics for the user interface and intelligent agents, (3) determining of the semantics and semiotics to be employed to display the database and convey meaning to the user, (4) determination of user intent to enable effective support of user tasks, (5) tools to enable real-time control, guidance, and assessment of data mining operations, and (6) support for collaboration between users and intelligent agents and collaboration among LSDB SDE users.

Part III

Integrating KDD and Visualization in Exploration Environments

Chapter 21

Discovering New Relationships
*A Brief Overview of Data Mining
and Knowledge Discovery*

Philip J. Rhodes

University of New Hampshire

Introduction

In recent years, the need to extract knowledge automatically from very large databases has grown increasingly acute. In response, the closely related fields of knowledge discovery in databases (KDD) and data mining have developed processes and algorithms that attempt to intelligently extract interesting and useful information (i.e., knowledge) from vast amounts of raw data. Such techniques are used in various application domains, ranging from department stores to catalogs of stellar objects. KDD and data mining are closely related to scientific databases in that they are concerned with analyzing raw data to extract new knowledge. The principal difference between them is that scientific databases are geared toward justifying a hypothesis, which is not necessarily true for KDD. For example, Wal-Mart has one of the world's largest databases of customer transactions, with over 20 million transactions being handled per day [Bab94]. Wal-Mart just wants to know to whom they should mail their next advertising circular; they are not trying to prove a hypothesis. On the other hand, the SKICAT system, a catalog of stars and galaxies, is used by astronomers who are presumably testing new theories and hypotheses [Fay96b]. Yet, both systems rely heavily on the techniques found in KDD. Fayyad et al. [Fay96a] give an overview of the fields of data mining and KDD. Chen, Han, and Yu [Che96] have also prepared a database-oriented overview of data mining. This chapter draws from various sources to provide a brief overview of knowledge discovery and to present some important concepts from the field.

There are a number of other fields related to or overlapping with KDD. Machine learning and pattern recognition also attempt to extract patterns from data, but with much less human interaction than KDD. Machine discovery is closer to scientific databases, in that it attempts to discover empirical laws or relationships from experimental observations [Shr90]. Data warehousing refers to a technique used in MIS in which records of customer transactions are collected and processed for on-line access. On-line analytical processing (OLAP) is often used in conjunction with data warehouses to provide multidimensional summaries of transaction data.

21.1 KDD Versus Data Mining

There is potential for confusion about the distinction between KDD and data mining. Fayyad et al. [Fay96a] claim that KDD is the *process* of discovering useful knowledge within data, whereas data mining is simply the application of algorithms for extracting patterns from data. Data mining is a class of methods used by the KDD process. KDD requires that the patterns found during data mining be "valid, novel, potentially useful, and ultimately understandable." Fayyad et al. define these several terms in detail, leading toward a definition of *interestingness*:

Data ■ A set of facts F.

Pattern ■ An expression E in some language L describing facts in a subset F_E of F. E is called a pattern if it is simpler than the enumeration of all facts in F_E.

Validity ■ The certainty that a pattern is valid when applied to new data. Certainty is defined as a function $C(E, F)$ that maps a pattern E in data set F to a fully or partially ordered measurement space called M_C.

Novelty ■ Refers to whether a pattern represents new information. For example, if a pattern is just a rephrasing of existing patterns, it is not novel. Novelty can be represented as a function $N(E, F)$ that returns either a Boolean or perhaps continuous value.

Utility ■ If a pattern is useful, it can be acted upon in some way. Utility is measured by a function $U(E, F)$ that maps a pattern E in data set F to a fully or partially ordered measurement space called M_U.

Understandability ■ Patterns should be understandable by humans, but this property is difficult to measure. (Presumably, it varies according to the human.) However, Fayyad et al. suggest that the *simplicity* of a pattern is an indication of its understandability. Accordingly, they propose a simplicity function $S(E, F)$ that maps a pattern E in data set F to a fully or partially ordered measurement space called M_S.

The very important concept of *interestingness* is defined to be a combination of validity, novelty, utility, and simplicity. Some KDD systems use a value $i = I(E, F, C, N, U, S)$ as a metric of a pattern's value. Other systems implicitly define interestingness by ranking the discovered patterns in some order. In either case, the notion of interestingness ultimately requires human judgment because several of its constituent functions cannot be objectively defined. Despite its subjective nature, interestingness is important because it plays a prime role in the definition of *knowledge* proposed by Fayyad et al.:

Knowledge ■ A pattern EL is called knowledge if for some user-specified threshold $i \in M_I$, $I(E, F, C, N, U, S) > i$.

In light of these new concepts, Fayyad et al. offer the following definition:

KDD Process ■ The process of using data mining methods (algorithms) to extract (identify) what is deemed knowledge according to the specifications of measures and thresholds, using the database F along with any required pre-processing, subsampling, and transformations of F.

They also give a list of the basic steps involved in this process, emphasizing the interactive nature of KDD when compared with other, more AI-oriented, techniques such as machine learning:

1. Developing a pool of expert knowledge and end-user goals.
2. Choosing the data for which KDD is to be performed.
3. Data cleaning and pre-processing (e.g., handling noise and missing data).
4. Data reduction and projection: reducing the number of attributes to the minimum necessary to meet the end-user goals.
5. Choosing the data mining task: deciding whether the end-user goals can be met by classification, regression, clustering, and so on.

6. Choosing the data mining algorithms: selecting one or more methods to be used to implement the task chosen in step 5.

7. Data mining: searching for patterns or rules within the data. Performing steps 1 through 6 well can very positively affect the success of this step.

8. Pattern interpretation: the user examines the results of the preceding steps, and may decide to repeat them if necessary.

9. Consolidating discovered knowledge: incorporating new knowledge into the database. This includes accounting for conflicts with previously acquired knowledge.

Note that the KDD process may contain loops between any two of these steps, and may involve several iterations of any subset of this list. Most KDD research has been concerned with step 7, data mining, but Fayyad et al. are firm in their conviction that all nine steps must be carefully addressed for KDD to succeed in practice.

21.2 Data Mining

Data mining involves fitting models to, or determining patterns from, observed data. A *pattern* is an instantiation of a model. In other words, a pattern can be viewed as a sort of template for a model. For example, the expression $y = 3x + 5$ might be a pattern fitting the model $y = Ax + B$. Fayyad et al. [Fay96a] give a definition of data mining:

Data Mining ■ A step in the KDD process consisting of particular data mining algorithms that, under some acceptable computational efficiency limitations, produces a particular enumeration of patterns E_j over F.

There are two types of models commonly used. A statistical model allows for some nondeterminism in the data (i.e., it allows a little "slack"). So, for the model $y = Ax + B$, a statistical model might say that B is a random variable, with stated mean and standard deviation. In contrast, the logical approach to model specification allows no such uncertainty. However, notice that in either case the language used to express a model may contain relational operators such as < and >, allowing greater flexibility in fitting models to data. The flexibility of the statistical approach should be very helpful in dealing with error. For example, error introduced by measuring instruments or a data representation could be modeled as a random variable so that an appropriate pattern can still be found.

21.2.1 Goals of Data Mining

The primary goals of data mining are to describe the existing data and to predict the behavior or characteristics of future data of the same type. Description entails finding patterns within the data that are human understandable. For example, in a bank loan data set, a clearly understandable pattern might be: "If an individual's income is less than $20,000, they will default on the loan." The goal of prediction can be met by discovering patterns with a high degree of certainty, as measured by the function $c = C(E, F)$. If existing data matches the pattern with few exceptions, it is more likely that future data will also behave in the same manner. Fayyad et al. [Fay96a] provide a list of the tasks used to meet the primary goals listed previously.

Classification ■ The process of assigning categories to features or trends within the data. Identification of interesting features within the data is a form of classification.

Regression ■ The development of a function that approximates the mathematical relationship between two numerical attributes. For example, regression could be used to determine the relationship between the infrared reflectivity of a forest from satellite images to the percentage of deciduous trees.

Clustering ■ Tool attempting to discern groupings within data. For example, in a financial database, we might notice that various groups of stocks tend to behave similarly. We might divide securities into three groups, depending on which group they most closely resemble. Notice that clustering is not the same as classification, where categories are usually defined by the investigator. Clustering attempts to extract categories from the data itself.

Summarization ■ The process of finding a compact representation for data. This may include simple statistics, such as mean and standard deviation, or may employ more complex methods, such as regression. Summarization often plays an important role in the visualization and interactive exploration of a data set.

Dependency modeling ■ The process of modeling dependencies between variables. The model may consist of a graph $G = (V, E)$ in which each node represents a variable, and each edge represents a dependency. The edges may be weighted to represent the strength of the dependency.

Change and deviation detection ■ A process of looking for significant changes in the data from previous values, or looking for data that falls outside some normal range.

We should point out that several of these processes are important in scientific databases. Classification is closely related to feature identification, an important tool in GIS and other scientific systems. Clustering and regression both have clear scientific applications, and summarization is one of the goals of multiresolution data sets. Of course, finding relationships through processes such as dependency modeling is an important part of exploratory scientific data analysis.

21.2.2 Components of Data Mining Algorithms

Fayyad et al. [Fay96a] give three components for any data mining algorithm: model representation, model evaluation, and search. The authors do not claim that this division is perfect, but rather offer it as a convenient way of understanding the basic components of data mining algorithms.

A model is represented in some language L used to describe potential patterns. If this language is too limited, no amount of training data or processing will produce an accurate model for the data. For example, consider a model consisting only of rules such as "if $A.x > n$ then Q," where Q is some claim about the data. Such rules can only model patterns that consist of a threshold value along a dimension; in this case, the X axis. If the dividing line between Q and not Q were $y = x$, this model would be unable to express this relationship.

The danger in making a model language too expressive and powerful is that the training data may be *overfitted*. This means that the model parameters are too specifically tailored to the training example, so that new data fits the model poorly. If the model is not too expressive, it defines a somewhat loose fit, making this problem much less severe.

Model evaluation measures how well a pattern, consisting of a model and its parameters, meets the requirements of the KDD process. Because validity is a metric of how well a pattern will match (and therefore predict) future data, it is an important evaluation criterion. The descriptive power of the model must also be evaluated, using a combination of certainty, novelty, utility, and understandability, among others.

Search methods can be broken into two levels. *Model search* looks for the model that best fits the data. Once a model has been chosen, *parameter search* looks for the model parameter values that provide the best fit for the data. Essentially, the model search process iterates over models and then invokes the parameter search process for each model. Because the space of possible models and parameters is infinite, exhaustive search is not possible. Therefore, various heuristics must be used.

21.2.3 Data Mining Methods

Based on Fayyad et al. [Fay96a], we now describe a loose taxonomy of data mining methods. In addition, the last two sections provide a more detailed account of two important data mining algorithms, C4.5 and self-organizing maps.

Data Mining Families

Perhaps the simplest data mining method uses decision trees and rules with single variable splits. Each rule is of the form "if $A.x > n$ then Q," where x is an attribute of the data and Q is some statement about the data. Such rules divide the data domain into two parts using a plane parallel to an axis. This method is easily understood by humans, but is rather limited in power. An example of this approach is shown in Figure 21.1(a). A rule for accepting or rejecting students applying to a university is based on whether previous students with similar SAT scores and GPAs were able to graduate. Extending the model, as in Figure 21.1(b), to allow planes of arbitrary orientation increases the expressive power at the expense of understandability. The question of how to build effective decision trees is not a trivial one. The section "The C4.5 Algorithm," which follows, addresses this issue in some detail within the context of the C4.5 algorithm.

There is a family of nonlinear methods that attempts to match the data using linear and nonlinear combinations of a set of basis functions. This allows distinctions to be made that do not fall along straight lines. For example, a classification of the data into two or more groups might be done using a spline or other polynomial that describes an elaborate curve through the data domain. Also in this family are feed-forward neural network methods, which use neural networks to select the parameters of the model, which could be the coefficients for a spline. An example is shown in Figure 21.2.

Figure 21.1

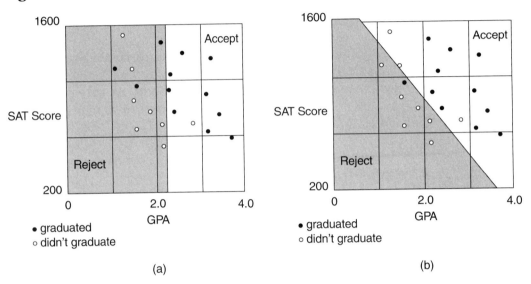

Two rule-based approaches: (a) plane parallel to an axis, and (b) plane of arbitrary orientation.

Figure 21.2

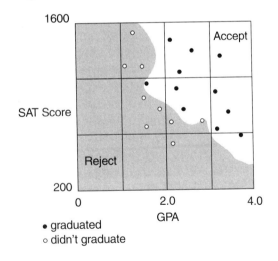

A spline-based approach.

Example-based methods are fairly simple in concept. The idea is to use existing data points to help classify and predict the properties of new data. That is, the properties of a new data point are taken to be the same as the properties of its nearest neighbor in the existing data set. Finding the nearest neighbor requires the existence of a distance measure, which is not always easy with nominal or categorical data.

Probabilistic graphical dependency models use a graph structure to represent the probability of a dependency between any two variates. The method arose out of AI work with expert systems in which experts set the probabilities according to their knowledge of the field. KDD researchers have focused on extracting values for these probabilities directly from the data during the model search process. Although this work is still experimental, its graphical structure should allow for clear visualization and understandability.

Relational learning models use first-order logic instead of the propositional logic of decision trees. Because first-order logic (e.g., Horn clauses) is more expressive, relational learning models are able to succeed in situations in which decision trees fail. For example, we have seen that a relation such as $y = x$ can cause trouble for decision trees, but it is easily handled by relational learning models. On the other hand, such models incur a considerable cost during search, and it can be difficult for humans to specify effective models. Shen et al. [She96] describe a system that automatically develops models (they use the term *metapatterns*), without requiring the user to specify whether particular data items are positive or negative examples of the pattern.

Self-organizing maps, originally developed by Teuvo Kohonen [Koh97], are another neural net–based data mining technique, but they do not set the parameters for a model as feed-forward neural nets do. Instead, they find clusters in the data by grouping similar items closely on a grid of neurons. For a bibliography of papers on self-organizing maps, see [Kas98]. The next section describes an application of self-organizing maps for very large databases of documents.

Self-Organizing Maps

The self-organizing map forms the basis for a variety of neural network recognition algorithms. As a data mining method, it is useful as a tool for classification and especially clustering, because it does not require predefined categories. The self-organizing map is described in [Kas97, Koh97].

Self-organizing maps consist of a grid of neural elements, each containing a vector m_i. The map is trained by presenting a series of new data vectors to the map, allowing neurons to change their m vector in response to the new information. Specifically, when a data vector x is presented, the neuron with an m value closest to x is located in the grid. This winning neuron's m value is adjusted to reflect the new data. In addition, the neurons in the neighborhood of this winning neuron also have their m values adjusted by an amount that decreases with distance from the winner. It is this training of neighboring neurons that gives the map its "self-organizing" property. After the map has been trained, neurons close together in the grid will have similar m vectors. Any data that belongs to a cluster will therefore appear in some neighborhood of the grid.

Kohenen [Koh97] describes a system for exploring very large databases of text documents called WEBSOM. The system employs self-organizing maps to locate documents that most closely satisfy a document query. Unlike traditional queries, which use methods such as keywords or bibliographic information, WEBSOM allows the user to write a short description of the type of document she is looking for.

The WEBSOM system actually consists of two separate self-organizing maps. We call the first map the *fingerprint map*, because it is used to produce a fingerprint (i.e., description) of the words in a document and how they are related. First, any articles (a, an, the) are discarded, as well as words that occur very infrequently. Next, the text is broken up into overlapping triplets of consecutive words, and each triplet is fed into the fingerprint map. When this process is complete, the vectors in each neuron serve as a fingerprint or histogram of the document. An important property of this approach is that triplets containing semantically similar words will map to nearby areas of the map because they tend to appear in similar triplets. This means that even if a query does not use exactly the same terms a document uses to describe a concept, the system can still properly retrieve the relevant document.

Once the fingerprint of a document has been generated by the first map, it is given as training data to the second map, which we call the *document map*. That is, the data vector x given to the document map describes the entire content of the fingerprint map. This process is repeated for each document in the database, after which the document map contains the accumulated fingerprints of all documents.

The user can then write a short description of the type of document he is looking for. A fingerprint of the description is then produced in the manner described previously. The document map is then searched to find the set of documents that most closely matches the query.

The C4.5 Algorithm

C4.5 [Qui93, Qui96] is a rule-based technique for classification of data. It uses a decision tree with tests X_i at each of the interior nodes, where each X_i

Table 21.1

A simple classification example.

Case	Outlook	Temp (F)	Humidity (%)	Windy?	Class
1	Sunny	75	70	True	Play
2	Sunny	80	90	True	Don't play
3	Sunny	85	85	False	Don't play
4	Sunny	72	95	False	Don't play
5	Sunny	69	70	False	Play
6	Overcast	72	90	True	Play
7	Overcast	83	78	False	Play
8	Overcast	64	65	True	Play
9	Overcast	81	75	False	Play
10	Rain	71	80	True	Don't play
11	Rain	65	70	True	Don't play
12	Rain	75	80	False	Play
13	Rain	68	80	False	Play
14	Rain	70	96	False	Play

has two or more outcomes. Before classification can begin, the decision tree must be constructed. We start with a set C of classes, and a set D of cases (i.e., samples) that have already been classified. That is, for each member of D, we already know to which class in C it belongs. The following recursive algorithm will construct the decision tree for a set of cases D [Qui96]:

1. If D satisfies a stopping criterion, the tree for D will contain only a single node. This node will be identified with the class most prevalent in D. An obvious stopping criterion is when all members of D belong to the same class, but this is not the only possibility. We may also stop when no test yields a non-zero information gain, described in the following.

2. A test X with outcomes $T_1, T_2, \ldots, T_k$ is applied to D that partitions D into disjoint sets $D_1, D_2, \ldots, D_k$, associated with each outcome. The tree for D will consist of the test X at its root, with a subtree for each T_i formed by applying the algorithm recursively on each D_i.

To illustrate the algorithm, Table 21.1 shows an example taken from [Qui93]. Each case consists of four weather attributes and belongs to one of two classes, shown in the last column. Using this table as training data, we

Figure 21.3

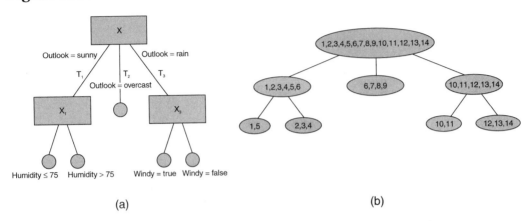

(a)   (b)

(a) A decision tree for the data in Table 21.1, and (b) the resulting partition of the data into subsets of a single class.

construct the simple decision tree shown in Figure 21.3(a). Suppose that the first test of a decision tree divides the data according to *outlook*, the first attribute. The result will be three sets, where the middle set is all of class *play* but the other two are still mixed. We can divide the first subset with a test with outcomes *humidity_75* and *humidity > 75*, giving sets each of a single class. We can finish the tree by testing the third set on the attribute *windy*, giving two sets of uniform class. In addition to the decision tree, Figure 21.3(b) shows another tree demonstrating how the original set of cases is divided through the three tests into subsets consisting of cases that are all of the same class.

It should be clear that the previously cited algorithm eventually generates a tree with each leaf corresponding to a subset of a single class, as long as each test *X* performs some non-trivial partition of its input set. Smaller trees are more understandable, and tend to give better results. To minimize the size of the decision tree, Quinlan uses a *gain ratio* criterion to decide which tests should be employed. Based on information theory, this criterion is the ratio between information gain and split information [Qui93]:

$$gain\ ratio\ =\ \frac{information\ gain}{split\ information}$$

Intuitively, after a test is performed, the input set *D* should be partitioned into several D_i that are somewhat less "mixed up" with regard to class. Information gain measures how much more we know about what class the cases in the D_i belong to. This measure is trivially maximal when there is one case in each D_i, because this guarantees that each partition contains cases of the same class. In [Qui86], the author describes a decision tree method predating C4.5 that uses only information gain to evaluate tests. To minimize the decision tree, however, it is much more desirable to divide D into fewer partitions while still maximizing the information gain. Split information measures how much information was added by partitioning D into the several D_i. Such information is essentially a cost, rather than a benefit. The motivation for gain ratio should now be clear: we want to choose tests that give us a larger gain in information and a smaller splitting cost.

Once the tree has been constructed, it may be pruned to replace less useful subtrees with leaf nodes. Such subtrees may be the result of noisy or erroneous training data, and will therefore not contribute to the performance of the decision tree. After construction and pruning, the decision tree is ready to be used in the classification of new data.

21.3 Summary

We have outlined the KDD process and the goals, methods, and algorithms of data mining. KDD is the process of discovering useful knowledge within data, and consists of a series of steps that includes data mining. Compared to related fields, such as machine learning, the KDD process is much more interactive. It requires the user to define clear goals and make decisions about the data and data mining algorithms to be used, and then interpret newly discovered knowledge.

Data mining methods are used to meet a variety of goals, including classification, regression, clustering, and dependency modeling, among others. The large selection of data mining techniques can be divided into several families that are well suited to meeting one or more of these goals. Decision trees, example-based methods, and relational learning models are often used for data classification. In contrast, probabilistic graphical dependency models are used for modeling dependencies between variates. Self-organizing maps are a powerful technique for clustering data into categories that are not known beforehand. This chapter concluded with an examination of the C4.5 and self-organizing map algorithms, giving a more detailed treatment to these two important data mining methods.

References

[Bab94]   C. Babcock. "Parallel Processing Mines Retail Data," *Computer World,* 1994.

[Che96]   M.-S. Chen, J. Han, and P. S. Yu. "Data Mining: An Overview from a Database Perspective," *IEEE Transactions on Knowledge and Data Engineering,* 8:6, IEEE, Los Alamitos, CA, 1996.

[Fay96a]   U. M. Fayyad, G. Piatetsky-Shapiro, and P. Smyth. "From Data Mining to Knowledge Discovery: An Overview," *Advances in Knowledge Discovery and Data Mining.* Menlo Park, CA. AAAI Press/MIT Press, 1996.

[Fay96b]   U. M. Fayyad, S. G. Djorgovski, and N. Weir. "Automating the Analysis and Cataloging of Sky Surveys," *Advances in Knowledge Discovery and Data Mining.* Menlo Park, CA. AAAI Press/MIT Press, 1996.

[Kas97]   S. Kaski. "Data Exploration Using Self-Organizing Maps," *Acta Polytechnica Scandinavica: Mathematics, Computing and Management in Engineering Series No. 82,* Helsinki University of Technology, Finland, 1997.

[Kas98]   S. Kaski, J. Kangas, and T. Kohonen. "Bibliography of Self-Organizing Maps," *Neural Computing Surveys,* 1998.

[Koh97]   T. Kohonen. "Exploration of Very Large Databases by Self-Organizing Maps," *Proceedings of ICNN'97, International Conference on Neural Networks,* IEEE Service Center, Piscataway, NJ, 1997.

[Qui86]   J. R. Quinlan. "Induction of Decision Trees," *Machine Learning, vol. 1,* 1986.

[Qui93]   J. R. Quinlan. *C4.5: Programs for Machine Learning.* San Francisco. Morgan Kaufmann, 1993.

[Qui96]   J. R. Quinlan. "Improved Use of Continuous Attributes in C4.5," *Journal of Artificial Intelligence Research.* San Francisco. Morgan Kaufmann, 1996.

[She96]   W.-M. Shen and B. Leng. "A Metapattern-Based Automated Discovery Loop for Integrated Data Mining: Unsupervised Learning of Relational Patterns," *IEEE Transactions on Knowledge and Data Engineering,* 8:6, IEEE Computer Society Press, Los Alamitos, CA, 1996.

[Shr90]   J. Shrager and P. Langley (editors). *Computational Models of Scientific Discovery and Theory Formation.* San Francisco. Morgan Kaufmann, 1990.

Chapter 22

A Taxonomy for Integrating Data Mining and Data Visualization

THOMAS H. HINKE
TIMOTHY S. NEWMAN

*Information Technology & Systems Laboratory
and University of Alabama, Huntsville*

Introduction

This chapter presents a visualization taxonomy that can be used to characterize the integration of data visualization and data mining. Examples from current research exploring data mining of remotely sensed satellite data are discussed.

The focus of our research is the application of data mining to large scientific archives, such as those being developed for NASA's Earth Observing System Data and Information System (EOSDIS). An initial focus of our work has been on the development of techniques and an associated system called AdaM (algorithm development and mining) to mine remotely sensed satellite data for phenomena of interest, such as mesoscale convective systems (large storms). We have used these mining results in a Web-based coincidence search engine called Eureka, which will permit scientists to identify the dates when a phenomenon, such as a mesoscale convective system, is coincident with regions of interest, such as the Amazon River basin in Brazil [Hin97a]. Using the resulting dates, the user can request data for the desired date(s) and region from one of the EOSDIS archives, with the assurance that it represents data that was captured when the desired phenomenon/region coincidence occurred.

In this initial application, mined phenomena were first presented as arrays of numbers and as images. These arrays and images can be visualized using a number of tools, or overlaid with geographical boundaries and ingested into the Eureka system, where the users of Eureka can view them for the days that show the desired coincidence.

One of the significant constraints of this mining application is the large time delay (minutes) required to retrieve the archived data from secondary storage, uncompress it, and then mine it. Hence, it is not conducive to a fast, interactive, user-involved visualization system. This problem is addressed to some extent in a paper presented at the KDD'97 conference [Hin97b], in which deviation and trend data is extracted from the archived data and stored on secondary storage, where it can be rapidly searched and visualized. We have shown that if approximately 2% of the data is extracted, approximately 92% of the mesoscale convective systems detectable in the original data can still be detected in the extracted data. Although this is a step in the right direction, additional compression will have to be achieved if deviation and trend data is to be extracted for a system such as EOSDIS, which has a projected growth rate of one terabyte of data per day [Ger93].

Our current research is focused on using AdaM for interactive data exploration at NASA's Global Hydrology and Climate Center (GHCC), where it will be used to perform mining on newly produced data buffered for a limited period on secondary storage. Interested parties can easily download this data from the anonymous FTP server of the GHCC. The availability of this data on fast-access secondary storage provides an opportunity for us to explore the applicability of interactive data mining without the large access time experienced to retrieve archived data from tertiary storage.

As we move into this second data mining application, we have focused on how to integrate data visualization into data mining. To provide a framework for analyzing this problem, we have developed the data mining/data visualization taxonomy described in the following section.

22.1 Taxonomy

This taxonomy is oriented around the axes of roles and architecture. Each of these is briefly described in the following sections.

22.1.1 Role

The role axis is concerned with how the visualization system empowers the user to participate in the mining process. The two roles are passive and active.

Passive Role

Under the passive role, the user is provided with a view into the mining process, but this view is not vital to the mining effort. For example, in our mining work, we create an image of mined phenomena overlaid with geographical boundaries. This provides a useful way for the user to view the results, but it is not used to significantly influence the mining, except during debug, where faulty results can be used to detect problems.

Active Role

Under the active role, the visualization system furnishes a view into the mining process that provides the user with information necessary to make decisions that affect the data mining process itself. Under this approach, having an adequate visualization approach is critical to the success of data mining.

An example of this type of role can be found in our trend mining [Hin97b]. For this mining, we overlay Earth with a grid of equal-degree bins and then for each bin calculate a month-to-month trend line that indicates the normal trend in values for each bin. Deviation data that potentially contains phenomena are data values that differ from these trend lines by some predetermined amount.

To mine the trend data, we create a 3D histogram, using the slope of the trend line as one dimension, the y intercept of the trend line as the second, and the count of the number of bins that have this particular slope and intercept as the third dimension. In our work with SSM/I (Special Sensor Microware/Imager) data, we discovered a very dominant mode for this data. The user could select this dominant mode, and then the data that contributed to this dominant mode would be retrieved and visualized. The resulting bins were generally over the oceans near the equator. In this particular case, the visualization was part of the mining effort, and thus placed the user in a critical decision-making position in performing the mining.

There is a very fuzzy line between a passive-role system and an active-role system, in that what begins as a passive-role system can begin to look like an active-role system as the user takes actions to change the nature of the mining based on what the user sees in initial mining results. An active-role system facilitates this change, whereas a passive-role system does not.

22.1.2 Architecture

There are three facets to the architecture portion of our taxonomy. These are cycles, realization approach, and seamlessness. Each of these is discussed in the following sections.

Cycles

When visualization is integrated with data mining, data mining furthers the visualization. This combination of a data mining phase followed by a visualization phase forms a cycle. In our taxonomy, a data mining system can consist of a single cycle or multiple cycles. In a single-cycle system, the data is mined and the results are visualized. An example of this is our current mesoscale-phenomena mining approach with AdaM, in which the results of the mining are transformed into images and viewed.

In a multicycle architecture, multiple mining/visualization cycles can be used. In this way, visualization can be applied to intermediate results and then additional mining operations performed.

Realization

There are three generic approaches for realizing an integrated data mining and data visualization architecture: visualization as a component of the mining system, the miner as a component of the visualization system, or a homogeneous mining/visualization system. Each of these is described in the following.

Visualization as Component of Mining System

Under this approach, a visualization module (i.e., a visualization tool) would be inserted at various stages of the data mining process. For example, our AdaM data miner is designed to support a pipeline of mining operators, selected from a repertoire of available or newly created operators. A mining plan can be interactively designed through a Java interface to indicate the mining operators and their order and plan-specific parameterization for each mining plan. The available operators can be roughly divided into data readers, data manipulators, and data writers. Several data readers and writers are available to read and write data in a number of formats. Numerous data manipulator operators are available to provide desired functionality; examples include transforming the data, detecting various phenomena, or subsetting the data. New operators can easily be added to AdaM's C++ based, extensible, object-oriented architecture.

Currently, we have data writers that write data in common formats that can be interpreted by many viewers. The data is written to a file, where a viewer or a visualization system can then access it. Under this approach, the visualization is at the end of the pipeline and the user need not be present as the files are written. At her leisure, the user can invoke desired visualization modules and view the files produced by the data mining system. This is an example of a single-cycle system.

We are also currently loading polygons representing mined phenomena into our Eureka system, along with low-resolution GIF images of the data that has been mined. Using the Eureka system, the user can find date(s) where the desired coincidence occurred and then view the image for that date. The user can also find river basins that have a high incidence of mesoscale convective system activity. This is another example of a single-cycle system, in that visualization comes only at the end of the cycle.

Another approach we have considered is to create a visualization module that can be inserted at one or more arbitrary points in the mining pipeline. Under this approach, the user would be able to view intermediate as well as final results. Because the data miner could perform its mining over an extended period, there would need to be a means of queuing these intermediate results such that the user would not have to be present during the entire mining period. This would be an example of a multicycle system.

Miner as Component of Visualization System

In this approach, the mining system would be included as a module of a visualization system. For example, in interactive visualization environments such as AVS or Khoros, users construct perceptually meaningful displays by choosing appropriate tools from a toolbox of functions. The tools are linked to form a data flow network in which data flows from function to function in a pipeline. We have employed the methodology of a pipeline of visualization functions to extract and render anatomical structures of interest from tomographic data [New96, Tan97]. If a data mining module or modules are available within a visualization environment, the data miner block(s) would be included within a visualization network. For example, you could envision that a data mining block could provide a gross-level data select feature, and downstream visualization modules could be used by the user in a passive or active mode to select part or all of the initially selected data for visualization.

For applications in which the data discovery process requires active re-combination of visualization components, the rich selection of ready-made visualization tools provided by an interactive visualization environment (or perhaps even visualization tools offered by a slightly less integrated and less visual toolkit of visualization functions) seems particularly useful.

Most environments that allow the incorporation of new functionality, such as mining modules, could also accommodate active cycling of mining and visualization. For example, the user could re-initiate mining with new parameters, based on the results of preliminary visualizations that result from an initial mining operation. This would provide another example of a multicycle system.

Homogeneous Mining and Visualization

The first two architectures we have described represent first-stage architectures for integrating data mining and visualization. These are attractive architectures to use in developing a prototype system to investigate the integration of data mining and data visualization technology. Once the issues inherent in this integration are well understood, this knowledge will provide the basis for designing a homogeneous mining and visualization system. Rather than starting with a mining or visualization system, the designers would start with the goal of an integrated system.

Seamlessness

In a truly seamless system, the user will be able to move effortlessly from mining to visualization and back. It would be expected that one of the goals of the homogeneous system would be to develop a seamless system in which the application of mining and visualization techniques would be naturally integrated in a seamless manner. It is also anticipated that the two other realization approaches would not have a particularly seamless architecture, because they would be merging to very different systems.

22.2 Conclusion

We have found the taxonomy described here to be useful as we contemplate the increased utilization and integration of data visualization into our data mining process. Our objective is to provide a means for the data visualization system to move from a passive to a more active role.

Acknowledgments

This chapter describes work from our ongoing phenomena-oriented data mining project supported under a NASA grant. The AdaM and Eureka systems described in this chapter are the work of the following members of the Information Technology & Systems Laboratory and/or the Universtiy of Alabama, Huntsville, Computer Science Department: Dr. Sara Graves, Dr. Heggere Ranganath, Mr. John Rushing, Ms. Shalini Kansal, and Mr. Evans Criswell.

References

[Ger93]   N. D. Gershon and C. G. Miller. "Special Report: Environment, Part 2: Dealing with the Data Deluge," *IEEE Spectrum*, July 1993.

[Hin97a] T. H. Hinke, J. Rushing, S. Kansal, and S. J. Graves. "Eureka Phenomena Discovery and Phenomena Mining System," *Proceedings of the 13th International Conference on Interactive Information and Processing Systems (IIPS) for Meteorology, Oceanography, and Hydrology*, February 1997.

[Hin97b] T. H. Hinke, J. Rushing, H. Ranganath, and S. J. Graves. "Target-Independent Mining for Scientific Data," *Proceedings of the Third International Conference of Knowledge Discovery and Data Mining*, August 1997.

[New96]   T. Newman, N. Tang, S. Bacharach, and P. Choyke. "A Volumetric Segmentation Technique for Diagnosis and Surgical Planning in Lower Torso CT Images," *Proceedings of the International Conference on Pattern Recognition*, August 1996.

[Tan97]   N. Tang and T. Newman. "High Performance Medical Visualization Tools in Kidney Assessment," *Proceedings of the Medical Imaging '97: Image Display*, February 1997.

Chapter 23

Integrating Data Mining and Visualization Processes

NANCY GRADY

Oak Ridge National Laboratory

LORETTA AUVIL

National Center for Supercomputer Applications

ALLAN BECK

Gentia Software

PETER R. BONO

Peter R. Bono Associates, Inc.

CLAUDIO J. MENESES

University of Massachusetts, Lowell

Introduction

This chapter discusses research issues and requirements for the overall process of data exploration to be under the control of end users. The creation of standards for data structures and of taxonomies for mining algorithms and visual representations would allow users to interchange data between the methods and visualizations of their choice. The creation of personalized "problem-solving environments" would thus give end users sophisticated yet user-friendly data mining capabilities.

23.1 Background

Integration of expertise between two different disciplines is a difficult process of communication and reeducation. Integrating data mining and visualization is particularly complex because each of these fields in itself must draw on a wide range of research experience. Data mining is the blending of the artificial intelligence, statistics, and mathematics fields. Information visualization draws from scientific visualization, human-computer interaction, and algorithm animation experience.

As a research field, data mining and visualization can draw on the years of development in these disciplines to investigate exciting issues relating to the user interface. Most data mining activities, however, are driven by application needs, the structure of the data needing to be explored, the amount of data needing to be considered, and the depth to which the data needs to be drilled. Organizations around the world are realizing that there is tremendous value in the legacy data generated within their daily activities. There is great demand for sophisticated end-user tools to address a widespread operational need.

For practical utility, end users need a problem-solving environment geared toward the manipulation and display of large data sets. Data mining applications have traditionally been developed as separate systems, with the data storage, retrieval, filtering, mining, and visual presentation residing within completely independent application environments. When the applications are within the commercial sector, there is a further complication in that individual components are often proprietary and thus not open for examination. Although elements of a given application may be useful for the problem at hand, no one technique will contain all of the approaches that could provide value for understanding a given data set. The user is typically left to select one programming system for a given step and to manually translate the data into a format useful for the next step. Sophisticated visualizations of the data are often an external action requiring additional manual manipulation to prepare the data for presentation within a separate visualization package.

23.2 Modular Problem-Solving Environment

The next generation of data exploration tools will need to work in a complete problem-solving environment in which data objects can be easily passed from one method to another at the user's direction. This would allow for testing of individual components in the mining process and for visualization of the data or method. To understand the actions of a mining tool, users need to have interactive control and visual presentation at each step in the process.

The individual steps in the knowledge data discovery (KDD) process have been outlined [Fay96] to understand the nature of the activities. Typically, visualization is considered primarily for the final interpretation step. What has not been emphasized is that users need access to direct visual representation for each task. Typical tasks needing visual representation include:

Raw data overview ■ Visual representation of size and complexity of the data

Metadata from tests ■ Results of initial data exploration to understand the range of the data or the correlations among attributes

Data cleaning ■ View of records/attributes requiring attention with easy interaction for their processing

Data reduction ■ Determination of how the dimensionality of the data can be lowered

Sampling ■ Display of data samples within the larger population, including views of each dimensionality or of higher-dimensional representations

Filtering/selection ■ View of records selected as important for the problem at hand

Transformation/normalization ■ Shows how the values are manipulated

Mapping/derivation ■ Distribution of additional attributes calculated from raw data

Mining algorithm ■ Exposure of manipulation of the data or the behavior of the parameters of the method

Arrangement/sorting/ordering of classifications ■ User control over views

Summarization (including granularity) ■ Visual representation of important conclusions

Within each of these tasks, users need both a suite of visual representation paradigms and interaction capability. (See, for example, box 15.2 in Shneiderman [Shn98], which lists data types and tasks from a visualization perspective.) The interactions listed by Shneiderman include overview, zoom, filter, details on demand, relationships, history of actions, and extraction of sub-collections. Each of these interaction tasks would be useful for understanding the data and the method(s) within each of the KDD tasks previously listed.

For each of these mining steps, the end user also needs to be able to view the actions of the method being used, through two separate visualization scenarios. The first views are of the data object, with views appropriate for the structure of the data and for the size of the data set. A suggested set of scaled representations would be needed as the quantity of data increased. The second set of visual representations would concern the methods themselves, including algorithm behavior and data subsetting. For example, in a clustering algorithm the user may want to watch the progress of the algorithm, how many records are falling into each group, or the most important variables on which the clustering is being based. This would provide greater understanding of the behavior of the technique and of the character of the data. The developer would be required to instrument his program to provide external access to this information so that it could be available for visualization.

23.3 Research Requirements

We see a number of requirements to be addressed by data mining systems to increase their usefulness to end users, particularly through visualization, and to allow the field to develop more rapidly from an applications viewpoint. We need to better understand the relationship between objects and rendering. By developing a taxonomy of visual paradigms and by understanding their utility for different data structures and data set sizes, we can better present to end users a range of choices for exploring their data.

We need to develop some standards for modularity. This would begin with guidelines for developers into the common general data structures needed for different mining algorithms. We need descriptions of the variables to be publicly accessible within a method to allow for understanding the performance of the method. This is needed to separate, for example, sampling patterns from optimization performance.

We also need methods to connect the algorithms with user interface operations for steering the method through data selection or for dynamic data selection. All programs should follow guidelines for the most useful user interactions, such as visual data selection, sliders for querying, and lists to choose from.

Data exploration systems should have control of the persistent state of the mining operation. This includes synchronization of cursors or regions and of highlighted data selections between differing visual representations. Finally, we should have session management through an overall environment that would capture the user interaction through scripts or logs.

23.4 Conclusions

From an end-user perspective, individual components needed for data mining are beginning to reach a good state of maturity. User interaction requirements for effective visualizations are also well understood. Some exciting data mining applications are beginning to appear that provide for the integration of selected methods and visual representations. What is greatly needed is the ability to understand the performance of the methods used in data mining and of interactive visual representations of the data and methods at each stage of the overall process. Through the development of standards for data representations and an understanding of taxonomies of visual rendering paradigms, we could approach a "mix-and-match" environment in which users could work with the best individual algorithms and visualizations for their data needs. In this environment, users could further obtain good feedback on the performance of tools they have chosen without having to understand such tools' internals. We feel the development of this type of general problem-solving environment would enable tremendous growth within the interdisciplinary field of data mining and visualization.

References

[Fay96] U. M. Fayyad, G. Piatetsky-Shapiro, and P. Smyth. "From Data Mining to Knowledge Discovery: An Overview," *Advances in Knowledge Discovery and Data Mining*. U. M. Fayyad, G. Piatetsky-Shapiro, P. Smyth, and R. Uthurusamy (editors), pp. 1–34. Cambridge, MA. AAAI Press/MIT Press, 1996.

[Shn98] B. Shneiderman. *Designing the User Interface: Strategies for Effective Human-Computer Interaction*. Reading, MA. Addison-Wesley Longman, 1998.

Chapter 24

Multidimensional Education
Visual and Algorithmic Data Mining Domains and Symbiosis

Ted W. Mihalisin

Temple University and
Mihalisin Associates, Inc.

24.1 Education: The Need

It is our view that the data mining community must strive to educate the business world concerning the nature of multidimensional data and the analysis thereof. Perpetuating the myth that data mining is "automatic" and provides information an untrained person can utilize as the basis for making important business decisions is not in the best interest of the field. A related myth is being propagated by some OLAP vendors, who would have corporations believe that fast, ad hoc queries by hundreds or even thousands of analysts, managers, and even sales representatives untrained in even low-dimensional rudimentary statistics can solve all of their problems, when in fact it may create more than it solves. In both cases, the motivation is clear. Corporations are enamored with flattening their organizational charts and distributing decision making—it's the "in" thing. They want the complex to be simple. In addition, they do not want training expenses (let alone, educational expenses) if they can avoid them. The temptation is clear, in that business wisdom dictates that vendors must give the customer what he wants, even if it is impossible.

24.2 Education via Visualization

We believe that the nested hierarchical visualization method covered by U.S. Patent No. 5,228,119 provides a means of educating people as to the nature of multidimensional data and its analysis. Business analysts with little or no statistical training are not the only ones in need of this education. Our experience is that a large fraction of Ph.D. statisticians do not understand the limitations of a variety of conventional multivariate statistical methods. This lack of understanding arises in large measure because people simply do not comprehend the richness of all possible data sets in a high-dimensional space, nor do they understand the combinatorial complexity involved when grouping variable values, or when aggregating over subsets of variables.

24.3 Data: Information Domains and Scalability

Using the tabular rows and columns language for a data set—with each row being a record corresponding to a uniquely defined entity or event, and each column being a variable—data sets can be "massive" because they contain many rows (narrow field), or many columns (wide field), or both. In many instances, transformations between narrow-field and wide-field formats can be made with a corresponding change of the meaning of a record (the entity). A massive data set is not necessarily complex. Complexity is determined by both the number of variables and (if discrete) the number of values for each. A perfectly scalable analysis engine would (after a pre-process) have a performance that would be independent of the number of records, the number of variables, and the number of values for these variables. To the best of our knowledge, no such engine exists. However, a fully recursive analysis engine that is scalable in respect to the number of records does exist, and is utilized by our visualization system. The logical way to define data information domains is in terms of a concatenation of the data specification just alluded to and the type of information you seek.

24.4 When to Use Visual Mining

We believe that when the number of multidimensional cells is on the order of 1 million or less (i.e., the product of the number of values for each included dimension is less than 1 million), our visualization method should be utilized, in that it is robust and fast and provides all results in context. Moreover, it is capable of virtually all types of information discovery. However, because a variable must have at least two values, and $2^{20} \sim 10^6$, we are limited to at most 20 dimensions. Of course, many variables may have more than two values.

24.5 When to Use Algorithmic Mining

When the number of multidimensional cells exceeds a million, algorithmic approaches are appropriate. This may occur because there are far more than 20 variables, or variables with a large number of values, or both. It should be noted that there is a great deal of confusion concerning the number of variables, number of dimensions, and number of measures. This confusion arises because of the possibility of wide-field/narrow-field transformations and their altering of the record entity.

24.6 Visual/Algorithmic Symbiosis and Type I Errors

When the algorithmic approaches are appropriate, visualization may be useful (1) at the outset, to limit the scope of the algorithmic endeavor, (2) during the endeavor to steer the algorithm, and (3) at the end, to provide a visual context of the result(s) in a space of related results. When the advantages of visual mining are desired, but the number of variables is prohibitively large, algorithms can be useful in selecting the best subset of dimensions to be used by the visualization. Because both visual and algorithmic approaches involve in general an extremely large number of comparisons, both types of mining systems must address the issue of type I errors.

Chapter 25

Robust Beta Mining

R. DOUGLAS MARTIN
TIM SIMIN

*University of Washington
and MathSoft, Inc.*

25.1 The Famous Beta

In the finance world, the quantity beta is a very well-known measure of risk and return. The portfolio view of beta is that it represents the contribution of an equity's risk to the systematic (non-diversifiable) risk of the portfolio, risk taken to be the standard deviation. The capital asset pricing model (CAPM) interpretation of beta is that beta is the slope of the linear relationship between the expected excess return (over the interest-free rate) of an equity and the expected excess return of the market. A beta value of 1 means that the equity behaves like the market, whereas a beta larger (smaller) than 1 means that the equity has a higher (smaller) expected return than the market and a corresponding higher (smaller) risk. For a nice textbook treatment, see [Hau97]. The original paper by [Sha71] is recommended, as is the paper by [Fam65].

25.2 Conventional Calculations of Beta

Investors routinely look at calculated values of beta for equities, such calculated values being supplied by various sources, such as ValueLine. Although any one of several adjustments may be applied in reporting a calculated beta, the calculation typically consists of using least squares (LS) to fit a straight line to the scatter plot of a time series of equity (excess) returns versus the S&P 500 (excess) returns, and taking beta to the slope of the straight-line fit. See [Hau97]. A discussion of the various adjustments may be found in [Elt91].

25.3 Impact of Outliers on Conventional Beta Calculation

It turns out that the scatter plot of equity returns versus the S&P 500 sometimes contains bivariate outliers, which may be quite large. These outliers have substantial influence on the least squares straight-line fit, and hence on the calculated beta. By substantial, we mean that the reported value of beta can change by as much as, say, .5, 1, or 2. These are differences that would certainly be viewed as financially significant by investors. For a discussion of influential data points in regression, see [Coo82] and [Rou87].

25.4 Robust Estimation of Beta

Robust estimation of beta can provide a very good fit to the bulk of the equity returns versus S&P 500 data, in the presence of one or more large outliers. It is important here that truly robust regression estimates be used. It does not suffice to use LS estimates or simple M estimates, in that they are not robust to outliers that occur with leverage; that is, with large independent variable values (negative or positive). The theory of bias-robust regression [Mar89] provides guidelines for the selection of good robust estimators. For calculating beta, either of the following two bias-robust estimators work quite well: (a) an adaptive least trimmed squares estimate, and (b) an MM estimate of [Yoh88], computed as suggested in [Yoh91]. Trade-offs in using these two estimators are briefly discussed in the following.

25.5 Test Statistic for Comparing Least Squares and Robust Beta Calculations

We provide a test statistic for testing whether or not the least squares and robust beta estimates are significantly different.

25.6 Visualization Issues

Of course, it is quite easy to identify large outliers in the scatter plot of a particular equity return versus S&P 500 returns, and delete them. This is particularly convenient in a high-interaction graphics environment that allows you to perform interactive what-if analysis. Furthermore, because the scatter plot consists of time-series data, it is very useful to have linked-views, high-interaction graphics that display both the scatter plot and the two individual time series, so that painting and/or labeling of outliers in the scatter plot result in painting and/or labeling of outliers in the time series. Then the time patterns of the outliers are easily identified, and you can determine whether or not they tend to be clustered in time (which they seem not to be) or associated with well-known effects, such as the January effect or the Monday effect (for which there is some tendency).

On the other hand, because there are in the vicinity of 8000 firms on the combined NASDAQ, NYSE, and AMEX exchanges, it is not practical to visually examine all scatter plots. You need some type of data mining tool to select the firms for which the conventional beta calculation differs significantly from a robust beta calculation.

25.7 Robust Beta Miner

We are using S-PLUS to build a robust beta miner tool that will allow the user to quickly isolate firms for which the conventional beta calculation is suspect, and to automatically provide visualizations of the time-series and scatter-plot data for such firms. The database consists of the time series of equity returns, along with the S&P 500 returns, on a weekly basis for intervals of up to five years (e.g., as with ValueLine). The prototype is using the CRSP data, but this can be replaced with data from any of the historical equity data suppliers. Obvious query types are to request visualizations (with displayed analytic quantities, such as the values of LS and robust beta estimates) for (a) all firms for which LS and robust beta estimates have statistically significant differences, using the test statistic mentioned previously, (b) all firms for which the absolute difference between LS and robust beta estimates is financially significant in the investor's eye (e.g., .5 or greater, 1 or greater, and so on), and (c) unions or intersections of (a) and (b). In addition, many other types of queries are possible; for example, on tests of bivariate normality (which we illustrate), tests for heteroscedasticity, and tests for nonlinearity.

25.8 Summary of (General) Main Points

The visualization required may be very simple, but because the number of such visualizations is large, data mining is required to select manageable subsets of all possible visualizations. Modern robust regression can be used as a powerful data mining tool to determine the important subsets of the data that contain outliers and hence require further analysis (the outliers could be bad noise or the most important information-revealing aspect of the data). In my experience, outliers occur quite frequently, and they can fool a popular data mining tool such as a (naive) neural network (i.e., based on least squares minimization) into thinking there is a nonlinearity when a nonlinear model is not the answer. A data set need not be in the gigabyte range to require data mining methods. It need only be large enough that it is not at all practical for a human to digest it sufficiently to find the interesting information (e.g., as in the beta estimation problem, maybe only a few megabytes).

References

[Coo82]   R. D. Cook and S. Weisberg. *Residuals and Influence in Regression.* New York. Chapman & Hall, 1982.

[Elt91]   E. J. Elton and M. J. Gruber. *Modern Portfolio Theory and Investment Analysis*, 4th ed. New York. John Wiley & Sons, 1991.

[Fam65]   E. Fame. "The Behavior of Stock Prices," *Journal of Business*, 38:34–105, January, 1965.

[Hau97]   R. A. Haugen. *Modern Investment Theory*, 4th ed. Upper Saddle River, NJ. Prentice Hall, 1997.

[Mar89]   R. D. Martin, V. J. Yohai, and R. H. Zamar. "Min-Max Bias Robust Regression," *The Annal of Statistics*, 17:4, pp. 1608–1630, 1989.

[Rou87]   P. J. Rousseeuw and A. M. Leroy. "Robust Regression and Outlier Detection." In Wiley series *Probability and Mathematical Statistics: Applied Probability and Statistics*. New York. John Wiley & Sons, 1987. (Reviewer: V. J. Yohai)

[Sha71]   W. F. Sharpe. "Mean-Absolute-Deviation Characteristic Lines for Securities and Portfolios," *Management Science*, 18:2, pp. B1–B13, October, 1971.

[Yoh88]   V. J. Yohai. "High Breakdown-Point and High Efficiency Estimates of Regression," *The Annals of Statistics*, 15:2, pp. 642–665, 1988.

[Yoh91]   V. J. Yohai, W. A. Stahel, and R. H. Zamar. "A Procedure for Robust Estimation and Inference in Linear Regression." In *Directions in Robust Statistics and Diagnostics, Part II*, W. A. Stahel and S. W. Weisberg (editors). New York. Springer-Verlag, 1991.

Chapter 26

Use of the Manifold Concept in Model Visualization

WILLIAM D. MAWBY

Michelin Tire Corporation

Michelin Tire Corporation in North America is currently constructing several data mining applications. Although one application is in the traditional field of marketing intelligence, there is also a production system application, to which I will confine my remarks in this chapter. Data mining in this context is an extension of the traditional decision support system providing queries and reports. It is necessary in such a view to provide interfaces to sophisticated data modeling methods in real time through a graphical interface. It must also be possible to guide or validate the methods by direct reference to the user's area of knowledge to promote acceptance.

The user community for this application could consist of plant managers, shop managers, line technicians, and research scientists at up to 20 separate geographical locations. The data will be distributed on several platforms (VAX, IBM, RISC, PC server) and will be accessed by a data warehouse structure. The data itself will be collected (and usually stored) at the sites, will have different frequencies of refreshment, and will be in the 5- to 10-gigabyte range. Typically it will include 100 input and 50 output variables, many of which will be correlated and will have missing values that may not occur completely at random. Access to the data (or to the results) will be through an intranet system or a PC server network and ideally will be client-server in nature. The following are some examples of the types of information that could be sought by these users:

- Patterns in quality results
- Time-series patterns

- Imputation of missing values
- On-line capability studies
- Pattern matching
- Patterns of probability
- Summarization of multivariate data
- Outlier screening

The statistical and modeling tools could include discriminant analysis, classification trees, neural networks, ridge regression, correspondence analysis, log-linear modeling, state-space modeling, and general estimating equations. A Bayesian paradigm may be applied informally as the user interacts with the flow of the analysis.

Specifically we see the graphical user interface as being the key to integrating these data mining operations into the decision support environment. There are open technical problems in the areas of data mining in a time-series environment, in the use of user knowledge to influence the mining, in the use of general algorithms (such as EM to impute values before or during the data mining operation), and in the proper sequencing of data mining steps.

Chapter 27

Data Warfare and Multidimensional Education

TED W. MIHALISIN

*Temple University and
Mihalisin Associates, Inc.*

Introduction

Humanity is about to engage in a new type of warfare. The participants are not countries seeking political dominance but are companies seeking economic dominance. Although battles of this type have occurred for centuries, a new era marked by new weapons is beginning. The weapons are tools for extracting information/knowledge from data. They come in several varieties, including OLAP, data mining, and visualization tools.

The key to selecting the best weapons is education; in this case, education concerning multidimensional data and the analysis thereof. You might assume that potential customers for these weapons are frantically struggling to understand the complex issues involved in extracting knowledge from very large multidimensional data. Yet this is not the case. Instead, companies are asking vendors to simplify their tools. Presumably, this will allow analysts with few conventional data analysis skills, let alone multidimensional skills, to effectively use the tools. The folly of arming hundreds or even thousands of troops with slingshots when your enemy is buying ICBMs and training its smartest troops how to launch them seems to have eluded many companies.

What is clearly called for is multidimensional education that will allow companies to discern which tools are powerful and which are not. This chapter is an attempt to start the educational process. Its main conclusion is that no current (or for that matter, future) tools will allow you to discover all of the information contained in one of today's typical large multidimensional data

315

sets in your lifetime, or for that matter, in the lifetime of the universe, even if you are using a teraflop computer. On the other hand, many methods can find all of the information of a tightly specified genre. It is important to understand that these methods can be flawless and yet lead to totally erroneous conclusions. This seemingly self-contradictory statement can be understood as follows: (1) the method finds the answer(s) to a particular question, subject to a number of constraints and assumptions; (2) the user wants the answer(s) subject to no constraints and no assumptions (and in fact is often totally unaware of them); and (3) the assumptions are not valid and/or the constraints are not appropriate. The ultimate folly is to believe that one method or the collection of all current and future methods can discover all information in an acceptable time frame. Hopefully, few readers would still fall prey to this type of deception.

The proper focus then is to realize that although there is no ultimate weapon some weapons are far more powerful than others, and it is essential to be able to distinguish them. Of course, the weapons will steadily grow in power, and this means that an arms race is inevitable.

27.1 Problem Overview

Four problems plague the process of extracting information from a large multidimensional data set. First, the size of the data set does not allow you to use conventional analysis methods that are computationally intensive. Second, many conventional multivariate analysis methods make unwarranted assumptions. Third, a combinatorial explosion of possible cases that must be explored occurs as you increase the number of variables (dimensions) and their cardinality (number of values). Fourth, humans have difficulty codifying knowledge even when they are experts in some information domain. This last problem is greatly compounded when you are asked to discover information in multidimensional data containing attributes (variables) associated with several different information domains (e.g., finance, marketing, and manufacturing). A brilliant analyst in one field may not realize the significance of a discovery in another field. It is difficult to believe that unattended algorithmic or neural net tools will soon be endowed with suitable expert rules that will allow them to discern which findings are trivial and which are earth-shattering. Data mining tools that output 10 or 100 or even 1000 findings for human evaluation may or may not be acceptable, depending on how intelligible the findings are. However, asking humans to evaluate obtuse or prolific discoveries is unacceptable.

27.2 Data Management, Data Access, and Data Analysis Are Three Different Issues

The exact same information can be stored and accessed in an infinite number of ways. We have all heard arguments as to why relational databases are superior to flat files and multidimensional databases in some respects, and for some purposes, and vice versa. These issues have also been transferred to OLAP tools (e.g., ROLAP versus MOLAP). Most serious data analysis tools want to "work on" flat files. We will not address these sorts of issues. You can of course produce flat files from relational or multidimensional databases. The fact of the matter is that the most important issues concerned with the analysis of large multivariate data sets have nothing whatsoever to do with data management and data access issues. For ease of communicating, we will speak in terms of flat files.

27.3 A Simple Example

Let's consider a relatively small, uncomplicated data set consisting of six columns and 100,000 rows. Each column is a variable, and each row is a record that corresponds to the sale of one product (quantity 1) in a particular territory via a particular sales channel, using a particular method of payment in a particular quarter. Hence, five of the columns (variables) are product, territory, channel, method of payment, and quarter. There are five products, five territories, two channels, two methods of payment, and five quarters. The sixth column is an otherwise meaningless unique identifier. For example, it could be the concatenation of a scanner's serial number and its "scan number" (i.e., the number of scans it has made in its lifetime). The total number of records that can be distinct (i.e., differ in at least one of their variable fields, other than the unique identifier) is $5 * 5 * 2 * 2 * 5 = 500$. Let's associate a cell with each of these 500 possibilities, as shown in Figure 27.1. Because there are 100,000 records and only 500 cells, on average there will be 200 records per cell. Of course, in the universe of all possible data sets of this type, any cell can have from 0 to 100,000 records, subject to the constraint that the number of records (the "counts") must sum to 100,000. This simple data set contains only discrete variables (i.e., no continuous variables). Two of these variables (namely, quarter and territory) may have been derived from one or two continuous variables via "binning"; time to get quarter, and longitude and latitude to get territories. The issue of how you bin continuous variables is an important one, but we will not address it here. The fact of the

Figure 27.1

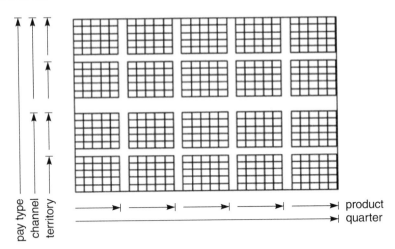

*One arrangement of 500 cells that can be used to display sales broken
down by five variables; namely, product (five values), territory (five
values), sales channel (two values), method of payment (two values)
and quarter (five values). This is an example of a five-way distribution.*

matter is that the problem is difficult enough even when we are presented
with all discrete variables, as in this example.

In Figure 27.1 we see the 500 cells arranged in one of many possible ways.
Note that each cell must correspond to specifying one particular value for
each of the five variables: product, territory, channel, method of payment,
and quarter. In Figure 27.1, the five quarters run along the horizontal. Nested
within each quarter is the set of five products; hence, we say that the product
variable is nested inside the quarter variable. Also in Figure 27.1, the two
methods of payment (namely, cash and third-party) run along the vertical.
Nested within each method of payment is the set of two sales channels (retail
and mail), and nested inside each sales channel is the set of five territories.
Hence, we say that territory is nested within channel, which is nested within
method of payment. There is nothing special about this particular nesting
scheme. It happens to be a useful one if you are interested in analyzing the
data from the point of view of how market share varies from territory to territory when further broken down via channel, method of payment, and time
(quarter). Other nesting schemes are better suited to different analysis points
of view.

We can imagine pouring 100,000 identical ping pong balls into the lattice
of cells, shown in Figure 27.1. The number of possible results when we pour
the balls is equal to the different number of ways we can add 500 numbers

(each being in the range from 0 to 100,000) to get a total of 100,000. Note that the cells are distinguishable by their set of five variable values, but the ping pong balls are identical and hence indistinguishable. The answer is that the number of different data sets is 100,499!/(100,000! * 499!). This can be estimated via Sterling's formula to be about 10 raised to the power 1350; that is, a 1 followed by 1350 zeros. This is a staggering number because it dwarfs the total number of atoms in the universe. When you consider typical data sets that people get from today's data warehouses, involving tens of millions of records and far more cells (originating from more variables and/or higher cardinalities), the number of possible data sets can exceed 10 raised to the power 1 billion.

We of course have only one data set to consider. So what is the relevance of there being 10 to the power 1350 different data sets of this type? The answer is that we must recognize the potential of such a data set to contain vast amounts of information. By way of contrast, consider the language of analysis. If A, B, and C are three ordinal variables, people ask whether A and B, or A and C, or B and C are correlated. If we have five ordinal variables to consider, more "sophisticated" people will ask what the 5-by-5 correlation matrix looks like. If the variables are nominal discrete (categorical) variables, they ask similar questions but refer to interaction instead of correlation. But wait a minute. A 5-by-5 correlation matrix, for example, has at most 10 distinct meaningful numbers, because each variable is perfectly correlated with itself, and the correlation of A with B is identical to the correlation of B with A. It is as if we are supposed to believe that 10 numbers between 0 and 1 can uniquely specify which of the 10 to the power 1350 data sets we are dealing with. That this is not so can be demonstrated by considering a correlation matrix that has all zeros for its off-diagonal elements, indicating "no correlation" between any two non-identical variables. This is a uniquely specified matrix, and yet there are many different data sets of our form that can give rise to this matrix, including cases such as "A and B are perfectly correlated when $C = C_1$ and perfectly anti-correlated when $C = C_2$," and so on. The number of different cases of this type is huge. That is, there is a small fraction of the 10 to the 1350 cases (but nonetheless a very large number of cases), all of which give the exact same correlation matrix.

27.4 Problems with Interactions: Subsets of Values and Chi-Square

Shown in Figure 27.2 is a much simpler set of cells; namely, a 5-by-5 array of cells corresponding to aggregating Figure 27.1 over the variables channel, method of payment, and quarter. Thus, each cell in Figure 27.2 contains the

Figure 27.2

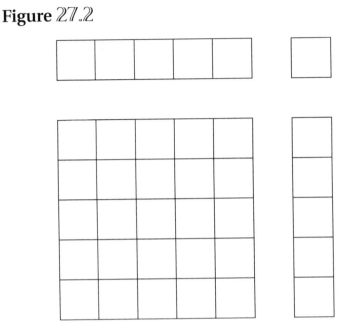

A cell arrangement that allows you to view a two-way distribution and two one-way distributions, as well as the global count.

number of sales of a particular product in a particular territory. Above this 5-by-5 array of cells is a horizontal set of five cells, one for each product. Each of these cells contains the total number of sales of a particular product, irrespective of territory. That is, territories have been aggregated. Similarly, to the right of the 5-by-5 array is a vertical set of five cells, each cell corresponding to a particular territory. Each of these cells contains the total number of sales in a particular territory, irrespective of product. That is, product has been aggregated. Finally, in the upper right-hand corner is a single cell. In that cell is the total number of sales of all products in all territories, or the "global" sales.

The next step is to divide the numbers (i.e., number of sales) in each of the cells (the cells in the 5-by-5 array, the cells in the horizontal and vertical sets of five, and the single cell in the upper right) by the global sales to obtain instead the fraction or frequency of the total sales that is in each of these cells. The set of five horizontal cells is known as the marginal distribution of sales by product (this equals % market share if you multiply each by 100). For example, f_{P1} is the fraction of all sales that are sales of product 1.

Similarly, the set of five vertical cells is known as the marginal distribution of sales by territory (e.g., f_{T2} is the fraction of all sales that were made in territory 2). The 5-by-5 array is known as a two-way distribution of sales; namely, by product and territory. For example, f_{P3T4} is the fraction of all sales that were sales of product 3 in territory 4, and so on. If there is no "interaction" between the variables, product and territory, or if, equivalently, they are "independent," any cell in the 5-by-5 array is given by $f_{PiTj} = f_{Pi} * f_{Tj}$.

Statistical measures exist for the degree to which the f_{PiTj} fractions or frequencies differ from what you expect by chance if P and T (product and territory) variables were indeed independent. In particular, you can form a "chi-square" statistic, which involves summing the squares of the deviations of f_{PiTj} from the expected values of $f_{Pi} * f_{Tj}$.

A wide range of behavior can be observed for the f_{PiTj}. First, all f_{PiTj} can be equal or not statistically different from the expected values $f_{Pi} * f_{Tj}$, for all i and j = 1 to 5. Second, for any row in the array, there might be one and only one column value that has a non-zero frequency, and at the same time for any column there is one and only one row that has a non-zero frequency. Because the two-way frequencies must obey "sum rules" (that is, f_{PiTj} must add to f_{Pi} when summed over T_j and must equal f_{Tj} when summed over P_i), it follows that the set $\{f_{Pi}\}$ must equal the set $\{f_{Tj}\}$, though the order of the elements in the set can vary. This of course is a very special case of perfect two-way interaction, and in general could either be highly significant or trivial. In this example, it says that each of the five territories sells a distinct product.

Third, a subset of the cells in the 5-by-5 array may show strong deviations from the frequencies $f_{Pi} * f_{Tj}$. For example, for ease of discussion, imagine that all cells show $f_{PiTj} = f_{Pi} * f_{Tj}$, except for the four in the upper right, corresponding to products 4 and 5 and territories 4 and 5. Again, to simplify the discussion, imagine that the two off-diagonal cells in the extreme upper right have zero frequencies. Because the sum rules must hold, it follows that $f_{P5T5} = f_{P5} * f_{T5} + f_{P4} * f_{T5}$ and that $f_{P4T4} = f_{P4} * f_{T4} + f_{P5} * f_{T4}$. Of course, the point here is far more general than this very special case. You can pick any two rows and any two columns to determine which four of the 25 cells are going to show deviations from the frequencies based on variable independence. Similarly, you can pick any subset of three, and so on. This may not seem like a large number of cases when you are dealing with variables of cardinality 5, but in real applications you might be dealing with 100 products and 100 territories. Then the total number of possibilities is astronomical, in that it goes as 2^{2C}, where C is the cardinality of each variable. Hence, there are on the order of 2 to the 200th or 10 to the 60th power for the case of 100 products in 100 territories, whereas it is only on the order of 2 to the 10th, or 1024, for two variables. Actually it is reduced to 961, or $(2^c - 1)^2$, in that one of the 2^c possibilities is the null set and further reduced to $(2^c - 1 - c)^2$ because the c choices for one value of each variable cannot violate independence; hence, for c = 5, you get $(2^5 - 1 - 5)^2 = 676$. For large cardinality, the difference between 2^{2c} and $(2^c - 1 - c)^2$ is not significant in a geometric sense. A more modest approach is to consider only all sets of two products and two territories, which for our case of 100 products and 100 territories gives us only about $(100)^4/4 = 2.5 \times 10^7$ instead of 10^{60}.

A key point that is not appreciated is that you can obtain significantly different chi-square values, depending on which products and which territories are included in the analysis. Going back to our simple example, when only the products 4 and 5 in territories 4 and 5 show deviations from the frequencies, $f_{Pi} * f_{Tj}$ (i.e., the case of the 2×2 array of four cells in the extreme upper right), you would obtain a significantly different chi-square if only the sales of these four cells were used to determine the marginal product frequencies, f_{P4} and f_{P5}, and the two marginal territory frequencies, f_{T4} and f_{T5}. Note that now there are only two products, not five, and only two territories, not five. Here the global sales would just be the total sales of these two products in these two territories, and a much larger chi-square would result. This point is far more dramatic when you consider the case of 100 products and 100 territories.

This brings us to another key point; namely, the issue of type I errors (false positives). Certainly, statistics dictates that if we look at enough cases (in this instance, all possible choices for 2×2 subarrays, 3×3, etc.) and we are testing at the 5% confidence limit, we will find many false positives. Roughly speaking, if we test 400 cases and we do not concern ourselves with the actual values of chi-square, but rather only that it is large enough to be significant at the 5% (or better) level, we would expect to get 20 false positives. But to not investigate these cases in some manner is irresponsible. One solution is to randomly split the records into several equal-size groups. The statistical power of the similar data sets is reduced, because it goes as $\sqrt{N}$, but the advantage is that you can test to see if the same choices of products and territories result. For our 5×5 example, using just pairs of products and pairs of territories, we have $(5 \times 4/2)^2 = 100$ cases, and hence we would expect 5 of the 100 by chance. But if, for example, we split the records into G equal-size groups and separately ran our test, the odds that one particular 2×2 would show a significant chi-square by chance in all G groups would be 1 part in 20^G (i.e., 1 in 400 for G = 2, 1 in 8000 for G = 3, 1 in 160,000 for G = 4, etc.). If a data mining tool is to avoid burdening the user with a plethora of "discoveries" that are in fact statistically spurious, it must automatically mine a sufficient number of subsets and perform proper tests to identify valid discoveries. Of course, even then the discoveries may not be useful.

27.5 Problems with Interactions: Groupings of Values and Chi-Square

A very similar problem arises when you face the issue of grouping values of a variable. If, for example, we have five distinguishable objects (e.g., products), the number of ways we can partition them into one, two, three, four, or five non-empty subsets is given by the sum over m = 1 to 5 of the Sterling numbers [Abr70] of the second kind S^m_5 and equals 52. But if we have, for example, 25 products, the number of ways they can be partitioned into one, two, three, and so on to 25 non-empty subsets is in excess of 10^{18}. Again, these groupings (of both product and territory values) alter the chi-square statistic in a non-trivial fashion.

27.6 Moving to Higher Dimensions

All of the problems associated with chi-square mentioned so far occur in low dimensionality (i.e., the 2D case of just product and territory). Let's discuss our 5D case of Figure 27.1 and extensions where we increase the cardinality of one or more variables.

Figure 27.1 can be described as consisting of $5 \times 2 \times 2 = 20$ product-territory 5-by-5 arrays of cells, each of which is identical to the 5-by-5 array of cells of Figure 27.2. However, in Figure 27.2, each of the 20 arrays (5-by-5) corresponds to sales in a particular quarter, via a particular sales channel, using a particular method of payment. That is, Figure 27.1 can be thought of as 20 product-territory arrays broken down or conditioned by quarter, channel, and method of payment. The sales numbers in all of the cells specify a five-way distribution function. In Figure 27.2, the marginal distributions (namely, sales by product and sales by territory) were shown, as well as the global sales cell. In Figure 27.1, you can imagine that a horizontal set of five cells and a vertical set of five cells, as well as a single cell (analogous to the global cell of Figure 27.2), are associated with each of the 20 product-territory 5-by-5 cell arrays. In this case, a horizontal set of five cells corresponds to sales for each product, irrespective of territory but for a particular quarter, channel, and method of payment. Similarly, the vertical set of five cells corresponds to sales in each of the territories, irrespective of product but again for a particular quarter, channel, and method of payment. The single cell corresponds to sales, irrespective of both product and territory (i.e., for all five products and all five territories, but again for a particular quarter, channel, and method of payment).

A key point here is that all of the problems associated with selecting subsets of products and/or territories and of grouping products and/or territories mentioned in connection with Figure 27.2 are present for each of the 20 5-by-5 product-territory cell arrays of Figure 27.1. Moreover, far more complicated behavior can occur. For example, some of the 5-by-5 arrays can show variable independence (i.e., no interaction), whereas others can display strong interactions. In the former case, we would speak of the product and territory variables as being conditionally independent (i.e., for certain quarter/channel/method of payment three-tuples). In the latter case, we would say that product and territory variables show conditional interactions.

The range of possibilities is great and can lead to surprising results. For example, it is possible to have a data set in which all 20 conditional product and territory two-way conditional distributions show strong conditional interactions, and yet when you aggregate over the conditioning variables (here, quarter, channel, and method of payment) to obtain the 5-by-5 array of cells of Figure 29.2 (i.e., the unconditional or marginal two-way distribution for product and territory), it shows no interactions. Moreover, it is possible to have a data set in which all 20 arrays are conditionally independent but the marginal 5-by-5 shows significant product-territory interactions.

In previous discussion we imagined summing each 5-by-5 array over territory to obtain the 20 conditional one-way distributions of sales (i.e., versus product and summing over product to obtain the 20 conditional one-way distributions of sales versus territory). However, this is only one of many ways you can play the chi-square game. If you have five variables (here treated as dimensions, not measures), you have $2^5 = 32$ possible aggregations. First, let's consider the number of ways you could calculate the expected frequency of a particular cell in Figure 27.1 based on a variety of models statisticians might wish to view in terms of a log-linear approach [Agr84]. First, $f_{PiTjCkMlQm} = f_{Pi} * f_{Tj} * f_{Ck} * f_{Ml} * f_{Qm}$ would be used if you were interested in the simplest model where all variables are "totally" independent. Second, you could consider models where f for the cell in question was of form $f_{PiTj} * f_{Ck} * f_{Ml} * f_{Qm}$. Here, f_{PiTj} is the i-th, j-th component of the observed "marginal" two-way sales (by product and territory) distribution, and f_{Ck} and so on are the observed marginal one-way distributions for channel, and so on. Because there are $5 * 4/2 = 10$ ways to pair two of five variables, there are

10 cases of this form. Next, consider forms such as $f_{PiTjCk} * f_{Ml} * f_{Qm}$. There are $(5 * 4 * 3/3!) = 10$ cases of this form. Next, consider forms such as $f_{PiTj} * f_{CkMl} * f_{Qm}$. There are $(5 * 4/2)(3 * 2/2) = 30$ cases. Next, consider forms such as $f_{PiTjCk} * f_{MlQm}$ having $(5 * 4 * 3/3!) = 10$ cases. Next, consider forms such as $f_{PiTkCkMl} * f_{Qm}$, having five cases. Finally, there is the single fully saturated form $f_{PiTjCkMlQm}$. The total number of cases is 67, but the number of ways of computing the "expected" frequency is 66. Keep in mind that chi-square is computationally intensive and that the subset and grouping issues are still present.

The relevance of pointing out the variety of ways you can compute the expected frequency of a single cell goes beyond the chi-square test of variable independence. Many data mining methods use the ratio of the observed frequency to the expected frequency, the "lift," to determine if they have found a "nugget" of information that should be brought to the attention of the user. Some mining methods also test the statistical significance of the difference between observed and expected frequencies. The question, of course, is whether or not all of the different models are being tested. Even more fundamental is whether or not the mining is even testing to "depth 5" (i.e., using five-way distributions) or stopping short by looking only at all possible two-ways (i.e., 10), or, in addition, all possible three-ways (i.e., 10), and so on. This is a vital point because, for example, we have seen that you can have no two-way interactions in a set of five variables and yet have a strong three-way, or have no two-way or three-way interactions and yet have a strong four-way, and so on.

It should be noted that the number of ways to compute the expected frequencies escalates with dimensionality, as follows: for d = 2 there is only 1 way, for d = 3 there are 4 ways, for d = 4 there are 17 ways, for d = 5 there are 66 ways, for d = 6 there are 257 ways, and for d = 7 there are 1611 ways.

27.7 Higher Dimensions with Multiple Ordinal Variables of High Cardinality: Randomness and Grouping

Consider a 5D space like that shown in Figure 27.1, but with 200 time periods, not 5. Let the cardinality of the other variables remain the same (i.e., five products, five territories, two channels, and two methods of payment). Consider the array of cells as 200 subarrays, one for each time period, each subarray consisting of $5 \times 5 \times 2 \times 2 = 100$ cells, with each cell specified by a product/territory/channel/method of payment four-tuple. Imagine that the numbers in each of the 100 cells look more or less random for each of the 200 subarrays. Now consider a set of possibilities of increasing complexity. First, consider changing the nesting so that the time variable, now having 200 values (formerly quarter with five values), is the nested variable along the horizontal. This new figure could be thought of as a collection of time series; namely, $5 \times 5 \times 2 \times 2 = 100$ time series, each with 200 values of time. Now, of course, a huge number of possibilities arises. First, all of the time series could look random. Second, some or all of the time series could show obvious patterns. Imagine, for example, that each time series is flat but at different values. This would mean that each of the 200 original subarrays, one for each time, of size 100 had identical sets of random numbers.

Consider the first case, where the time series all look random, but instead of plotting "sales of product i, in territory j, sold in channel k, via method of payment l" versus "time for all i, j, k, and l 4-tuples," consider selecting two cells from the original figure that correspond to two different values of the four-tuple but at the same time. Then plot the number of sales for the first cell versus the number of sales for the second cell for the 200 different times, thus eliminating time as a variable.

Here, even though all of the data looked random in the original 5D plot, we might see a perfect correlation in the new, simple 2D plot. For example, the sales in PiTjCkMlQm cell could be 3.17 times the sales in cell Pi'Tj'Xk'Ml'Qm (note that these have equal times Qm), though each is varying randomly with time Qm. To check for information of this type, we would need to investigate $100 \times 99/2 = 4950$ cases. Moreover, it may turn out that these sales are correlated but with a finite time lag; hence, we might need to consider up to, say, 100 time lags, which would still leave 100 points to analyze. Now you have in effect 100 times as many time series that could be analyzed via the cross-correlation function. The complexity does not stop there, however. What if the sales in two cells are correlated over a subdomain of time or are correlated conditionally; for example, depending on the sales in a third cell, and so on?

The complexity can be escalated further by considering the elimination of variables other than time. For example, consider whether or not sales in two cells specified by PiTjCkMlQm and Pi'TjCk'Ml'Qm' (same territory T_j) are correlated over the territory variable, and so on. In our example, there are $5 \times 2 \times 2 \times 200 = 4000$ choices for each four-tuple, and hence about 16 million choices of pairs of cells. (Issues of this type are discussed in more detail in the next section.)

Another issue relevant here is the issue of grouping. Consider the following case. The sales in a particular PTCM cell versus time consist of a set of random numbers $R_1(t)$. The sales in a second cell of this type versus time consist of a different set of random numbers $R_2(t)$ (different seed). Sales in a third cell of this type versus time consist of yet another set of random numbers $R_3(t)$. However, the sales in a fourth cell are given by $R_1(t) + R_2(t) - R_3(t)$. Hence, if you were to group cells 1 and 2 and also cells 3 and 4 and plot the number of sales in the first group versus the number of sales in the second group, you would obtain a perfect correlation. The number of ways of selecting the groups is $(100 * 99)/2 * (98 * 97)/2 = 23{,}527{,}350$. Of course, larger groups may be relevant. Moreover, cross-dimensional grouping may also be relevant.

The considerations in this section are clearly relevant to many fields, most notably finance and portfolio analysis. However, they also apply to any field in which the "fluctuations" are really the signal and the "trends" are the noise.

27.8 The Ultimate Transformation: Wide Fields Versus Narrow

In the last section, we in effect were transforming records from a narrow field form, with each entity (record) being a sale to a variety of wider-field formats, and analyzing a subset of the narrow field records that corresponds to two values of n-tuples with $n < 5$, or equivalently a subset of wide-field variables. For example, when we "plotted" the number of sales in the cell PiTjCkMl versus the number of sales in the cell PI′Tj′Ck′Ml′ at equal times, we were in effect transforming the entity to be time (time becomes the unique identifier) and looking at just two of the possible variables (columns); namely, the number of sales in each of the two cells. The logical extension to make, of course, is to include as variables all $5 \times 5 \times 2 \times 2 = 100$ possible sales as columns, hence transforming the original narrow flat file that had five meaningful columns (variables), plus the unique identifier column by 100,000 rows, to a new wide-field format consisting of 101 columns; namely, time plus the number of sales in each of the 100 product/territory/channel/method of payment four-tuples by only 200 rows (times). Because the column variables (other than time) are number of sales and we now have the constraint that the $100 \times 200 = 20{,}000$ entries in the "spreadsheet" must add to 100,000, we could compute the number of possible data sets of this type [i.e., $119{,}999!/(100{,}000!19{,}999!)$]. But I think you will agree that it is a larger number. In our original calculation, we had $100{,}499!/(100{,}000!499!)$ possible data sets, but that was when the number of times was 5, not 200, so that the total number of cells was $5 \times 5 \times 2 \times 2 \times 5 = 500$. If we were to recalculate based on 200 times, we would get $5 \times 5 \times 2 \times 2 \times 200 = 20{,}000$ and, as we must, we would compute the exact same number of data sets; namely, 119,999!/ (100,000!19,999!). The number of possible data sets is invariant to field transformations.

Returning to our wide field, it is no longer practical to speak of the cardinality of the variables, in that each is a number of sales that in principle can range from 0 to 100,000. However, the numbers in all 20,000 cells must sum to 100,000. Hence, it may often be the case that the numbers will be about 5, which is too small for meaningful analysis. Hence, we must either increase the number of narrow-field records or reduce the number of wide-field cells. First, let's increase the number of records. For example, if we had a total number of sales equal to 100 million, each of our new wide-field cells would have, on average, 5000 sales. Now we could engage in a process of setting up bins for our new variables that are now all ordinal and best thought of as quasi-continuous. For instance, let each variable have 10 bin ranges (i.e., 0 to 1000, 1000 to 2000, . . . , 8000 to 9000, and > 9000).

Now we would think of our new data set as consisting of 100 variables, each of cardinality 10 plus time, and we have only 200 records (times). If we were to attempt to set up an array of cells like those in Figure 27.1, it would consist of 10^{100} cells, among which we have only 200 records to distribute. This obviously leads to a very sparse problem, in which the most likely outcome is that $10^{100} - 200$ cells are empty and 200 cells have count (number of times) of 1. Clearly, going to the complete depth of 100 dimensions is silly. Even if we were to create only two bins (e.g., < 5000 and > 5000 for each variable), there would still be $2^{100} \sim 10^{30}$ cells and we would still be in the extremely sparse limit. This, of course, leads us to realize that for wide field/ small number of records (here, number of times) we need to greatly reduce the dimensional depth of the problem by selecting small subsets of the 100 variables. This is the topic of the next section.

Next we will consider a number of other ways to widen the original flat files. The "total" widening just discussed is not the only "total" widening case. By total widening we mean that the number of records is determined by the number of values (cardinality) of one of the original variables. In the previous example, we used the time variable but, as mentioned in the last section, we could have chosen any other variable; for example, the product variable. The other aspect of a "total" widening is that the non-unique identifier variables are counts (here, number of sales) for a concatenation of the other original variables. For example, when product is chosen as the unique identifier variable, we would have only five records and, as pointed out in the last section, the number of all other variables (columns) would be $5 \times 2 \times 2 \times 20 = 4000$. Of course, any one of the five variables can be chosen.

Next, consider a case in which both time and product are used to define the records. That is, time and product are concatenated to form $5 \times 200 = 1000$ records, each record corresponding to a particular product and particular time. Then, for instance, the other variables can be concatenated to form variables that are the number of sales for each territory/channel/ method of payment (i.e., $5 \times 2 \times 2 = 20$ count variables).

Because one variable—or concatenations of two, three, four, or all five of the original meaningful variables—can be used to form the number of records, there are $2^5 - 1 = 31$ cases. In each instance, the remaining variables are concatenated to form a set of count (here, sales) variables. Thus, the nature of the transformations for a given number of original variables (in the narrow field) has to do with how the possible concatenations are partitioned between generating new record entities and generating new count variables. If all are concatenated to form the record set with $5 \times 5 \times 2 \times 2 \times 200 = 20,000$ records, the only variable left is count itself, and each record would consist of a five-tuple unique identifier column (i.e., P-T-C-M-Q and a count (number of sales) column). This is "close" to our original narrow record case, except that there are only 20,000 records, not 100,000 (or more recently, 100 million). Our original records had "count = 1" and many identical records (five-tuples), but this case has no repeated five-tuples and count equal to the number of original records with a specified five-tuple.

The cells of Figure 27.1 correspond to the records of this case and allow us to recursively compute an enormous amount of information about the original narrow-field record entities (sales), as discussed at length in [Mih95]. Remember that our original narrow records had five meaningful variables that were attributes of sales. Our new records have only one attribute variable for the new record entity (which is the P-T-C-M-Q five-tuple); namely, count (number of sales). Instead of using these new records to uncover information about our old record entities (sales), we could bin the single count variable (i.e., the old count variable, number of sales, which is now an attribute variable for our new entities, the five-tuples) to the 10 bins alluded to earlier; namely, 0 to 1000, 10 to 2000, . . . , 8000 to 9000, and > 9000. We would uncover information about our new record entities (the five-tuples).

Because we now have 20,000 records, on average we would have 2000 records per bin. Note that each record is now a particular product, in a particular territory, sold via a particular channel, using a particular method of payment, and in a particular time frame (i.e., day, month, quarter, and so on), so that our 10 count bins show the number of these P-T-C-M-Q entities with sales in each of the 10 sales (count) bins. Thus, the data has been totally convoluted to be about these five-tuple entities, and count (sales) is the single attribute that characterizes them. Our new array of cells is now a single (say, horizontal) set of 10 cells, and the numbers in the cells give the marginal distribution of these five-tuple entities P-T-C-M-Q. That is, the numbers in the cells (the "counts") are not the number of sales (the old entities) but rather are the number of five-tuples. For example, if the number in the first of the 10 bins were 3120, it would mean that 3120 of the 20,000 product/ territory/channel/method of payment/quarter five-tuples had sales between 0 and 1000.

27.9 Depth of Analysis, Computational Hardness, and Recursive Computing

Throughout the previous sections it has been clear that increasing the cardinality and/or number of dimensions (variables) leads to a variety of explosions in complexity. These include a simple geometric explosion in the number of cells and a variety of severe combinatorial explosions. Each explosion impacts computation time, requiring in essence one computation or one set of computations per case. The size of each computation set can explode combinatorially at the same time the number of cases explodes combinatorially. If you have to return to the original data set (which for realistic data involves millions of records and many variables) for each computation, the compute time will become hopelessly long at a very early stage. If, on the other hand, you can recursively perform the new computations utilizing the counts in the cells (which in the dense limit are far fewer than the number of records), all operations can be done in RAM and only a single pass over the records is necessary. Although there appears to be no hope that even this method can cover all cases in a finite amount of time, it nonetheless can provide enormous performance boosts over the multi-pass, disk-based approach.

Another point that should be clear from the preceding section is that the depth of analysis you can engage in depends critically on the number of records. More precisely, it is the number of cells that dictates how many records are required. That is, you can go to depth 2 with two variables each of cardinality 100, or to depth 4 with four variables each of cardinality 10 (say, with 10 million records) and on average have 1000 records per cell in each case. If you try to add a third variable of cardinality 100 to two existing variables also of cardinality 100, you have 1 million cells and 10 million records, and a problem. The problem is that on average there are 10 records per cell, making statistical analysis dubious.

As discussed earlier, the depth to which an analysis is done determines the class of information that can be discovered. Many algorithmic data mining tools go to far less depth than a given number of records would allow. Instead, they focus on multiple shallow analyses. If you have a large number of variables n, and the number of records and cardinalities would allow a depth of k variables, the number of ways of selecting k variables from n variables can become prohibitive. The strategy taken by many mining algorithms is to look only at all possible pairs, or perhaps triplets, of variables (even though $k > 3$) to narrow the problem.

Next, consider nonrecursive conventional analysis methods in particular as they are applied to data involving continuous variables. For example, consider simple routines, such as finding a linear correlation coefficient r for two variables x and y. This calculation scales with the number of points. Reducing the number of points by taking a small random subset of points rules out the possibility of constraining the points using other variables (i.e., it limits the depth of analysis, so that you cannot see if r_{xy} depends on u, v, w, and so on). You may be confused on the issue of data subsets, in that in an earlier section, "Problems with Interactions: Subsets of Values and Chi-Square," we stressed that taking G equal-size random subsets was desirable in order to rule out type I statistical errors. Now we are saying that a "small random subset" limits analysis depth. The key here is the word *small*. If, for example, we have 100 million records, reducing it (e.g., by a factor G = 4) to 25 million may be adequate for discovering/ruling out type I errors, but will not severely limit analysis depth. However, many methods force you to analyze 50,000 or fewer records. Even then, they may be extremely slow; but more to the point, reduction from 100 million to 50,000 records can severely limit analysis depth.

Hence, a better approach is to bin u, v, w, and so on and let the binning form the x-y subsets, leaving the full complement of points in the data set. However, we are considering cases in which the full data set is too large to fit into RAM. Hence, these data subsets must be swapped in and out of RAM from disk, a very slow operation. Contrast this approach with one in which x and y are binned, as well as z, u, w, and so on. Let's bin x, y, z, u, v, and w so that each has five equal-width bins. The corresponding array of cells can then be arranged to form $5^4 = 625$ arrays of cells (each 5 by 5). Each 5-by-5 array corresponds to the x and y variables, and the count is displayed in each cell. Each 5-by-5 array shows an x-y two-way distribution that you can test in a variety of ways for correlation. The total number of cells is $5^6 = 15,625$. Let the total number of records be 10 million; hence, on average there are 640 records per cell, and the computation load has been reduced by a factor of

640. Moreover, the 16,625 cell counts can be easily handled in RAM. No disk swapping is required.

Next, consider more computationally intense calculations, such as clustering, that scale as N^2 or worse. Here, a similar analysis would show a factor of $640^2 = 409,600$ reduction in computation time, and again no need to perform slow disk operations.

It is beyond the scope of this chapter to describe in detail an extremely fast, fully recursive computational engine that can perform a wide variety of computations relevant to this exploratory type of analysis. Here, we simply want to discuss in the next section how visualization can greatly assist in the information discovery process by guiding the analysis process.

27.10   How Multidimensional Visualization and Recursive Computing Can Expedite Analysis

Consider again Figure 27.1 and extensions to Figure 27.1 that occur when you increase the cardinality of one or more variables. Instead of placing numbers in each cell, place a vertical bar with a height proportional to the number in the cell. You then have a collection of vertical bar charts that shows how the sales depend on product, territory, channel, method of payment, and quarter. You can visually detect trends more easily if the products are sorted in ascending order of marginal sales. Similarly, territories should be sorted on the basis of marginal sales, as should channels and methods of payment. Quarter generally should not be sorted on the basis of sales, because it is an ordinal variable with its own intrinsic order.

Before discussing this case further, consider Figure 27.3, which is similar to Figure 27.2, except that two marginal distributions (i.e., the vertical set of five cells and the horizontal set of five cells) and the global cell of Figure 27.2 are not present in Figure 27.3, and vertical bars are in the cells. In Figure 27.3, the products and territories are not sorted based on marginal sales. In Figure 27.4, they are.

In Figure 27.4, each row of five cells is a graph of sales versus product (one for each territory). If there are no interactions between products and territories (i.e., these variables are independent), each of the five graphs of sales versus product (one for each territory) in Figure 27.4 should be monotonically increasing, because products have been marginally sorted. Moreover, each graph should be identical, except for a scale factor. This follows immediately, in that independence implies that $f_{PiTj} = f_{Pi} * f_{Tj}$ and the actual number of sales is simply $N_{global} * f_{PiTj}$, which should equal $N_{global} * f_{Pi} * f_{Tj}$. Hence, as you move from one territory to the next, you get identical

Figure 27.3

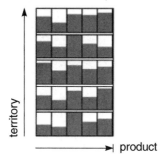

product

*A graphic representation of a two-way
distribution using vertical bars. Shown are
number of sales versus product and territory.*

Figure 27.4

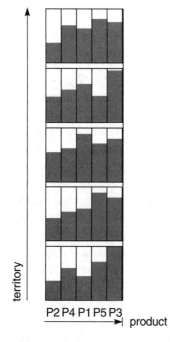

P2 P4 P1 P5 P3
product

*The same graphic as in Figure 27.3, except that
the products and territories have been sorted on
the basis of number of sales. The products with
greater number of sales are to the right. The territories with greater number of sales are at the top.*

Figure 27.5

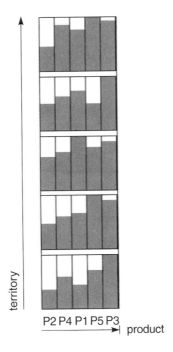

The same as Figure 27.4, except that each of the five graphs of sales versus product (one for each territory) has its own scale.

numbers, except that the j-th territory numbers are scaled by f_{Tj}, whereas the j'-th territory numbers are scaled by $f_{Tj'}$. If you let each of the five graphs have its own scale, you should obtain five graphs that appear to be identical. Figure 27.5 shows this case; that is, each of the five graphs has its own scale (not shown), determined by its maximum rather than having one common scale for all five graphs, which is the case in Figure 27.4. By inspection of Figure 27.4 and, especially, Figure 27.5, it is clear that a marginal interaction between product and territory is present, in that the five sales-versus-product graphs in Figure 27.5 (one for each territory) are clearly not identical.

In Figure 27.6 we show a specific example of Figure 27.1, with data represented by vertical bars [USP01]. The variables have not been sorted by ascending marginal sales. Figure 27.7 shows the same data, except that the nesting has been changed so that time (quarter) is nested within product. Note that although all we have done is to reshuffle cells, new information is obvious that was not apparent by casual inspection of Figure 27.6. Figure 27.8 is the same as Figure 27.7, except that each graph of number of sales versus time now has its own scale. This transformation of scales is referred to as

Figure 27.6

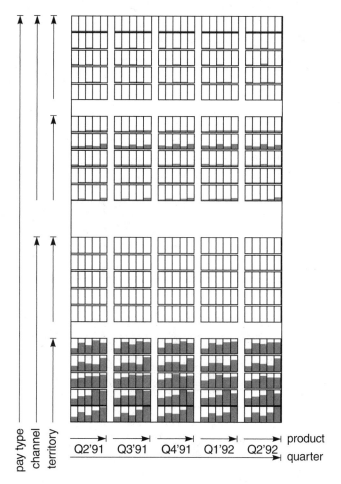

One possible graphic representation of the five-way
distribution of sales by product, territory, sales channel,
method of payment, and quarter.

normalization, and it makes it easier to look at time trends in the second
channel, where sales are small, and, as mentioned previously, to look for
interactions. In particular, note the sudden drops in sales for some products,
in some territories, for the first method of payment, via the second channel.

Figure 27.9 is a textbook example of a three-way interaction in a four-
variable space. Unfortunately, the vertical bars are too small to be seen away
from the center of the graph. In Figure 27.9, all cells have the same scale. In
Figure 27.10, the normalization is turned on and the three-way interaction is

Figure 27.7

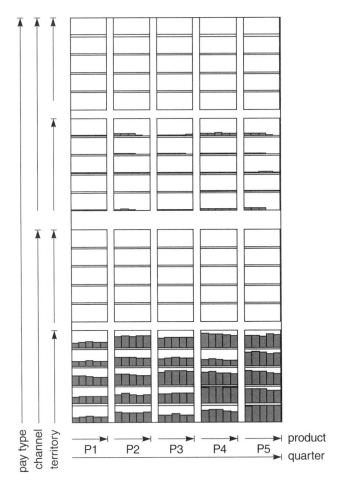

*The same data as in Figure 27.6, but in this figure the time variable
quarter) is nested within the product variable. This figure can be
thought of as a collection of simple time series, one for each of the
100 product/territory/channel/method of payment four-tuples.*

obvious. With the normalization tool, a user with a trained eye can quickly
identify the presence or absence of two-, three-, four-, five- and even six-way
interactions, and combinations thereof, in spaces of higher dimensionalities.

In Figure 27.11, we show a totally different type of graph [Mih95]. Here,
the vertical bars in the cells are related to the mean income of people (1990
Census), plus or minus the standard error of the mean; the independent
variables or dimensions—namely, age bracket, education level, and gender

Figure 27.8

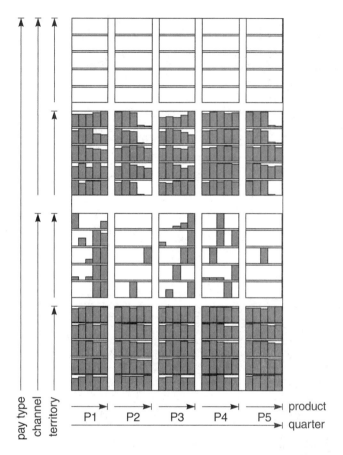

The same as Figure 27.7, except that each of the 100 time series has its own scale, making it possible to see the time trends of sales in product/territory/sales channel/method of payment four-tuples that have low sales and to compare them with the trends for other four-tuples.

(males are black symbols, females are gray)—are all along the horizontal. Clearly this data is radically different from previous examples. We can in fact visually infer that mean income grows exponentially with education, grows but saturates exponentially with age, and differs radically with gender. The gender differences in fact reflect substantial differences in the amplitudes of the variation of income with both age and education.

These examples and the cases discussed previously but not explicitly shown as graphs (such as the "random" cases) demonstrate a very important

Figure 27.9

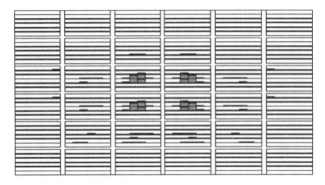

A textbook case of a three-way interaction in a four-variable (dimension) space. Here, all cells have the same scale.

Figure 27.10

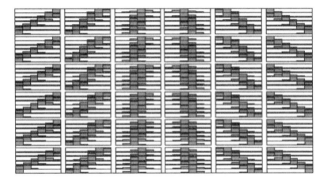

The same data as in Figure 27.9. Here, however, the "normalization" tool has been applied so that each "small graph" has its own scale, making the three-way interaction obvious.

point about the roles of multidimensional visualization. These visualizations can "steer" our information search in the vast multidimensional space. They can save enormous amounts of time by telling us instantly whether the data shows very clear patterns involving ordinal variables (such as the Census data) and that hence modeling by simple mathematical forms is appropriate and that looking for cells with the greatest "lift" is a waste of time. Alternatively, they may indicate the presence of a highly conditional correlation of two variables. They may also show random-looking patterns for all

Figure 27.11

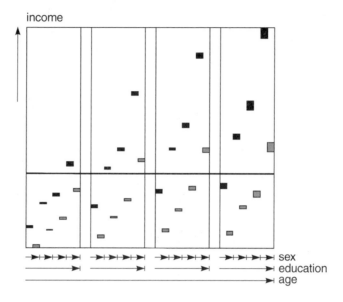

A graph of how the mean income (plus or minus the standard error of mean) varies with education, age, and gender.

possible variable nestings, indicating that correlations between cell pairs over one or more variables should be sought. Although in earlier discussions of this type of random data we pointed out that this redirection of our analysis efforts was in some sense equivalent to pursuing all possible narrow-field to wide-field data record transformations, this in fact is not the best way to implement the new analysis, in that it is extremely time consuming. Instead, the numbers in the cells (sales) are streamed out of the visualization engine, are reorganized, and then reenter the engine in the context of a new set of cells.

Consider, for example, the case in which we are interested in whether or not the sales of product 1 in territory 3 are correlated over time with the sales of product 3 in territory 2. Here, we have simplified the problem by aggregating over both channel and method of payment. In this case, the cell structure is very simple; namely, there is only one cell. However, that cell contains a normal *x-y* plot, with the number of sales of product 1 in territory 3 along *x*, and the "same time" number of sales of product 3 in territory 2 along *y*. If we had not aggregated the two channels and the two methods of payment, we would have four such graphs, each of which would display the same type of plot, but with the sales broken down by channel and method of payment.

Note that here both product-territory pairs must have the same channel and method of payment. We could of course choose to make comparisons, such as sales of product 1 in territory 3 via channel 1 with sales of product 3 in territory 2 via channel 2. In this case, we could either aggregate over method of payment and show one graph, or not aggregate and show two graphs, one for each method of payment, and so on.

The vital point here is that in all of these cases not only can visualization steer the information discovery process but it can rapidly provide new graphics suitable for the new direction of investigation. This is because all computations are done recursively in RAM, and the cell data need only be redirected, not recomputed from the records.

27.11 Real Business Problems, Optimization, and Combinatorics

The discussion to this point has been abstract. The nature of particular business problems you may wish to consider has not been explicitly addressed. An obvious question to ask is which business problems can be solved (utilizing data in a warehouse) in a relatively straightforward fashion and which problems cannot. This may be an obvious question, but it does not have an obvious answer. You can of course pose particular business problems that are simple to solve. For example, if all five products in Figure 27.1 are products of a single company rather than products of five competing companies, an executive might ask a question such as "If I had dropped some of my worst-performing units [a unit being a particular product in a particular territory sold via a particular channel and method of payment], how would it have affected my return on investment?" Assume the costs associated with each of the 100 units were the same. Let's call this the ROI question. To find the answer, you simply find the total sales for each product/territory/channel/method of payment unit and sort these 100 numbers in descending order to form a series (call it series I). Next, you form a new series II, as follows: the first entry is the sales of the top unit divided by 1, the second entry is the sum of sales for the top two units divided by 2, and so on, with the last entry in the series being total sales for all 100 units divided by 100. Next, you form a series III, as follows: subtract the 100th entry in series II from each entry in series II, divide each result by the 100th entry in series II, and then multiply each result by 100. Series III then gives a list of percentage changes in return on investment. For example, the 99th entry is the percentage change in return on investment that would have occurred if the worst unit were dropped (i.e., the 100th unit). The 98th entry is the percentage return on investment that would have occurred if the worst two units were dropped, and so on. For this simple question, there are only 100 cases, and its solution is trivial.

However, the presence of the data warehouse has allowed you to break down revenues by the four variables (i.e., product, territory, channel, and method of payment), and hence to form revenues for the 100 units. In the absence of such data, you would have to resort to assumptions. For example, if only the marginals were known (i.e., revenue by product, revenue by territory, revenue by channel, and revenue by method of payment), you would have to assume that the four variables were independent and answer the question on that basis. If strong interactions of a two-way, three-way, or four-way nature were in fact present, an answer based on an independent variable model could lead to disastrous decisions.

But how has "data mining" helped here? What "nuggets" of information have been discovered that might affect decisions? This is a semantic issue. You can say that the discovery of significant interactions is the "nugget." You might also take the point of view (correct or not) that the executive can only decide which units to drop based on a unit being defined via product, territory, channel, and method of payment, and hence it is not a matter of nugget discovery, but rather of information utilization. As I said, this is a semantic issue.

However, what if the costs involved for the ROI question were not this simple? The distance, and hence shipping costs, may differ for each product-territory pair. The sales cost may differ for each product/territory/channel/method of payment four-tuple. There may be complex economies of scale, and so on. In addition, what if constraints were put on, such as requiring a minimum amount of total revenue or a minimum revenue for each product or each territory? The only feasible approach may be to evaluate the ROI for all $2^{100} \sim 10^{30}$ cases, and to then filter them via the criteria.

To gain a perspective, let's grossly underestimate the computation and say that each case requires only one floating-point operation (in reality, it could be millions). Then, at least 10^{30} floating-point operations would be required to solve the problem. Using a one-teraflops supercomputer would require $10^{30}/10^{12} = 10^{18}$ seconds. Each year has $\sim 3 \times 10^7$ seconds. Hence, $10^{18}/3 \times 10^7 \sim 3 \times 10^{10}$ years would be required. This could easily be low, by a factor of 10^6. But who cares? Clearly this is not how business decisions are made. Instead, complex but linear optimization routines are utilized, and multi-dimensional data is oversimplified by modeling it to forms that have minimal interactions without differing radically from known data, at least to a dimensional depth of two, or possibly at most three, variables.

27.12 What's the Value of Data Mining?

What is the point of data exploration (mining) if utilizing information leads to computations that are too complex to be performed? The "answer" of course is that there are a myriad of different problems (other than the ROI type problem previously discussed) that can be solved, and a myriad of opportunities that can be exploited, which can be shown to have a net positive effect on the bottom line. That is, large revenue-generating opportunities with known and small incremental costs can be discovered. The ROI problem just discussed can become a full-blown combinatorial optimization problem that can be shown to be N-P complete. Data warehouses, data mining, OLAP, and visualization do not solve N-P complete problems, but that does not mean they are not valuable. They are leading to major discoveries in marketing, finance, manufacturing, and research in a variety of industries. The key issue is how you can discover important information that is difficult to find.

Knowledge discovery is a search problem. The area to be searched is vast, but presumably there are many prizes to be found. Unfortunately, the density of prizes per unit area is very small. How are you to proceed? A Ferrari is good because it will allow you to cover a lot of ground in a short period of time. A telescope is good because it will allow you to view large areas from any vantage point, especially if it has rapid-focus scanning capabilities. Clearly, mounting such a telescope on a Ferrari that can traverse distances comparable to the range of the telescope in short times is ideal. If we can locate our Ferrari essentially anywhere on the terrain, where should we start our search? Given that starting point, when should we beam ourselves (*Star Trek* "beam") to a vastly different location to start phase II of the search? The terrain is too vast to be completely searched in the lifetime of the universe, but clearly with our Ferrari and telescope we will discover far more prizes than Mr. Magoo in a Model T Ford. Recursive computing is the Ferrari, and multidimensional visualization is the telescope with fast-focus scanning. Ferraris will get faster, and telescopes will improve. Pick your own metaphor.

27.13 Evaluation of Discovery Tools

So far we have used two metaphors, the weapons metaphor and the search metaphor (Ferrari and telescope). The term *data mining* is itself a metaphor. *Data prospecting* is probably a better term. Both "mining" ("prospecting") and "searching" are good metaphors to use when attempting to discuss how to evaluate tools. Two prospectors may have very different tools to assist them in their search for gold. If we have a contest to see which prospector can find gold first, the winner may have the best tools, but it is far more likely that he was just lucky.

Consider the case of data mining tools. If we use two different tools on the same data set, we might be tempted to conclude that the tool that found more information and/or information of greater value in a given amount of time is the superior tool. This conclusion has precisely a 50-50 chance of being correct. Much like our prospector example, luck is involved. The luck involved here has to do with the nature of the data set. For instance, tools vary greatly in respect to the type of information they can discover in a pre-determined amount of time, or for that matter, in any amount of time. As mentioned earlier, tools vary in respect to their emphasis on dimensional depth versus dimensional breadth. If you use a shallow tool on a data set with 100 variables that has several important nuggets of information in widely different two-variable subspaces, you are likely to achieve a "good result."

On the other hand, if you use a deep tool designed to look to a maximum depth of, say, six variables, you can expect such a tool to take much longer to discover the shallow information. Basically, it is a case of comparing $100!/(98!2!) = 4950$ to $100!/(94!6!) = 12,547,920$, the latter being more than 2534 times larger. In reality, the deeper search will take far longer because the size of the spaces escalates geometrically and the number of possible types of interactions escalates combinatorially, as discussed at length previously. However, if the most important information in the data set occurs at a depth of five variables, the shallow tool will never find it, but the deep tool will. Moreover, the discoveries made in a fixed amount of time by two tools that are essentially identical in their performance (algorithmic efficiency) and in respect to their scope can vary widely if the tools are not run to completion. This is simply a luck phenomenon (i.e., which tool stumbles upon the information first).

You might be tempted to create a suite of test data sets with differing types of information planted within them. These data sets could then be used to benchmark mining tools. Unfortunately, I seriously doubt that this is a viable methodology, except perhaps to weed out tools that totally fail on even the simplest data sets. The possibilities are simply too enormous for this approach to work. The only way I can imagine making an intelligent choice of weapons (tools) involves multidimensional education and the willingness of the vendors to reveal their methodology. Even then, it will not be easy.

References

[Abr70]   M. Abramowitz and I. Stegun (editors). *Handbook of Mathematical Functions.* New York. Dover, 1970.

[Abr84]   A. Agresti. *Analysis of Ordinal Categorical Data.* New York. John Wiley & Sons, 1984.

[Mih95]   T. Mihalisin, J. Timlin, E. Gawlinski, and J. Mihalisin. "Visual Analysis of Very Large Multivariate Databases," *Proceedings of the Section on Statistical Graphics,* pp. 18–27. Orlando, FL. American Statistical Association, 1995.

[UPS01]   U.S. Patent No. 5,228,119 (Figures 27.6 through 27.11 herein).

Chapter 28

Document Mining and Visualization

ALEXANDER G. GEE

University of Massachusetts, Lowell

JOHN LIGHT

Intel Architecture Labs

Introduction

Providing access to documents for the purpose of analysis is a current issue for the data mining and visualization communities. This chapter focuses on how to provide content information for image and textual material. Metadata is introduced as a unification mechanism providing access to the various document types. In addition, a generalization about documents is made to provide the possible future analysis of more complex documents.

Computer applications for the analysis of numeric records are abundant in both commercial and research areas. However, tools are needed for the analysis of document collections. What are the application requirements needed for the mining and visualization of the rich information contained in large textual works and other such documents? The term *documents* will be loosely used here to refer to any data source that contains text, images, or both. The current state of applications and research involving the mining and visualization of documents is minimal, at best. Applications of data mining and data visualization do not handle significant amounts of textual material well.

Although similar to the work currently under way by information retrieval experts, the area of data mining and visualization attempts to draw generalizations about documents in a collection rather than obtain those documents from the collections that contain specific information. Data mining has heretofore been primarily concerned with finding numerical needles in database haystacks. Mining techniques have been aimed at large arrays of records, containing information that is primarily numeric or that can be easily converted to numbers. This is understandable, in that the earliest mechanisms for data mining involved mathematical analysis. Likewise, visualization tools require numeric values for their graphical presentation of data. Examples include MineSet by SGI and Diamond by SPSS. Documents, on the other hand, contain a large number of basic elements—words in text or pixels in images—set in some form of layout that represents a self-contained source of data.

Our concern is the design of text and image representations for data mining and data visualization. This chapter discusses two important questions pertaining to document mining. How do you extract and map document content information into data structures for analysis? What important metadata is required for the various types of documents to be analyzed?

28.1 Indexing Images

The mining and visualization of image collections require an understanding of what each image represents. The comparison of images is the process of comparing the content of each image. Current techniques for extracting image content originate from the field of computer vision, a child of the artificial intelligence community. Computer vision experts are developing computer systems that have the capability of understanding their surroundings through image analysis tools.

There are three standard approaches for image analysis: segmentation, feature extraction, and shape recovery. Segmentation is an edge-based method, a process that locates discontinuities across the image, or a region-based method, a process that groups pixels based on similarities [Kas91]. Feature extraction attempts to locate particular regions of interest in the image. Shape recovery goes beyond feature extraction to cluster regions that describe an object. The most important of these approaches is segmentation, which is typically the starting point to any image understanding application and includes the extraction of colored regions, object edges, and textured areas.

To provide useful information for mining and visualization tools, image content information needs to be concisely summarized. Such summaries should exploit the various image attributes (such as color distribution, motion, shape, structure, and texture), which can be used to gauge similarity and perhaps used to index the image [Rav95]. The exact information needed to provide a useful image comparison is currently not known, and different systems tend to use a variety of basic techniques. An example high-level retrieval system, the QBIC system developed by IBM, uses segmented objects (composite regions that form a known shape) as its index to images [Man97]. Another technique for indexing images involves representing images with vectors used as representations of appearance [Rav95]. Here, each pixel of the image is associated with a vector of values corresponding to the application of several Gaussian derivative filters applied to the image.

The Image Retrieval for Information Systems (IRIS) project developed at the University of Bremen, Germany, combines methods and techniques of computer vision and knowledge representation for the automatic generation of textual content descriptions of images [Kla95]. This system combines color, texture, and contour analysis with graph grammars to provide a taxonomy of the content space. By establishing an arbitrary, homogeneous size grid across each image and analyzing these images for color, texture, and edges, this system classifies the collection of images into discrete image types.

Because images are represented as arrays of numerical values, the mining and visualization of images can readily be performed with a minimal amount of effort in comparison to text documents. Yet, current tools handle only the actual content and not the interpretations of the content. It could be of great value to provide tools that can access all levels of information provided in images.

28.2 Indexing Text

As document collections grow, the need to understand and organize such collections requires new tools. New advancements in both document storage and algorithm design will be required to permit the analysis of text. Text is an important medium for storing complex information using natural language. Consisting of letters, words, and sentences, text documents are not created for computers but for humans. The appropriate encoding of such text is required to provide computers with easy access to a text's underlying content.

In contrast to analyzing images, the mining and visualization of text-based documents have only just started. Because most mining and visualization systems to date use numerical values, text cannot be analyzed. One approach is to extract information contained in such text documents and encode the information numerically. The trick is to represent each document with sufficiently detailed information that covers all relevant content yet totals less than the entire document in size.

As text documents are typically large, it has been impractical to index entire documents. It was standard practice to index a document from a subset of terms found in the text. The chief drawback to full-text indexing has been its expense, which is associated with storage space, time requirements, and computational resources [Wit94]. Consequently, index terms or other tags that reflect the content of the text have been used to retrieve documents from a collection [Smi90]. For information retrieval purposes, similar documents will have overlapping terms. Thus, it is important in the extraction of index terms that they all reside closely in an information space of terms that covers the entire document collection. Too little a selection of terms for each document means the resulting information space could be quite sparse.

The selection of terms from a document should involve not human effort but rather an automated process preventing the possibility of personal bias toward information. The automatic derivative indexing is to extract or derive appropriate index terms from the text, providing a consistent set of indexes across the document space [Smi90]. Early experimental work by Luhn broke the process of indexing into several steps. First, count the frequencies of all words in a document and then discard the most frequent and the least frequent words. Next, for each sentence in the document, compute a score based on the number of terms remaining. Use the index terms from those sentences with the highest scores [Smi90]. A possible improvement results from the use of relative rather than absolute frequencies; such frequencies take into account the entire document collection [Smi90]. Another variation is the use of only stem words. Proposed by Sparck Jones, a more appropriate weight for a term is the difference between a term's frequency in the document and its frequency in all documents. The resulting list of terms and their corresponding weights distinguishes the more important terms from the less important [Smi90]. There is now a new trend toward full-text indexing. Because of modern compression techniques, it is now possible to index every word in a text document [Wit94]. The compression of text reduces text storage while at the same time providing fast indexing information to the words.

Full-text indexing is a powerful and mature method for finding records in a text archive. It has limitations in many of the places it is used, but its limitations become burdensome in the data mining environment. First, indexing does not integrate well with other technologies. Indexing is a highly optimized mechanism for a specific class of problems, and its methodology does not easily adapt to other purposes. Second, indexing does not scale well in either space or time. The process of indexing involves essentially inverting a very large matrix. As the size of the archive increases, the storage and processing time required for creating the index becomes enormous. However, the recent use of compression techniques does provide a means of circumventing the storage problem. Next, indexing successfully works for taking specific input and providing specific output, though this is not the data mining paradigm in which the search for the right question is often as important as any of the answers. Finally, there is no satisfying visualization of the indexing; indexing is used primarily for a text-in/text-out process. Consequently, further research needs to concentrate on the storage and representation of text documents that removes such limitations.

Presented next is one idea for providing additional information about documents that could help current mining and visualization systems. Although still in its infancy, the idea of using the compressed version of a document might provide other benefits. It might also be possible to have data mining and visualization techniques that directly access these compressed text files. There could also be a hybrid solution. Such a solution would involve a hierarchical representation of text documents, ranging from a few index terms to the full compressed document. The following idea attempts to extract text information that can be directly used by current mining and visualization tools.

The key to integrating text mining and data mining is the conversion of textual material into numbers that can be handled like any other numerical field in a database record. Because most databases react poorly to having additional fields added on short notice, the general solution is to create a proxy record for every record in the database. This is done currently in data mining when the database itself is too large and not all fields are needed, or when the database is sampled to create a smaller number of records to deal with. By applying data mining and visualization to the set of proxy records instead of to the original records, mining queries can refer to both original and generated fields, allowing analysis of both textual and nontextual fields in the original database.

The critical issue in creating useful proxy records is how we create numeric fields from text fields. The pressing issue is how to handle the larger amounts of textual material that increasingly occur in our databases. The challenge is to explore and understand the possible methods for summarizing the textual information with numbers that can be used in the mining process. The standard information retrieval method for reducing text to numbers is to represent the document as a term vector. The total size of a term space for a typical document is many thousands (N), each document can be thought of as a point in N space, and clusters of documents in N space represent similar documents. Often, the distance in N space is used as a metric for similarity among documents.

The naive way to approach turning text into numbers is to drop the N vector for each document into its proxy record. Although this may prove interesting, current data mining applications do not appreciate many thousands of fields and are not optimized to handle such a large number. What we would really like to do is summarize each document with a reasonable (10 to 100) number V of numeric fields that could then be used in the mining process. One possible technique is to find those terms in a document set that are most effective at distinguishing clusters. You might apply such a term selection method, then pick the most distinguished terms and drop them into the proxy record. Another idea is to perform a full clustering on the document set for an arbitrarily large number of clusters. Here, for each document, you would build a vector of the distances to the centroids of each cluster and drop the result into the proxy record to represent the document content. A third possibility involves authoring a representative set of V topics for the document set. Here, you would represent each topic with an "ideal" document, either chosen or authored by an export, and represent each document with a vector of similarity functions between the document and each of the V topics.

28.3 Metadata

Indexing is really one type of metadata—representative terms that provide additional information about a document. It was mentioned that "metadata has to be generated in addition to the data it relates to" [Lan96]. The effort of creating metadata would imply that it has a useful purpose. Although seemingly important, the topic of metadata requirements has only appeared within the last five years. Initiated by a metadata workshop held at the Center for High Performance Computing in Austin, Texas, in August 1993, the discussion of metadata still has a relatively small following. However, metadata will become an important key to integrating the various document types within data mining and visualization applications.

Metadata provides supporting data to a corresponding document and can be used to help relate different documents. There is also the possibility of comparing across different document types by implementing similar metadata formats. Table 28.1 provides a comparison of some basic metadata elements between text and image documents. This table is important for the

Table 28.1

Comparing image and text data.

Image	Text
Pixel Count	Word Count
Format	Layout
Regions	Keywords
Automatic Semantic Representation	Automatic Natural Language Summarization
Feature Extraction	Term Extraction
Mood	Tone

comparison between document types and the analysis of documents containing both types.

Mining a document archive may seem entirely amenable to indexing methodology, even when considering the issues discussed in the preceding section. For most query purposes, this may be true, but for data mining, more forms of information should be considered. A partial list of explicit nontextual metadata for general document sets includes document size; number of paragraphs, lines, and words; publication date (modification date); number of images, figures, and tables; language enumeration (English, etc.); standard complexity analysis (grade level, etc.); and number of authors. The availability of this additional metadata is especially useful in data mining, where the object is to find something new rather than something you have seen before. The result is that all text mining can benefit from a combination of objective metadata and more subjective evaluations of the document. Thus, there is really no difference between the ideal milieu for mining databases containing textual information and mining document archives. They form a continuum that has varying degrees of objective and subjective information, all amenable to standard data mining practices, including visualization.

28.4 Documents

The future trend of tools for data mining and visualization will eventually provide the ability to analyze document collections that contain various media formats. The general document will contain text, images, layouts, sounds, and video. The introduction of metadata provides the initial linkage method needed to bring the various data types together for analysis. Recent research has started this generalization by analyzing documents containing both text and images. Current work at the University of Maryland aims at looking at the decomposition of documents into regions that contain text and images. The structural analysis of documents involves the derivation of the logical or semantic meaning of regions, which requires the labeling of document components by a document class or type (memo, letter, newspaper, etc.). Other projects, such as those at the University of Massachusetts, Amherst, are involved with the extraction of text from images [Wit94].

28.5 Conclusion

The application of data mining and visualization tools to textual material is a topic of increasing interest as the number of text document collections continues to increase. The unification of text retrieval and data mining techniques will allow the broadening of tools for data mining, including visualization, to be used in mining text archives. To use current systems, the representation of textual material in the standard record form of data mining by summarizing each document or text field as short vectors is required. Further research for alternative document storage techniques and corresponding mining and visualization tools are also required. Document mining is only the cap of the iceberg and represents the proving ground for mining and visualizing rich media such as videos and Web sites.

References

[Kas91]   R. Kasturi and R. C. Jain. *Computer Vision: Principles*. Los Alamitos, CA. IEEE Computer Society Press, 1991.

[Kla95]   C. Klauck. "Graph Grammar Based Object Recognition for Image Retrieval," *Proceedings of the Second Asian Conference on Computer Vision*, December 1995.

[LAM97]   Language and Media Processing (LAMP) Lab, University of Maryland. "Page Decomposition and Structural Analysis," 1997. *documents.cfar.umd.edu/ LAMP/Media/Projects/PageDecomp.html.*

[Lan96]   U. Lang, G. Grinstein, and R.D. Bergeron. "Visualization Related Metadata," *Lecture Notes in Computer Science*, vol. 1183, pp. 26–34, A. Wierse, G. Grinstein, and U. Lang (editors). New York. Springer-Verlag, 1996.

[Lig97]   J. Light. "A Distributed, Graphical, Topic-Oriented Document Search System," *Proceedings of the Sixth International Conference on Information and Knowledge Management* (CIKM'97), November 1997.

[Man97]   R. Manmatha. "Multimedia Indexing and Retrieval Research at the Center for Intelligent Information Retrieval," *Proceedings of the Symposium on Document Image Understanding Technology*, 1997. *hobart.cs.umass.edu/~mmedia /postscript/sdiut97.ps.gz.*

[Rav95]   S. Ravela, R. Manmatha, and E. M. Riseman. "Scale-Space Matching and Image Retrieval," *Proceedings of the ARPA Image Understanding Workshop*, 1995. *hobart.cs.umass.edu/~mmedia/postscript/iuw95.ps.gz.*

[Smi90]   P. D. Smith. *An Introduction to Text Processing.* Cambridge, MA. MIT Press, 1990.

[Wit94]   L. H. Witten, A. Moffat, and T. C. Bell. "Compression and Full-Text Indexing for Digital Libraries," *Abstracts for the 1994 Workshop on Digitial Libraries: Current Issues*, 1994. *www.cs.umbc.edu/conferences/dl/abstracts.html.*

Chapter 29

Research Issues in the Analysis and Visualization of Massive Data Sets

CLAUDIO J. MENESES

University of Massachusetts, Lowell

GEORGES G. GRINSTEIN

University of Massachusetts, Lowell

Introduction

In this chapter, we identify and discuss some research issues related to the analysis and visualization of massive data sets, in the context of the KDD process. Mainly, we discuss the lack of adequate definitions and models to deal with massive data sets, and the need to evaluate, characterize, and adapt existing data analysis methods and visualization techniques to address the challenge presented by massive and complex data sets.

29.1 Background

Recent advances in the technology available to society (such as sensors, satellite systems, telephone networks, global computing networks, etc.), are generating huge data sets. These sets, called massive data sets—with a large number of dimensions and an even larger number of observations (records)— are challenging the ability of the scientific community to measure, analyze, and visualize data. New methods, tools, and perhaps definitions from diverse disciplines are needed to address this challenge. In addition to the need for a wider variety of statistical models to analyze massive and complex data sets, new methods to mine knowledge from data and novel visualization techniques are essential to advance toward a new generation of tools that integrates both approaches.

The collection of observations that compose the database of many organizations is today growing exponentially. Examples of such huge and high-dimensional databases are being generated by systems from different fields, such as earth observation systems [Kah96], marketing systems [Sch96], crime data sets [Kin96], health care systems [Goo96], atmospheric systems [Lev96], and on-line textual database systems [Dum96], among many others. However, techniques and tools used in the analysis and visualization of small and medium-size data sets are inconvenient, and in some cases are simply not applicable to large and high-dimensional data sets. The main obstacles are human limitations (resolution of the human visual system), computational complexity (which tends to increase faster than linearly with data sets), and lack of software (for massive parallelism).

In this chapter, we discuss some issues in which further research is required in order to deal with massive data sets. First, we need precise definitions of the means of massive data sets and their relationship to small and medium-size data sets. There is also the need to evaluate and characterize data analysis methods and multidimensional visualization techniques to determine their frontier of aggravation, and if it is feasible to adapt them in the analysis and visualization of massive data sets.

29.2 Concepts and Definitions

Although a definition of *massive* can be found in any dictionary, it is not useful to define objectively what it means for a data set to be massive. Some classifications proposed and based on the size of the data [Hub96] are subjective, and they clearly depend on the available computing resources. In this sense, an objective model that captures the basic properties of the data set, the available computational resources, and the type of task (e.g., visualization, data analysis, and data processing) to be performed on the data set is required in order to formulate an objective definition of the concept "massive" applied to data sets.

In addition, in relation to the modeling process, there is the urgent need of knowing and understanding the relationship between the complexity of the data and the power of prediction and description of the model. In other words, we need to know how, when, and why models that predict and describe adequately data sets of small and medium complexity are exceeded for massive data sets of high complexity. For example, data processing is a task commonly performed in batch mode with little or no participation of humans, but data analysis typically requires human steering, and for that reason is an interactive work; thus, the limit in which problems start to appear, in relation to the size of the data set, may be different for processing, analysis, and visualization of data sets, and currently it remains diffuse and not well defined.

29.3 Scaling Data Analysis Methods

In the context of the KDD process, a wide variety and number of data mining algorithms from fields of statistics, pattern recognition, machine learning, and databases are described in the literature. However, massive and high-dimensional data sets create combinatorially explosive search spaces for model induction and increase the probability that a data mining algorithm will find spurious and invalid patterns [Fay96]. Thus, there exists the need of adapting the existing techniques and inventing novel methods to handle high dimensionality and the huge number of observations inherent in massive data sets.

Most of the current data mining algorithms (e.g., rule induction and neural networks from machine learning) assume that the data set is of moderate size and can be loaded in memory, because they need to take all data at once in order to create a hypothesis based on this data. Of course, this is a serious limitation when we want to analyze and extract patterns from massive data sets. Thus, an evaluation and better characterization of these methods may provide the necessary insight in adapting or discarding them when we are dealing with massive data sets.

29.4 Scaling Visualization Techniques

Most of the modern visualization techniques (e.g., parallel coordinates) work well with a small number of dimensions and records, but they usually do not scale to massive data sets. How can these techniques be adapted to visualize data sets with large numbers of dimensions and huge numbers of observations?

For massive data sets, we would like to use the human visual system in the process of discovering knowledge, because it is a powerful pattern recognizer and perhaps the best pattern discoverer we currently have. However, a serious limitation is the resolution of the human visual system, which is poor and is limited to small and medium data sets. Thus, as in the case of data analysis methods, there exists the need to adapt multidimensional visualization techniques to work with massive data sets or to create novel methods. It is essential, as a first step, to elaborate a robust evaluation and characterization of the current techniques and tools used to visualize multidimensional data sets.

References

[Dum96]   S. T. Dumais. "Information Retrieval: The Promise and Problems." *Massive Data Sets*. Washington, DC. National Academy Press, 1996.

[Fay96]   U. Fayyad, G. Piatetsky-Shapiro, and P. Smyth. "The KDD Process for Extracting Useful Knowledge from Volumes of Data," *Communications of the ACM*, November 1996, vol. 39, no. 11, pp. 27–34.

[Goo96]   C. R. Goodall. "Massive Data Sets: Guidelines and Practical Experience from Health Care," *Massive Data Sets*. Washington, DC. National Academy Press, 1996.

[Gri96]   G. G. Grinstein. "Harnessing the Human in Knowledge Discovery," *Proceedings of the Second International Conference on Knowledge Discovery and Data Mining*, August 1996, Portland, OR. E. Simoudis, J. Han, and U. Fayyad (editors), pp. 384–385, 1996.

[Gro93]   M. H. Gross and F. Seibert. "Visualization of Multidimensional Image Data Sets Using a Neural Network," *Visual Computer*, 10, pp. 145–159, 1993.

[Gro94]   M. H. Gross. "Subspace Methods for the Visualization of Multidimensional Data Sets," *Scientific Visualization: Advances and Challenges*, L. Rosenblum, R. Earnshaw, J. Encarnacao, H. Hagen, A. Kaufman, S. V. Klimenko, G. Nielson, F. Post, and D. Thalmann (editors), pp 171–186. London. IEEE Computer Society Press/Academic Press, 1994.

[Hag94]   H. Hagen. "Visualization of Large Data Sets," *Scientific Visualization: Advances and Challenges*, Rosenblum et al. (editors), pp. 187–198. London. IEEE Computer Society Press/Academic Press, 1994.

[Hin92]   G. E. Hinton. "How Neural Networks Learn from Experience," *Scientific American*, September 1992, pp. 145–151.

[Hub96]   P. J. Huber. "Massive Data Sets Workshop: The Morning After," *Massive Data Sets*. Washington, DC. National Academy Press, 1996.

[Kah96]   R. Kahn. "Earth Observation Systems: What Shall We Do with the Data We Are Expecting in 1998?," *Massive Data Sets*. Washington, DC. National Academy Press, 1996.

[Kin96]   C. R. Kindermann and M. M. DeBerry. "Management Issues in the Analysis of Large-Scale Crime Data Sets," *Massive Data Sets*. Washington, DC. National Academy Press, 1996.

[Kni90]   K. Knight. "Connectionist Ideas and Algorithms," *Communications of the ACM*, November 1990, 33:11, pp. 59–74.

[Lev96]   G. Levy, C. Pu, and P. D. Sampson. "Massive Data Assimilation/Fusion in Atmospheric Models and Analysis: Statistical, Physical, and Computational Challenges," *Massive Data Sets*. Washington, DC. National Academy Press, 1996.

[Sch96]   J. Schmitz. "Marketing," *Massive Data Sets*. Washington, DC. National Academy Press, 1996.

Chapter 30

Toward Smarter Databases
A Case-Building Toolkit

Marc Ringuette

Inference Corporation

Inference Corporation is an industry leader in deploying Case-Based Reasoning (CBR) systems for problem solving. In the past, we have encouraged our customers to create their case bases by hand by using our CBR Express authoring environment, and we have become experts in the institutional process of turning problem-solving experience into case bases. Still, we continue to look for ways to provide more powerful tools to our customers for building case bases.

We have deployed software, the CBR Generator, which uses text indexing to create case bases from textual problem logs. However, our production code is not yet taking advantage of the structured information available in our customers' in-house databases.

Our vision is the Case-Building Toolkit: the fusion of a data mining and visualization front end operating on SQL databases, inductive learning, and clustering routines that can be applied to SQL tables of data to produce new columns (features) from existing data. Our vision also incorporates the CBR paradigm, which operationalizes problem-solving knowledge.

We believe this final step is critical. We believe that data mining is not just a matter of extracting knowledge and placing it in an expert's head or in a glossy report. When an organization hopes to achieve a real return on its investment, it must have some tools to operationalize that knowledge for problem solving. CBR is such a tool, and there are several decades of research and deployed systems demonstrating its effectiveness. Our Case-Building Toolkit is intended to enable the expert to

- Identify, extract, categorize, and cluster data that is potentially useful to problem solving

- Generate a case base of prototypical problem descriptions and solutions

- Test and refine that case base to improve its coverage and usability for problem solving

- Deploy the case base for use by individuals in day-to-day problem solving

Only the first of these steps is given much attention in data mining research! We hope to change this.

Chapter 31

The NASD Regulation Advanced Detection System

Integrating Data Mining and Visualization for Break Detection in the NASDAQ Stock Market

TED E. SENATOR
HENRY G. GOLDBERG
PING SHYR

NASD Regulation, Inc.

SCOTT BENNETT
STEVE DONOHO
CRAIG LOVELL

SRA International, Inc.

Introduction

As part of its responsibility as a self-regulatory organization in the securities industry, the National Association of Securities Dealers (NASD) Regulation, Inc., is responsible for surveillance of the NASDAQ stock market. The NASDAQ market involves a complex series of electronic interactions between multiple market participants in diverse geographic locations. Market makers provide quotations, which represent prices at which they are willing to buy or sell shares in a particular security, and size, which is the number of shares they are willing to buy or sell. Market makers also execute trades, either with other market makers or with customers, for their own or for customer accounts. NASDAQ participation is governed by a complex set of rules, designed to ensure a level playing field so that the market is fair to all participants and to facilitate maximum trading liquidity.

This chapter discusses a system under development by NASD Regulation, Inc., and SRA International, Inc., for use by NASD Regulation, Inc., as part of its responsibility for surveillance of the NASDAQ stock market. The system, known as the Advanced Detection System, or ADS, integrates data mining and data visualization as essential components of a break detection system. (Break detection systems are a particular form of fraud detection system that alerts a user to complex scenarios of activity that may represent violative behavior. Break detection systems are discussed in [Gol97].) ADS is built around a data warehouse containing NASDAQ trades and quotes, associated source and derived attributes, and summary and profile information about issues and firms. Application programs update the warehouse on a daily and weekly basis, and detect breaks using two pattern matchers, one of which matches patterns expressed as rules and the other of which matches patterns expressed as time sequences of events. Data mining components include parallel and scalable decision trees and association rule implementations; visualization components include a series of custom-tailored 2D displays, 3D landscapes based on a commercial product, and pseudo-natural language and graphical displays of rules discovered by the data mining components.

31.1 Rule Generation and Visualization

The decision tree and association rule modules are used to generate rules that may represent patterns of regulatory interest in the trade and quote data. A rule-filtering and management module is used to reduce the set of generated rules to those that are most general across multiple firms. Analysts and developers review the generated rules to determine their utility and validity as patterns for break detection. The rules are presented to NASD Regulation analysts through the use of custom visualization software, implemented in Java. The visualization is essential to summarize the transactions underlying the rule to the analysts, to present the context of the rule (including positive and negative examples to the analyst), and to clearly identify the features contained in the discovered rule. The same visualization used to present discovered rules is used to present breaks; that is, sets of trades and quotes that match the approved patterns used for break detection. (Patterns are simply rules that have been "promoted" or activated for use in break detection.)

Figure 31.1

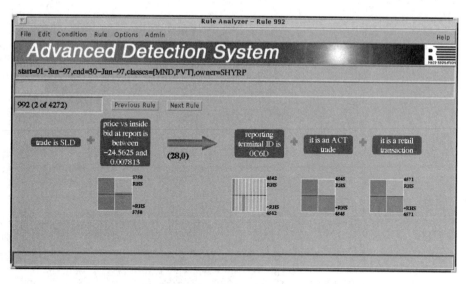

Rule analyzer. (See also color plate.)

A rule consists of a left-hand side and a right-hand side, both of which are a series of conditions. The rule visualization depicts each of the conditions as a box, indicating all possible values of the variable in the condition on the horizontal axis, and using a bar graph above and below the horizontal axis to indicate the number of trades/quotes corresponding to the truth and falsity of the entire rule, respectively. The conditions are described with a pseudo-natural language translation of the variable name and values. An arrow pointing from the conditions on the left-hand side to the right-hand side is labeled with a pair of numbers corresponding to the number of instances of the left-hand side for which the right-hand side is true and false, respectively. Clicking on the arrow brings up a tabular display of all trades/quotes referenced by the rule, with the positive examples in black and the negative examples grayed out. Our experience in presenting the results of rule generation to the analysts led to the development of this display. We have found that visualizing the conditions of the rule has allowed our analysts to determine which rule conditions are important and which are not, making it possible for them to suggest modifications and generalizations to the mined rules, which make them more useful for break detection. The analysts can also edit rule conditions to create new rules, and view the results of these new rules with the same display. This rule display is illustrated in Figure 31.1.

Figure 31.2

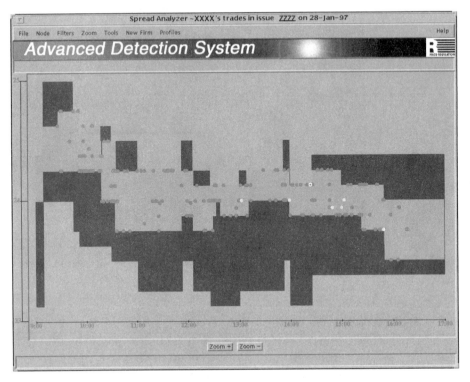

Spread display.

31.2 2D Displays

To effectively interpret breaks generated by the system, analysts need to be able to rapidly and comprehensively review the state of the market during the time around the suspected violation. We have developed a "spread display" that depicts the market in a particular security as seen by a specific market participant. It is a sequence display that depicts the flow of shares between market participants, and a firm relationship display that depicts relationships between market participants. Because the key relationship in market surveillance is temporal, these displays (except for the firm relationship display) are based on time.

The market context around the time of a suspected violation in a security is determined by three things: the trades in that security, the bids and asks of the market makers in that security, and the "inside" bid and ask (the lowest ask price and the highest bid price). The difference between a bid and an ask-

Figure 31.3

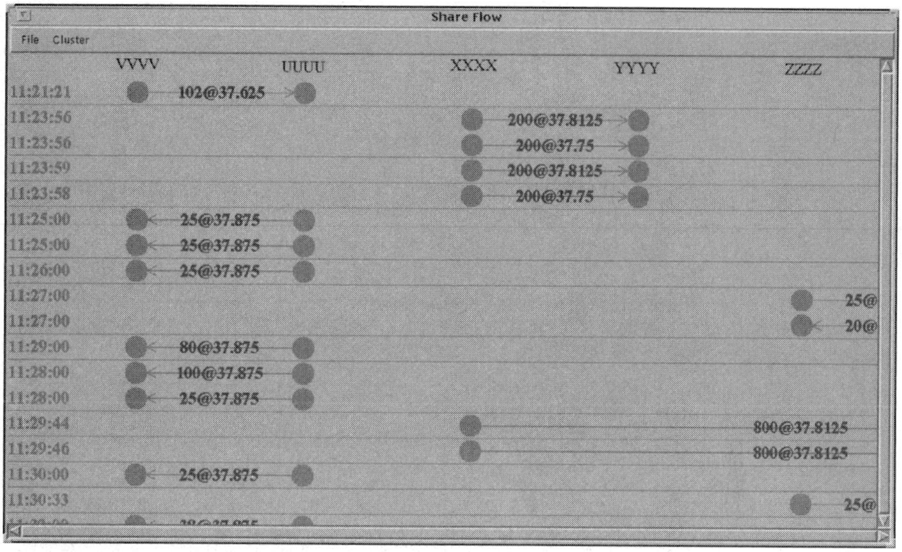

Share flow.

ing price is called the "spread." This context is captured visually in the "spread display" tool (Figure 31.2). A market maker's bid price and ask price in an issue are plotted against time in blue. The inside bid prices and ask prices are plotted in green over the market maker's quotes. This shows the market maker's quote with respect to the inside—specifically, at what times that market maker had the best bid or ask. A trade is a discrete event occurring at a specific time at a specific price, and thus is displayed as a dot plotted at that point. Running the mouse over or inside a trade or quote causes the details of that event to be displayed at the bottom of the screen. This allows analysts to quickly identify important events visually, such as the inside spread being narrowed, multiple small trades being executed against a market maker, and a market maker buying up a lot of shares in an issue.

The sequence display (Figure 31.3) shows a group of trades in order by execution time. Each trade has a buyer, a seller, a price, a number of shares, and a time at which the trade occurred. A trade is represented as an arrow from the buyer to the seller, marked with the number of shares and price. When a group of trades is sorted by time, patterns of share flow are visible. A firm may collect shares through multiple medium-size buys, and sell them in one large sale. Shares may pass through multiple firms before reaching their final destination. These patterns of share flow are crucial for analyzing potential violations.

Figure 31.4

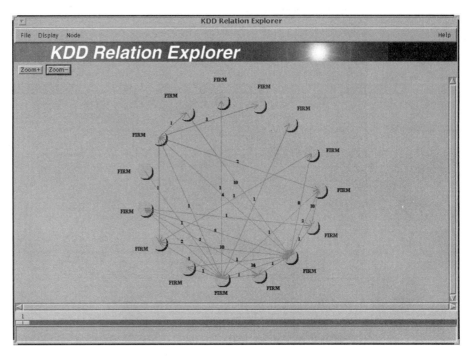

Relationship display.

The firm relationship display (Figure 31.4) shows aggregate trading statistics among firms for a given time period. Firms are represented as dots and are arranged in a circle. If firm 1 had three sells to firm 2, this is represented as an arrow from firm 1 to firm 2, with a weight of three. The arrows as a group show which firms trade heavily with which other firms. Unusually heavy trading among a small group of firms during a time period may be interesting to an analyst.

31.3 3D Displays

In addition to specific rule violations, NASD Regulation must detect any potential conventions or regularities in market behavior that might indicate improper coordination by market participants. Detecting such possible, unknown conventions is key task for the discovery components of the system. By definition, any convention involves regularities of behavior in

Figure 31.5

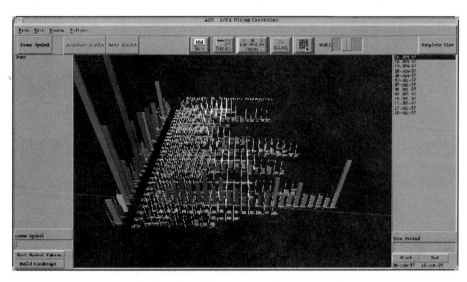

Pricing landscape. (See also color plate.)

many market actions by groups of market participants. Detecting any such conventions requires the ability to rapidly review large amounts of market data for patterns and anomalies.

To provide this ability, Visible Decisions' Discovery software was selected as the basis for 3D displays of market activity. (See [Mar96] for a description of this off-the-shelf software package.) Two 3D "landscapes" have been developed. The first, called the Pricing landscape (Figure 31.5), displays a large amount of summary data regarding quotation activity by multiple market makers in many issues. This landscape was designed to highlight the possible existence of pricing conventions in portions of the market. These may be agreements among market makers to quote only in specific price intervals. When these "agreements" are enforced by peer pressure or harassment, they become anticompetitive and are violative practices. These and similar practices have been identified as resulting in less favorable markets for the customer, and are the subject of a major surveillance effort by NASD Regulation.

A visual examination of this display permits an analyst to rapidly determine patterns of quotations in an issue and similarities between the quotation behavior of different market makers. The landscape focuses on the securities issues quoted by a particular market maker. Then all quoting behaviors for all other market makers are displayed. This allows the analyst to view how a particular market maker stacks up against the others with

Figure 31.6

Spread landscape. (See also color plate.)

whom he competes. Situations in which the pricing conventions hold for all but a few market makers are those most likely to result in anticompetitive behavior, warranting the closest review. In addition, new conventions are more easily visible, in that the display may be adjusted by various thresholds and filters to show how a price convention may correlate with certain market conditions.

The second display, called a Spread landscape (Figure 31.6), allows an analyst to view the quotation and trading behavior of a set of market makers in a particular issue over a specified time period. This display may be viewed as a generalization of the 2D spread display previously described. It immediately allows an analyst to focus in on anomalies in behavior by a particular market maker or at a particular time. The data from the NASDAQ stock market arrives as a series of updates to the market's "state." Yet, brokers/dealers view the market as a dynamic entity. In order for regulatory analysts to recapture this viewpoint, the data updates must be merged back into a unified entity they can visualize as a whole. This landscape is designed to accomplish this within the limits of data processing and graphics capabilities. Even when limited to a single security, there may be a few thousand trades, and many hundreds of quote changes, during a trading day. The interrelationships among market makers are made visible, and the analyst can "drill down" by maneuvering and zooming in 3D, as well as by displaying data details in pop-up windows provided for this purpose.

31.4 Conclusions

ADS demonstrates that visualization and data mining are complementary components of a useful break detection system. Visualization is necessary to present the results of discovery to analysts so that they can determine which results are of interest. The exact same visualization mechanisms that aid in this discovery process are those that are of value to the break evaluation process. This "dual-purpose use" of the visualization provides a developmental economy, the value of which cannot be discounted in a real application. Visualization is also used as a discovery tool to suggest patterns of activity to analysts. These patterns then become the basis for automated discovery in the data.

References

[Gol97]   H. G. Goldberg and T. E. Senator. "Break Detection Systems," *Proceedings of the Workshop on AI Approaches to Fraud Detection and Risk Management.* Providence, RI. AAAI Press, 1997.

[Mar96]   J. Martin. "Beyond Pie Charts and Spreadsheets," *Computerworld*, May 27, 1996.

Index

About the Authors

Loretta Auvil is currently working in the Automated Learning Group at the National Center for Supercomputing Applications (NCSA). She specializes in applying data mining and visualization techniques to real-world problems from industry as well as academic areas. Her main research interest is information visualization approaches for multidimensional data. Ms. Auvil received an M.S. in computer science from Virginia Tech in 1992 and a B.S. in applied mathematics and computer science from Alderson-Broaddus College in 1990. Prior to working for NCSA, she spent several years creating tools for visualizing performance data of parallel computer programs at Rome Laboratory and Oak Ridge National Laboratory.

Sheila B. Banks is president of Calculated Insight, a company providing research and development, consulting, and educational services for businesses and organizations. Dr. Banks received a B.S. from the University of Miami, Coral Gables, Florida, in 1984 and a B.S. in electrical engineering from North Carolina State University, Raleigh, in 1986. Also from North Carolina State University, Raleigh, she received an M.S. in electrical and computer engineering in 1987 and a Ph.D. in computer engineering (artificial intelligence) from Clemson University in 1995. Her research interests include artificial intelligence, human behavior and cognitive modeling, intelligent computer-generated forces, associate and collaborative systems, distributed virtual environments, intelligent human-computer interaction, and man-machine interfaces.

Allan Beck has around ten years' experience in all aspects of quality software delivery, covering architectures and project management. He has managed and delivered projects in most application and business areas and in recent years has focused on the delivery of analytical and CRM products and solutions. Allan is currently a technical consultant with MoTech Software Europe, a technical and e-business consultancy. Prior to that, he was a technical and development manager at thinkAnalytics Corporation, where he was responsible for delivery of the thinkCRA suite of analytical applications.

He was also involved in the development of the K.wiz knowledge discovery and data mining platform. Allan has also worked with British Telecommunications on projects as diverse as telecommunications network monitoring and repair software and satellite management systems. Allan graduated from the University of Aberdeen, Scotland.

Barry Becker is currently manager of a data visualization group at Blue Martini Software, a maker of e-commerce software. Prior to this, he spent four years at Silicon Graphics, Inc., developing the MineSet decision support product. As a computer scientist at Lawrence Livermore National Laboratory from 1990 to 1995, he worked on scientific visualization research. He graduated from Rensselaer Polytechnic Institute in 1990 and received an M.S. in computer science from U.C. Davis in 1992.

Scott Bennett is vice president and director of research and development at SRA International. Since joining SRA in 1993, he has focused on creating high-value advanced technology solutions for government and commercial clients. This has included work on the design, development, and deployment of large-scale data and text mining systems. Dr. Bennett's data mining experience includes work with very large structured and unstructured data sets, parallel architectures for data mining, a variety of discovery and detection algorithms, and graphical tools for analysis of mining results. He has worked on fraud detection in a number of domains and worked closely with NASDAQ in architecting and developing the Advanced Detection System (ADS), which uses a combination of discovery and detection algorithms to surveil the market. He helped to design and build SRA's core multistrategy data mining toolset on which applications like ADS are based as well as those for the mortgage, insurance, and brokerage industries. Dr. Bennett also helped to build a computer security offering that utilizes data mining to proactively discover potential intrusion patterns and to deploy them for real-time detection of intruders. In the area of bio-informatics, he has worked to bring unique data analytic capabilities to bear in the area of microarray data analysis and serves as a principal investigator in grant work with the National Institutes of Health. Dr. Bennett is now working to enhance user productivity on mobile devices through a combination of technologies, including the use of automated text analysis. Dr. Bennett received his Ph.D. in electrical and computer engineering from the University of Illinois at Urbana-Champaign in 1993.

Peter R. Bono is president of Peter R. Bono Associates, Inc. His current consulting activities encompass collaborative computing, data mining, data visualization, and general volume visualization. He uses his experience in user-interface design and software project management to plan and direct Web-related activities like corporate portal development and services for wireless information appliances. He has hands-on familiarity with HTML, DHTML, Java, JavaScript, VBScript, Active Server Pages, XML, and SQL. He served as chairman of the U.S. Computer Graphics Standards Committee (X3H3) from 1979 to 1994 and as chief delegate for the U.S. to ISO/IEC JTC1/SC24 from 1979 to 1989. Dr. Bono received his A.B. cum laude in mathematics from Harvard College and his M.S. and Ph.D. in computer science from the University of Michigan. He has coauthored two books and has written, taught short courses, and lectured widely on topics related to standardization and systems integration. Dr. Bono is associate editor of the refereed journal, *Computers & Graphics*. He is a member of ACM, ACM-SIGGRAPH, the IEEE Computer Society, and IFIP and is a Fellow of the Eurographics Association. In 1989, Dr. Bono received NCGA's Award for the Advancement of Standards in Computer Graphics.

Ken Collier is vice president of technology services with KSolutions, Inc., a full-service knowledge management consulting and solutions provider with core competencies in business assessment, strategy, implementation, and measurement. With over ten years of experience in data mining, quantitative analytics, and knowledge discovery in databases, Dr. Collier extends his expertise across industries to assist businesses in converting stored information into corporate wisdom. Prior to KSolutions, Inc., Dr. Collier was senior manager in KPMG Consulting's Knowledge Management Solutions, where he was responsible for the business intelligence practice and helped line-of-business consulting teams deliver data mining solutions to clients for customer care, supply chain management, manufacturing, financial management, and resource management needs. Prior to joining KPMG, Dr. Collier was an associate professor of computer science engineering at Northern Arizona University. He cofounded and was the technical director of the Center for Data Insight, a leading center of excellence in data mining and advanced data analytics. Dr. Collier holds a Ph.D. in computer science engineering from Arizona State University and an M.S. in computer science from the University of Oregon. His specialties include software engineering, database theory, and machine learning.

Dennis DeCoste is senior member of technical staff and technical group leader of the Machine Learning Systems Group at the Jet Propulsion Laboratory/California Institute of Technology. He received his Ph.D. in artificial intelligence and computer science from the University of Illinois, Urbana-

Champaign, in 1994. At JPL, he has been principal investigator of several data mining projects, involving both large-scale engineering time-series data (e.g., Space Shuttle fault detection) and science image data (e.g., detecting volcanoes on Venus). His ELMER anomaly detection software flew onboard the recent Deep Space 1 mission as part of the Beacon autonomy experiments. His current research interests include scalable support vector machines and kernel methods, high-dimensional indexing and visualization methods, and graphical models.

Peter Docherty has been senior vice president of research and development at K.wiz Solutions since 1996. He has over 12 years' experience in software development, specializing in telecommunications and real-time systems. He led the development and delivery at K.wiz Solutions of the knowledge discovery and data mining platform that is at the core of thinkAnalytics' products. Prior to that, Mr. Docherty was a technical manager for Hewlett-Packard, responsible for the development of high-performance telecommunications signaling monitoring software. He has also held various lead engineering positions at British Telecommunications, including system designer for all projects within the award-winning BT Airline Interactive Services program. Mr. Docherty graduated from the University of Strathclyde, Scotland, and is a Chartered Engineer.

Steve Donoho is a research scientist at SRA International. He received his Ph.D. in 1996 from the University of Illinois, focusing on automated change of representation techniques. His work at SRA has included customizing KDD techniques to detect stock market manipulation, developing data visualization tools for analyzing suspected fraud cases, and creating link analysis approaches to antimoney laundering.

June M. Donato received her Ph.D. in applied mathematics from UCLA in 1991, specializing in numerical methods for simulating scientific phenomena. She also earned a B.S. in computer science and a B.S. in physics from the University of California, Irvine. Since 1998 she has been a senior programmer analyst at SAIC, where she has consulted on various projects in the industries of telecommunications and transportation. From 1991 to 1998, she was a researcher at Oak Ridge National Laboratory (ORNL), where she was technical lead for the data mining project on credit card bankruptcy, designed and implemented algorithms for data mining applications utilizing techniques such as decision trees and artificial neural networks, and participated on other data mining applications in the areas of transportation and consumer products.

Usama Fayyad is cofounder, president, and CEO of digiMine, a data warehousing and data mining ASP. Prior to digiMine, he founded and led Microsoft Research's Data Mining and Exploration Group (DMX), where he developed data mining prediction components for Microsoft Site Server, developed and customized scalable algorithms for mining large databases, and helped establish a new standard in data mining based on Microsoft's OLE DB API. Prior to Microsoft, Usama founded the Machine Learning Systems Group and developed data mining systems at the Jet Propulsion Laboratory/California Institute of Technology, where he received the most distinguished excellence award and a medal from NASA. Dr. Fayyad holds a Ph.D. in engineering from the University of Michigan, two B.S.E.'s in electrical and computer engineering, an M.S.E. in computer science and engineering, and an M.S. in mathematics. He is editor-in-chief of several technical journals and newsletters and served as program co-chair of KDD'94 and KDD'95 and as general chair of KDD'96 and KDD'99.

Madeleine Fillion is cofounder and president of Livetech Research International, Inc., a company doing research on building software for applications considered too difficult by normal standards, especially for risk management, derivatives, and trading systems. Madeleine has worked with high management to introduce and manage technological change in financial companies and has been researching linguistic and usability issues for user interfaces. She studied English linguistics at the University of Toronto, obtaining a B.S. in education (B.Ed.) in French linguistics and pedagogy.

Raymond E. Flanery, Jr., is director of the Advanced Visualization Research Center at Oak Ridge National Laboratory, developing effective means of viewing and interpreting results contained in scientific data sets that are both complex and massive. Mr. Flanery received his M.S. in applied mathematics at Youngstown State University. His research interests are scientific computing on vector and massively parallel machines, visualization of massively parallel and networked environments, and graphical user interfaces and scientific databases in networked environments.

David Law Yuh Foong is a Research Fellow with the Department of Decision Sciences of the Business School, National University of Singapore (NUS), and has been research associate with the Centre for Management of Innovation and Technopreneurship, NUS, since 1998. In addition he manages the faculty Knowledge Management and Enterprise Modeling Research Programmes. He was presented with the inaugural Singapore Internationale Award by the Singapore International Foundation in 2000 for his contribution to establishing Singapore as part of the global research network in the field of knowledge management. Prior to this, Mr. Foong was a research scientist with the Centre for Natural Product Research of the Institute of Molecular and Cell Biology, NUS, for four years. His research interests, publications, consulting, and work experiences cover areas in knowledge engineering, expert systems, knowledge discovery and data mining, enterprise modeling, information systems research, applications in pharmaceutical domains, organizational learning, and knowledge management. He is a member of various computing and knowledge professional bodies, including AIS, AAAI, BCS, CKIMPS, and IKMS. He has collaborated with Singapore-based organizations; was involved in the organizing of various events, including seminars and academic and executive conferences; and has published in or served as reviewer for a number of internationally refereed conferences (e.g., PACES/SPICIS'97, SCI/ISAS'99, AMCIS'99, PACIS'2000, and ICIS'2000) and journals (e.g., ESWA, Informatica, JITTA, JNCA, and DSS). Mr. Foong has authored over 30 research articles and reports related to his areas of research.

Mike Foster received his M.S. in computer science from MIT in 1996. At the time "The Data Visualization Environment" was written, he worked in the Artificial Intelligence Group at the Jet Propulsion Laboratory/California Institute of Technology, developing a time-series data visualization tool. Mike is currently working at Maxager Technology, a startup developing advanced profit analysis solutions for manufacturing companies.

Alexander G. Gee is currently pursuing a doctorate degree in computer science at the University of Massachusetts, Lowell. Working for the past five years as a research fellow within the Institute for Visualization and Perception Research, he continues to be involved with numerous consulting projects, including development of various visualization techniques, visualization system designs, numerous user-interaction approaches, and several data visualization and data mining projects. As a consultant to Anvil Informatics, Inc., Mr. Gee provides visualization expertise to bioinformatic problems. His doctoral research focuses on the generalization and formalization of visualizations. His educational background includes an A.A. from Saint Petersburg Junior College in 1991, a B.S. in mathematics from Northern Arizona University in 1994, and an M.S. in computer science from the University of Massachusetts, Lowell, in1996.

Henry S. Gertzman helped to develop one of the world's first successful terabyte data warehouses for MCI and is working to integrate the data warehouse with state-of-the-art data mining and data visualization tools. Dr. Gertzman wrote this chapter while at MCI Telecommunications Corporation. He can now be contacted at High Summit Consulting in Colorado Springs, Colorado, 719-548-1982.

Henry G. Goldberg is an assistant director in the market regulation department of NASD Regulation, where he heads a team of knowledge engineers and data miners responsible for knowledge discovery, development, and maintenance in support of several regulatory surveillance systems. His prior work for the U.S. Treasury also focused on computer systems for detection of financial crimes. He holds a B.S. in mathematics from MIT and a Ph.D. in computer science from Carnegie-Mellon University, where he worked on pattern recognition and speech understanding systems. His current research interests include architectures for integrated AI and data analysis, AI techniques for link analysis, and discovery of temporal patterns in data. He has served as co-chair for the fall 1998 AAAI Symposium on AI and Link Analysis.

Nancy Grady, as vice president of advanced development and chief scientist at 212 Studios, leads the advanced development group in data analysis and data mining. She has over 20 years' experience in research on modeling and mining of data from her background in computational and mathematical physics. Prior to 212 Studios, Dr. Grady was a Wigner Fellow at the Oak Ridge National Laboratory and taught physics at Case Western Reserve University. While at ORNL, Dr. Grady led teams that were awarded two significant event awards for their data mining and analysis work. She has a B.S. in the College Scholars Program from the University of Tennessee, with an emphasis in physics and honors math. She was a recipient of the chancellor's citation for research, the first Alvin H. Nielsen College Scholars Scholarship, and the freshman and senior physics awards. Her Ph.D. is in mathematical physics from the University of Virginia, where she won the Gwathmey award for the outstanding research paper by a graduate student in the physical sciences.

Georges G. Grinstein is a professor of computer science at the University of Massachusetts, Lowell, and director of its Institute for Visualization and Perception Research. His research interests include computer graphics, sonification, data mining, virtual environments, and user interfaces with the emphasis on the modeling, visualization, and analysis of complex information systems. Dr. Grinstein received his Ph.D. in mathematics from the University of Rochester in 1978. He has over 25 years in academia with extensive private consulting, has over 50 research grants, has products in use nationally and internationally, has numerous publications in journals and conferences, and has been the organizer or chair of national and international conferences and workshops in computer graphics, visualization, and data mining (e.g., co-chair IEEE Visualization conferences, program committee AAAI conferences in Knowledge Discovery and Databases, co-chair IEEE Workshops on the Integration of Databases and Visualization, co-chair IEEE and AAAI Workshops on the Integration of Data Mining and Visualization, co-chair ACM Workshop on the Psychological and Cognitive Issues in the Visualization of Data, and co-chair SPIE Visual Data and Exploration and Analysis Conferences). He is on the editorial boards of several journals in computer graphics and data mining, has been a member of ANSI and ISO, a NATO Expert, and a technology consultant for various government agencies. He is currently the chief technologist for AnVil Informatics, Inc., a data exploration company that provides professional data mining and visualization services in bioinformatics to leading pharmaceutical and biotech companies initially focused on genomics/functional genomics and drug discovery.

Howard J. Hamilton is an associate professor in the Department of Computer Science at the University of Regina, Saskatchewan, Canada, where he has served since 1991. He received his B.Sc. (High Honours) and M.Sc. in computational science from the University of Saskatchewan and his Ph.D. in computing science from Simon Fraser University. He is director of the University of Regina's Institute for Computational Discovery. He is a project leader with the Institute for Robotics and Intelligent Systems, which is associated with PRECARN Associates, and the Networks of Centres of Excellence program of the Government of Canada. His research interests include knowledge discovery in databases, machine learning, temporal representation and reasoning, and natural language processing. Some issues investigated in knowledge discovery are performance of knowledge discovery software, knowledge interestingness issues, parallelization of knowledge discovery tasks, domain generalization graphs, share-based item sets, and visualization of results. He was co-chair of the TIME'94 and TIME'95 International Workshops on Temporal Representation and Reasoning. He is currently treasurer of the Canadian Society for Computational Studies of Intelligence (CSCSI) and the Canadian national AI society. He is a member of the American Association for Artificial Intelligence, the Association for Computing Machinery, CSCSI, and the IEEE Computer Society.

Robert J. Hilderman received his B.A. in mathematics and computer science from Concordia College at Moorhead, Minnesota, in 1980. He worked as a consultant in the software development industry from 1980 to 1992 developing financial and management information systems. In 1995, he received his

M.Sc. in computer science from the University of Regina at Regina, Saskatchewan, and was selected as the Governor-General's Award Nominee from the Department of Computer Science for 1994. From 1995 to 2000, he worked as a professional research associate in the Department of Computer Science at the University of Regina and received his Ph.D. in computer science from the University of Regina in 2000. He is currently a research faculty member with the Saskatchewan Population Health and Evaluation Research Unit and an assistant professor with the Department of Computer Science, both positions located at the University of Regina. His research interests include knowledge discovery and data mining, parallel and distributed computing, and software engineering. He has authored research papers and articles in the areas of knowledge discovery and data mining, data visualization, parallel and distributed algorithms, and protocol verification and validation.

Thomas H. Hinke performed this work as an associate professor of computer science at the University of Alabama, Huntsville. Currently he is a senior scientist at the NASA Ames Research Center in California, developing a data mining system to operate on NASA's information power grid. In 1999, he was one of the co-organizers of the NASA Workshop on Issues in the Application of Data Mining to Scientific Data. He completed his Ph.D. in computer science at the University of Southern California in 1991 and holds a master's in computer science from the University of California at Los Angeles (1975) and an M.S. in business administration from Oklahoma City University (1971). His B.S. in electrical engineering was completed at the University of California, Berkeley, in 1967. His primary research interests center around knowledge extraction from data, including the development of high-performance data mining systems and developing security-oriented inference-detection systems for databases.

Patrick E. Hoffman is a senior scientist in charge of data mining at AnVil Informatics. His latest research focuses on visualization and data mining in the bioinformatics field, such as gene expression and chemical fingerprints. His novel high-dimensional information visualization techniques, such as dimensional anchors and radviz, are being successfully applied to many application areas. Over the years, Dr. Hoffman developed a broad range of technical expertise in the software and communications area, including virtual reality visualization and multimedia environment setup, network security software and interactive Web site development, pattern recognition and artificial intelligent, and networking and communications. Before joining AnVil, Dr. Hoffman was the president of System Solutions, an information technology consulting firm. He also served as director of engineering at

Clinical Data, Inc. Dr. Hoffman taught computer courses in several New England universities and colleges and held various key R&D positions at GRI Computer Corporation and Sanders Associates. Dr. Hoffman received his Sc.D in computer science from the University of Massachusetts, Lowell, his M.S. from Northeastern University, and his B.S. from the University of Connecticut.

Wesley Johnston is a senior information disciplines analyst in Chevron's Mathematical and Modeling Disciplines Center of Excellence. He first studied artificial intelligence under Dr. Jurg Nievergelt at the University of Illinois in 1968, inspired by John von Neumann's conception of iteratively improving machines designed by machines. He now applies his interest in machine learning to complex analytical problems in all areas of Chevron's business, with special interest in the complex business-driven trade-offs between many candidate models, as well as methods of combining models into ensembles where the whole is greater than the sum of the parts.

Ron Kohavi is the senior director of data mining at Blue Martini Software, where he heads the engineering group responsible for the data collection, analysis, reporting, and campaign management modules in the company's Customer Interaction System. Prior to joining Blue Martini, Kohavi managed the MineSet project, Silicon Graphics' award-winning product for data mining and visualization. He joined Silicon Graphics after earning a Ph.D. in machine learning from Stanford University, where he led the MLC++ project—the machine learning library in C++ now used in MineSet and at Blue Martini Software. Kohavi received his B.A. from the Technion, Israel. He co-chaired KDD 99's industrial track with Jim Gray and the KDD Cup 2000 with Carla Brodley. He was an invited speaker at the National Academy of Engineering in 2000 and a keynote speaker at PAKDD 2001. He co-chaired WEBKDD 2000 and WEBKDD 2001 and co-taught a tutorial on e-commerce and clickstream mining at the SIAM Data Mining conference in 2001. He co-edited with Foster Provost the special issue of the journal *Machine Learning on Applications of Machine Learning* and the special issue of the *Data Mining and Knowledge Discovery* journal on applications of data mining to electronic commerce, now available as a book. He has been a member of the editorial board for the *Data Mining and Knowledge Discovery* journal from its inception and has served as a member of the editorial board for the journal of *Machine Learning* from 1997 to 1999.

Sharon J. Laskowski is a computer scientist and manager of the Visualization and Usability Group in the Information Technology Laboratory at the

National Institute of Standards and Technology, where she manages projects that involve evaluation methodologies, benchmarks, and metrics. Her research has included the development and evaluation of 3D visualization for document collections. She directs the Web Metrics Testbed Project, which is developing proof-of-concept tools to support rapid, remote, and automated usability evaluation of Web sites. She also leads the Industry Usability Reporting (IUSR) Project, which is creating and validating a common format for summative user test reporting. Dr. Laskowski directed the research NIST performed for the evaluation of collaborative systems as part of the DARPA Intelligent Collaboration and Visualization Program. Prior to joining NIST, she was employed by the MITRE Corporation, where she conducted research in expert systems, information fusion, plan recognition, and text analysis. Dr. Laskowski was a faculty member in the computer science department at Pennsylvania State University and received her Ph.D. in computer science at Yale University.

Liangchun Li received an M.Sc. in computer science in 1998 from the University of Regina in Canada. He previously received a B.Sc from Shanghai Jiaotong University and an M.Sc. from Harbin Shipbuilding Engineering Institute in China. His research interests include data visualization, artificial intelligence, data mining, and distributed systems. His M.Sc. thesis, entitled "Web-Based Data Visualization for Data Mining," won the Governor-General's Academic Gold Medal for best thesis at the University of Regina in 1998. He currently works as a software developer in the United States.

John Light received a B.S. in mathematics in 1970 and a B.A. in psychology in 1973 from California State University at Los Angeles. He worked in both system software and user-interface design for a variety of firms before joining Intel in 1995. At the Intel Architecture Labs, he researches information management, information visualization, and ubiquitous computing.

Craig Lovell graduated with a masters in logic and computation from Carnegie-Mellon University in 1994, where he studied artificial intelligence and automated theorem proving. He worked at SRA developing knowledge discovery algorithms and architectures for fraud detection domains. Craig is currently a software architect at IGEN International, a Maryland biotech company.

R. Douglas Martin is professor of statistics at the University of Washington and chief scientist of Insightful Corporation, both in Seattle. He is an author of many publications in the areas of time-series and robust statistical methods, including two invited Royal Statistical Society Discussion papers and one invited Annals of Statistics discussion paper. Martin's recent research focus has been on applications of statistical methods in finance and financial engineering, particularly the application of robust methods in finance, and on data mining. Martin was a professor of electrical engineering at the University of Washington prior to becoming a professor of statistics in 1981. He was a consultant in the Mathematics and Statistics Research Center at Bell Laboratories from 1975 to 1985 and chair of the statistics department at the University of Washington from 1983 to 1986. In 1987, Martin founded StatSci, Inc., to develop and market the S-Plus system for data analysis, based on the S language from Bell Laboratories. In 1993, Martin sold StatSci to MathSoft, Inc., located in Cambridge, Mass., and in 2001 the MathSoft business was consolidated as Insightful Corporation, an S-Plus data analysis and data mining products and services business in Seattle. Martin holds B.S.E. and Ph.D. degrees in electrical engineering from Princeton University.

William D. Mawby received a Ph.D. in biomathematics from North Carolina State University at Raleigh in 1980. After working as a postdoctoral on ecological modeling, he was a private contractor for several years in applied mathematical modeling. He joined Michelin Tire Corporation in 1985 as principal statistician for research and development. He is currently manager of statistical and mathematical services for Michelin in North America, supervising work in statistical consulting, software development, and process analysis. His interests include applications of data and text mining in a manufacturing environment.

Muralidhar Medidi is an assistant professor in the Department of Computer Science and Engineering at Northern Arizona University in Flagstaff, where he has taught since 1994. Dr. Medidi received his Ph.D. in computer science from the University of Central Florida, his M.Tech. in computer engineering from the Indian Institute of Technology, and his B.Tech. in electronics and communications engineering from J. Nehru Technical University. His research interests are in parallel algorithms and data structures, reliability analysis, simulation, and algorithmic graph theory. Dr. Medid is a member of the ACM, IEEE, and Sigma Xi.

Claudio J. Meneses earned his computer engineer degree (equivalent to a B.S. in the United States) at Northern Catholic University in Antofagasta, Chile, in 1990 and his M.S. and Ph.D. in computer science at the University of Massachusetts, Lowell, in 1996 and 2001, respectively. His research interests include data mining and knowledge technologies. Currently, he is a full-time professor in the Department of Computer Science at Northern Catholic University. Dr. Meneses is a member of the ACM and the AAAI.

Ted Mihalisin received a Ph.D. in physics from the University of Rochester in 1967, joined Temple University as an associate professor in 1969, and became professor of physics in 1975. Dr. Mihalisin was named an Alfred P. Sloan Fellow in 1972 and received Temple University's Faculty Research Award in 1987. He has also been the recipient of a National Science Foundation Creativity Award. Dr. Mihalisin is one of the inventors of a method for visualizing very large multidimensional data sets (U.S. Patent 5,228,119, July 1993, and Re. 36,840, August 2000). Since 1989, Dr. Mihalisin has published about a dozen papers on data visualization.

Timothy S. Newman is an associate professor of computer science at the University of Alabama, Huntsville. He received a Ph.D. in computer science from Michigan State University and was the recipient of a National Research Council postdoctoral fellowship with the U.S. National Institutes of Health. His interests include visualization, medical imaging, computer graphics, computer vision, and applications of high-performance computing to problems in these areas. Dr. Newman is a senior member of the IEEE and a member of the ACM.

Ronald M. Pickett is a professor of psychology at the University of Massachusetts, Lowell, where his area of special interest and expertise is applied visual pattern perception. Besides working on problems of data visualization, he has worked extensively on the evaluation and enhancement of image-based medical diagnosis. Dr. Pickett is currently collaborating in studies of the effectiveness of stereo mammography in the detection and diagnosis of breast cancer.

Michel Pilote, cofounder and head of research and development at Livetech Research International, Inc., has tested, refined, and extended data warehousing, data mining, data visualization, object-oriented development, and knowledge representation techniques and methodologies. He researched and applied user interface design, interactive programming languages, and rapid development methodologies. Dr. Pilote has been a knowledge engineering consultant for many large financial companies and a systems engineer at IBM, Canada. He has presented many academic papers to international conferences and contributed to professional DP publications and conferences. His current research interests focus on improving financial engineering theory and practice. Dr. Pilote holds a Ph.D. in artificial intelligence from the University of Toronto, a M.Sc. in computer science, and a B.Sc. in mathematics.

Philip J. Rhodes is a doctoral candidate in computer science at the University of New Hampshire. He received his B.A. in philosophy from the University of Virginia in 1991. After developing a mathematical visualization tool for educational use, he received an M.S. in computer science from the University of Rhode Island in 1995. His current research interests include scientific databases, multiresolution representation of large data sets, and visualization of scientific data.

Marc Ringuette is a computer science researcher, inventor, and software playboy, currently semiretired in Sacramento, California. He spent seven formative years in Carnegie-Mellon's Computer Science Department and has worked in machine learning, information filtering, search engines, robot agents, and speech understanding. He is currently in mad scientist mode, building a heliostat mirror solar power system out of Lego Technic parts, fishing line, and old music CDs.

Donald Sautter is a consulting manager in the business intelligence group at KSolutions, Inc., where he specializes in data mining and advanced analytics. Prior to joining KSolutions, he was a manager within the business intelligence group at KPMG Consulting, Inc. He also participated in the creation and implementation of the Center for Data Insight at Northern Arizona University. In 1998, the Arizona Board of Regents designated the Center for Data Insight as the premier data mining and knowledge discovery research center in the state of Arizona.

Jack Schryver received a B.A. in psychology in 1974 from the University of California at Los Angeles and a Ph.D. in cognitive/experimental psychology in 1982 from the University of California at Irvine. Since 1986, he has been with the Computer Science and Mathematics Division at Oak Ridge National Laboratory. His research interests at ORNL include data mining, machine learning with emphasis on artificial neural networks, discrete event systems simulation, and human-computer interaction. He has applied data mining and machine-learning techniques to financial, transportation, waste transfer, and bioremediation data.

Ted E. Senator is a program manager at the Defense Advanced Research Projects Agency (DARPA), responsible for development, evaluation, and transition of technologies for the analysis of relational (i.e., structured and/or linked) data, specifically, evidence extraction, link discovery, and pattern learning. He previously established and directed the Knowledge Discovery in Databases Group of the National Association of Securities Dealers (NASD) Regulation and the Artificial Intelligence Division at the Financial Crimes Enforcement Network (FinCEN) of the U.S. Department of the Treasury. He is a three-time winner of the Innovative Applications Award from the American Association for Artificial Intelligence for his work with NASD Regulation, FinCEN, and the U.S. Navy. He has served on the program committees for the Innovative Application of Artificial Intelligence (IAAI) and Knowledge Discovery and Data Mining (KDD) conferences for several years. His technical interests include the development and application of AI and KDD techniques, systems, and processes, particularly as applied to finance, fraud detection, and other areas of critical importance. He holds degrees in physics and in electrical engineering from MIT and has done additional graduate work in physics, computer science, and finance.

Ping Shyr is a senior knowledge discovery in databases specialist in the Market Regulation Department of NASD Regulation, responsible for several domains of ADS and leading a new project. He has worked in the area of AI applications for the past 15 years. He is also a Ph.D. student in the School of Information Technology at George Mason University (GMU). His dissertation concerns multistrategy learning and knowledge acquisition and is closely associated with research projects in the Learning Agents Lab at GMU.

Tim Simin graduated summa cum laude from the University of Texas at Dallas with a B.S. in economics and finance in 1992. Between 1992 and 1994, he worked in the Division of Monetary Affairs at the Federal Reserve Board of Governors in Washington, D.C., and has since been at the University of Washington working on a Ph.D. in finance. Mr. Simin has taught finance and economics at the University of Washington, held a visiting position at the University of North Carolina at Chapel Hill, and is currently in the Department of Finance at Pennsylvania State University. His research interests include empirical issues in asset pricing, robust econometric methods, and international finance. Tim has published research in the *Journal of Economics and Business* and the *Journal of Financial Markets* and serves as a referee for the *Journal of Financial and Quantitative Analysis*, *The Review of Financial Studies*, and *Management Science*.

Dan Sommerfield's experience with machine learning and data mining began at Stanford University, where he graduated with a B.S. in computer science, a B.A. in psychology, and an M.S. in computer science in 1995. From 1994 to 1995, he was a research assistant in the Robotics Lab, working with Ronny Kohavi on MLC++, a machine-learning library in C++. They published papers on feature subset search and accuracy estimation. In 1996, MLC++ moved to Silicon Graphics as part of the MineSet project. Mr. Sommerfield joined SGI to continue work on the project. Through MineSet, he coupled MLC++'s algorithms with state-of-the-art visualization techniques. The visualization of the simple Bayesian classifier that appeared in the paper was the product of joint work by Ronny Kohavi, Barry Becker, and Dan, all members of the MineSet team. "Visualizing Data Mining Models" grew out of a focus group at the KDD'97 workshop on mining and visualization. In 1999, Dan left the MineSet project to start up a data mining group at Rubric, a marketing automation company. Rubric was acquired by Broadbase in 2000, which was in turn acquired by Kana in 2001. He is currently a senior engineering manager at Kana and in charge of developing data mining solutions for business users, which is to be distributed as part of Kana's CRM applications.

Martin R. Stytz is a chief principal research scientist and engineer at the Air Force Research Laboratory. He received a B.S. from the U.S. Air Force Academy in 1975, an M.A. from Central Missouri State University in 1979, an M.S. from the University of Michigan in 1983, and a Ph.D. in computer science and engineering from the University of Michigan in 1989. He is a member of the ACM, SIGGRAPH, SIGCHI, the IEEE, the IEEE Computer Society, Simulation Industry Association of Australia, American Association for Artificial Intelligence, and the Society for Computer Simulation. His research interests include information visualization, data understanding and valuation, virtual environments, distributed interactive simulation, distributed systems, modeling and simulation, large-scale system architecture, design and development, distributed software development, cyberwarfare and modeling, computer graphics, graphical user interfaces, distributed virtual environments, user-centered decision support, human-computer interaction, computer-generated actors, intelligent agents, medical virtual environments, information security, and software engineering.

Kurt Thearling is senior director of development at Wheelhouse, a marketing services technology company, where he is responsible for leading software development. He spent much of the last decade evaluating, designing, and building customer relationship management (CRM) and data mining applications. Most recently he was director of analytics at CRM software vendor Xchange, Inc., where he was responsible for integrating data mining, reporting, and optimization into a suite of marketing automation applications. Prior to Xchange, he held senior technology positions at Dun & Bradstreet, Pilot Software, and Thinking Machines Corporation. Dr. Thearling received his Ph.D. in electrical engineering from the University of Illinois and has multiple undergraduate engineering degrees from the University of Michigan. He is a regular speaker at industry events and has written numerous articles on decision support and CRM technology.

Matthew O. Ward received his B.S. in computer science from Worcester Polytechnic Institute (WPI) in 1977 and his M.S. and Ph.D. in computer science from the University of Connecticut in 1979 and 1981, respectively. He is currently a full professor in the computer science department at WPI. Prior to coming to WPI in 1986, he worked at the AT&T Bell Laboratories in the Visual Communications Research Laboratory and at Skantek Corporation. His research interests are in data and information visualization. He has published more than 60 papers and is the author or coauthor of several public-domain visualization packages, notably XmdvTool, XSauci, SpiralGlyphics, and SimCortex. He is a member of the IEEE Computer Society.

Andreas Wierse is the managing director of VirCinity, a spin-off company from the Computing Centre of the University of Stuttgart, focusing on and consulting in advanced visualization software. Previously at the Computing Centre, Dr. Wierse designed and implemented the distributed data management for the COVISE visualization system and maintained a wide range of graphics workstations. Dr. Wierse's initial background in mathematics led to work in computer graphics, mainly scientific visualization. He developed the GRAPE (GRAphics Programming Environment) user interface, as well as parts of its device-independent graphics drivers.